Renaissance Retrospections

Medieval Institute Publications is a program of
The Medieval Institute, College of Arts and Sciences

WESTERN MICHIGAN UNIVERSITY

Renaissance Retrospections
Tudor Views of the Middle Ages

Edited by Sarah A. Kelen

Studies in Medieval Culture LII

MEDIEVAL INSTITUTE PUBLICATIONS
Western Michigan University
Kalamazoo

Manufactured in the United States of America
This book is printed on acid-free paper.

Library of Congress Cataloging-in-Publication Data

Renaissance Retrospections : Tudor Views of the Middle Ages / edited by Sarah A. Kelen.
    pages cm. -- (Studies in Medieval Culture ; 52)
  Includes bibliographical references and index.
   ISBN 978-1-58044-173-5 (clothbound : acid-free paper) -- ISBN 978-1-58044-174-2 (paperbound : acid-free paper)
  1. English literature--Early modern, 1500-1700--Criticism, Textual. 2. Manuscripts, Renaissance--England--Editing. 3. Literature and history--England--History--16th century. I. Kelen, Sarah A., 1968- editor of compilation.
  PR418.T48R44 2013
  820.9'003--dc23
                              2012051399

1 2 3 4 5 C P 5 4 3 2 1

Contents

Acknowledgments   vii

Abbreviations   ix

Introduction: The Body and the Book in Early Modern Readings   1
of the Medieval English Past
     Sarah A. Kelen

The Resurrected Corpus: History and Reform in Bale's *Kynge Johan*   16
     Dan Breen

When Polemic Trumps Poetry: Buried Medieval Poem(s)   37
in the Protestant Print *I Playne Piers*
     Kathy Cawsey

The Work of Robert Langland   70
     Thomas A. Prendergast

The Monkish Middle Ages: Periodization and Polemic in   93
Foxe's *Acts and Monuments*
     Jesse M. Lander

"That auntient authoritie": Old English Laws in the Writings   111
of William Lambarde
     Rebecca J. Brackmann

The Rebel Kiss: Jack Cade, Shakespeare, and the Chroniclers   127
     Kellie Robertson

At Hector's Tomb: Fifteenth-Century Literary History and Shakespeare's   141
Troilus and Cressida
     William Kuskin

Owning the Middle Ages: History, Trauma, and English Identity   174
    Nancy Bradley Warren

Bibliography   199

Notes on Contributors   217

Index   219

Acknowledgments

I would like to express my appreciation to the Medieval Institute for the 2004 Visiting Fellowship where I began work on this collection, and to Medieval Institute Publications for their support through the process of collecting and editing the essays. My particular thanks go to David Matthews, who was a meticulous and insightful reader of the manuscript, who identified himself as the peer reviewer, and from whose scholarship I have learned so much in the years since our first meeting over Tyrwhitt in the BL Rare Book Reading Room. I could not have asked for a better reader for this collection, and I know that the final version was much improved by his suggestions.

This volume has been several years in production, during which time the authors of these essays have welcomed many new additions to their families. Collectively, we have gained seven children, three spouses, and even four chickens. This volume is dedicated to our families. Our work would not be possible without your support.

Abbreviations

OED   *The Oxford English Dictionary.* Edited by J. A. Simpson and E. S. C. Weiner. 2nd edition. 20 vols. Oxford: Clarendon Press, 1989.

STC   Pollard, A. W., and G. R. Redgrave, compilers. Revised by W. A. Jackson and F. S. Ferguson, completed by Katherine F. Parker. *A Short-Title Catalogue of Books Printed in England, Scotland, and Ireland, and of English Books Printed Abroad, 1475–1640.* 2nd edition. 3 vols. London: Bibliographical Society, 1976–91.

Wing   Wing, Donald. *Short-Title Catalogue of Books Printed in England, Scotland, Ireland, Wales, and British America, and of English Books Printed in Other Countries, 1641–1700.* Ann Arbor, MI: University Microfilms International, 1978.

Introduction: The Body and the Book in Early Modern Readings of the Medieval English Past

Sarah A. Kelen

Like Hollywood screenwriters who create movies based on television shows, comic books, and video games, writers in the premodern and early modern periods mined antecedent texts for narrative models. For medieval and Renaissance authors, writing very frequently meant rewriting. Some adaptations and revisions obscure their own origins, but some openly reveal their intertextual affiliations. In the most explicitly bookish of the *Canterbury Tales*, Chaucer's Oxford Clerk invokes "Frauncesy Petrak, the lauriate poete" as the source of his rhyme royal tale, lamenting that Petrarch "is now deed and nayled in his cheste."[1] The image of Petrarch's physical body is supplanted immediately in the Clerk's retelling of the Griselda story by what the Clerk calls "the body of his tale" (*CT* IV.42). The Clerk's phrasing here makes explicit an analogy buried in the initial reference to Petrarch. Corpses, after all, were not the only things to be enclosed in a "cheste": an Oxford clerk likely stored his own books in an *armarium*, a chest. For the Clerk, the body of the poet and the body of the tale are not dead artifacts to be left in the past. Both could better be described as "undead": simultaneously absent and present, expired and enabling. Through both his presence and his absence, Petrarch (figured both textually and corporeally) enables the Clerk's tale of Griselda, herself a character quite explicitly and repeatedly embodied within the tale.

Like Chaucer's Clerk, early modern writers self-consciously used antecedent texts to enable their own work, but then struggled (not always successfully) to keep earlier social, religious, literary, legal, and political systems "nayled in [their] cheste." The ghost of the Middle Ages continued to haunt the early modern period because neither the tomb nor the text could wholly contain its occupants. A major plot element within the Clerk's Tale is the return of Griselda's children, seemingly from the grave, an event that shocks Griselda herself into a pseudo-death:

Whan she this herde, aswowne doun she falleth
For pitous joye, and after hir swownynge
She bothe hir yonge children unto hir calleth,
And in hir armes pitously wepynge
Embraceth hem, and tendrely kissynge
Ful lyk a mooder, with hir salte teeres
She bathed bothe hir visage and hir heeres.

O, which a pitous thyng it was to se
Hir swownyng, and hir humble voys to heere!
(*CT* IV.1079–87).

The repeated reference to Griselda's swoon, three times in nine lines, emphasizes the drama of Griselda overcome with emotion at having her children returned to her from their seeming grave. Griselda swoons "[f]or . . . joye," but the reiterated image of her lying unconscious on the floor raises the possibility that Walter may finally have tormented Griselda to death.

Griselda is joyful, but the Clerk is rather more ambivalent about the emotions associated with this happy reunion.[2] Just as Griselda's swoon is referred to three times within nine lines, so too is the Clerk's claim that her joy is "pitous." It is not Griselda who feels pity but the Clerk. He even inserts himself bodily into the scene, casting himself as both spectator and auditor by reporting how pitiable it was "to se / Hir swownyng and hir humble voys to heere" (lines 1086–87). The Clerk himself has not seen or heard Griselda, however. He has read about her in Petrarch's book. And while he demonstrates his desire to resuscitate Griselda from her "pitous" swoon, in the envoi to the Clerk's Tale he (or Chaucer, or the pilgrim-narrator) unceremoniously kills her off: "Grisilde is deed, and eek hir pacience" (line 1177).[3] The Clerk's narrative of Griselda's life and death animates her imaginatively for the Clerk's audience of fellow pilgrims, and it brings her into the Chaucerian present from the Petrarchan past.

In his tale the Clerk alternately animates and kills off his protagonist, just as his prologue first invokes Petrarch then consigns him to his grave. The Clerk's reference to his poetic predecessor as both a textual authority and a corpse manifests (if in unusually explicit terms) a Bloomian anxiety of influence also visible elsewhere in Chaucer's negotiations with an inherited literary tradition.[4] Interestingly, that literary tradition is almost entirely Continental. Chaucer's source texts are predominantly non-English, and where he does refer to the native English literary tradition, he is often disparaging, as in his mockery of rhymed romance in The Tale of Sir Thopas. For Chaucer, writing at the end of the fourteenth century, earlier English writers provoked neither anxiety nor admiration.[5] On the other hand, for the literary generation to follow, neither Chaucer himself nor medieval English literature as a whole was so easily dismissed. The Chaucerian fixation of many fifteenth-century English writers is the best-known feature of that generation's literary output.[6] Sixteenth-century English writers, however, were more vocal about their debt to Continental models than to the English literary tradition. The idea of a sixteenth-century "rebirth" of learning looks back to a classical age in which England was a remote outpost of the Roman Empire, and home to no native literary tradition of its own.[7] Despite this, the English medieval literary tradition was a strong, if not always acknowledged, presence for early modern authors.

A century and a half after Chaucer's Clerk both revived and buried his literary predecessor, William Baldwin's introduction to the *Mirror for Magistrates* (1559) reiterates the Clerk's strategy. The *Mirror for Magistrates* is a translation and expansion of Lydgate's *Fall of Princes*, itself a translation of Boccaccio's *De Casibus Illustrium Virorum* (by way of Chaucer's Monk's Tale). The *Mirror* begins with a scene of composition that invokes Lydgate's spiritual presence through the physical volume that contains his text. In this scene Baldwin recounts a gathering of the authorial syndicate in the early stages of compiling the *Mirror*: "Whan certayne of theym to the numbre of seuen, were throughe a generall assent at an appoynted time and place gathered together to deuyse therupon, I resorted vnto them, bering with me the booke of Bochas, translated by Dan Lidgate, for the better obseruacion of his order."[8] Baldwin's image of a medieval text being used both to invoke a dead literary exemplar and to enable future literary composition recapitulates the Clerk's conflation of Petrarch's dead body and the "body of his tale." The two images are emblematic of the ways that early modern readers and writers responded to medieval textual history.

Some early modern uses of medieval literary models are well known—for example, Shakespeare's multiple uses of Chaucerian sources, and the influence of Petrarch on the early modern sonnet tradition. These borrowings and adaptations tend to be seen in isolation, however, as particular choices made by individual writers, rather than as part of a significant and extended literary and cultural engagement with the antecedent period. Moreover, the intertextual connections between early modern and medieval texts extend beyond literary fictions to historical, theological, and political writings. A simplistic view of English history would divide feudal, Catholic, medieval England from its early modern, post-Reformation counterpart. However, Tudor writings made reference to the medieval past or to medieval texts to justify any number of religious and political positions, as the essays in this volume demonstrate. Early modern readers of all factions used medieval texts to authorize postmedieval ideologies. As with any authorial attempt to control hermeneutics, early modern invocations of medieval texts opened the possibility for alternative interpretations.

Early modern historiographical writers espoused ethical certitudes about the utility of history writing, but the essays that follow certainly show that historical texts were no less subject to reinterpretation by later readers than were literary texts. Thomas Blundeville's *The true order and Methode of wryting and reading*

Hystories (1574) argues that there are three purposes for which histories ought to be written: "First that vve may learne thereby to acknovvledge the prouidence of God vvherby all things are gouerned and directed. Secondly, that by the examples of the vvise, vve maye learne vvisedome vvysely to behaue our selues in all our actions . . . . Thirdly, that vve maye be stirred by example of the good to follovve the good, and by example of the euill to flee the euill."[9] The first purpose for history writing—demonstrating God's providence—sets the stage for the other uses Blundeville cites, in which humans use history to pursue virtuous ends. Surely, God wishes for readers of history to behave with wisdom, to follow the good, and to flee the evil. Nevertheless, even setting aside the question of the relationship between God's providence and human action, these three uses of history are not as straightforward as they may initially seem. Learning the proper moral lessons from history requires a historical record with a stable and universally agreed upon meaning, and a record that provides clear examples of good and evil actors and of wise and unwise behavior. The rapid and radical political and religious transformations of the Tudor period ensured that readers of history knew better than to trust such an ideal of interpretive stability.

Tudor authors rewrote the Middle Ages to their own advantage, but with the knowledge that their source texts could just as easily be remobilized for contrary purposes. Even if an account is true, a text can be interpreted in many ways, but the truth of medieval texts was already suspect (as Jesse Lander's and Dan Breen's essays in this collection make clear). In his account of Jean Froissart's fourteenth-century chronicle, the Tudor historian Edward Hall encourages his readers to adopt an attitude of suspicion toward the medieval text, even though Hall is reticent about identifying any particular errors or untruths: "Iohn Frossart wrote the liues of kyng Edward the third, and kyng Richard the seconde, so compendeously and so largely, that if there were not so many thyngs spoken of in his long woorkes, I might beleue all written in his greate volumes to bee as trewe as the Gospel. But I haue redde an olde prouerbe which saithe, that in many woordes, a lie or twayne sone maie scape."[10] One might well encounter "a lie or twayne" in Froissart's *Chronicles*, not to mention Hall's *Chronicle*, but at such a historical remove, how can those lies be identified and excised? Historical records tell biased stories, but they are also often the only possible means of access to the past. The materiality of the book might seem to fix the text to some extent.[11] However, as early modern readers negotiated the literary and documentary records of the medieval past, they were well aware that competing interpretations as well as author biases destabilized the meaning of any text.

Raphael Holinshed comments both implicitly and explicitly on the subjectivity of the historical record in his massive *Laste volume of the Chronicles*. In his account of the reign of Richard II, Holinshed itemizes numerous instances of the king's misrule: "he was prodigall, ambitious, and muche giuen to the pleasure of the bodie"; he overspent; he maintained too many servants; members of his household dressed beyond their degree; he advanced illiterate prelates; and he was guilty of "lecherie and fornication."[12] Immediately after this extended censure of Richard, Holinshed qualifies it somewhat: "Thus haue ye heard what wryters do report touching the state of the time and doings of this king. But if I may boldly say what I think: he was a Prince the most vnthankfully vsed of hys subiects, of any one of whom ye shal lightly read. For although through the frailtie of youth he demeaned himselfe more dissolutely than seemed conuenient for his royall estate ... yet in no kings days were the commons in greater wealth, if they could haue perceyued their happie state."[13] Holinshed's remarks on the injustice of Richard's deposition implicitly call into question the veracity of the complaints against him, complaints Holinshed distances from himself by marking them as others' words: "what wryters do report." Holinshed carefully neither disputes these reports nor endorses them. History may serve the ethical and exemplary functions assigned to it by Blundeville, but the written records of past deeds are not entirely transparent.

As is apparent throughout the essays collected here, Tudor authors made frequent use of both literary and nonliterary texts from the medieval period, and the authors' responses to those texts range from suspicion to imitation, from criticism to appreciation.[14] For literary, historical, legal, and religious writers in the early modern period, the medieval written record provided not only models but also sources of potential conflict, given the cultural and historical distance between the two periods. In the anecdote quoted above Baldwin shows great deference to Lydgate's book, ceremoniously bearing it into the room where the *Mirror* writers are to meet and presenting it as an exemplar. Yet Baldwin's actions can also be seen as an assertion of his ownership of the text, and his physical (and thus spiritual) control of his literary predecessor's material, which he and his collaborators were soon to reshape for their own purposes. In reworking Lydgate's medieval text, the *Mirror* syndicate would confront the specter of Lydgate the author as well as confronting the durable, material substance of Lydgate's text.[15] In Baldwin's anecdote the book stands in for Lydgate himself, whether the medieval poet is seen as an implicit participant in the writing of the early modern text or as the antecedent who will be superseded and replaced by his younger successors. The book borne into the room thus functions as a medium to transmit the posthumous voice of the antecedent poet, even as it manifests his necessary absence. The book is a metonym for its author, yet in this case the volume's author points to an even more distant textual past. Baldwin describes *The Fall of Princes* as "the booke of Bochas, translated by Dan Lidgate," subsuming Lydgate's authorial labors in the chain of literary history and providing an exemplar for the syndicate's own act of cultural translation. "[T]he booke of Bochas" twice lives on past an author's death, as Lydgate transmits (and replaces) Boccaccio's work and the *Mirror* transmits (and replaces) Lydgate's.

Baldwin's introduction manifests ambivalence about *The Mirror*'s relationship to its literary model. Paul Strohm refers to the *Mirror* as "Janus-faced," for looking backward toward its antecedents while seeking an opportunity to present itself as authoritative in its own historical and political context.[16] Gordon McMullan and David Matthews identify a similarly divided attitude toward the literary past in the prologue of *The Two Noble Kinsmen* (1634). The prologue at once acknowledges the play's adaptation of Chaucer's Knight's Tale and worries that an unfavorable response to the play might make Chaucer cry out from his grave. As Matthews and McMullan point out, this prologue's professed anxiety is merely for show: "Chaucer does not actually pronounce the speech of complaint the prologue puts in his mouth which is in any case contingent on the play failing in performance, something which the prologue, at its end, seems confident will not happen."[17] In *The Two Noble Kinsmen* Shakespeare and Fletcher, like Baldwin and Chaucer before them, situate their literary antecedent in a tomb.

For early modern readers of medieval texts, as well as for Chaucer's Clerk, the literary and historiographic past is recorded not only in books but on bodies, and the twin images of body and book recur throughout this volume. That books simultaneously stand in for and create the absent past is perhaps an unremarkable observation for a post-Derridean reader. However, the proliferation of dead bodies throughout this volume might give one pause. While the body count in this collection does not rival that of most action movies, corpses or tombs appear in the essays by Dan Breen, Nancy Bradley Warren, Kellie Robertson, William Kuskin, and Thomas Prendergast, with metaphors of death or burial in the essays by Kathleen Cawsey and Rebecca Brackmann. As these examples should demonstrate, Chaucer's Clerk is not the only reader for whom the invocation of a source text leads to images of death, nor is he the only one for whom the reuse of a literary work by a now-dead antecedent provokes a very apparent anxiety.

In Dan Breen's analysis of John Bale's *Kynge Johan*, the abuses of the estates of England are allegorically legible in the corpse of King John on stage at the end of the play, even if the historiographic record is distorted by the biases of the monastic chroniclers. As Breen points out, when King John's dead body is removed from the stage, his place is taken by the character Veritas, who speaks on behalf of a true and unbiased historiography: one distinct from the existing monastic chronicles that were, in Bale's opinion, falsified by their Catholic authors. In place of the flawed textual record, Veritas offers physical monuments to John's kingship, like London Bridge. John's body and the durable and tangible witnesses named by Veritas record the true history that has been obscured by monastic textuality. It may be appropriate to a play, an embodied text, to valorize the physical, but it is noteworthy for a writer to denigrate textuality in this way.

For John Foxe, Bale's successor in Protestant historiography, the relative values of body and book are reversed; in Foxe's formulation the errors of Catholicism are literally embodied in corporeal ceremonies. Jesse Lander argues in his essay that Foxe uses the rhetorical figure of *accumulatio* (or heaping) to replicate and indict the proliferation of nonbiblical practices in Catholicism. As Lander points out, when Foxe lists the practices of which he disapproves, many of them are explicitly bodily: "crepyng the crosse, carying Palmes, takyng ashes, bearyng candels, pilgremage goyng, sensyng, kneelyng, knockyng."[18] In this list the Catholic body is the instrument of a misguided and idolatrous religion, one that emphasizes the corporeal over the spiritual. Lander demonstrates that the iconography of the woodcuts in Foxe's editions as well as Foxe's rhetoric consistently associate Catholicism with the body (and thus with physical excess) and Protestantism with the book. Yet Foxe's *Acts and Monuments* was better known as the *Book of Martyrs*, a double title that complicates the associations between Catholicism and carnality, and between Protestantism with textuality. The monuments of the martyrs are their acts, their embodied deeds, and their martyrdom invests their (dead) bodies with the spiritual authority that their Catholic tormentors with their carnal practices lack.

A fascination with Catholic carnality of a more scandalous sort is evident in Thomas Robinson's *The Anatomie of the English Nunnery in Portugal* (1622), discussed here by Nancy Bradley Warren. Robinson claims to have worked as a copyist at the Brigittine abbey of Syon (then in exile in Portugal) and thus to have eyewitness evidence of the community's vices. As proof of the Brigittine nuns' licentiousness, Robinson claims to have discovered hidden within the nunnery walls the bones of the nuns' illegitimate children. These bodies are legible as remnants of an only partially forgotten past, and their physical continuation serves in place of absent texts that would have represented the past truthfully. To that extent, the bodies are unofficial "documents" that correct the biased official records of the abbey. Although the title of Robinson's work invokes very directly the analogy between books and bodies, Robinson denies that his *Anatomie* will present a "profound Lecture upon a dissected body." Yet he does perform a kind of mental autopsy on the bones he has found, concluding them to be evidence of the nuns' illicit sexuality.[19]

The body can be legible, a kind of book, but so too can a text be a kind of tomb. Rebecca Brackmann discusses a 1583 address by legal theorist William Lambarde, who laments that the native Anglo-Saxon laws cannot "bring unto us any good at all whilst they lie shut up in our books only as dumb letters and dead elements."[20] As Brackmann shows, Lambarde differentiates between later (Rome-influenced) and early (non-Roman) medieval English history, emphasizing the continuity of English common law from what he terms "auntient" times. For Lambarde, it is the more distant early medieval period, not the proximate later Middle Ages, that should be recognized as authoritative in shaping English legal thought. Anglo-Saxon law can protect the English body politic from foreign corruption, provided that law is treated as a living entity, not a dead body.

Lambarde's sepulchral metaphor highlights the difference between a work's physical and intellectual preservations. Texts from the past may persist, but they are only valuable insofar as they circulate and are used. John Leland raises this very concern in his discussion of Henry VIII's dissolution of England's religious houses, which put so many of the records of the medieval past at risk. In his *Newe Yeares Gyfte* to King Henry, Leland describes his labors to preserve the "monumentes of auncient writers" from abbey libraries: "I have conservid many good autors, the which other wise had beene like to have perischid to no smaul incommodite of good letters."[21] Leland's terminology here is significant. Although his actual accomplishment is the preservation of endangered manuscripts (and thus of the works those volumes contain), he describes his labors as the conservation of authors who would otherwise perish. Of course, the human authors of the books in question are long dead, and no amount of book collecting by Leland will resuscitate them. Metaphorically, however, the "auncient writers" live on because of their textual survival, the textual "monumentes" that they have left behind. The metaphor of extant books as living bodies is made all the more explicit by Leland's statement of his intention to bring those works "owte of deadly darkenes to lyvely light."[22] If the Renaissance was a "rebirth" of classical learning, it was also a continuation of a more proximate medieval tradition that was still very much alive (despite polemical attempts to bury it).

Early modern uses of medieval books bring their texts to life, keeping them vital for a new generation of readers, and early modern editions or quotations of medieval works make long dead authors speak again. In Kellie Robertson's analysis of the accounts of Jack Cade in chronicles and in Shakespeare's *2 Henry VI*, she focuses on an episode in which dead bodies rather than dead texts are reanimated: the (alleged) puppetry that the rebels performed by making the decapitated heads of their enemies "kiss" in a gruesome public spectacle. The macabre puppetry ascribed to the rebels by both medieval and early modern historiographers acknowledges and exploits the extent to which bodies can be seen (and also scripted) as texts. The kissing heads, like the bodily remains of illegitimate children that Thomas Robinson claims to have seen at Syon, are dead bodies made to tell stories to the living. The stage rebels are themselves reanimated corpses, given that actors in history plays represent medieval events for early modern viewers. In the rhetoric of the late sixteenth-century antitheatrical tracts that Robertson cites, the theatre tends toward idolatry because it involves real actors playing fictions, mistaking the inanimate for the animate. The rebels' puppets differ from the enacted historical figures only by being more obviously but no less significantly the living dead.

Robertson's essay notes that Shakespeare's depiction of Jack Cade highlights Cade's awareness of theatricality, and argues that *2 Henry VI* is therefore metadramatic, calling into question the nature of dramatic representation. William Kuskin too highlights a Shakespearean meditation on the nature of artistic representation. While Robertson considers the metadramatic elements of the Cade plot in *2 Henry VI* as an indication that Shakespeare's concerns as a playwright are different from those of a medieval chronicler, Kuskin's essay argues that the questions about the nature of representation staged in Shakespeare's *Troilus and Cressida* are already apparent in Shakespeare's late medieval sources. In the case of *2 Henry VI*, Shakespeare is translating an ostensibly nonliterary genre for the stage, although Robertson also notes the way Holinshed's narration of the Cade rebellion engages in literary patterning. In the case of *Troilus and Cressida*, Shakespeare begins with a historical (or pseudo-historical) narrative already primarily literary in its generic affiliations. Both Robertson's essay and Kuskin's emphasize the importance of genre as influencing the way early modern writers reused medieval texts.

In Kuskin's essay the twin metaphors of body and book, that is corporeality and textuality, once again come into contact. Kuskin analyzes the ekphrasis on Hector's tomb in Caxton's translation of the *Recuyell of the Histories of Troye*, noting that the tomb's double image of Hector—the effigy and the embalmed body—calls into question the nature of representation and the indeterminate hierarchy of value connecting artifice and nature. For Kuskin, the description of Hector's tomb in the *Recuyell* functions metonymically to represent what it means to write Trojan history from the early modern period, looking back to a classical past that is necessarily mediated through texts from the Middle Ages. The medieval manuscripts and early printed books that make up the corpus of Trojan historiography in the early modern period also entomb that history, and stand as monuments to both artifice and actuality.

While Kuskin proposes an early modern historiography that is hyperaware of its own origins, Kathy Cawsey's essay demonstrates that early modern texts may instead suppress textual history, even as they preserve their medieval antecedents. Cawsey argues that *I Playne Piers*, a Protestant polemic published first around 1550, and again in 1589, is a compilation of prior poetic texts, at least some of which seem to be medieval in origin. Both editions of *I Playne Piers* are printed as prose, however, suggesting that the printer did not recognize the composite text for what it was. While perhaps not an exquisite corpse, *I Playne Piers* does serve as a monument to an enduring medieval literary culture, despite the printer's misunderstanding of the text. The printed editions thus engage in an unrecognized act of remembering, even as the text's poetic format is dismembered by its presentation as prose.

While Cawsey's essay focuses on the Protestant appropriation of medieval texts (some texts more orthodox than reformist in their theology), Thomas Prendergast argues that even *Piers Plowman*, a poem notoriously interpreted as proto-Protestant by its sixteenth-century editor, also appealed to some Catholic readers. Nicholas Brigham, whom the Protestant propagandist John Bale cites as a source of information about the author of *Piers Plowman*, seems to have been a

Catholic sympathizer as well as a reader of medieval literature. Langland was not the only object of Brigham's literary historical affections; as Prendergast notes, it was Brigham who had a new tomb built for Chaucer in Westminster Abbey (yet another intersection of text and tomb).[23] Prendergast argues that the group of scholars who "discovered" the identity of Robert Langland, the author of *Piers Plowman*, shared a humanist set of reading practices and approaches to textual scholarship, despite their religious differences. The research of these scholars reembodies the past textually, through the preservation and correction of manuscript texts, and corporeally, recovering the author as a person through research on authorial identity and biography.

Prendergast's example of a scholarly community in which the commitment to humanist practice overshadowed the scholars' individual political and religious affiliations is unusual. Narratives of the medieval past were more often constructed precisely to bolster one or another ideology. Indeed, this is true in the case of one of the writers in the community of scholars Prendergast discusses: John Bale may have been committed to nonfactional scholarship in the interest of uncovering the author of *Piers Plowman*, but he also treats the anonymous medieval chroniclers as collectively mistaken and thus subject to correction, in both their historiography and their religion. Similarly, when William Lambarde reads the Anglo-Saxon law codes, as a Protestant writer he attempts to "de-Catholicize" the medieval English past. As Rebecca Brackmann's essay demonstrates, Lambarde calls into question whether the pre-Reformation English were truly Catholic (and thus under Rome's control) or somehow proto-Protestant. This debate about the religious identity (and relative "Romishness") of pre-Reformation England appears in many early modern discussions of English history. Even when Catholics and Protestants shared an understanding about the catholicism (and Catholicism) of medieval England, they could disagree about how that past related to the present.

Nancy Bradley Warren demonstrates the way that the (Catholic) Lancastrian support for the Brigittine abbey at Syon proved troubling for (Protestant) Tudor attempts to affiliate themselves with their Lancastrian predecessors; such a visible commitment to Roman Catholicism made the Lancastrians a problematic model for the Protestant Tudors. From the other side of the religious divide, the Catholic Robert Parsons sought to delegitimize the Tudor claim to a Lancastrian pedigree. By doing so, he hoped to purge England's Protestant monarchs from the (Catholic) Lancastrian line. Sixteenth-century debates between Catholics and Protestants over how to understand the religious sentiments of pre-Reformation England call into question who "owns the Middle Ages," in Warren's terminology.

The essays in this volume deal with truths revealed or obscured in the medieval past, and with the interpretive strategies early modern authors used to choose among the potential meanings of their source texts, as they sought to make sense of or to stake a claim to the past. Earlier I used the term "undead" to describe the way Petrarch's corpse and his tale are simultaneously absent and present for Chaucer's Clerk. Perhaps I should rather have used the term "uncanny." Nancy Bradley Warren, for example, speaks of the Lancastrian history in terms of the return of the repressed—a useful concept for all of the essays in this volume, insofar as they show the medieval past to be a consistent (if contested) presence for Tudor writers. To use a Freudian critical language that far postdates the Tudor writers here described may not be as anachronistic as it seems on the surface.[24] The uncanny, the return of the repressed, and melancholia are themselves all explicitly subjects of early modern writing. The best known literary figure from Tudor England is also its most famous melancholic: Prince Hamlet, whose father's ghost, both horrifying and familiar, seems a perfect icon of Freud's concept of the uncanny.[25] Indeed, as noted above, Shakespeare's history plays quite literally reanimate the past. The Middle Ages are, in fact, an uncanny but continuous presence in the early modern period both culturally and textually.

The essays collected here should, therefore, remind scholars of the early modern and medieval periods that the line drawn between literary periods is a professionally convenient fiction, and not always a very consistent one. Once again, Chaucer's Clerk's Tale provides a telling example: in this text, a medieval English writer imitates and updates a narrative by his Italian humanist predecessor Petrarch. In an odd twist of international chronology, a poet from the English "Middle Ages" writes a generation after one from the Italian "Renaissance."[26] Scholars on both sides of that disciplinary divide are beginning to recognize the value of work that acknowledges the interconnectedness of the premodern and the early modern. The scholars included in this volume represent those who work primarily on medieval England, those who are primarily early modernists, and those who have published in both fields; their arguments below are thus important additions to the growing dialogue between the disciplines of medieval and early modern studies.[27]

Because scholarly interchanges between the medieval and early modern fields are still relatively infrequent, it is easy to overlook the deep dependence of early modern culture on its medieval predecessor.[28] Seth Lerer, for example, argues for the influence of a medieval literary figure on the behavior of later readers (not merely later characters); he claims that for early Tudor court culture Chaucer's Pandarus represented "a model of advisory friendship and political sagacity," even as he functions also as "a creature of voyeurism and surreptitiousness."[29] In Lerer's view, Troilus is not Pandarus's only student: early modern courtiers also depended on his teaching to learn their craft. Medieval literary forms, characters, and narratives had a continued presence in Tudor England. The essays in this volume speak to all three of these continuities.

When they look back at the texts of the English Middle Ages, the Tudor writers discussed in this volume express anxieties that are both deeper and more public than the Oedipal anxiety of influence. The Reformation (and Counter-Reformation), the printing press, sixteenth-century enclosure riots, and the increasing possibility of socioeconomic mobility all made the act of looking backward politically fraught. Despite the eighteenth-century picturesque imagination of the Renaissance in clear opposition to the Middle (or even "Dark") Ages, England's present was inevitably linked to its medieval past for Tudor readers.[30] The meaning of that medieval past was disputed, however, and potentially dangerous as well as potentially useful.

If the variety of Renaissance retrospections discussed in this collection manifest the complexities of the early modern understanding of the past, they also demonstrate the great scholarly potential that early modern medievalism still holds. Far from being superseded by the Renaissance, the Middle Ages remained important in that new cultural milieu. In studying, responding to, and reprinting medieval texts, early modern readers were not just looking backward, as the title of this volume might imply. The very fact that Tudor writers used their medieval antecedents in all of these ways kept the medieval literary and historical tradition present and active. Historical retrospection is thus a way of looking at the writer's own time as well. It therefore seems no coincidence that the Clerk's twin images of book and body, text and tomb, recur throughout this collection. Both graves and texts are monuments of the past, as the essays in this volume repeatedly demonstrate. As such, these monuments attempt to fix the meaning of that earlier time for successive ages.

Antecedent texts help enable future composition, but to do so they need to be contained, entombed. However, the Middle Ages, like Griselda and her children, refused to stay dead.[31] Far from being a buried past, irrelevant to later periods, the literature, historiography, politics, religion, and law of the Middle Ages remained deeply bound up with some very contemporary concerns of the Tudor era. The title of this volume uses the metaphor of early modern readers looking backward to their medieval antecedents, but texts from the Middle Ages were not trapped in the past; they were the still-present material from which early modern authors constructed their own works. Medieval authors may have been relegated to their tombs by the mid-sixteenth century, but many of their books continued to circulate and be read.[32] Books outlast their authors and their initial context; keeping this in mind can help scholars of premodern and early modern England better understand the ongoing and changing cultural significances of the texts that we study.

NOTES

1. Chaucer, *Riverside Chaucer*, *CT* IV.31, 29. Subsequent citations will be parenthetical in the text.

2. Much has been written comparing the tone and emphasis of the Clerk's Tale to those of antecedent versions of the story (including Petrarch's). See, for example, Emma

Campbell, "Sexual Poetics and the Politics of Translation," 191–216; David Wallace, "'Whan She Translated Was,'" 156–215; and Dinshaw, "Griselda Translated," chap. 5 in *Chaucer's Sexual Poetics*.

3. The envoi is consistently designated "Lenvoy de Chaucer" in the manuscripts. Of course, the Clerk and the pilgrim-narrator of the *Canterbury Tales* are both Chaucerian fictions; the *Canterbury Tales* is by Chaucer, but within that text Chaucer does not speak in his own voice. I refer to the Clerk, rather than the pilgrim-narrator, as the speaker, since the Clerk introduces this passage in the first person: "I wol with lusty herte, fressh and grene / Seyn yow a song to glade yow, I wene" (lines 1173–74).

4. Bloom, *Anxiety of Influence*.

5. The same may not be the case for the later readers of both Chaucer and Langland, his English contemporary. On the later construction of the two poets as rivals, see Bowers, *Chaucer and Langland*.

6. See, for example, James Simpson, *Reformation and Cultural Revolution*; Lerer, *Chaucer and His Readers*; or Lawton, "Dullness and the Fifteenth Century."

7. At least in the case of the early Middle Ages, the understanding of England as marginal was not simply the projection of a condescending later age. Nicholas Howe has argued that Bede himself understood early medieval Britain as marginal within the Roman Empire; see Howe, "From Bede's World to 'Bede's World.'"

8. The quotation is taken from the work's modern edition: Lily Campbell, *Mirror for Magistrates*, 69. This passage is discussed by Paul Strohm in *Politique*, 88–89. In an unpublished conference paper ("The *Mirror* Syndicate Reads Lydgate, 1553"), Strohm argued that this scene treats Lydgate as "apparitional" in two senses of the word: in the etymological sense of being a presence that appears in response to a summons, and in the spiritual sense of being an apparition or ghost (*OED*, s.v. "apparitional"). I am grateful to Strohm for the permission to paraphrase his argument here.

9. Blundeville, *True order and Methode*, fols. Fiiv–Fiiir. Of course, Sir Philip Sidney makes the opposite point about history as an ethical genre in the *Defense of Poesy*: "history, being captived to the truth of a foolish world, is many times a terror from well-doing, and an encouragement to unbridled wickedness"; Sidney, *Major Works*, 225.

10. Ellis, *Hall's Chronicle*, vi.

11. The stability of a text is itself only approximate, however. Both manuscripts and printed texts were subject to variation in the processes of production (authorial, scribal, and printing variants) as well as circulation (marginalia, rebinding, damage, or loss). Adrian Johns has argued strongly against the notion that an early modern printed text is "fixed"; Johns, *Nature of the Book*, especially chap. 1, "Introduction: The Book of Nature and the Nature of the Book." My point here does not presume unanimity of print or manuscript exemplars so much as the relative durability of any single, physical book (which, it is true, could be altered over time).

12. Holinshed, *Laste volume of the Chronicles*, 1116–17.

13. Holinshed, *Laste volume of the Chronicles*, 1117. For a more detailed discussion of Holinshed's historiography and his awareness of divergent interpretations of the events he records, see Annabel Patterson, *Reading Holinshed's Chronicles*. See also Kelen, "'It is dangerous (gentle reader).'"

14. The distinction between literary and nonliterary texts is conventional but inexact: there are literary elements not simply in drama or verse but also in historical and legal texts. In their essays below, Kellie Robertson invokes Hayden White's notion of the "emplotment" of historical narrative, and Rebecca Brackmann discusses the extended metaphors

William Lambarde uses in his legal writing. Moreover, some narratives recognized as historical in the Middle Ages would today be classified as literary fictions (for example, the Trojan history that William Kuskin discusses in his essay below).

15. To use Strohm's definition of Lydgate as "apparitional," if an apparition appears as a response to a summons, the summoner holds the power; if the apparition is a spirit that returns of its own volition, the apparition and not its observer is the controlling agent.

16. Strohm, *Politique*, 89.

17. McMullan and Matthews, *Reading the Medieval in Early Modern England*, 2.

18. Foxe, *Ecclesiastical History*, C1r; Foxe's complete list of Catholic practices is much longer.

19. Robinson, *Anatomie of the English nunnery at Lisbon*; for a discussion of this passage, see Warren, below.

20. Lambarde, *William Lambarde and Local Government*, 117–18; For a discussion of this passage, see Brackmann, below.

21. John Leland, *Newe Yeares Gyfte . . .*, printed in Smith, *Itinerary of John Leland*, xxxvii–xxxviii.

22. Leland, *Newe Yeares Gyfte*, quoted in Smith, *Itinerary of John Leland*, xxxviii.

23. Prendergast has also explored the intersection between text and tomb in *Chaucer's Dead Body*.

24. One need not posit (as Freud did) the literal and universal applicability of his paradigms in order for them to provide interpretive schemata for analyzing texts from a premodern age. Freud's own "proofs" for his theories derive frequently from figures within the Western literary tradition (e.g., Oedipus, the Sandman). Lee Patterson has argued against the application of Freudian concepts to premodern literature; Patterson, "Chaucer's Pardoner on the Couch," 656. However, because Freud often conceptualized his theories by reference to premodern Western literature, I would argue for their continued applicability in medieval and early modern literary studies, even as Freudianism has been largely supplanted in Freud's own field of psychology.

25. Interestingly, *Hamlet* could be said to share with the works discussed in this volume the metaphorical conjunction between body and book. When Hamlet encounters Polonius in act 2, scene 2, Hamlet is reading a book (which forms the initial subject of their dialogue); later in the play, Hamlet exits his mother's closet dragging the body of the murdered Polonius. The bookish Hamlet has turned Polonius from a kind of walking commonplace book to a common corpse.

26. It is also worth recalling that Petrarch (who from a twenty-first-century perspective seems a near contemporary to Chaucer) may have been distant enough in both time and nationality to be unfamiliar to Chaucer's readers. As Theresa Tinkle points out, manuscripts of the *Canterbury Tales* frequently misspell Petrarch's name in ways that suggest the scribes had not heard of the author; Tinkle, "Wife of Bath's Sexual/Textual Lives," 65. Manuscript spellings of Petrarch's name when the Clerk introduces him at line 31 range from "Perak" (San Marino, Huntington Library, MS Ellesmere 26 C 9) to "Partrake" (London, Bodleian Library, MS Laud 739) to "Patrik" (London, Bodleian Library, MS Laud 686); there is a similar range of spelling variants across the manuscripts at line 1147 of the Clerk's Tale, where the Clerk closes his tale with the claim that Petrarch wrote the story of Griselda to counsel constancy amid ongoing adversity. See Manly and Rickert, *Text of the "Canterbury Tales,"* pt. 3, p. 330 (the first introduction of Petrarch's name) and pt. 3, p. 370 (the reference to Petrarch in the tale's conclusion).

27. Scholarship that speaks to multiple academic disciplines might not always rise to

the level of "interdisciplinary," as David Scott Kastan has pointed out (*Shakespeare After Theory*, 51). However, the essays in this volume, bringing together as they do texts, cultural phenomena, and reading practices from two distinct periods, might (by virtue of spanning medieval and early modern studies) fulfill Kastan's definition of the "truly interdisciplinary": work that "would expose the limitations of disciplinary knowledge formations and work to undermine the disciplinary culture of the modern academy" (47).

28. McMullan and Matthews survey recent work in this area in their introduction to *Reading the Medieval* (1–14). One noteworthy example of scholarship with a deep investment in both medieval and early modern studies is Summit, *Memory's Library*. As Elizabeth Scala pointed out in a review of Curtis Perry and John Watkins's collection, *Shakespeare in the Middle Ages*, work that spans the period divide is more usually written by medievalists looking forward than by early modernists looking backward. Her review opens: "It isn't often that one has breaking news to share in a book review, but to readers of *TMR* the news that Shakespeareans and other early modernists now appear interested in the Middle Ages feels much like that. Perry and Watkins's collection intimates, alongside other recent volumes [her footnote cites the McMullan and Matthews collection], that the medieval period is finally starting to attract its disciplinary neighbors" (*The Medieval Review*, 10.05.21).

29. Lerer, *Courtly Letters in the Age of Henry VIII*, 3.

30. The word "medieval" does not enter the language until the eighteenth century. *OED*, s.v. "medieval." On the semantics of "medieval," see Matthews, "From Mediaeval to Mediaevalism."

31. Gordon McMullan and David Matthews make a similar point, with a particular focus on the unquiet ghost of Chaucer in the prologue to the printed edition of *The Two Noble Kinsmen*; McMullan and Matthews, *Reading the Medieval*, 2.

32. See similarly, Ernst Gerhardt's study of John Bale's rhetoric in describing England's loss of manuscripts after the dissolution of the monasteries: "While Bale attempts to mark a decisive break in England's history—radically differentiating himself and his contemporaries from the Catholic past—his attempt fails to the degree that manuscripts survive as remnants of the past." Gerhardt, "'No quyckar merchaundyce than lybrary bokes,'" 420.

The Resurrected Corpus:
History and Reform
in Bale's *Kynge Johan*

Dan Breen

John Bale's *Kynge Johan* is frequently recognized as the earliest extant play to stage a representation of an English king—in fact, of two English kings.[1] Recognized far less often is that the play is also one of the earliest to stage an English historian—in fact, two English historians. The first of these is the character Veritas, who enters after the historical plot has concluded with John's assassination, and delivers a speech that is part eulogy, part political prophecy. To aid in recounting John's reign and to serve as his muse, Veritas invokes the second English historian: "Leylonde, out of thy slumber awake, / And witness a trewthe for thyn owne countrey's sake."[2] This is John Leland, a friend and antiquarian colleague of Bale's who died in 1552, at least six years before Bale made his final revisions to *Kynge Johan*.[3] The effects of Veritas's (and Leland's) entrance on the remainder of the play are remarkable. Not only is King John's reputation rescued from the libels of Catholic historians but political order is restored to a realm in crisis, the Protestant reformation is set back on course, and Sedition (the character as well as the political concept he represents) is purged from England, cursing Veritas as he is led to the gallows: "I sought to haue serued yow lyke as I ded kynge Iohn, / But that veryte stopte me. The deuyll hym poison!" (lines 2575–76). As Sedition observes here, Veritas seems to exercise the kind of power we might expect in a monarch.

Why, then, does the play send a historian to do a monarch's job? The broader question here of the role of medieval historiography within an England newly separated from the jurisdiction of the Church of Rome was one of crucial currency for post-papal royal politics, largely because medieval history—or the Crown's version of it, at any rate—served as one important evidentiary source upon which Henry VIII and his counselors drew in order to justify England's ecclesiastical and political independence. From the very beginning, even before its

16

course was set, the English reformation was represented as an act of resurrection. Scholars summoned to London to aid in crafting arguments for the annulment of Henry's marriage to Catherine of Aragon contributed research for the *Collectanea satis copiosa*, a manuscript anthology of selections from mostly historical texts that asserted the temporal and spiritual rights of the monarch against those of the pope.[4] The Act in Restraint of Appeals, a piece of Parliamentary legislation that formally severed temporal ties between England and Rome, commenced with the assertion that the work of historians attested to the authenticity of Henry's claims of primacy: "Where by divers sundry old authentic histories and chronicles it is manifestly declared and expressed that this realm of England is an Empire . . . governed by one supreme head and king."[5] And Henry himself, assuredly recognizing the political value history offered for his cause, informed Charles V's imperial ambassador that he intended to challenge the pope's jurisdictional claims in order to "repair the error of Kings Henry II and John who, by deceit, being in difficulties, had made this realm and Ireland tributary."[6] Indeed, if it might fairly be wondered why Bale's historian is doing a king's work, it is at least clear that in the 1530s king's work was not easily distinguishable from historian's work, and that the two were in fact interdependent.[7]

One element of this interdependence, shown in the examples cited above, derives from historiography's usefulness as a source of political propaganda.[8] A second, particularly important for the present discussion, relates to the specific designs that Protestant reformers—courtiers, theologians, and historians—had on claiming the king's favor. While eager to ally themselves with the king in Henry VIII's break with the Catholic Church, the reformers were equally eager to draw Henry over to their theological and ecclesiastical views, an intellectual and spiritual trajectory about which the king was at first reluctant, and then antipathetic.[9] Bale's *Kynge Johan* has for some time been regarded by critics as an excellent example of such an attempt at confessional encroachment.[10] Both the title character and Imperial Majesty are presented as virtuously engaged in a political and religious struggle with Rome, like Henry. Both characters are also—as the reformers hoped Henry would become—decisively Protestant: they oppose auricular confession and vigorously support preaching of the gospel.[11] Despite the tension produced by recognizing the monarch as a source of ultimate authority and then attempting to alter the constitution of this authority by attributing to it beliefs it does not hold, *Kynge Johan* seems to acknowledge a need to secure the monarch's support in order to provide a dispensation for its religious reforms—to work the system from within, as it were. Andrew Hadfield pithily sums up Bale's (and the reformers') attitude toward the monarch's role in the reformation: for Hadfield, Bale is "king-worshipping Bale."[12]

Yet if the monarch can be said to be the most important figure in the English reformation, there is also a sense in which the reformation merely begins with him or her. Despite whatever personal virtues or dispositions a monarch may possess toward Protestant ideals of godliness, the measure of a monarch's success as a reformer is the degree to which he or she is able to secure the political and ecclesiastical conditions necessary to enable widespread evangelization. It is curious, then, that this is the capacity in which Bale's King John is most strikingly deficient. Though he is certainly virtuous and well-versed in both history and scripture, his reforms invariably fail.[13] Moreover, this failure seems to be related to the terms according to which the king attempts to implement his new policies: John tries to inaugurate his reforms by insisting on the preeminence of his own political authority—indeed, very much as Henry did.[14] Though Imperial Majesty, the play's other monarch-figure, fares better politically, he is off stage when the estates of council repent their wrongdoing and again at the very end of the play when they discuss the political and religious future of the nation. If the monarch is an important figure for Bale, then it also seems clear that this importance is qualified in significant ways.

Veritas, of course, is a key figure in these political developments, and it is the purpose of this essay to examine his overall influence in the play and the effects of his influence on our reading of the outcome. In what follows I hope to offer a different perspective on Bale's politics by reading *Kynge Johan* against the background of Bale's work as an antiquarian and historian in the 1530s and 1540s. Embracing John Leland's comprehensive research methodology, Bale seeks to further Leland's work in reconceiving historiography by redefining the limits of textuality and conducting historical inquiry based on the evidence of royal and civic documents, topography, and architecture, as well as the more traditional history. Unlike Leland, however, Bale attempts to draw the discipline of historiography into a specifically public domain. Bale identifies works of history written during the Middle Ages as a potent intellectual resource that must be harnessed by English readers of different social degrees in order for the reformation to succeed. Manuscripts of histories kept in monastic libraries must be preserved, submitted for publication in print, and disseminated widely as evidence of the corrupting influence of the Catholic Church. In Veritas Bale creates the historian capable of effecting such a monumental cultural shift, which in turn creates a surprising political change. Veritas's intervention in *Kynge Johan* amounts to a powerful critique of political centralization, and the potential consequences of this centralization on the authority to produce, preserve, and interpret scriptural and historical texts, specifically works of history written during the Middle Ages. In *Kynge Johan* historiography and literature are represented as social imperatives, as arenas in which subjects of the crown can and must exercise their political and religious duties and contribute to the progress of the reformation and to the stability of the nation.

Histories of Power: Bale, Leland, and the
Politics of Medieval Historiography

The starting point for this discussion, then, is the staging of multiple sources of political authority with which *Kynge Johan* presents its audience, and more specifically the roles that Veritas and Leland play in mediating and structuring these sources. Why does Bale choose to highlight this multiplicity through a historian in *Kynge Johan*? This question acquires a special immediacy given the context in which the play was originally composed. As noted above, in the 1530s historians were central to the project of the Royal Supremacy and as such were engaged in defending the king's prerogative against the church's claims for mutually exclusive levels of legal and financial jurisdiction—in other words, the historians were trying to prevent a particular form of political plurality.[15] The political bent of the supremacy exerted such considerable force on historiography that it drew together writers of very different ideological commitment.[16] Humanist scholars (such as Leland) were attracted by the possibility of winning preferment at court, and Protestant reformers (such as Bale) by the opportunity for evangelization afforded by the break with Rome. That these two groups did come together did not, of course, result in either abandoning its intellectual and spiritual principles per se. Instead, as James Simpson observes, Henry's move toward political centralization provided a broad banner under which humanists and religious reformers might pursue their discrete agendas, provided they did so in the king's name.[17] Perhaps the question at the top of the paragraph might then be restated: what motive might a historian have to challenge a political dispensation that authorizes his work?

One possible answer lies in the ways in which Henrician historians understood their relationship to the royal policy that gave the most direct material impetus to their work—namely, the dissolution of the monasteries. Very recently, critics have drawn attention to the generally ambivalent stance taken particularly by Leland and Bale toward the dissolution, broadly considered.[18] Though each looks with favor on the breakup of the monastic and fraternal orders, both write with considerable regret regarding the destruction of the libraries, which in Bale's words contained "infynyte treasure of knowledge."[19] The consequences of Bale's and Leland's conflicted attitudes are examined in considerable depth by other scholars, but it is important here to note the one concern that each identifies as an especially troublesome consequence of the dissolution: both Leland and Bale are notably anxious about the ways in which books have become scattered and potentially irretrievable.[20] For both, this massive diffusion constitutes an intellectual crisis with inescapable political dimensions, and both make the recovery and analysis of monastic books a matter of national import. However, the specific scholarly projects that each envisions are very different, and embedded within these projects are remarkably different assumptions about the social role of history, the relationship of historiography to political power, and the nature of the English polity.

For Leland, the task of gathering manuscripts and printed books in the wake of the dissolution was closely analogous to Henry's broader political project, of which the dissolution was one expression: the solidifying of his political control over Parliament, the church, and the outer territorial reaches of his domain. Leland's understanding of the link between his work as a historian and Henry's brand of royal politics emerges most clearly in the "Newe Yeares Gyfte," a short précis of the historiographical work Leland intends to produce as a synthesis of his researches in monastic and collegiate libraries in the 1530s and early 1540s.[21] For him, there is no historiographical project without Henry's authorization. Although it is conventional enough for Leland to identify his patron as the inspiration for the project, it seems curious that in so doing he divests himself of virtually all generative agency. Henry becomes more than the patron who "encoraged me, by the authoryte of your moste gracious commyssion" (B.8r);[22] by the time Leland begins to describe the full extent of his writing, he represents it as work to which "your grace moste lyke a kyngeley patrone of all good learning ded anymate me" (C.6v). His choice of the verb "animate" here is especially suggestive because it conveys two distinct connotations: that Henry is a metaphorical spirit which imbues Leland's researches, and that he is in a very real sense responsible for creating those researches. Indeed, the deference to Henry and the attendant rhetorical gesture—to envision Leland's writing as an enactment of Henry's political dispensation—are remarkable throughout the text and help to construct a particular model of history's political role.[23]

In the "Newe Yeares Gyfte," the historian labors within a political space that the monarch has already carved out for him, both materially and methodologically.[24] The historian performs a kind of work that is also generated by the monarch's prerogative, and which produces results that must first be presented to the monarch through an audience-specific medium. Further, the monarch retains a reversionary privilege over the elements that make up this labor. According to Leland, of all the texts he has collected, "parte remayne in the moste magnyfycent libraryes of your royal palaces. Part also remayne in my custodie" (C.2r). These texts no longer lie "secretely in corners" (C.2r) of monastic libraries; like the monasteries themselves, they have been appropriated to the king's discretion, for him to parcel out as he chooses. Additionally, the historian in the "Newe Yeares Gyfte" is continually performing labor that is triumphal in nature. As Henry has come to power over his kingdom and its church in such a way as to redefine the office of monarch according to terms that the examples furnished by his predecessors cannot provide, so too must Leland craft a narrative of English history that is unmistakably of the present, one which draws upon and ultimately surpasses its predecessors in the historical tradition. In other words, the primary importance of the medieval texts Leland has collected is defined by their usefulness for inclusion in the monumental history of the nation that he hopes to undertake, but once realized, this massive narrative will supersede its constituent elements as an authoritative text and reduce these elements to the status of historical curiosities. By my count, Leland informs Henry in the "Newe Yeares Gyfte" that his historiographical project will consist of sixty-four books once completed—including a fifty-volume history of every county in England and Wales—as well as a quadrate table of silver engraved to represent the territorial extent of Henry's power.[25]

For Bale, the monarch is also of course an important figure, and it is tempting to suggest that Bale understands this importance in the same way that Leland does. As a client of Thomas Cromwell in the 1530s, Bale would have appreciated that his fortunes at court depended largely on his ability to satisfy his patron. Moreover, he certainly thought highly enough of Leland and his work to edit and publish the "Newe Yeares Gyfte" in 1549, with a dedication to Edward VI. However, *The Laboryouse Journey and Serche of Johan Leyland*—Bale's edition of the "Newe Yeares Gyfte," which includes Bale's own commentary and apparatus—offers strong indications that Bale, far from echoing Leland, is using his work to offer strikingly different models of readership and polity. If the surviving corpus of works of medieval history defines a specific and unique relationship between monarch and historian for Leland, historiography for Bale represents a social and political imperative, one that reaches across the boundaries of social degree.[26]

In his dedication to Edward, Bale writes that chronicles have value both as material embodiments of tradition and as objects of interpretive study: "I shall not nowe neade to recite to your learned maiestie, what profyte aryseth by continuall readinge of bokes, specially of auncyent histories. . . . They treat what is in ych commenwelth to be followed, and what to be chefely eschewed" (A.3r–v). This "profyte," it is clear, is not reserved only for Edward or members of the nobility and gentry who hold high office. As Bale presents Leland's account of his geographical study of England, he remarks in the apparatus: "out of [this work] myght men of sondry occupienges, fatch most wonderful knowledge, for their necessary affayres euery where" (D.5r). Elsewhere the usefulness of Leland's work is redefined in terms that reach beyond the conceptual boundaries of occupation or social estate. In discussing Leland's plan to include as part of his finished product a narrative tracing the histories of the "Isles adiacent to [the king's] noble realme," Bale comments that the effect of this inclusion will be that Leland's "natural countrey men, myghte knowe the sytuacion and hystorycall commodities of [these islands], and afterwardes that all men dwellynge undre the worthy dominion of Englande, myghte of his studyouse labours take profyte" (E.2r). In other words, historical narrative is uniquely suited to convey to all readers a sense of a national past and to translate that sense into a series of lessons applicable to the present.

This perception conforms exactly to traditional understandings of the pragmatics of humanist historical thought.[27] What is interesting here is these observations are made not by the emphatically humanistic Leland but by the emphatically non-humanistic Bale.[28] Certainly Leland did envision his project, once completed, as working within humanist standards of education and aesthetics. He writes, for example, that he hopes his histories will be judged to have "pleased, but also profyted the studyouse, gentil, and equal reders" (E.4r). But again, Leland's interpretive authority derives from his understanding of his work as a product of Henry's political authority. Bale, by contrast, stakes out a role for the historian—or more properly, for historiography—that exists outside the patron-client economy of the court, a role that lays claim to an interpretive authority in which both monarch and subjects participate.

By emphasizing that the benefits of diligence in historical study extend across the social spectrum, Bale intimates that the didactic potential of historical narrative is so capacious that the act of interpretation acquires a curious specificity for the reader. Edward VI may look into a chronicle and find the causes of the rise and fall of political dynasties, but in so doing his experience is different only in degree from that of "men of sondry occupienges." Those who read histories are at the moment of textual engagement readers first, who then look to apply the lessons of the past "for their necessary affayres euery where." Further, having established the preservation and reproduction of chronicle texts as necessary for the perpetuation of national tradition and the advancement of political and religious reform, Bale's emphasis on the importance of broad social participation in the act of textual consumption creates a readership whose very constitution makes it complicit in the project of nation building, and indeed in the development of an empire.[29] To read English history is to learn one's social role, and so by acting upon the principles gleaned from historical study to make the shape of English society more coherent.

What is especially remarkable about this concept is the degree to which the task of contributing to the moral and political health of the nation by disseminating and interpreting texts devolves upon the members of the gentry, rather than the monarch. As noted above, the king is complicit in and necessary to the project of recovering and reestablishing the nation's sense of its own past, but in precisely the same way that every other reader demonstrates this complicity—that is, by reading. Bale exhorts the gentry to demonstrate their regard for England's historical traditions by participating in his expansive historiographical project, and also to take more direct action by providing material support for the reproduction of medieval historical and exegetical texts. In his "Preface to the Reader" he issues a call to the nobility and merchants of the country: "Steppe you fourth now last of all, ye noble men & women (as there are in these dayes a great nombre of you most nobyllye lerned, prayse be to God for it) and shewe your naturall noble hartes to your nacyon. . . . [B]rynge you into the lyghte, that they haue kept longe in the darkenes, or els in these dayes seketh utterly to destroye. As ye fynde a notable Antyqvyte . . . let them anon be imprented, & so brynge them into a nombre of coppyes, both to their and your owne perpetuall fame" (B.2v).

It is extremely important here to note the specificity of this exhortation. Bale does not use his discussion of printing to praise the wide availability of scripture, as John Foxe does in his *Acts and Monuments*; instead he writes solely about medieval works of history.[30] Further, the act of reading these histories is for the time being second in importance to the task of searching them out and printing them, with no apparent restrictions on content or authorship.[31] Readers who do successfully bring medieval histories into print are, strikingly, granted a share of historical memorialization. For Bale, the process of exhaustively surveying the available material seems to lie at the heart of the historian's enterprise.[32] His collective call to the gentry is again echoed in his conclusion, wherein Bale enlists readers to contribute to his own ongoing work by inviting them to peruse the catalog of writers he includes at the end of the text in order to inform him, of any omissions: "sende me the names, tymes, tytles, nombres, and beginninges of their workes. I wyl register them, as I haue don those" (H.7v).[33] The exhaustive comprehensiveness that characterizes Leland's approach to his sources and is for him a precondition of writing history is for Bale always a future goal, never a present reality. The work of this bibliography will never be fully completed, and the measure of its success depends largely upon a strikingly articulated collaboration among the members of the social degrees wealthy enough to have access to medieval texts.[34]

In the *Laboryouse Journey* then, Bale envisions a thoroughly textual political culture, in which there would be at least "in euery shyre of Englande, but one solempne library, to the preservacyon of these noble workes, and preferrement of good lernynges in oure posteryte" (B.1r). And yet, as much as he is concerned to implicate multitudes of readers and printers in the project of nation building, he reserves an important role for the historian.[35] Significantly, he articulates this role in a way that allows him to distance himself from it—unlike Leland, Bale does not suggest that he himself can bring closure to the antiquarian enterprise in which he is engaged. Rather, the historian he envisions as being able to interpret the chronicles and set them in "good order"—that is, to free them of the influence of Catholic interpretive bias—is consistently represented in abstract, inclusive terms.[36] The ideal English historian for Bale is a figure rather than a person. He laments the fact that, as yet, "no studiouse persone" (C.3v) has come forward to inaugurate a campaign of transliterating manuscripts into print, and the fact that during the dissolution "men of learning & of perfyght loue to their nacyon, were not then appointed to the serche of [monastic] lybraryes" (A.2v). Conversely, he hopes that Leland's work "shoulde come to some learned mannes hande" (D.7r).[37] Through his own exhortations to the gentry, Bale construes his work as a search for both histories and historians, and as a way for literate members of the commonwealth to provide the historical framework through which the reformation can proceed.

The Resurrected Corpus

Bale's *Laboryouse Journey*—the first work in which he resurrects Leland— is haunted by a pervasive air of philosophical and political crisis. The historical Leland disappeared into the sheer impossibility of the task he sets for himself. For all that he had accomplished in his travels and researches, he left the production of an authoritative history of England undone; the fully comprehensive narrative becomes, like its author, a poetic figure. However, the very existence of Leland's work allows Bale to reconsider the relationship between history and reform and to approach certain aspects of this relationship with a kind of hopeful speculation. The figure of this single, masterful historian provides Bale with symbolic capital that energizes his thinking about the nature of polity. In the *Laboryouse Journey* Bale's idealized England rises from its medieval past with a sense of urgent realization. National history cannot—indeed, must not—exist through the prerogative of one person, project, or institution. Such centralization helped the Catholic Church to maintain its hegemony for hundreds of years. At the same time, Leland's efforts allow Bale the opportunity to conceptualize the English polity in metaphorical terms that suggest a library under construction. Leland's researches represent work already undertaken, and Bale makes it clear that it falls to English subjects to pick up where Leland left off.

Seen in this light, it is clear that the monarch plays a pivotal role in this biblio-commonwealth. While appreciating the utility of historiography for understanding his or her own responsibilities, in addition the monarch must recognize that reading national history is imperative across the social degrees. In *Kynge Johan* Bale presents his audience with a monarch who comprehends the former but addresses the latter with considerable uncertainty. From the beginning of the play, questions of history, authority, and interpretation are central to the crisis facing John and his subjects. Initially, this crisis seems to derive from the king's misunderstanding of the gravity of the country's collective difficulties. John perceives a need for reform, but he first suspects that this need is related to the fact that the extent of his empire has made the extant English legal system an insufficient and parochial instrument of government. Early on, then, he confines his aims "To reforme the lawes and sett men in good order / [So] That trew iustyce may be had in euery bordere" (lines 20–21); that is, he calibrates his changes to the legal system according to what for him are absolute standards of truth as defined by scripture and by the English chronicles. However, upon John's meeting with the character England, the audience begins to discover that the nation's problems run considerably deeper than the king seems to suppose. In the first of several such moments, King John is unable to recognize England because of the poverty to which she has been reduced by the abuses of the clergy. Even after she reveals her identity, the king appears to experience momentary doubt: "I mervell right sore how thow commyst chaungyd thus" (line 42).

The parallel themes of misrecognition, misperception, and doubt become central to the early action of the play.[38] King John constantly has to ask for clarification when speaking with Sedition, the chief vice figure; Nobility is consistently fooled into thinking Sedition is a member of the clergy when the latter dons ecclesiastical apparel; and Civil Order is unable to understand or elaborate on the character of his transgressions when the king calls him to account during the first attempt at political reform.[39] The nature of this constant misperception remains ambiguous and somewhat suspended early on. Despite not addressing this constant undercurrent of uncertainty, the king forges ahead with his attempt to reorient the law toward scriptural precepts and forces the estates of council to swear a formal oath rededicating their allegiance to him. Interestingly, the terms of the oath lead the estates to affirm by locating its power entirely within the person of the monarch. After King John has addressed each individually, Clergy, Nobility, and Civil Order all respond in unison, acknowledging: "To be faythfull, than, ye us more streytly compell" (line 526).

Some critics read this model of reformation onto the end of the play, asserting that Imperial Majesty succeeds where John fails because Imperial Majesty is successfully able to rid England of the influence of the Catholic Church, and so consequently can exercise an unchallenged control over the estates of council.[40] It is also possible, however, that King John's attempts at reformation are unsuccessful for different reasons—reasons closely related to the pervasive problem of misperception, which remains ambiguous and unresolved in spite of the king's attempts to push past it. As the action of the play develops, this misperception is increasingly linked to problems with the dissemination and interpretation of scriptural and historical texts. King John develops his approach to political and religious reform through an intensive program of reading and rereading scripture and the English chronicles. Because his secular estates of council have no experience with these forms of textual interpretation, they are unable to grasp the rationale that underpins his reforms, and so John enforces them by insisting on the eminence of his political prerogative. Political power, then, attempts to fill the gap that separates John's understanding from that of the estates, and so to employ the estates in achieving political ends that are fully comprehensible only to the king. Ironically,

John's administrative strategies here demonstrate a curious symmetry with those of the church, which also seeks to use the estates in order to enhance its political prestige and maintain the luxuriant lifestyles to which its clergy are accustomed. Like John, the agents of the church are willing to appeal to the prerogative of political authority when necessary, but in the play this is rarely the case. The contest for political control of England is carried out among the estates, between the king and the church, and at issue are the strategies that each political pole employs to secure the allegiance of the estates.[41]

The most effective method by which the church exerts its authority is by keeping a careful material and interpretive control over the very texts from which John develops his programs of religious and political reform. During the congress of the vices, it becomes evident that the suppression of the Bible is essential to the church's control over England. The vice figures vow to continue this campaign both in a material and in a metaphorical sense. The character Dissimulation, for example, announces the pope's intent to support the proliferation of liturgical ceremonies in order "To drowne the scriptures for doubte of heresye" (line 999), and to call an ecclesiastical council to declare that "Gospell prechyng wyll be an heresy" (line 1023). Shortly afterward the pope himself, during his symbolic condemnation of King John, reduces the Bible to an icon in order to represent excommunication: "As this boke doth speare by my work maanuall, / I wyll God to close uppe from hym his benyfyttes all" (lines 1038–39). Presumably, at this moment on stage the book is shut in a demonstration of the church's control over interpretive authority, which extends beyond the boundaries of scripture to works of secular history. Even before Veritas's appearance at the end of the play, Nobility is aware that the potential for considerable abuse exists when textual production and interpretive practice are entirely centralized. He addresses Clergy thus: "Yow pristes are the cawse that Chronycles doth defame / So many prynces and men of notable name, / For yow take upon yow to wryght them evermore" (lines 585–87). History itself, as far as Nobility is able to understand, is located within the textual dominion of the church, and it is because the church is aware of the need to safeguard this dominion that the vice figures in the play are able to maintain their control over England and the estates.[42]

Such a monopolization of textual culture damages attempts at reform by creating an irremediable gap between King John and the estates of council. The king, who has an estimable command of scripture and the chronicles, is unable to marshal these traditions as evidence against the corruption of the vice figures because the vices (and, it should be added, Clergy) have been so successful at keeping the Bible and works of history from secular society. Denied a common discursive field, King John and England on one hand and the estates on the other can only cleave to the textual authority that each group is able to recognize. That these authorities (i.e., the church, as well as scripture and history) are evidently at odds with one another creates the climate of miscommunication, uncertainty, and misperception that invariably frustrates King John's attempts to establish justice and order and leads ultimately to his death. Throughout the play, as he is consistently unable to recognize the treachery intended him by members of the clergy, the king ultimately accepts a lethal dose of poison offered as a cordial by Dissimulation, disguised as the monk Simon of Swynsett.

It is at this moment, however, when the related problems of political and interpretive authority seem most insoluble, that the play seems to begin to offer a novel solution. On stage with the dying king, the widow England takes custody of his body and delivers a short speech that looks ahead to the monastic works of historiography that she knows will misrepresent King John and his deeds:

> Oh horryble case, that ever so noble a kynge
> Shoulde thus be destroyed and lost for ryghteouse doynge
> By a cruell sort of disguysed bloud souppers—
> Unmercyfull murtherers, all dronke in the bloude of marters!
> Report what they wyll in their most furyouse madnesse,
> Of thys noble kynge muche was the godlynesse.
> (lines 2187–92)

England's lament presents two entirely new perspectives on the problem of the church's textual dominion. First, in order to create an alternative version of John's kingship, she explicitly challenges this dominion by invoking the rhetoric of martyrdom and appropriating the conventions of hagiography—in other words, by engaging with monastic historians on their own formal terms.[43] More crucially, however, England also gestures toward the existence of a newly generated and competing tradition of historiography, one that is properly the dominion of the nation rather than of the Catholic Church. The textual basis of this new tradition is none other than the king's body, which is transformed in England's own interpretation into an emblem of the consequences of ecclesiastical oppression. As John speaks his last words, England vows that she "wyll not leave ye thus, / But styll be with ye tyll [God] do take yow from us, / And than wyll I kepe your bodye for a memoryall" (lines 2181–83).

This last line is particularly striking because it identifies so clearly the link between the act of memorialization and historiographical production. The king's actual body, still lying on stage, assumes a potent symbolic identity as England asserts that it will generate a body of text that will challenge Catholic interpretations of history. This new historiographical tradition, England hints, will be distinguished by the kind of methodological comprehensiveness that Veritas articulates during his entrance. In particular, readers and writers in this new tradition will be willing to extend conceptions of textual production beyond the generic boundaries of the chronicle and, indeed, beyond the material boundaries of the codex.

England's use of the term "memoryall" conveys a sense of this comprehensiveness. Here the word connotes a written document, but it also, perhaps somewhat surprisingly, evokes the language and apparatus of funerary monuments. Bale was, however, sensitive to the symbolic power of the tomb; in fact, at some point during the late 1540s or early 1550s he composed a Latin poem on the subject of the historical King John's reburial in Worcester Cathedral.[44] The poem identifies itself as an epitaph—as part of John's funerary architecture—and urges the reader to remember the king. This injunction is, however, prefaced by a rhetorical assertion of the poem's claim to memorial authority. Before concluding, the reader (or viewer) is informed that the catalyst for this occasion of remembrance is the king's body lying underneath the stone that displays the epitaph—under *hoc saxo*. As in Bale's play, the king's body must be somehow materially "kept" in a form that is at once textual and nontextual so that it can be constantly revisited, reinterpreted, and reflected upon.[45]

Immediately after the widow England bears the king's body offstage, Veritas enters and inaugurates the new tradition of historiography that England had predicted. Like England, Veritas addresses both history writing and other forms of historical evidence; however, he invokes an additional guiding spirit for his enterprise, namely John Leland. Yet Leland's role here has implications that prove puzzling. Why should Veritas, himself an abstraction called upon to oversee the reformation of historiography, need Leland's symbolic assistance? Why should one muse need to invoke another? In part, Leland's function is to clarify further the nature of Veritas's project. As the ghost of a specific English historian, Leland represents a body of work that has already begun, but which remains unfinished. At the time of his death in 1552, Leland left behind voluminous catalogs of texts and authors, notes on English history, and his "Itinerary"—an enormous collection of notes he made while traveling to monastic and collegiate libraries in the late 1530s and early 1540s. This research was to provide the raw material for the sixty-four books of English history that he had promised Henry VIII in the "Newe Yeares Gyfte," but at Leland's death and later (when Bale made his final revisions to *Kynge Johan*) most of Leland's notes remained unsynthesized, his work largely unpublished. Veritas's gesture toward Leland, then, adds a dimension to the new tradition of historiography that he introduces: history writing must be cumulative as well as comprehensive. Like Leland himself, Veritas begins his attempt to refashion historiography by incorporating work that is already extant.

Within the framework of *Kynge Johan*, however, Veritas acts to change and clarify Leland's view of historiography just as much as Leland does Veritas's. After listing eight chroniclers whose work (supposedly) stands as a testament to King John's character,[46] Veritas goes on to insist that readers and writers of English history must look to additional sources in order to gather an account of John's reign that is free from monastic bias:

Great monymentes are in Yppeswych, Donwych and Berye,
Whych noteth hym to be a man of notable mercye.
The cytie of London through hys mere graunt and premye
Was first privyleged to have both mayer and shryve,
Where before hys tyme it had but baylyves onlye.
In his dayes the bridge the cytiezens ded contrive.
(lines 2212–17)

The image of London Bridge recalls the widow England's determination to commemorate King John in both textual and nontextual forms. As the king's body becomes for England sublimated in different kinds of "memoryall," so too for Veritas is the bridge meant to stand as a testament to John's excellence: "Though he now be dead hys noble actes are alyve" (line 2218). The fusion of royal body with historical artifact, first proclaimed by the widow England, is here reaffirmed and lent an important sense of contemporary relevance.

As far as method is concerned, Veritas's inclusion of London Bridge and other "monymentes" is perfectly consonant with the broad understanding of historical evidence that he and Leland both favor. However, the symbolic and historical value of London Bridge is not confined to the edifice itself. For Veritas, the bridge is a fitting tribute to John both because it provides a material link between his reign and the sixteenth century and because of the nature of its construction—because "the cytiezens ded contryue" it. If the bridge is identified specifically as one of John's "acts," then it is also the case that Veritas's representation of that act allows for a much different understanding of kingly virtue than that which Leland advocates in the "Newe Yeares Gyfte." Where Leland attempted to catalog the English past and present in order to assist Henry VIII in asserting his proprietary and political rights—to translate "youre realme" into text—Veritas's view of the monarch's historiographical identity is fuller and more inclusive. As one of the physical remains of John's reign, London Bridge must be understood as a tribute both to the king and to the citizens who planned and built it. For Veritas, the measure of remembrance lies in objects and texts that bear the stamp of broad social collaboration.

It is here that the differences between Leland and Veritas begin to emerge most clearly. In Veritas's understanding, English historiography is the product of more than a patron-client relationship between monarch and historian. John is the subject of memorialization here not simply because of the personal virtues he may have possessed. He is also remembered because of the degree to which he was willing to limit his own authority and to devolve political and social responsibility onto his English subjects. In addition to London Bridge, Veritas identifies other "monymentes" in East Anglia as further historiographical evidence of John's excellence. These are not statues or sculptures but charters—written documents wherein the supervening authority (in this case the king) agrees to create a legal space for civic or local politics by withdrawing carefully articulated measures of his own power.[47] The charter that the historical John granted to Ipswich specifically addresses this issue. Along with a series of legal and economic privileges, John also allows for the creation of a political system in which Ipswich burgesses elect and have the power of removal over a number of their own civic officials.[48] Significantly, this is precisely the aspect of the charter's legal instrumentality in which Veritas seems most interested.[49] His short discussion of the specifics of John's 1215 London charter, for instance, mentions only that the king created the new political offices of mayor and sheriff, offices to be monitored and occupied by the citizens of London.[50]

In his antiquarian work, Bale was certainly familiar with the historical King John as a granter of charters; in his *Index*, Bale in fact identifies John as the author of the Magna Carta.[51] However, it is interesting to note that the magnanimous and politic King John whom Veritas exhorts his audience to remember (while providing them with a reference list) is remarkably different from the well-meaning but myopic and single-minded king in Bale's play. In one sense, the sharpness of this contrast highlights the intellectual value of Veritas's historiographical project. Absorbing Leland's methodological comprehensiveness, Veritas here uncovers truths that the work of Catholic historians attempted to obscure, both rhetorically and materially. By broadening the canon of historiography to include architecture, topography, and town and city charters, Veritas is able to identify Catholic traditions of history writing as overly exclusive, and inaccessible to most readers. This relative inaccessibility, coupled with the temporal distance that separates medieval historical figures from the sixteenth-century present, lends the interpretations within these texts an air of remote and definitive authority. For Veritas, history is just the opposite: it is a means to a clearer understanding of the present and plays a central role in forming key political and religious decisions.[52]

This sense that history must be read and regarded as ineluctably of the present adds a pragmatic urgency to Veritas's work. It is not enough for Veritas merely to reclaim King John as a potent exemplum providing symbolic authorization for the political and ecclesiastical policies of the House of Tudor. The reexamination of historical texts and the historiographical method itself must be shown to exert a palpable influence on the practices of—and theoretical structures underlying—government and religion. Veritas begins to demonstrate this urgency by incorporating an additional textual category into his historical survey: the narrative of the play itself. As *Kynge Johan* moves into a wholly allegorical mode during the last scene, Veritas takes advantage of this temporal indeterminacy in order to make explicit the historical link between past and present. In his confrontation with the estates of council, he rebukes them by both calling attention to their actions and by challenging the biographical portrait of King John that develops at the hands of the clergy: "Ye have raysed up of hym most shamelesse lyes, / Both by your reportes and by your written storyes" (lines 2289–90). Significantly, Veritas's account of the estates' treachery then shifts focus to the violence done to the king's body: John has been "cruelly slayne" (line 2287); subjects should be executed who "On a noynted kynge . . . [laye] handes violent-lye" (line 2296); and Veritas insists that "I could shewe the place where yow most spyghtfullye / Put out your torches upon hys physnomye" (lines 2301–2). The connection between the bodily harm done to King John and the historiographi-cal tradition that continues to reenact this harm is, for Veritas, unmistakable: "Ye were never wele tyll ye had hym cruelly slayne, / And now, beynge dead, ye haue hym styll in disdayne" (lines 2287–88).

Presented with the comprehensive historical record for which Veritas serves as a figure, the estates undergo a remarkable transformation, the essence of which Clergy articulates: "All the worlde doth knowe that we have done sore amys" (line 2307). The diffusion of interpretive authority throughout the estates makes the vices' position completely untenable—the world is only able to "know" the extent of the church's corruption because Veritas has broken its dominion over textual production and interpretation. Made appropriately contrite by this histori-cal knowledge, the estates are now prepared for the kind of political reform that in the first scene of the play King John attempts to enforce. However, as Imperial Majesty takes the stage, the reenactment of John's oath of allegiance takes place according to strikingly different terms. John's oath demands an affirmation that locates the power for political action squarely with the person of the monarch. The affirmation with which the estates respond to Imperial Majesty makes a strong claim for their own political agency: "By the helpe of God, yche shall do hys func-tion" (line 2649).[53]

Certainly, this act of political reconfiguration is not represented as one that consists solely of redemption. In order for political and religious reform to proceed (and indeed, even before the estates can be prepared to swear the reconstituted oath of allegiance), the character Sedition must be purged from the common-wealth and executed.[54] However, it is important that Bale does not end the play here.[55] Immediately after the oath, Imperial Majesty exits the stage, leaving the estates to provide a brief commentary on the narrative. For Bale, this is a signifi-cant formal departure, with equally significant implications for the intellectual and emotional effects of the play upon its audience. In three of his four other extant plays a single character—in fact, Bale himself as Baleus Prolocutor—remains on stage at the end to provide definitive interpretations of the plays' most valuable moral lessons.[56] At the end of *Kynge Johan*, Bale cedes his interpretive authority in the same way that Imperial Majesty limits his political authority: by highlight-ing the roles and responsibilities of the estates of council.[57] After recounting what they have learned at Veritas's hands, the estates close by urging the audience to remain vigilant against Catholic sedition by knowing "their pestylent wayes" (line

2669) and by offering a prayer that Elizabeth, her counselors, and her posterity will beware of potential Catholic treachery. Strikingly, the effects of Veritas's historiographical project allow the estates to articulate aspects of the monarch's political role as well as their own roles.

Kynge Johan thus implicates itself in an ongoing project of reform by offering itself as a model for political and religious change. However, the model that the play formulates at the end is considerably different from that which it seems to advocate in the beginning. A political culture that favors reform— in which the monarch and his or her estates of council share broad, clearly defined duties across the political spectrum—is not conceivable under the reign of Bale's King John because the intellectual resources the estates need in order to understand the rationale for reform are unavailable to them. John's response is to retreat to the vagaries of monarchial prestige and to exercise an uncompromising and seemingly arbitrary authority. Significantly, of course, this was also Henry VIII's response, and the result for England in the 1530s (and also for England in *Kynge Johan*) was a reformation that stalled and then reversed.[58] For Bale to again revise the play after Elizabeth's accession suggests a perception on his part that the status of the Church of England remained uncertain, and, further, the importance of Elizabeth's active participation in furthering the reformation. That he locates the mechanism for reformation within the reading of scripture and history undertaken among different social degrees, however, suggests a model of social authority that incorporates but goes beyond the office of monarch. In *Kynge Johan* reformation, if it is to succeed, is a political duty that cannot lie only with the monarch.

This essay is not meant to suggest that Bale's play advocates anything like a democracy of readership. Yet the connections between historiography and political agency are frankly compelling. In particular, the emphasis that Veritas places upon reading and reinterpreting an extant historical tradition generates a perspective on mid-Tudor historiography that allows for considerable interrelation among strands of historical inquiry traditionally thought to be discrete. The chronicle, the martyrology, the civic humanist survey, and accounts of national topography all combine in a methodological comprehensiveness that is replicated in the biobibliographical and topographical comprehensiveness that Veritas makes essential to his historical project. Further, the nature of this correspondence between method and practice in Veritas's project suggests an ideological coherence that draws its force from a confidence in the inviolable integrity of the interpretive act itself. Reading history thus becomes a potentially powerful—indeed, in *Kynge Johan* one of the two most powerful—sources of political unity. The status of this unity is, however, contingent upon the diffusion of interpretive practice throughout the estates of the realm, not simply or even chiefly upon the person of the monarch. Following this understanding of historiography in *Kynge Johan*, the politics of the play can be read less as a glorification of the office of the monarch and more as a gesture toward the political potential of the estates. The success of reformation in *Kynge Johan* depends upon the dissemination of scripture and of secular historical texts, and on the systematic and collective reinterpretation of the latter. Reformation cannot truly begin until the body of the murdered king is removed from the stage, returning in diffuse and abstract form through the work of the historians.

NOTES

1. The first of course is the Angevin King John; the second is the character Imperial Majesty who, though he has no discrete historical identity, performs the function of an English monarch, much like the title character in John Skelton's *Magnyfycence* (ca. 1515–16).

2. Bale, *King Johan*, lines 2198–99. Hereafter, the text of the play is cited parenthetically.

3. *Kynge Johan* has a complicated textual history. The fullest accounts are in Adams's edition of *King Johan*, 1–24; Happé, *John Bale*, 89–92; and Walker, *Plays of Persuasion*, 170–78. The fairly confident consensus is that the play was originally written ca. 1535, then revised at some point in the 1540s and again after 1558.

4. On the *Collectanea* see Guy, *Tudor England*, 128–29; MacCulloch, *Thomas Cranmer*, 54–55; 59–60.

5. Act in Restraint of Appeals, 1533. *Statutes of the Realm*, vol. 3, p. 247 (24 Hen. 8, c. 12), reprinted in C. H. Williams, *English Historical Documents*, 738.

6. Eustace de Chapuys to Charles V, March 15, 1533, printed in Great Britain, *Letters and Papers*, vol. 6, no. 235.

7. One compelling reading of the nature of this interdependence is Betteridge, *Tudor Histories of the English Reformations*, esp. 28–39. Betteridge suggests that historians may, on occasion, exercise a kind of political authority that the monarch cannot, though the purpose of doing so is to reassert the monarch's political prerogative.

8. Bale's play has long been read as propaganda in relation to his role as a client of Thomas Cromwell. For one prominent such reading, see Pineas, "Polemical Drama of John Bale," 194–208.

9. Rex, *Henry VIII and the English Reformation*, 133–66. Rex's reading reflects what has been the scholarly consensus for some time, but more recent studies have questioned the degree to which Henry might be said to have turned against his own Reformation; see, for instance, Ryrie, *The Gospel and Henry VIII*, esp. 248–58.

10. Walker, *Plays of Persuasion*, 208–10; see also Forest-Hill, *Transgressive Language*, 165–66.

11. For Bale's dramatic work as literature of conversion aimed at king and subjects alike, see Paul Whitfield White, *Theatre and Reformation*, 12–41.

12. Hadfield, *Literature, Politics, and National Identity*, 53. See also Shrank, "John Bale," esp. 187–90.

13. Peter Womack has observed that John "is shown as *willing* but *unable*" to enact what from the reformers' point of view are necessary reforms. It is one of the purposes of the present discussion to investigate the source of this incapacity. Womack, "Imagining Communities," 118.

14. This suggestion—that the crises in *Kynge Johan* are to some degree brought about by John himself—is a departure from readings of the play which argue that King John cannot be a flawed ruler because of his personal virtue; see, for example, Pineas, "Polemical Drama of John Bale," 196; Peter Happé, "Dramatic Images of Kingship," 250.

15. The view of Henry VIII as an autocrat attempting over the course of his reign to concentrate political power in his own hands finds considerable favor among historians. See Rex, *Henry VIII and the English Reformation*, 167–75. For an especially vigorous opinion on the subject, see Bernard, "Tyranny of Henry VIII."

16. James Simpson, *Reform and Cultural Revolution*, 29–31. Though note also Cathy Shrank's claim that understandings of humanism at Henry's court in the 1530s were capacious enough to allow for what she reads as Leland's committed Protestant nativism; see Shrank, *Writing the Nation in Reformation England*, 20, 76–77.

17. James Simpson, *Reform and Cultural Revolution*, 30–31.

18. Gerhardt, "'No quyckar merchaundyce than lybrary bokes'"; Ross, *Making of the English Literary Canon*, 51–62; Schwyzer, "Beauties of the Land."

19. Bale, *Laboryouse Journey and Serche*, sig. A2v. Passages quoted in the body of the essay are hereafter cited parenthetically.

20. See Bale, *Laboryouse Journey and Serche*, sig. B1r–v. According to the Oxford historian Antony á Wood, Leland wrote a letter to Cromwell in 1536 urging him to aid in Leland's search for medieval books because the "Germans perceiving our desidiousness and negligence, do send daily young scholars hither, that spoileth [the books] and cutteth them out of libraries, returning home, and putting them abroad as monuments of their own country." The letter does not survive; see á Wood, *Athenae Oxonienses*, 83.

21. Leland, "A Newe Yeares Gyfte to King Henry the viii. in the xxxvii Yeare of his Raygne" [1546?]; available in print in Lucy Toulmin Smith, ed., *Itinerary of John Leland*, 1:xxxvii–xliii. A manuscript copy in Leland's hand—from which Henry VIII's presentation copy might have been made—survives, dated 1546. No printed text is extant (it is possible that Leland presented his book to Henry in manuscript form), and Leland seems not to have published it.

22. Because Bale reprints the "Newe Yeares Gyfte" in full in his *Laboryouse Journey and Serche*, I have chosen for the sake of convenience to cite Leland in Bale's edition rather than in Smith's.

23. Cf. Schwyzer, "Beauties of the Land," 109: "[Leland] seems to have been genuinely seduced by the vision of Henry VIII as an enlightened monarch bent on restoring the nation to its ancient and imperial glory."

24. This characterizes the approach Leland took to his researches, as well as to his writing. A surviving letter from one monastic official to another, asking the recipient to allow Leland access to library materials "yn setting forth such matiers as he writith for the King's Majeste" is included in his *Itinerary*. As Leland traveled, he made it clear that he traveled with Henry VIII's authority; see Smith, *Itinerary of John Leland*, 2:148.

25. See Ross (*Making of the English Literary Canon*, 54) on the significance of the silver table as an emblem of empire.

26. For a relevant discussion of notions of monarchial citizenship, see Shrank, *Writing the Nation in Reformation England*, 97.

27. On humanist understandings of the aesthetic and utilitarian qualities of history writing, see Levy, *Tudor Historical Thought*, 50–68; Kelley, "Humanism and History."

28. For a contrary view of Bale as committed to humanist ideals of scholarship, at least in the case of discovering the author of *Piers Plowman*, see Thomas Prendergast's essay in this volume.

29. See Shrank, "John Bale," 184.

30. Cf. Foxe, *Acts and Monuments*, vol. 3, pp. 718–22. See also Gerhardt, "'No quyckar merchaundyce than lybrary bokes,'" 420.

31. This is particularly surprising given the attention Bale devotes elsewhere to issues of interpretation. See Summit, "Monuments and Ruins," 9–15.

32. Andrew Jotischky suggests that Bale's approach to antiquarian method began to develop during his researches into the history of the Carmelites; see *Carmelites and Antiquity*, 259–60.

33. For an account of Bale's bibliographical labors, see Bale's *Index*, which contains short entries covering most of the texts catalogued in the *Summarium* and the *Catalogus*. Brett and Carley, introduction to *Index Britanniae Scriptorum*.

34. For a specific but useful assessment of Bale's approach to the task of bibliography, see Hudson, "*Visio Baleii*."

35. Bale's approach to the role of "reforming" historian is discussed thoroughly in Summit, "Monuments and Ruins," 10–15; and Kastan, "'Holy Wurdes' and 'Slypper Wit,'" 274–78. Both argue that Bale envisioned himself as the historian best suited to revise the chronicles and remove the effects of Catholic interpretive bias. I attempt to offer a further perspective by suggesting that Bale's constant deferral of this task is itself significant and suggestive.

36. For a different reading, see Summit, "Monuments and Ruins," 10–15. See also n. 54 below.

37. The hope that "some" historian will be able to accomplish the crucial work of synthesis is present elsewhere in Bale's writing. In *A Brefe Chronycle Concerning the Examination and Death of . . . the Lord Cobham*, he calls upon "some learned Englishman . . . to set forth the English Chronicles in their right shape"; see Bale, *Select Works of John Bale*, 8.

38. For a different reading, see Griffin, "Birth of the History Play."

39. Dermot Cavanagh argues that the pervasive uncertainty in the play reflects the arbitrariness of royal favor which *Kynge Johan* is attempting to confront (*Language and Politics*, 16–35). The present essay suggests that this uncertainty may also bear upon our understanding of the king as a flawed character.

40. Fairfield, *John Bale*, 108–9; Walker (*Plays of Persuasion*, 210–21) offers a much different account of the end of the play but holds Imperial Majesty to be the key reforming figure.

41. Cavanagh, "Paradox of Sedition."

42. Cavanagh, "Paradox of Sedition," 171–91. Dillon (*Language and Stage*, 70–87) discusses the vices' misuse of language as a form of disguise.

43. Betteridge, *Tudor Histories of the English Reformations*, 77–78.

44. Both the Latin text of this poem and a translation are available in Bale, *Complete Plays of John Bale*, 1:151.

45. The role of literature in the immaterial—and sometimes material—preservation of the dead is a constant preoccupation among sixteenth- and early seventeenth-century writers. See Schwyzer, *Archaeologies of English Renaissance Literature*.

46. The question of whether the sources Veritas cites do in fact suggest the depiction of John he claims to derive from them is a subject for a separate piece. The best account of the sources is Bale, *King Johan*, 26–30; 202–7.

47. I am indebted to Diarmaid MacCulloch for calling my attention to this definition of "monument" during the summer 2004 Folger Institute seminar he directed entitled "The English Reformation, 1500–1640: One or Many?"

48. Canning, *Principal charters*, 2–4.

49. King John's provisions for Bury St. Edmunds are somewhat different, insofar as they relate to the status of a hospital rather than a town corporation. However, the same

principle applies: the king recognizes a specific limit to his own authority. See the charters granted by John to St. Savior's Hospital in Harper-Bill, *Charters of the Medieval Hospitals*, nos. 168, 176.

50. See Bale (*King Johan*, 192) for a discussion of the London charter.

51. Bale, *Index Britanniae Scriptorum*, 173.

52. Bale's deployment of theater in this way may anticipate by several decades the relevance of drama to the development of practical ethics. For a recent discussion, see Angus Fletcher, *Evolving Hamlet*.

53. On the two oaths sworn by the estates, see Hunt, *Drama of Coronation*, 105, 109.

54. For Thomas Betteridge, this is the act at the center of the model of reformation that the play advocates. See Betteridge, "Staging Reformation Authority," 55–58

55. Cf. Betteridge, "Staging Reformation Authority"; Forest-Hill, *Transgressive Language*, 173–74; Vanhoutte, "Engendering England," 70–72.

56. Shrank assigns this role in *Kynge Johan* to the Interpreter, who appears at line 1085 to offer a commentary on the symbolic excommunication of King John during the congress of the vices. While this is no doubt a figure of significant interpretive authority, it is equally important, I suggest, that Bale does not reintroduce him at the end of the play. See Shrank, "John Bale," 191 and n. 57.

57. Cf. Pineas, "Polemical Drama of John Bale," 201; Betteridge, "Staging Reformation Authority," 53. Both authors argue that Veritas is a figure for Bale himself. I am suggesting, on the other hand, that it is significant that Veritas is *not* Bale at the end of *Kynge Johan*, and that since his other plays encourage us to expect to see Bale delivering the final moral, it is important that that role is reserved for characters other than the Baleus Prolocutor.

58. For a different reading, see Ryrie, *The Gospel and Henry VIII*, 248–58.

When Polemic Trumps Poetry: Buried Medieval Poem(s) in the Protestant Print *I Playne Piers*

Kathy Cawsey

The ways in which Tudor Protestants appropriated *Piers Plowman* and turned William Langland's work to their own purposes have increasingly gained scholarly interest in recent years. Piers has proven to be a remarkably adaptable character: first presented in the mid-fourteenth century by Langland as a primarily orthodox figure through which to criticize abuses within the church, he was quickly adopted by the rebels of the 1381 uprising as a representative figure of social and economic justice. The Lollards of the late fourteenth and fifteenth centuries pushed Piers's radical religious views over the edge into heterodoxy, in texts such as *Pierce the Ploughman's Crede*. By the sixteenth century the plowman was sufficiently recognizable as a figure of rustic wisdom that the convention could be mocked in Wynkyn de Worde's 1510 print *How the Plowman lerned his pater noster*.[1] For the reformers of the mid-sixteenth century, the advertising power of Piers's name was so evocative that it was used in titles of works in which the character himself plays only a minor part, such as *Pyers Plowman's Exhortation*, printed by Antony Scoloker in the 1550s.[2] Langland's more radical figure merges with Chaucer's plowman when the spurious Plowman's Tale is introduced by William Thynne into the *Canterbury Tales* in 1542.[3] Finally, *The Vision of Pierce Plowman* was printed by Robert Crowley in 1550, who was interested in establishing Langland's medieval credentials and using those to support the Protestant cause.[4] The Protestants of the sixteenth century pointed to Piers as a kind of pre-Lutheran Protestant in order to counter Catholic claims of Protestant "new-fangledness," and to prove that Protestant beliefs, not Catholic, were the more ancient and hence more authoritative ones.[5] Piers also became a symbol of "Englishness" and English Protestantism in the face of Continental Catholicism, and so his status as a symbol of an earlier, English reforming movement catered to feelings of English nationalism as well.

Because of these many transformations, Piers the plowman is a good figure through which to study not only the early modern understanding of medieval Lollardy and other reforming movements but also the early modern and Renaissance understanding of medieval literature and poetry. In the introduction to his edition of *Piers Plowman*, Robert Crowley explains to his Tudor audience the unfamiliar medieval poetic form of the alliterative long line: "[Langland] wrote altogether in miter: but not after the maner of our rimers that wryte nowe a dayes (for his verses ende not alike) but the nature of hys miter is, to haue three wordes at the leaste in euery verse which begyn with some one letter."[6] Crowley's explanation of this medieval poetic form is significant. Other editors in the Piers Plowman tradition had insisted on the antiquity of their texts: Wendy Scase writes of *Pyers Plowman's Exhortation* that "to authenticate the old age of the text, the editor has ostentatiously retained the old orthography and vocabulary, providing a glossary of obsolete words."[7] Crowley, however, was unique in his attention to the poetic *form* of the medieval text. His desire to make Langland's text accessible to his readers seems to be warring with his desire to retain as many of the work's markers of antiquity as possible, thus bolstering the Protestants' claim to be representatives of an older tradition. Crowley therefore retains the obscure poetic form and explains it for his readers; likewise he modernizes Langland's spelling and grammar but does not update the by-now archaic vocabulary.[8] After Crowley's edition of Piers Plowman appeared, Reynald Wolfe printed an edition of *Pierce the Ploughman's Crede* in 1553. Like Crowley, Wolfe needed to balance his reader's unfamiliarity with medieval vocabulary and form with a desire to avoid obscuring the indications of the text's medieval origin, and so printed a glossary of "certayne hard wordes used in this booke" to make the medieval work more accessible to his sixteenth-century readers.[9]

Not all of the printers of Protestant plowman texts were as learned as Crowley about medieval poetic forms and styles, however. In the mid-sixteenth-century print *I Playne Piers*, a rhyming, alliterative long-line, medieval poem has been combined with several other poems (along with long sections of prose) to produce a polemical work that draws on the antiquity of the plowman figure—but without making use of the antiquity of the medieval work's form. This poem has hitherto not been examined in detail, and since the text was printed as prose, many scholars have completely missed the fact that it is made up of several kinds of poetry, including alliterative long line, rhyming couplets, and tail rhyme.[10] Barbara Johnson notes the combination of verse and prose in the work and mentions the rhyme, but makes no comment on the alliteration; Andrew Wawn states that "I Playne Piers" is "basically a poem yet was printed entirely as prose," and lists some lines from the Plowman's Tale which were incorporated into the work; John Bowers comments that "the pervasiveness of submerged rhymes through the text suggests ... that one or more other verse-works from the Wycliffite underground were also incorporated," but provides no further exploration of those works; Anne Hudson mentions a "mocking use of proverb or rhyming tag" and suggests that the "frequency of alliteration in these prose works may owe something to Langland's poem," but does not analyze the alliteration or rhyme structure fully. Other scholars fail to notice the poetry entirely: James Simpson states unequivocally that "I Playne Piers Which Cannot Flatter (c. 1547) is written in prose" although he acknowledges its debt to the Plowman's Tale; Bruce Holsinger, while condemning Simpson's dismissal of any "literary" characteristics within "I Playne Piers," writes that "the tract is indeed written overwhelmingly in prose," other than the four-line poetic jingle in the title; and White, Edwards, and Kelen make no comment on the poetry.[11] None of these scholars, even those who note some of the poetry or "submerged rhymes," provide any analysis or discussion of the poetry.

In this article, therefore, I propose to address this scholarly lacuna by providing a preliminary analysis of the poem or poems contained within "I Playne Piers." The poem(s) are printed for the first time in poetic layout in the appendix to this article (prose sections of "I Playne Piers" have been omitted for reasons of space, but entire work can be accessed via Early English Books Online, *STC* 19903a). In her 1985 article on the Protestant plowman prints, Anne Hudson asks,

> Why did the sixteenth-century reformers resort to these old texts? How did they regard the ideas of an earlier reforming movement? How did they treat the texts—respectfully, or in cavalier fashion, interpolating their own preoccupations and altering the medieval terms to accord with sixteenth-century ideas? Most importantly for a literary critic, can the claims of the unattested works to be medieval compositions be sustained, or are they forgeries?[12]

The buried medieval poems in the print "I Playne Piers" provide answers to some of these questions. The different political and religious concerns which appear in "I Playne Piers" probably belong to different original works, and therefore point to the shifting concerns of the Reformers and to the changing use of the figure of Piers over time. "I Playne Piers" provides fascinating evidence for the way in which early Protestant writers and printers created new works and plundered a hodgepodge of medieval and postmedieval sources in doing so.

The *STC* dates "I Playne Piers" to 1550, presumably by association with Robert Crowley's printing of Langland's *Piers Plowman* and the other cheap plowman pamphlets printed around that time.[13] However, "I Playne Piers" was probably printed earlier, and thus predates Crowley's printing. Because of references to contemporary events and personages within "I Playne Piers," Anne Hudson dates it to "soon after" June 1546, while Andrew Wawn argues for a date of 1546–48, after the recantations of Nicholas Shaxton and Edward Crome but before the return of Miles Coverdale from exile in 1548.[14] Clearly, the various works that have been amalgamated into "I Playne Piers" date from even earlier, and it is difficult to know at what point the poetic form(s) were lost. This makes "I Playne Piers" among the earliest of the plowman texts of the Reformation period.

"I Playne Piers," like many of the Protestant plowman prints, argues for the antiquity of Protestantism. The writer states that "This hath bene the plow-ghemannes faythe euer sythe Joseph of Aramethee that buried Christe in graue, was by gods good prouysion, sent into this region, the olde bryttons for to saue" (lines 591–96).[15] However, the print does not make use of the markers of age that are buried within its own text: the medieval verse forms, vocabulary, and archaisms. Indeed, the various editors and compilers have carelessly updated or obscured these, to the point that the medieval poetry becomes nearly invisible. Other plowman texts make similar claims to antiquity but do not attempt to evince that antiquity linguistically.[16] The hidden poems in "I Playne Piers," therefore, at least one of which is almost certainly medieval, may provide evidence for the pre- and post-Crowley understanding of medieval poetic forms. Crowley's explanation of alliterative verse may have been a watershed in the Protestant Tudors' use not only of medieval *symbols* but of medieval *forms* in their contention that Protestantism endorsed an older set of beliefs than Catholicism.

After a four-line jingle on the title page emphasizes the "plainness" of Piers and the fact that his speech—unlike, presumably, the speech of clerics and friars—is "fowle" and does not "flatter," the text of "I Playne Piers" proper opens with the line, "I Piers plowman folowyng ploughe on felde." This phrase forms the first line of a seven-line alliterative long-line stanza, rhyming in the form *ababcac*:

> I Piers plowman folowyng ploughe on felde,
> my beastes blowing for heate, my bodye requyrynge rest,
> gapynge for the gayne my labors gan me yelde,
> vpon the plowgh beame, to syt me thought it beste,
> agayne the hayle I lened, my face to heauen I cast,
> to that greate Lorde aboue, my buckcler and my shelde,
> who always after labors sendeth ease at the laste.
> (lines 1–7)

Four further stanzas of the same poetic form follow (see appendix A). Although the alliteration is sporadic at times, it is consistent enough to make the form recognizable: line 1 alliterates on *p*, line 2 on *b*, line 3 on *g*, line 4 on *b*, line 5 on *h*, line 7 on *l*, line 10 on *c*, line 13 on *w*, line 14 on *s*, line 15 on *l*, line 16 on *f*, line 19 on *f*, line 26 on *b*, line 28 on *b*, line 29 on *s*, line 30 on *s*, line 31 on *h*, line 32 on *d*, line 33 on *h*, line 34 on *s*, line 35 on *p*.

In some cases the alliteration may have been lost because the compositor of "I Playne Piers" did not recognize the form—so, for example, in line 14 one can speculate that the original might have been "to serue theyr lyuing Saviour with out stryfe or hate" rather than to "serue theyr lyuing God," so that the *s* alliteration is strengthened. Similarly, the original version of line 6 might have read "to that greate God aboue, my buckler and my shelde" rather than to that "greate Lorde aboue," although this emendation is more speculative since there is no *g* alliteration in the second half of the line. Some medieval forms have survived: for example, the use of "nyghte" in line 27 to mean "ne might." Some of the alliteration is, of course, proverbial, and I would be reluctant to place too much weight on it; "Piers plowman" itself in line 1, for example, has become well known by this point, and phrases such as "bote vn to our bale" (line 28) or "pore plowman" (line 35) cannot be taken as evidence for more than the fact that proverbial phrases often alliterate. Nonetheless, the alliteration seems pervasive enough to suggest there is at least an attempt here to emulate Langland's poetic form.

This first section of the poem is relatively well written: the combination of alliteration and rhyme requires some poetic skill, as does the relatively complex rhyme scheme (a scheme much more intricate than the couplets or *abab* form that appear later in "I Playne Piers"). More importantly, the rhyme is not merely decoration or a gesture to the requirements of a conventional form but actually works in tandem with the content, especially in the first stanza: "felde" and "yelde" rhyme with "shelde," for example, linking the labors of the poor plowman with God's protection and the respite of heaven. "Rest" rhymes with "best," and the meaning here, that the plowman needs a break, foreshadows the message of the next few lines: the true, "best" rest that will come in heaven. The same progression is found in the rhymes "endure . . . creature . . . cure"—if they endure the labor of the earth, God's creatures will find their cure for earthly pains in heaven. The rhymes, therefore, in a reasonably skilled manner, follow the progression of the logic of the first two stanzas, from the labor and pains of the plowman on earth to his salvation and rest in heaven.

This section of "I Playne Piers" also uses some sophisticated imagery and inversion of convention in a way that indicates a poet of some skill. God himself is portrayed as a laborer through his making of the world, and his act of creation becomes an "Image to mannes doynge" (line 21), an ideal that earthly creatures are to emulate. The conventional image of God as the creator and the source of light is played with and inverted, as the poet—rather shockingly—emphasizes God's role of the creator of *darkness*: "thys lorde him selfe first the darke dyd frame and make" (line 9). This startling inversion of the convention is then explained in the following lines, as the speaker reminds the reader that for a laborer it is nighttime, not day, that brings rest and relief. The speaker argues that God provided for "the comforte of his creature" before such creatures were even made, by "commaundynge the night for euer al labors to abate" (lines 10, 12). Heaven, for this speaker, is a dark, comforting place, far from the light of day which brings "labors and bysy care" (line 15). In this inversion of convention, therefore, the poet brings home to the reader the reality of a plowman's life in a subtle, powerful way.

In the next stanzas, in contrast to the godly labor of creation, earthly labor is shown to be a result of Eve's transgression: man's "careles lyfe in innocency" becomes the "bondage, vile labor and trauell" (lines 24, 26) of the poor plowman. Christ is evoked as the "womanes sede" that will be "bote vn to our bale" (line 28), and is instantly paired with his Old Testament prefiguration, Noah. Up to this point the poem has been relatively orthodox, even conservative, in its theology, despite its at times unconventional use of poetic images; only here do we get a hint of more radical, even Lollard, thinking, as the poet obliquely criticizes the Church's criteria for canonization and sainthood. While the poet in this part never explicitly ventures into a full-blown Lollard or Protestant criticism of the cult of saints, he does suggest that "poor plowmen" would choose different saints from those the church has traditionally chosen: indeed, the plowman would canonize the man who brought "bull to yoke," which gave "mykell ease" to the poor laborer (line 33). Only in the last line of this section does the speaker mention any kind of clerical authority figure, when he suggests that "yf euer pore plowman of pope myght get the keys" (line 35), different saints would be chosen from the ones the pope has been choosing.

The themes in this section clearly revolve around the value of honest poverty and labor, and draw on the same social aspects of Langland's *Piers Plowman* that the 1381 rebels adapted. Aside from the final line, "yf euer pore plowman of pope myght get the keys" (line 35), there is little anticlericalism or antifraternalism, much less the polemical anti-Papist sentiment the Tudor Reformers often advocated. One can assume that the poor laboring plowman is meant to provide a contrast with the wealthy landlords and clerics, or that the "blynde" ones who were "drenshed not regardynge goddes dome" (lines 31–32) during the flood prefigure the corrupt clerics of the present, but these comparisons are left latent. Indeed, the tone of this section is surprisingly mild and provides a sharp contrast with later sections that explicitly condemn priests who are "Sodomite[s] . . . in beastly buggery" who go "an whore hyntynge" (lines 64–67)—changes in poetic form aside, this shift in tone alone would provide strong support for the argument that "I Playne Piers" is made up of several different works. The first section of "I Playne Piers" seems to come from an alliterative long-line poem which was not necessarily Lollard or even religiously radical but which used the figure of the plowman to express an economic and social complaint.

That this poem was medieval is almost certain. The alliterative poetic form was virtually unknown in the sixteenth century; according to A. S. G. Edwards, prior to Crowley's 1550 printing of Langland, only one work of alliterative verse was printed.[17] Crowley's detailed description of the alliterative form in his preface to *Piers Plowman* likewise indicates that his readers were unfamiliar with the form and needed an explanation of it. It thus seems highly improbable that someone might have deliberately written in an obscure, archaic form that would not even have been recognized; moreover, if this had in fact been the case, one would expect the archaisms to be emphasized and highlighted. Instead, the printer of "I Playne Piers" did exactly the opposite, obscuring the poetic form in prose format, seemingly eliminating some of the alliteration and possibly updating some of the medieval language. (We can speculate, for example, that the final word of line 20 should be "heir" rather than "ruler," to rhyme better with "care" [line 15] and "fayre" [line 17]. While such a change does not indicate that the original text was in Middle English, since 'heir' would have been understandable in the sixteenth century, it does raise the possibility that other changes to the vocabulary were made which have been rendered invisible by the fact that the words are not in rhyming positions.) Again, it is highly unlikely that a writer would go to the trouble of deliberately creating a work in an archaic form and then further obscure the archaisms by printing it as prose. The balance of probabilities suggests that the first section of "I Playne Piers" draws on an authentic medieval poem.

After a section of tail rhyme (discussed below), the alliterative long line intrudes once more into "I Playne Piers," at line 150 (see appendix A). The tone of this section is different from that of the earlier alliterative section, explicitly thanking God for the "grace to sle the Sodomyte" and for having escaped "Sodome" (lines 151, 153). However, the rhyme structure is almost the same as the earlier stanzas (*ababcxc*), suggesting that this is a different part of the same original poem as the first section of "I Playne Piers." Since the word "Sodomyte" is in a position which both alliterates and rhymes, it is probably original and implies that we should not place overmuch weight on the difference in tone from the first section to later sections. The *x* rhyme along with the poor rhythm in line 155 suggests that someone has meddled with this stanza; the alliteration also disappears in the final lines after alliterating on *l* in line 150, *g/s* in line 151, *l/g* in line 152, and possibly *s* in line 153. The following stanza has the same *ababcac* rhyme scheme as the first section of "I Playne Piers," but the alliteration almost completely disappears. However, this stanza evokes the dream vision form of Langland's poem, although no reference to this form had been made earlier: "All this whyle me thought I slept" (line 157). One can speculate that this line in the original poem marked a transition back to the poor plowman, perhaps after a more vivid vision of Sodomites and other evildoers. This stanza also returns to the same images and themes of the first section of "I Playne Piers": the trials of honest labor, and the comfort and ease of night. At this point the plowman takes "a boke . . . in hande" (line 162) to cure his insomnia, in a manner reminiscent of Chaucer's dreamers.

Although the following lines (164–72) seem to lead on smoothly from this stanza and traces of alliteration remain, the rhyme scheme changes to *abab* or couplets, and thus we cannot consider this section to have been part of the original alliterative long-line poem. The subject matter also changes, shifting away from the issue of labor to a subject nearer and dearer to the hearts of Protestant Reformers: the Bible. The poet reminds us that the speaker is still Piers Plowman, for he says "I Piers" (line 164); however, this Piers is not concerned with the same issues on which the previous speaker dwelt. Instead of the trials of labor, this Piers reminisces about a time "thre yeres paste" (line 91) when he could read the scriptures himself, presumably in English, and teach them to his wife, children, and servants. As the leader and "shepherd" of the household, it was his job to feed them both on "broth and bacon" and on the "bread of the Byble" (line 167); and here the word "Bible" does not rhyme in the new rhyme scheme, and hence may be an even later interpolation. This section of couplets therefore seems to have been tacked on to an older poem and registers a shift in concern from the issue of labor to the issue of vernacular scriptures.

So far, therefore, we have an original medieval poem in alliterative long lines, using the stanza form *ababcac*, relatively orthodox and conservative in tone, although with a possible shift to a more polemical tone against sodomy. This poem evokes Langland both in the name of its speaker, Piers the plowman, and in the mention of a dream vision form at line 157. Several lines of couplets have been appended to this poem, lines which mark a change in interest from social and economic issues to a concern with the Bible and vernacular scriptures. Another poetic form has been included into this mix, and continues after the couplets: from lines 36–149 (apart from four lines of couplets in 95–99) and then again after line 174 (see appendix A), we have another metrical form, possibly tail rhyme; like many tail-rhyme poems, the rhyme scheme and meter are irregular, so the verse form is hard to identify. For the most part, these lines are rather jog trot, a far cry from the more elegant poetry in the first section:

> But wel I wot
> and I durst rowt,
>   why this good man and other
> from Nohe to Christe,
> and all the rest
>   were unholy and prophane,
> because they
> were maried aye,
>   & knew not of that gere,
> which of alate,
> by Christes mate,
>   dyd brynge in mykell gayne.
> Yf Peter had ben found,
> in scripture sounde,
>   or Paule to had a wyfe,

nether shulde haue be saint
I do you waraunt,
    not yet thys thousande yere.
(lines 36–54)

The rhymes are often poor ("wot" and "rowt," "Christe" and "rest," "saint" and "waraunt") and the rhythm is clearly inconsistent. Nevertheless, the attempt is consistent enough to be considered poetry—if rather badly constructed poetry. In these sections, more than in the alliterative long-line sections, prose often intervenes, and at times the poetry is so poor that it is difficult to discern what is poetry and what is prose. The text also shows evidence of tampering and interpolations, which often affect the rhythm and rhyme scheme.

    This section uses the concept of sainthood as a transition from the alliterative long-line poetry. In contrast with the subtlety and humor of the alliterative poem, which advocates the canonization of the man who invented the yoking of oxen to a plow, the tail-rhyme section takes the concept of sainthood at face value and uses it to launch directly into a condemnation of the Catholic doctrine of clerical celibacy. The argument is straightforward: if only celibate people can be saints, then none of the Old Testament figures "from Nohe to Christe" (line 39) could have been saints; furthermore, if Peter or Paul had had wives, the church would have refused to canonize them as well. This topic is different in both tone and subject matter from the text's earlier concern with social inequality and labor, and the polemical tone ramps up into a diatribe against priests who "burne . . . boyle . . . [and] tomble the tayle," engaging in sodomy, "beastly buggery," masturbation, or "whore huntynge" (lines 60–69) instead of taking wives. Here both the condemnation of clerical celibacy and the polemical tone seem more typical of Tudor Protestantism than of radical or heterodox medieval works, and so both the poetic form and the subject matter of this section indicate it was taken from a later, sixteenth-century source. The text goes on to condemn "popyshe playe" and "Antychristes abuse" and register a disapproval of courts and assizes at which the speaker runs the risk of condemning himself—again, both language and subject matter suggest a later date for this section. The tail rhymes have also come from a different original dialect than the alliterative long lines: in line 35 of the alliterative lines, the word "keys" rhymes with "ease," but in line 108 of the tail rhymes, "kays" rhymes with "sayes."

    An *abab* stanza intrudes at line 96 and shifts the subject from the corruption of priests to the role kings and rulers play in supporting those corrupt priests. The *abab* stanza is relatively mild, calling on "kynges & Princes dere" to "consyder . . . nowe your flocke how that ye lede," and telling them that they shall answer for "al defaultes, lewdenes and yll honoure" (lines 98–99). The tone then heightens, as the speaker condemns "popyshe sayes" and states that kings who are

"Antechristes protectour(s)" are "lothely" things (lines 102–5). The following lines mention the burning of those who attempt to save people from "that Sodomiticall rowte" and "bryng them to lyght that shineth bryght" (lines 124–27). Again, we have none of the subtlety of light and dark imagery here—or of rhyme—that the alliterative long-line section demonstrated. However, there is the introduction of the character Raffe the raven, who is followed by "many blacke byrdes." When the raven says "I am Raffe," the other birds, "lytle knaues," cry "so am I, so am I" (lines 137–39). Whether this is a reference to a particular individual is unclear, but the author says that the birds are like priests who "counterfaite" the pope "al the world throughout" (lines 142–43). Whoever Raffe might represent more particularly, the character fits into the tradition of using birds as symbols for people, as is manifested by the pelican in the Plowman's Tale.[18]

After the alliterative long lines appear for two stanzas, the tail rhyme returns. Now the subject is the Latin the priests use, which no one understands: the "popysshe pryes" (probably "priests," but possibly "pies" [i.e., magpies]) "clatter in the kyrke" and speak in "combred rydles" (line 177–82). These lines recall not only the "church-chatterers" of the orthodox Tutivillus tales but also the bad Latin spoken by the demons in the medieval play Mankind.[19] The poor Latin spoken by many of the untrained Catholic priests was a common target for Reformers: another Tudor "plowman" print, *A godly dyalogue & dysputacyon betwene Pyers plowman, and a popysh preest*, features a Piers who debates the issue of transubstantiation with a priest. Piers wins the debate by quoting St. Augustine in Latin, which the priest does not understand.[20] In "I Playne Piers," however, the issue of Latin is different. The target of satire is not the fact that the priests speak poor Latin and do not understand the words they themselves speak; instead the speaker condemns the priests for speaking in a language the congregation does not understand. "We must come to mattens masse & euensonge," the speaker later complains

> and harken them bable I wot not how longe,
> we vnderstand neuer a worde
> whether they vs curse,
> or do they worse,
> they saye euen what they lyste.
> (line 546–51)

He also calls the priests' Latin "huther mother" (line 584). The "pratye playes" of the priests are a problem, the speaker says, for if the priest gets something wrong, the congregation is not even aware of the fact and therefore "worshipe we a false christ" (lines 544–54). The writer believes this obfuscation is deliberate: he argues that priests "cloke what thei can" so that they "maye closly lye" (lines 577–78). The congregation must put faith in the priests' honesty, but it is the priests' "natur . . . by theyr father"—presumably the father of lies, the devil—"to lye" (line 556). By contrast, if the priests spoke in English, the congregation could catch them in their lies: "wolde God we myght here what they do say, in our englyshe tonge they coulde not playe, but some of vs sholde espye" (lines 573–75). One of the touchstone issues for both medieval Lollards and for Protestant Reformers, the language of the Bible and of the church service, is thus explored relatively fully in this text.

At line 191 the tail rhymes break off and a prose section several pages long intervenes. No rhyme or alliteration is evident in this section, and many of the references seem to be to events of the 1530s and 1540s: Richard Hunne and the Lollards' tower is discussed, along with the Act of Six Articles; and More, Rochester, and Forest all receive mention. There is also reference to the imprisonment of printers during Henry VIII's reign: "And the poore Prynter also whiche laboreth but for his lyuynge, is cast into prison and loseth all he hath which seameth very sore." The compiler of the poems which make up the text of "I Playne Piers," whether or not he knew his sources were poetry, seemingly had no compunction about inserting his own prose into the text before returning to his sources for the end of the work.

When the poetry returns, the subject is again the problem of Christian kings supporting "ydollatry / pardons pylgrymages and popetry" along with the popish "antychristes" whose authority "he had nether of Peter nor Paule" (lines 195–96, 218, 222). Here the poetry, like the prose which came before, has become more specific to the concerns of the Protestants in the 1530s and 1540s: John Massey of Leeds is mentioned, who spread "suche slaunder" that the people of Leeds returned to Rome; a few lines later William Tyndale and Myles Coverdale are discussed (this section breaks the rhyme scheme, however, and may be a later interpolation). Throughout the rest of the text the image of the shepherd is regularly evoked to protest the conversion of people through force:

> my shepparde in the felde
> an hoke in hande shall welde,
> to take a shepe wyth that

the speaker says, and then contrasts his image of sheepherding with the methods used by those who which to enforce Catholicism:

> yf he come to the shepe a knyffe,
> and ryd a pore lambe of his lyffe,
> this were lytle grace.
> (lines 273–75, 279–81)

This change from the image of the plowman to the image of the shepherd as the dominant exemplar for a virtuous Christian life is yet another indication that "I Playne Piers" is made up of several different original works that have only imperfectly been woven together.

The issue of vernacular scriptures also returns, albeit from a different approach: the speaker condemns the church for allowing people to read

> legenda aurea,
> Roben Hoode, Beuys & Gower,
> & al bagage be syd
> (lines 385–87)

but forbidding the reading of the Bible in English. He calls the other literature "lyese," the "dowerie" of the church when she was "maried to Antychrist"—in other words, when the English church still belonged to Rome (lines 389–90). Again, we can see the text of the poem has been changed, since "dowerie" should be "dower," to rhyme with "Gower" in the previous line. Furthermore, another section of prose interferes, and rather than taking "dowry" in a figurative, sarcastic sense, as being a poor heritage of lies and fables, this section takes it straight, as the material wealth of the church. This section's writer again launches into polemic: "The dowerie eke ye cal with lies great and small, that patrimony of saynte Peter … and christ him self for bad the twelue al such lordly rowte." Apparently this prose interloper barely understood or chose to ignore the figurative meaning of "dowry" in the previous lines.

At line 405 the verse form changes again. First there is a section of shorter, randomly rhyming lines, then a section of primarily *abab* rhyming short lines, which once again returns to the subject of priestly lechery. Here the subject changes to the problems of maintenance men and giving alms unto the rich. At line 483 the tail rhymes reappear, and at line 609 the longer-line couplets return. Clearly, by this point the author of "I Playne Piers" is pillaging indiscriminately from a variety of sources, hardly caring if his text makes much sense, and either oblivious or indifferent to the verse forms in which his original sources were written. The couplets, although varying in length, continue with interposed sections of prose until the end of the text.

As Andrew Wawn has noted, at least some of these lines are taken from the pseudo-Chaucerian Plowman's Tale.[21] In addition to the lines Wawn notes, lines 301–3, 781–90, 815, and 821–26 of the Plowman's Tale have also been absorbed into "I Playne Piers." The extent of the use of the Plowman's Tale and the way in which it has been interpolated into "I Playne Piers" suggest the author of this section of "I Playne Piers" knew at least parts of the Plowman's Tale nearly by heart, for while the lines are close enough to be recognizable, individual words are often changed and additional sections have been added. So, for example, the lines "Some lyueth nat in lechery / But haunten wenches, wydowes & wyues" (lines 285–86 in the Plowman's Tale[22]) become in "I Playne Piers,"

> somme lyueth not in lechery,
> for we cannot proue it in court nor in assyse,
> thoughe we se it wyth our eye,
> howe they haue wenches wydowes and wyues.
> (lines 435–38)[23]

As I noted before, the final composer of this text had little regard for the poetry of his sources: "lyte" in the Plowman's Tale is changed to "lytle" in "I Playne Piers" (line 425), destroying the rhyme with "dyspit"; and the word "byte" a few lines later, which also rhymes with "dispyte" in the Plowman's Tale, has been replaced entirely by "stryke" (line 427). "Maximyen" has been change to "Mamyaunce," losing the assonantal rhyme with "them" in line 295 of the Plowman's Tale. Dialect differences are also apparent between the writer of the Plowman's Tale and those of "I Playne Piers," although of course this could be scribal—the Plowman's Tale uses the form "her" for the third person genitive plural and "hem" for the third person accusative plural, while "I Playne Piers" uses "theyr" and "them." Rhymes point out further dialect differences: in the Plowman's Tale "buckette in to the wall" rhymes with "fall" (lines 298, 300), but the "I Playne Piers" author has been forced to insert the line "they shall haue stones the truth wyll tell" to maintain the rhyme with "boket in to the well" (lines 448, 450). Adding another layer of confusion to this text, this insertion indicates that someone involved in the process of transforming and editing this work cared about maintaining the rhymes, even if the final compositor did not. Likewise, the writer of "I Playne Piers" has changed the lines "Why cleymen they holy hys powere / And wranglen ayenst all his hestes" (PlowT lines 525–26) to "why do thei claime christes power, & wrangle agaynst him euery hower" (IPP lines 429–30)—again, the change seems designed to keep the rhyme in a rhyme scheme that has been simplified. The author of "I Playne Piers" completely changes the next two lines of the Plowman's Tale, but retains the rhyme "beastes" with "feastes." If we place one section of the two texts side by side, we can see the kinds of changes the author is making:

They ben so roted in richesse	they be so roted in riches
That Christes pouert is foryet	that christes pouertye is forgotton
Serued with so many messe	serued wyth so many messe
Hem thinketh that Manna is no mete	that poore Christ is no meate,
All is good that they mowe gete	poore people out of the dore they shutte
They wene to lyue euermore	they sette vp a sygne for a sauyoure
But when god at dome is sette	and when God at his dome shall syt,

Suche treasour is a feble store	thys they shall repent ful sore,
Unneth mote they matyns saye	vnneth he mattens say
For countyng and for court holdyng	for countynge & for court holeynge.
And yet he iangleth as a iaye	And yet must he Jangle lyke a Jaye,
and vnderstont hym selfe nothyng	tho hys mynde be of another thynge,
He woll serue both erle and kyng	he wyll saye both Erle and Kynge,
For his fyndyng and his fee	for fyndyng, of his fee
And hyde his tythynge and his offryng	and gyue vs nought where he hath his lyuynge
This is a feble charite	this is I trowe feble charytie
(PlowT lines 781–96)	(IPP lines 459–74)

Several conclusions can be made based on this comparison. First, the writer either had a different manuscript of the Plowman's Tale than the one that has survived, or, more probably, he was not working from a written text but from memory. Second, as I have noted before, at least one person in the rewriting process cared about the rhyme, since when changes were made, the emendations fit the rhyme scheme ("sauyoure" for "euermore," for example). However, another person may have emended the text after it was written as prose, for changes such as "foryet" to "forgotton" betray a carelessness with the rhymes. Third, the changes do not seem to make either text more or less radical: "I Playne Piers" places slightly more emphasis on poverty with the line "poore people out of the dore they shutte," but both bring up Christ's poverty in the first line of the section; the line "they sette vp a sygne for a sauyoure" in "I Playne Piers" seems to be echoing the typical Protestant claim that Catholics turn the bread of mass into a false idol, but the Plowman's Tale seems more heterodox in its accusation that the priest does not understand the Latin he uses, rather than just having his mind elsewhere.

As the preceding analysis demonstrates, the text of "I Playne Piers" is a messy patchwork of various sources. More work needs to be done in tracking down other borrowings and the sources on which the author, or authors, draw. But the imperfect—indeed, often crude—seams in the weaving of this work leave clear traces of the way in which printers and writers in the Tudor period used and adapted medieval and postmedieval texts. The process seems to be remarkably similar to the way in which a modern plagiarizing university student cuts-and-pastes off of the web (I was tempted to submit "I Playne Piers" to Turnitin.com to see if other sources could be traced!). Drawing not at random but without much discrimination either on a haphazard assortment of sources—some of high quality, some of decidedly poorer quality—changing the sources to fit his argument better, weaving them together hastily and imperfectly, the final author of "I Playne Piers" seems to have pulled an all-nighter in order to meet his printer's due date. We may not be able to generalize, therefore, from the author's apparent obliviousness to the poetry in his sources, any more than we could conclude that because one student thinks Wikipedia is a perfectly good source, all students share that opinion.

Nevertheless, there is an alternative explanation—other than sheer igno-rance—to the printer's and author's disregard for the medieval forms in "I Playne Piers," especially when other Tudor printers were so keen to draw on the "antiq-uity" of their texts to support their Protestant project. Robert Crowley and his group may mark a turning point in the printing of plowman texts, since they rec-ognized the value of the *form*, not just the content, of medieval sources in arguing the case for the antiquity of Protestantism. If this is case, the printing of "I Playne Piers" helps demonstrate a transformation in the ways early modern printers and polemecists responded to their medieval source texts. Scholarship on "I Playne Piers" has primarily analyzed it in terms of early modern uses of the medieval Plowman figure; however, "I Playne Piers" is just as important as a witness to the early modern understanding (or misunderstanding) of medieval poetic texts.

NOTES

1. Here begynneth a lytell geste, STC 20034.

2. Pyers plowmans exhortation, STC 19905. For some of the fifteenth-century plow-man poems, see Barr, Piers Plowman Tradition; for discussion, see Bowers: "Piers Plow-man and the Police"; Hudson, "Lollard Book Production"; and Gradon, "Langland and the Ideology of Dissent." For good summaries of the use of the plowman figure in the later medieval and Early Modern periods, see Hudson, "Legacy of Piers Plowman"; Hudson, "'No Newe Thyng'"; Kelen, "Plowing the Past"; White, chap. 1 in Social Criticism; and Scase, chap. 4 in Literature and Complaint.

3. An earlier print of the Plowman's Tale exists, printed by Thomas Godfray: [Geoffrey Chaucer], [The Plowman's Tale], STC 5099.5. Since the title page and introductory lines are missing it is unclear whether the tale was intended to be considered one of the Canter-bury Tales. Joseph Dane argues that the tale was originally printed as a separate work and only later was absorbed into the Chaucerian canon, perhaps as a means of avoiding censor-ship; see "Bibliographical History Versus Bibliographical Evidence."

4. Thomas Prendergast's essay in this volume discusses Crowley's biographical informa-tion on "Robert Langland." For further discussion, see Hailey, Giving Light to the Reader," 489; Hailey, "'Geuyng light to the reader'"; King, "Robert Crowley"; King, "Crowley's Edi-tions of Piers Plowman," 344; and Scanlon, "Langland, Apocalypse."

5. Kelen, "Plowing the Past," 112–13; see also Prendergast's essay, "The Work of Robert Langland," in this volume.

6. [Langland], Vision of Pierce Plowman, fol. *iir.

7. Scase, Literature and Complaint, 155.

8. See Scanlon, "Langland, Apocalypse," 58.

9. On Wolfe's glossary, see Kelen, "Plowing the Past," 109.

10. The later, 1589 edition of I Playne Piers does print parts of the work as poetry, although the printer and I disagree about which parts are actually poetry. The two editions of the poem are I Playne Piers which can not flatter and O read me for I am of great antiq-uitie. For discussion, see my earlier article, "'Protestant Plowman Prints." In that article, I designate one of the buried verse forms as fourteeners; I have since reconsidered on the basis of the medial rhymes and now think they came from a tail-rhyme poem or other met-rical source. Thanks to David Mathews, who reviewed this volume for Medieval Institute Publications, for encouraging me to explore the forms further.

11. Johnson, Reading "Piers Plowman" and "The Pilgrim's Progress," 86; Wawn, "Chaucer, The Plowman's Tale and Reformation Propaganda," 185; Bowers, "Piers Plowman and the Police," 40; Hudson, "Legacy of Piers Plowman," 259; James Simpson, Reform and Cultural Revolution, 369; Holsinger, "Lollard Ekphrasis," 85; Helen White, Social Criticism, 31–32; Edwards, "Early Reception of Chaucer and Langland," 12; and Kelen, "Plowing the Past," 117–20.

12. Hudson, "'No newe thyng,'" 227.

13. For a discussion of the Protestant plowman pamphlets, see Cawsey, "Protestant Plowman Prints." Several scholars argue that the STC's assumption that other prints were capitalizing on Crowley's success may be fallacious: he himself could have been capitalizing on a growing interest in the plowman figure. See Cawsey, "Protestant Plowman Prints"; and Kelen, "Plowing the Past," 120, 125.

14. Hudson, "Legacy of Piers Plowman," 158; Wawn, "Chaucer, The Plowman's Tale and Reformation Propaganda," 186; see also Kelen, "Plowing the Past," 120, 125; and Helen White, Social Criticism, 31.

15. All line references to I playne Piers are to the transcript printed in the appendix to this article, based on STC 19903a.

16. For discussion, see Kelen, "Plowing the Past."

17. Edwards, "Early Reception," 14.

18. Thanks to Anne Hudson for help with this section and for this observation.

19. See Cawsey, "Tutivillus and the 'Kyrkchaterars.'"

20. A godly dyalogue & dysputacyon.

21. Wawn, "Chaucer, The Plowman's Tale and Reformation Propaganda," 185.

22. All quotations from the Plowman's Tale, including those in the appendix, are taken from McCarl, Plowman's Tale.

23. Wawn attributes "thoughe we se it wyth oure eye" to line 882 of the Plowman's Tale, but this seems virtually proverbial to me; see, "Chaucer, The Plowman's Tale and Reformation Propaganda," 185.

Appendix: "I Playne Piers"

I playne Piers which can not flatter
A plowe man men me call
My speche is fowlle, yet marke the matter
Howe thynges may hap to fall

[A.ii] I Piers plowman followyng ploughe on felde,
my beastes blowing for heate, my bodye requyrynge rest,
gapynge for the gayne my labours gan me yelde,
vpon the plowgh beame, to syt me thought it beste,
agayne the hayle I lened, my face to heauen I cast,   5
to that greate Lorde aboue, my buckcler and my shelde,
who always after labours sendeth ease at the laste,

because I tell you playne without rest nought can endure,
thys lorde him selfe first the darke dyd frame and make.
Fyrst of all prouydyng the comforte of his creature,   10

before that thynge earthlye hys forme and shape dyd take,
commaundynge the night for euer al labours to abate,
that wery workemen al theyr bones might salue & cure,
to serue theyr lyuing God with out stryfe or hate.

Then doth he make the lyght for labours and bysy care,   15
the firmament he framed betwixt the waters twayn,
the sees, the earth, the erbes, the trees, the frutes, bryght & fayre,
the sonne, the moone, the starres for our profyte and gayne,
the fyshes in the floddes, the brydes in the ayre flowynge,
all kynde of bestes, and man as lorde and ruler   20
them reaseth he eftsones an Image to mannes doynge,

he knewe full well the labors to man afore appoynted,
thoughe at the fyrste a whyle of good & bad not knowyng,
man led a careles lyfe in innocency then graunted,
unto the tyme that Eue to the old serpent assentyng   25
brought him into [A.iii] bondage, vile labour and trauell,
which skarcely nyghte restrayneth the body sore turmented
onles the womanes sede be bote vn to our bale.

This seede to Nohe than shadowed, reliffe to no man can fynde,
with comforte of the grape, and shipp that saued some   30
even those that hym beleued, & wold not styll be blynde,
al other then were drenshed not regardynge goddes dome
by bringyng bull to yoke, ye broughte in mykell ease,
happy therfore be he, a saynt he myght be shryned,
yf euer pore plowman of pope myght get the keys.   35

But wel I wot
and I durst rowt,
        why this good man and other
from Nohe to Christe,
and all the rest   40
        were unholy and prophane,
because they
were maried aye,
        & knew not of that gere,
which of alate,   45
by Christes mate
        dyd brynge in mykell gayne.
Yf Peter had ben founde,
in scripture sounde,
        or Paule to had a wife,   50
nether shulde haue be saint
I do you waraunt,

not yet thys thousande yere,
suche holynes
it is to lyue wyueles,   55
    and herefore do they stryue,
death it is to saye,
that a preste maye,
    haue wyfe in any case,
though he burne, thoughe he boyle,   60
thoughe he tomble the tayle,
    as Astalande dothe in Maye,
a Sodomite tho he be,
& in beastly buggery,
    hym selfe he muste nedes solace,   65
but let them go on styll
an whore huntynge, as they wyll
    and let no man saye naye,
The careles carions
shal ende the stryffe ones   70
    of thys ye maye be sure.
In the meane season
it wyll be lytle reason,
    goodes and lyfe to daunger aye,
let them kepe from our houses,   75
and shape vs no hooddes
    [A.iiii] and take this popyshe playe.
It is no artycle of my belefe,
thoughe the preste hange it on hys sleue
    and publyshe it in courte an assyse   80
it makethe me oft
of courte to be dofte,
    lest I my selfe accuse,
for I wold not swere
for my greate graye mayre,   85
    that prestes can so hyghe ryse,
to doo of man,
which now & then
    of nature wyll his course peruse,
but let it go,   90
God chaungethe it not so
    thoughe new beleffes they deuise
whyche haue al wolde,
in blyndnes holde,
    & Antychristes abuse.   95

Consyder o kynges & Princes dere for you we toile and labour
consyder I saye eftsones, nowe your flocke how that ye lede

you shall make answere, for al defaultes, lewdenes and yll honoure
eyther myght ye fyght on Chrystes syde, who is our guide & hed

or elles youre wepons   100
whet and sharppe
        to mayntayne popyshe sayes
and how lothely a thynge
is a christen kynge,
        to be Antychristes protectour,   105
we stryue not for the name
whome all men hate for shame,
        for hys forged kays,
the prestes wyll him mayntayne,
as theyre cheffe captayne,   110
        so long as they haue possession,
of them dyd he sprynge,
to him wyll they brynge,
        what so euer the hande can fynde,
rather then he   115
sholde peryshed be,
        in hys decrees and lawes canon.
Therfore do they burne,
        against the course of kind
which wolde do them good,   120
with theyr hart bloode,
        yf they coulde take it so,
to call them out,
of that Sodomiticall rowte,
        that helly synfull nacyon   125
to bryng them to lyght
that shineth bryght,
        which the scrypture leadethe to.
I hard [A.v] a tale of late,
howe a captayne cam to prate,   130
        and set a rauen in colours ryche,
wyth many blacke byrdes hym aboute,
who his consent sholde vtter oute,
        an hart of no smal pryde,
his uncleane cage began to speke,   135
the rauen dothe open hys beke,
        and saythe I am Raffe,
the lytle knaues standyng by,
so am I, so am I,
        euerych one they cryede.   140
Thus playe the prestes withouten doubt,
al the world throughout

the pope to counterfaite,
marke theyr lyfe, marke theyr lernynge,
marke theyr order and euery thynge,   145
    and yonge popes they bene lyche,
they lose they bynde,
they haue bothe sworde and keys, after the same kinde
    that olde Raffe had of late

I thanke my Lorde God the lyuyng Lord for euer,   150
that he hath geuen me grace to sle the Sodomyte,
I was longe in her lore, but I thanke my god the geuer
I haue escaped Sodome, and in god is my delite
I speke it of no rage, but as I wyll answere make,
so theyr owne selues be not Judges, in theyr owne cause and matter,   155
for then agaynst the dredfull daye, wyth clere hart I wyll it vndertake.
All this whyle me thought I slept, but the boye can prycke his beest.
Agayne I take the plough in hande folowynge myne honest labour,
tyll nyght commeth on, and sonne goynge downe causeth me to cease.
In the meane season, I tosse many thinges, as I were of porte and hauour,   160
when I came home, all that nyghte longe, I coulde not slepe a wynke,
a boke therfore I toke in hande, my selfe somthynge to ease,
wherin I wrote of sun [A.vi] dry ryte, as my hart doth iuge & thynke.
Aboute thre yeres paste when I Piers scripture myghte reade,
and render and reporte to my wyffe and to my barnes,   165
it semed then a goodly lyffe a houshold then to kepe and feade,
both with broth and bacon, and bread of the Byble,
to tel forth Christes trade, and trade of oure christenyng
(before were we called chrysten, and knewe of Christe nothyng)
Then was I syr, then was I father, then was I shepherd and all,   170
then nothinge fayled vn to my byddyng, nether in boure nor hal,
my wyfe for my wysdom dyd counte me her hed, my chylder theyr father, my seruauntes
    theyr syre,
then al did obbaye me in the feare of the lorde, more then for meade or hyer,

thys pleased the lorde
I dare recorde   175
    agaynst the popysshe pryes,
which clatter in the kyrke,
and cannot worke
    nothynge that good is,
whyche had dyspyte in harte,   180
that we to Christ dyd starte,
    leuynge theyr combred rydles,
and cryed as theyr fathers dyd before,
out, out alas, therfore
    all the worlde foloweth hym, and hys,   185

seinge vs of the lewde fee,
breke into heuen so violently,
    whiche they were sory for,
but of the herdes thei recked nothynge,
beyng occupyed wyth other thynge,   190
    as gentlemen and other,

[extensive prose passage omitted]

Answere to me this questyon,
ye shall not be far from reason,
    you can tel it if you please,
what droue downe ydollatry   195
pardons pylgrymages and popetry,
    and caused it to cease,
what gaue the kynge his power
and caused you to louer,
    but onlye Goddes wholi worde,   200
whiles you stoppe this,
full certayn it is
    you wolde haue him vnder the borde,
your blacke byrde coulde spreade
in the popet of breade,   205
    that the worste wretche of you al
was better by farre,
then all the kynges are,
    that werren purple and paull,
his reasons were this   210
full wysely guys.
    You knowe where he fetched it,
because his holy blessing
his blowynge and hys kyssynge,
    God from heauen coulde call,   215
the whiche auctoritie
I dare affyrme boldly,
    he had nether of Peter nor Paule,
what there oyle is I neuer wyst,
but you kynges are annoynted of Christe,   220
    agaynste his foes to fyght,
these antychristes hate you both,
be they leafe be they loth,
    I must hit the naile full strayght.
They sperade it so far   225
that they wyl make no warre
    to haue al there bagage agayne,
the knaues of oure kynge,

hathe spreade leasynge,
    to abhomynable for to layne.   230
Johnn Massey [E.i] your man,
from Leades be gan,
    suche slaunder for to spreade,
the holy byshope there,
and poole with lowrynge chere,   235
    retornynge then to Rome,
caused this deuyll to write,
as it maye apere ful tyte
    to him that hath dome,
this hath bene his workinge   240
and foule lurkynge,
    against .x. christen kynges,
this legerdemayne,
hath gotten you great gayne,
    myter staffe and ringes,   245

I wold not that you could pyke oute
in syckenes atale,
    by vs plowghwagges your vnder lowres,
then myght you worthely cause vs to stoupe,
whyles you the candle had put oute,   250
    and leaue vs as blacke as boroles,
well I wold that were the worst
that you coulde do to hym that durst
    tell you more of these
for we regardyng your curseynges,   255
as we do youre blessynges
    bothe not worth one pese,
but you haue gotten a sworde,
wherewyth ye make a ferde,
    bothe good men & bold,   260
more fete were a shepe hoke
in youre hande or eles a boke,
    yf you care for Christes folde,
the worde of God,
as the shepardes rod,   265
    the sworde and eke the staffe
that Peter hadde in dede,
when Christe bad hym these fede,
    and power to him he gaue.
This sworde temporall,   270
is fete to kyll wyth all,
    the shepe somdele fatte,
my shepparde in the felde

an hoke in hande shall welde,
    to take a shepe wyth that,   275
he shal it tarre, he shall it grease,
he shal do the poore shepe mykell ease,
    with outen sworde alas,
yf he come to the shepe a knyffe,
and ryd a pore lambe of his lyffe,   280
    this were lytle grace,
a bocherly knaue, then wold I saye,
pyke the hence gange [E.ii] forth awaye,
    I shall breake thy pate,
and I wene ye byshoppes bolde,   285
yf it be trewe as I harde ones told
    shal haue lyke answer at hauen gate,
Piers can tel you mykel more
whiche he kepeth yet in store,
    to se yf you wyll amende,   290
eles must here
suche maner of gere,
    euen to the worldes ende.
Stones sayde the lorde
shall beare recorde,   295
    yf other wytnes fayle,
you kyll the wytnes trewe,
God sendethe euer newe,
    lytle to your aduayle.
Trewe Tyndale was burned,   300
Myles Couerdale banyshed,
    by whose labors greate,
we haue the hole byble,
in dispyte of the deuel
    and truste to kepe it yet,   305
and you with your brall,
to make vs thral
    and loute vnto your becks,
haue styred lande and fees,
to stynge you lyke bees,   310
    and brought al in youre neckes,
we syghe for oure hony come,
goddes worde and dome,
    against these gredi waspes
whiche seke euery hower,   315
when they may deuoure,
    and for that gaines and gaspes.
But lincolen shyre saythe full well,
the truthe I do you tell,

that ye shalbe fayn at the laste,   320
wyth donge hydynge your crownes,
and castynge of your gownes,
    to stande ful agast
and thou Crome
haste gotten a crowne,   325
    mete for thy dotynge yeres,
if to thy furred hood,
a bel thou haddest sowed,
    and a payre of Asses eares.
Thou foole Sharton,   330
thy self thou hast vndon,
    thy byshoprike when thou forsoke,
thou myghte home kepte it styll,
and playd the lorde at thy wyll,
    and sayde what thou lyste a lone in a noke,   335
But the blynd byshope of norwyche
was [E.iii] a prophet belyche,
    that coulde tel so longe before,
that he kylled Abel,
and suffred Cayme to lyue styll,   340
    for the mayntenance of the great whore.
Good Bylnaye was brunt,
who for vyce was neuer shente,
    his enemes to wytnes,
but for Gods holy word,   345
for preachynge Christ only lorde,
    dyed he wyth mekenes,
o that eyther of you twayne,
had played Eleazar agayne,
    for the honeste of youre graye heares   350
it myght haue semed you ryght well,
to haue died for the gospel,
    in these your laste yeres,
why do we the pope hate,
only for his names sake,   355
    or for his wycked workes.
These brynge you in agayne,
condepnynge oure kynges dedes playne,
    more cruelly then turkes
yf the pope be raced oute,   360
which was to fel to ferse to stowte,
    to stable hys decrees,
why wyll ye styll,
agaynste Goddes holy wyl
    mayntayne popyshe lyes,   365

yf you burne the newe testamente,
of any good entent,
    it wolde haue done ryght well,
to haue shewed some cause,
or where it is false   370
    to monyshe of Errors fell,
haue ye nought to saye,
but tyrantes play
    stet pro racione uoluntas.
let reason stand styll,   375
for I wyll haue my wyll,
    out, out, alas,
no christ en boke,
maye thou on loke,
    yf thou be an Englishe strunt   380
thus doethe Alyens vs loutte,
by that ye spreade aboute,
    after that old sorte and wonte,
you allowe they saye,
legenda aurea,   385
    Roben Hoode, Beuys & Gower,
& al bagage be syd,
but Gods word ye may not a byde,
    these lyese are your churche dowerie,
when she was maried to [E.iiii] Antychrist,   390
al lyes & Errours in to her he thrust,
    he gaue them in possessyon,
and youre prelates
with whole hearte
    and wyl doth them mayntayne by succession.   395

The dowerie eke ye cal with lies great and small, that patrimony of saynte Peter whiche by youre proctores and by your pollynge youre ipocrisy and dyssemblyng where ye haue gotton wyde, wher in Moyses lawe, the byshoppes did not knowe, no suche lordeshyppes state, and christ him self for bad the twelue al such lordly rowte, that all the worlde maye se, who that ye be, the proude aduersaryes of Christe who wyth braggynge, and wyth lyinge, wyth torment, and burnynge, must mayntain youre hethenesse deuyle,

Christ if that he had wolde
myght haue had syluer & golde,
    & swordes for hym to fyghte,
but he forsoke bothe,   400
though Peter were loth,
    & so taught his scholers straight,
Christ bad Peter kepe,

and feede his shepe,
     and wyth hys sworde for bad hym to smyte.   405
Sworde is no toole wyth shepe to kepe,
but for shepardes that shepe wyll byte,
me thynke suche shepardes bene to wyt,
against there shepe wyth great dyspyte,
whome they oughte with there hart blood to cherishe, and kepe alyue,   410
none of Christes apostles were euer so bolde,
suche greate lordshyppes to them to imbrace
but somered theyr shep and kepe theyr fold,

and folowed Christes owne trew trade, but oures saye yet that they mai for the honour of the Realme, doo cleane contrary, to oure great vyllany slaun [E.v] der spyte and shame,

for yf oure realme be Christened right and haue not the name for noughte,   415
we must cal him the best and eke the wysest, whiche with his blod vs bought,
and all his workes and wordes also mayntayne obserue and kepe,
for therin onelye cn we espye the gootes from the shepe,
if it had ben glory to the christen communaltye byshoppes to be rych and so dysguysed,
Christ of his goodnes, nor his apostles Iwys, wolde it haue cleare dyspysed,   420

but oures be but counter fait
men maye knowe them by theyr frute,
theyr greatnes maketh them God to forgette
and take Christes mekenes in dyspit
where yf they were pore and had but lytle   425
they wold not deme the outwarde face,
but noryshe the shepe and them not stryke
God amende them for his grace,
why do thei claime christes power,
& wrangle agaynst him euery hower,   430
in lyfe so brutysshe as bene beastes
lyuynge in delyte
hauynge the pore in dispyte
     & no God in their feastes,

somme lyueth not in lechery,   435
for we cannot proue it in court nor in assyse,
thoughe we se it wyth oure eye,
howe they haue wenches wydowes and wyues.
so theyr proctores are so bolde,
so shamles, so graceles, and couytous eke,   440
that for a small syluer or golde,
their wytnesse shall not be worth a leke.
There was more mercye in Mamyaunce
and Nero that neuer was good,

then is nowe in many of them   445
that wereth myter and furred hoode,
they followe Christ thus that shed his bloode
to heauen as boket in to the well [E.vi]
I muste thus speake tho they be wood,
they shall haue stones the truthe wyll tell   450
they gyue theyr almose to the rytche,
to maynteneres and men of lawe,
for vnto the lordes they wyll be lyche,
beggers barnes I burne,
I trow yf Christ dyd teche suche maner of playe,   455
yf he lyued thus let them me shende,
the wot full well the truthe I saye,
but the deuel hath foule them blende,
they be so roted in riches,
that Christes pouertye is forgotton,   460
serued wyth so many messe,
that poore Christ is no meate,
poore people out of the dore they shutte,
they sette vp a sygne for a sauyoure,
and when God at hys dome shall syt,   465
thys they shall repent ful sore,
vnneth he mattens say,
for countynge & for court holeynge.
And yet must he Jangle lyke a Jaye,
tho hys mynde be of another thynge,   470
he wyll saye bothe Erle and Kynge,
for fyndyng, of his fee,
and gyue vs nought where he hath his lyuynge,
this is I trowe feble charytie
where we poore wretches in heate and colde,   475
do suffer paynes and mani a wrong,
they of our labours do heape vp gold,
against theyr founders they make them stronge,

we did found them, they counfounded vs,
with their dispensacyons,   480
with their non residence they clerely robbe vs,
by pluraly testotouotes & impropriacions.

Such vnproper gere
was neuer had
        before this generacyon,   485
who wyth their wylles
eche man begyles,
        with slyght and subtyl fasshon,

wolde God our kyng,
wold downe them brynge,   490
    and take their temprallties awaye,
an inpropriacion,
or forty marke pencyon
    [E.vii] were ynoughe for a popyshe iaye
it is no meruel   495
tho they ofte fall
    in that they take in hand,
offices they haue,
nether asketh aslaue,
    but hym that can vnderstande   500
Goddes worde to minyster,
and temporalties to order,
    either asketh a whole man,
half a man is ynoughe
to holde the ploughe,   505
    or kepe shepe in the felde,
therfore can, they
by no fayre playe,
    bothe there offices welde.
This all the worlde sayth,   510
but none beleueth,
    except god open the eyes,
yf they raygne styl,
they wil make vs at their wil,
    beleue their fables and lyes,   515
what is at the courte I wot nere,
but in the countrye both here and there,
    we haue monckes and frirysshe luskes,
which tellig the people ful playne,
that all there popery shall vp agayne,   520
    themself to no good buskes
These are oure shepherdes euery wher
it is no maruel tho motton be dere,
    good shepardes ar so skant,
some go to the pot   525
some dy of the rotte,
    other fode they want,
what lerned monke or fryer
but onelye popyshe gere
    in his sodomitecall lyfe,   530
thus do they teache a brode,
with vnyforme accorde,
    bothe the good man and the wyfe,
all oure counsell this must knowe,

thys shrift they call I wot not howe,   535
        for Christ he kenned nothynge of theyr gere,
Christ vnto Peter his sinners forgaue,
and Mari Magdelyn prest neuer shraue,
        yet must we new doctryne learne,
is nether the olde testament good,   540
nor yet the newe in Christes blod,
        but we must feare lawes of oure owne makyng,
which by man his owne founde wayes,
and suche pratye playes,
        shal vs to the blesse bring [E.viii]   545
we must come to mattens masse & euensonge,
and harken them bable I wot not how longe,
        we vnderstand neuer a worde
whether they vs curse,
or do they worse,   550
        they saye euen what they lyste,
yf they at the alter
do not ryght patter,
        then worshipe we a false christ
oure faythe is of theyr honestye,   555
whose natur is by theyr father to lye.

As I haue shewed before,
if the saye ryght it is God hole,
yf they say wrong it is an Idol,
to cause god to stryke vs for.   560

I was at masse not longe ago
where the prest had forgotten in his challyce to do
        the wyne that shulde haue bene a god,
the sellye folles knocke hande and breste,
theyr belefe was fullye vpon the prest,   565
        they honored for God they wyst not what,
so do they many a tyme mo,
God forgaue them that causeth it so,
        it maketh me muche agast,
for whether the wine be good or no   570
when they haue al their charmes Ido,
        it restethe to proue at laste,
wolde God we myght here what they do say,
in our englyshe tonge they coulde not play,
        but some of vs sholde espye,   575
this causeth them
to cloke what thei can,
        that they maye closly lye,

yf it be good geare,
why shuld they feare,   580
    that I poore Pears and other
shulde vnderstande,
this they kepe in bande,
    and it hyde in huther mother,
we haue soules to saue,   585
and heauen do craue,
    throughe the blod of the lambe vnspotted,
whom here we eate
in forme of bred,
    by faith that neuer fayled.   590
This hath bene the plowghemannes faythe
euer sythe Joseph of Aramethee
    that buried Christe [F.i] in graue,
was by gods good prouysion,
sent into this region,   595
    the olde bryttons for to saue,
I tell you that wylbe harde to cause
hob my hoggeherde my gossybe
    and cramer the olde syre,
to beleue transsubstancyacyon,   600
accident without subiect and lyke suggestyon
    wythout sworde or fyre,
whiche is a pretye beleuer,
crepte in withoute scrypture, euen lyke a thefe,
    and murther agaynst gods holy wyll,   605
yf this fayth nede so be stablysshed,
to be Christes faythe it maye be doubted,
    who came to saue and not to kyll,

for James and Johnn when thei went to Samaria,
and the men of the cytye wolde not receue Christe in no waye,   610
they sayde shal we command the fyre
them to destroye lyke as at Elyas desyre.
Christ retornyng dyd answere them sharpely rebukynge them, and sayde certaynly
ye do not know whose sprytes ye are,
the sonne of man, mens liues wil spare,   615
Christe them assigneth ii. maner of spirites,
the one that sufferethe, the other that byteth.

This bytyng adder is the serpentes seede,
who at the heart or boodye hysseth in dede,
but the sprite and the soule hateth he neuer,   620
of them that to Christ wyll suerly cleaue.
Truly no such is he able to greue,

for Christ at the lengthe shall breake his head,
shall hym & all his captaynes leade,
the spirit of his mouth whiche is hys worde certayne, 625
hath ben his sworde alwayes whiche his enemyes hath slayne.
The other sword let them use that be not his,
for stablysheynge Christe we knowe none but this,
we must be suffrers the scripture saythe playne,
yf we entende with Christ to rayne, 630

the persecutours we knowe howe they were [F.ii]
from the begynnynge, & yet tary styl.
The byshoppes and priestes kepynge Christ affarre,
not wyllynge to receue him but against theyr wyll,
I speke not agaynste Justice nor in power elles, 635
but let them shake swordes wher wickednes dwelles,
that is (as I haue sayde before)
to kepe the wolues from our dore,
who for theyr gaine theyre shepe gane byte,
the mylke & woll and all is to lyte, 640
to serue theyr lustes and gredy paunches
but to the poore carkase the theues do lashe.
And as the prophet sayth, truth in dede,
they boyle the fleshe as in a leade,
thys iustice to mynistre swinke and & swete, 645
and you shall haue all poore Pyers can get,
if you pul them not downe they wyl cause to rebel
in euerye contrey the papystes fel,
consider that ye kyll him that stealeth a horse
& wyl you suffer him to lyue that doth mykell worse, 650
they robbe the pore people of theyr lyuely bread
they robbe christes folke of their only foode,
Judge not them heretykes that breaketh mens sawes
and deme them not good men that brekes gods lawes,
no no mens inuencions rather must be heresy 655
for christ sayth in vaine with mens doctrine, do they worshyppe me,
and whom thei count most to despyse theyr decrees,
ar such as wil gladly followe no lyes,
but rune to theyr shepharde as fast as thei can,
besydes him they wyll heare no other man, 660
they do not knowe the voyse of a straunger,
therfore wyll they neuer harken to other
these are sheperdes of Christes shepe,
and al such christ his owne gan clepe,
al such therfore heretykes to deme, 665
is Christ him self an heretyke to esteme,

to burne them is to burne him, so ment he by [F.iii] saynge to Paule o Saule, saule, why doest thou persecute me, and at the dom he shal say to some, that ye haue done to the lest of myne ye haue done it to me,

I am the pastour I knowe my shepe,
myne heres my voyse, my wordes thei kepe,
I am the dore, euen I allone,   670
he that commeth not in by me, astray is gone
Theues or such murtherers fel,
my shepe wyl heare them neuer a dele,

they robbe they slaye, and distroie and not cease thei sley vs in soules, pynynge vs to deade, because they wyll nether preache thy word, nor let vs scriptur read they dystroye vs with sterueship to bryng vs into drede, they sparkell vs a brode, to the mouthes of wolues, so are we swallowed vp wyth deuouryng gloses, and who may saye that the mayntener of suche shephardes, is not the mayntener of theues & robbers,

Paule sayde there shoulde be men,   675
that wold not allowe God for to kenne,
these wyll god geue to mynd reprobate,
to do the thing that he dyd hate,
lyke Sodomytes and to abbuse an other,
without regarde of the course of nature,   680
Increasynge in theyr wycked mynde,
against god to be vnkinde,
fulfilled with al vnrightuousnes,
whoredome craft and covytuousnes,
ful of enuy slaughter and debat,   685
tale bearers, backebyters and full of disceyte,
euen haters of god, disobedyent to their parentes, to al men approbryous
men without knowlege, breakers of promyses, proude braggynge and glorious,
vnmerciful not pytyfull, farre frome all kynde of charytie,
onles we be blynde, we maye well fynde, that thefe oure popysshe be they, 690
yf we know the rightuous law, that al who such [F.iiii] thynges do,
are worthy of death not only that worketh, but also that assentythe them to,
beware of thys o Lordes, doubtles ye are vnder the wrathe of God,
so manye of you as wyl loute & bowe, to geue them your aduenging rod,
& you people al both gret & smal,   695

that seeth it with your eye
that in euery paryshe you about,
they be sterne, thei be stout,
thei prat thei cracke they lye,
some be proude some be couetuouse,   700
some be herde, some lewde, some be lecherous
some be medlynge with marchandise,

some mayntayners of men with mastery,
or stewardes, cownters or pleders,
and serue god, in hipocrisie   705
so followe they Judas, but vnto christ false traytors,
they be false they be vengeable,
& legyle [beguile?] men vnto christes name,
[half line missing] thei be vnstable,
to betraye theyr Lorde they thynke no shame,   710
to serue God they be full lame,
gods theues & falsly stele
gods worde thei do defame.
Antechrist they serue all,
with antechrist such shal fal,   715
thei know them selfes that thei do euel,
against christes commandement,
& a mend them neuer they wyl,
but serue Sathan bi one assent,
who saith soth he shal be shent,   720
or speketh agaynst their false lyuing,
God graunte vs al eyes to espye, eres to here & mouthes to speke,
that lernynge in herte to beleue trulye, oure wordes to goddes glory furth may breke,
& vttryng al their lecheri, at the laste leauing Babilon & al whorishnes eke
may worshyp god in hert truly, lest God his wroth vp on vs do wreke. 725

God saue the kynge & speede the ploughe.
And sende the prelates care ynoughe.
ynoughe, ynoughe, ynoughe.

The Work of Robert Langland

Thomas A. Prendergast

... he's the man we were in search of, that's true; and yet he's not
the man we were in search of. For the man we were in search of was
not the man we wanted.[1]

If medievalists recall Robert Langland at all, they probably remember him as a
mistake. Along with his neighbors John Malvern and William Langley, Robert
Langland was one of the many possible candidates for authorship of *Piers Plowman*.[2] Unlike his neighbors, however, it took him four hundred years to die.[3] Robert
Crowley, the first to print the poem as well as the first to identify Robert Langland
publicly, compared him to John Wyclif, saying that, like Wyclif, he did "sharply
rebuke the obstinate blynd."[4] And John Bale would later characterize him as being
"one of the first followers of John Wyclif."[5] None of these characterizations will be
of any surprise to most medievalists. Indeed, *Piers Plowman* has been seen as something of a byword for reformist literature—both in its anticipation and realization
of the English Reformation. One critic has gone so far as to characterize those who
discovered "Robert" as "a rabid group of Protestants who were interested in the
poem as propaganda."[6] Certainly, Crowley's associates at this time (William Seres
and the evangelical printer John Day) and his own reformist works would seem to
bolster the claim that Crowley et al. "kidnapped" the poem (as one writer put it)
in order to put it in the service of a reformist agenda.[7] More recently, however, a
number of critics have taken a more nuanced position on Crowley's dealings with
the poem. R. Carter Hailey argues that "evidence is abundant that Crowley was
diligent in his attempt to get the text right."[8] And Larry Scanlon has argued that
the goals of Crowley's edition were "much closer to those of modern editors than
to those of Reformation polemic."[9] But if early modern treatments of the text
tended to respect the historical evidence of the manuscripts, what of the name
of the author? I would suggest that far from simply creating "Robert" in order to

70

further a reformist agenda, the means by which the group of men discovered him were reflective of the humanistic methods of Erasmus, and involved the creation of a homosocial community that valued the sharing of intellectual work and the recovery of a rapidly disappearing past. The group's shared goal was to stabilize the past at a moment when ancient records and monuments were vanishing, or, more worryingly, being forged to promote spurious claims about pre-Protestant history.

Recovering Robert

In his "Preface to the Reader from the Printer" Crowley claims that "being desiryous to know the name of the author of Peers Ploughman," he consulted "such men as I knew to be more exercised in the study of antiquities, then I myself have ben" (fol. 2r). There are at least two things that we take away from the preface. First, it seems clear that whomever Crowley consulted, it was important to give the impression that some authority (even if unnamed) backed up his claims about Robert Langland. Second, he begins his work claiming that the desire to know the name of the author is his own. Why did Crowley want to know the identity of the author? It is possible that he had a humanistic desire akin to the desires of modern scholars to uncover the name of the author of *Piers Plowman*. But it is also important to keep in mind the historical context of Crowley's edition. In 1546 a royal proclamation made it illegal to publish a work without including the printer and the place of publication. This proclamation was in response to the illicit printing and circulation of works that were critical of Henrician policies. In many ways the act was a recapitulation of the earlier act of 1529, but there was one important difference: in the 1546 act not only the printer and place of printing must be included but also the name of the author.[10] The names of the authors explicitly forbidden to be printed or circulated in England—John Wyclif, William Tyndale, and John Bale, among others—make it clear that the act was partially the result of Henry's increasing religious conservatism and was certainly an attempt to regain control of discourse in the public sphere.

When Crowley's editions were published in 1550, the religious atmosphere was quite different than it had been in 1546. With Edward's accession, serious reformers like Bale were able to return to England and censorship restrictions were relaxed. The 1546 act was never repealed, however, and Crowley's desire to know the name of the author of *Piers Plowman* might well have been influenced by this act.[11] Perhaps more to the point, the ability to attach a historical name to the work might be seen to give the work an air of historical validity—something that was clearly important to those who wished to see in *Piers Plowman* not merely a conscript to the side of reform but something special, outside the traditional Reformation propaganda that had been produced by Bale and others.[12]

This humanistic formulation might appear naive to some. After all, humanist "truth" had itself always carried a certain amount of ideological baggage.[13] And, as Jonathan Woolfson has put it, there is something of a scholarly consensus that in England "humanism caught on not because of a Petrarchan longing for the ancient world, whose authentic reconstruction required some act of forgetting about a troubled present, but, on the contrary, because of the perceived relevance and utility of selected ancient texts . . . in the public sphere."[14] But there is a difference between ideologically inflected textual criticism and outright propaganda. I would make the case that for a brief time in the 1540s a small group of men both reformist and conservative (and perhaps motivated by their differences) more resembled the scholarly community imagined by Erasmus than the pragmatic humanism of the English Reformation. What makes claims about idealistic humanism difficult to swallow, I would argue, is less a belief that humanism was always subordinated to religious belief in the mid-sixteenth century and more the apparent involvement of John Bale in the discovery of Robert Langland. Though recent work has taken a more measured approach to "Bilious Bale" (as he was known), his reputation has long been as one who would subordinate virtually anyone or anything to his goals of reform.[15] Bale's biography of Robert Langland in *Scriptorium Illustrium Maioris Brittanie Catalogus* conscripts the purported poet to the Wycliffite cause and clearly had an effect on the subsequent reception of the poem.[16] Given the suspicion with which Bale is viewed, it is worth reexamining just how involved he was in the discovery of Robert Langland.

Skeat was the first to assert that Bale was almost certainly the source of Crowley's information about Robert Langland, and a scholarly consensus has emerged that more or less goes along with this insight, amending it only so far as to admit that there may have been other sources.[17] Yet though it is true that in the *Index Britanniae Scriptorum*—Bale's autograph notebook, not published until 1902—Bale's notes are very close to what Crowley had published in his address to the reader at the beginning of his 1550 editions of *Piers*, the timing of the notes in Bale's unpublished manuscript is troubling. Though the *Index* is not precisely datable, Bale began his notebook sometime after 1546; thus he would have had three years before the publication of Crowley's edition to enter notes about the author of *Piers Plowman*.[18] Yet as late as 1548 Bale claims in his *Illustrium maioris Brytannie* that John Wyclif is the author of *Piers Plowman*.[19] And seeing as none of the entries regarding Robert Langland are located in the original section put aside for the letter R, the conclusion seems to be that it would be difficult to date Bale's entries early enough to have influenced Crowley. Samuel Moore suggested as much almost a century ago and George Kane, perhaps following him, reported that "the entries in the *Index* do not appear to be among the earliest."[20]

A close look at Bale's notebook, however, suggests another possibility. The notebook was set up so that he could record his entries seriatim under each letter. At various spaces in the manuscript there are rubricated initials at what he thought would be sufficient intervals. *A* begins at folio 1r, *B* at folio 13r, and so on. The place in the manuscript where we would expect to find the entries for "Robert Langland" (under the rubricated letter *R*) runs from folios 153r to 164v. As stated above, none of the entries for Langland are found in this space. The reason is that (as the modern editor of the notebook puts it) "when Bale had reached a certain stage in bringing together and transcribing his collections, he discovered that he had allowed quite insufficient space for the letters *R* and *G*. The articles under *R* had already had to run back to folio 150r over three of the leaves assigned to it, but not required by *Q*; and *G* had in like manner overflowed on to the last page of *F*. Both letters therefore needed supplements, and these are inserted alternately on the leaves from [folios] 200–216, ff."[21] There are four entries having to do with *Piers*: one entry appears in this supplemental section but the other three appear in other parts of the manuscript.[22]

Crowley's printer's address to the reader from the first of his 1550 editions clearly has some kind of relationship to Bale's entries. It reads:

> Beynge desyerous to knowe the name of the Autoure of this most worthy worke (gentle reader) and the tyme of the writynge of the same: I did not onely gather togyther suche aunciente copies as I could come by, but also consult such me*n* as I knew to be more exercised in the studie of antiquities, then I my selfe haue ben. And by some of them I haue learned that the Autour was named Roberte langelande, a Shropshere man borne in Cleybirie, about viii myles from Maluerne hilles . . . the firste two verses of the boke renne upon .1. as thus.
>
>   In a somer season whan sette was the Sunne,
>   I shope me into shrobbes, as I a shepe were.
>
> (fol. 2r)

The note from Bale's *Index* that is closest to this address is attached to the entry from William Sparks. Bale's information and the faulty version of the beginning of the poem, "In a somer season whan *set* was the sun" (my emphasis), almost exactly match Crowley's address to reader. In addition, Crowley repeats the error (which is common to three of Bale's entries) of "viij myles" (probably for xviij). It would seem either that Crowley obtained his information from this entry or that Bale was copying Crowley's information after he printed his editions. As the information from Sparks is on the final leaf of the notebook and thus was presumably added quite late, I would incline towards the latter explanation. The information from John Wisdom is also late in the notebook (on the penultimate leaf), so, though it would later provide part of the entry in Bale's *Scriptorium Illustrium Maioris Brittanie Catalogus* in 1559, I likewise think it unlikely that this entry could be the source of Crowley's information about Robert Langland.

The two entries from Brigham seem to offer the most promise of being some record of what Crowley saw (or heard about).[23] One, as I mentioned above, appears in a supplemental section for the letter *R*, so though it may be earlier than the entries from Wisdom and Spark, it still is not among the earliest entries. The other entry from Brigham does not appear under *R* either. But if we look back at the entries in Bale's notebook, another possibility presents itself. Though Bale often categorized his authors under their Christian names he did not always do so. The "ex collectis Brigam" entry on folio 186r that begins "Uisio Petri Ploughman" seems to be one of those entries that Bale entered under the work rather than the author. Moore thought that this entry (made with other entries on visions, on the third folio of the section that begin with the rubricated *V*) demonstrated that Bale could not have known about the manuscript before 1550. Moore's reasoning here is not completely clear to me, but it appears that he argues that the entry is late on the assumption that it is only a kind of cross-reference to the other Brigham entry on folio 204v that he believes is later than 1550. Thus the argument is that both entries refer to one manuscript and that we must date both entries by whichever one appears to be later.

There are at least two problems with Moore's reasoning. First, even if both entries describe the same manuscript from Brigham's collection (by no means a certainty), there is no reason why he could not have added the entry on folio 204v after the entry on folio 186r. In fact, by Moore's own logic, the entry on folio 204v would have to be later than the entry on folio 186r. Second, the entry on the "Uisio" is unlike Bale's entries on "Robert Langland" in that his incipit to *Piers Plowman* is in Latin. In this it follows the other entries in the main part of the notebook rather than Bale's tendency to retain the English incipits in the later part of the notebook. This is not a decisive difference but might suggest that the other entries were seen as different precisely because they were supplemental. What we seem to have then is a relatively early entry in Bale's notebook that identifies the author of *Piers Plowman* as Robert Langland. It is probable then that this entry was among the sources, if not *the* source, of Crowley's attribution. The only real problem with this is that the incipit quoted by Bale is not the incipit quoted by Crowley in any of his editions.

If Crowley did not obtain his reading of the first line from Bale, then he must have obtained the peculiar reading of the opening line from San Marino, Huntington Library, MS Hm 128, the only manuscript that reads "set" in the first line.[24] Suggestively enough, Bale has written a note in Hm 128 which reads:

> Robertus langlande natus in comitatu Salopie in villa Mortymers Clybery in the claylande, within viij myles of Malborne hylles, scripsit, piers ploughman,
> Ii.I.
>   In somer season whan set was sunne.

The implication seems almost undeniable—that even if Crowley did not receive information from Bale orally or via another medium, Crowley must have seen Bale's note and reported more or less what it said in his first edition of the poem. This would assume that Bale had written the note in the manuscript sometime between the time he attributed the poem to Wyclif (1548) and the publication of Crowley's version of *Piers* (1550), and that Crowley had seen the manuscript and incorporated the note into his edition. Though this is not impossible, the timing is a bit tight. And Crowley's attribution of the poem in his edition differs in a small but perhaps telling detail: Crowley does not repeat the peculiar spelling of Malvern that one finds in Bale's note.[25] More likely is that among the "aunciente copies" that Crowley consulted was Hm 128, but that he saw the manuscript before Bale added the note. This timing would also fit in well with the entries in Bale's notebook. For as noted above, the entry from William Sparks whose incipit reads "In a somer season whan set was the sunne," etc. (and thus is closest to Crowley's entry *and* Hm 128), is on final folio of Bale's notebook and thus was added quite late.

The evidence that Bale influenced Crowley's selection of Robert Langland as author of *Piers Plowman* is, then, probably limited to the earliest note that Bale made in his notebook. He claims that he got this information from books out of Nicholas Brigham's library, and this, it seems, is all we know of the volume that Bale apparently examined. Fortunately, a small and seemingly casual note in London, Bodleian Library, MS Laud 581 gives us a clue as to where Brigham got his information. The note on folio 93r of the manuscript reads "Memorandum that I haue lent to Nicholas Brigham the Pers Ploughman which I borrowed of Mr. Lee of Addyngton." The person who wrote the note was Ralph Coppinger, knight of Davington (Kent), who died in Portsmouth in 1551. Ralph Hanna and Hoyt Duggan speculate that he was there because he had been appointed November 6, 1546, as second collector of custom and subsidy of wool, leather, and fells in the port of London.[26] The man from whom he had obtained the manuscript (Mr. Lee of Addyngton) was probably, as Duggan and Hanna tell us, Nicholas Leigh (1495–1581), lord of the manor of Addington (Surrey) and the builder of Addyngton place. But little else is known about him except that his brother-in-law Thomas Hatcliffe (d. 1540) was one of Henry VIII's four masters of the household.

We know a bit more about Nicholas Brigham, the man who borrowed the manuscript from the custom collector, Ralph Coppinger. John Bale describes Brigham as "Anglicarum antiquitatum amator maximus."[27] And Brigham apparently wrote the historical treatise "De Venationibus Rerum Memoribilium," some Latin poetry, and a twelve-volume work entitled "Memoirs by Way of a Diary." Unfortunately, all of these works have been lost. From what we know of his library and the books he borrowed, he had an interest in medieval English history and poetry. His most salient act was to raise a new tomb to Chaucer in 1556. Derek

Pearsall connected this translation of Chaucer's bones with a decidedly Catholic turn in England's destiny.[28] He argued that while Chaucer had been appropriated for the reformist cause in the 1530s and '40s, Chaucer's movement from the floor in front of St. Benedict's Chapel to the altar tomb against the east wall may have been an act of religious reappropriation during the short reign of Queen Mary, which attempted to "fix" the resting place of Chaucer as that of a "Catholic" poet.[29] What I would like to explore here is how Brigham's religious conservatism fit in with other more reformist searchers for the identity of the author of *Piers Plowman*. Specifically, I would assert that, contrary to expectations, conservative and reformist readers found at least some common ground in their recuperation of English literary history, particularly in their humanistic interest in who wrote *Piers Plowman*.

As we have seen, John Bale initially thought *Piers Plowman* to be a work by John Wyclif. Bale's move away from his belief that Wyclif wrote the poem, and his dependence on Brigham, a religious conservative, may suggest, then, that something other than a reformist agenda was at work here. Both Bale and Brigham were products of university culture. Though they were not at Cambridge at the same time (Bale took his bachelor of divinity in 1529 and Brigham probably took his bachelor of civil law in 1524), they certainly shared the same enthusiasm for antiquities that had university and, hence, humanistic underpinnings. As others have already argued, this attempt to recapture the past was given a new urgency in the 1530s, as Henry VIII seemed bound to efface that past in the dissolution of the monasteries.[30] One of the men of learning who felt this urgency most keenly, as a number of scholars have pointed out, was John Bale. Though a violent reformer, he, like his close literary companion Leland, had "a deeply divided consciousness," in that "he applauds the destruction of the [monastic] buildings but deplores the attendant loss of book."[31] Bale felt so bitterly about the loss of manuscripts and books during the dissolution that he could "scarsely utter it wythout teares."[32] Thus he seeks to bring forth monuments of learning "from darkenesse to a lyvely lyght."[33] Even if some might not precisely call him a humanist, he (like the Italian humanists Ciriaco of Ancona and Flavio Biondo, who wished to "wake the dead") sees learning as an ability to resurrect the past.[34] The Catholic Brigham, of course, would have had no sense of divided consciousness. His loss was not only "the lyvely memoryalles" but quite possibly a religious culture with which he had sympathies. In fact, his library, as well as the tomb that he raises to Chaucer, suggests even more of an attempt to bring to life, memorialize, and perhaps reconstitute a past that has been lost. Despite the differences between Bale and Brigham, they were clearly attempting to make connections with the vernacular poetry that lay in England's past.

In this attempt to reconnect with the English past, they certainly had a model in William Thynne, the editor of Geoffrey Chaucer's works. Thynne had served as second collector of custom and subsidy of wool, leather, and fells in the Port of London at the same time that Nicholas Brigham's father-in-law was customer in the Port of London's custom house. In addition, Ralph Coppinger (the man who lent Laud 581 to Nicholas Brigham) succeeded William Thynne as second collector after Thynne's death. Finally, the name John Thynne (William Thynne's nephew) appears in Laud 581 (as well as London, British Museum, MS Additional 10574), so it is likely that Brigham, at least, was acquainted with the Thynne family. As James Blodgett points out, the preface to Thynne's 1532 edition of Chaucer "accorded to the works of Chaucer the same respectful treatment that humanist scholars had been according to classical Greek and Latin writings."[35] Like those scholars of the classical languages, Thynne (or rather his spokesperson Brian Tuke) says, "I was moved and styred to make dilygent sertch / where I might fynde or recover any trewe copies of the sayd bookes."[36] Hence he is enlivened "to put my helping hand to the restauracion and bringynge agayne to lyght of the said workes / after the trewe copies and exemplaries aforesaid" (fol. A3r). The language here is of recovery, the disclosure "of things already known, though sometimes forgotten," as Tony Davies puts it.[37] There is a respect, in other words, for the past—even the Popish past. The attempt to recover this past is based perhaps, as Davies suggests, on "friendship—rather than allegiance to a shared ideological or intellectual programme."[38]

In terms of *Piers Plowman*, this friendship (as Bale's notes make clear) both enabled and was enabled by the exchange of manuscripts. Indeed, both Bale and Crowley apparently ascribed *Piers Plowman* to Robert Langland because they had seen multiple copies of the poem—from Brigham, Coppinger, and others. What were they doing with these multiple copies? Clearly they understood that different manuscripts had different readings even if Bale, Brigham, and Crowley, et al., didn't appreciate that they occasionally contained different versions of the poem.[39] And just as editors had long understood that there were true and false copies, they undoubtedly understood that some readings were wrong and some were right. How, then, as Will's name is actually inscribed in the text, did they settle on Robert instead of William?

William was clearly taken seriously as a candidate for authorship of *Piers Plowman*. The note by John Bale in Hm 128 (claiming that Robert Langland is the author of *Piers Plowman*) seems a response to a note just above it that states "Robert or william langland made pers plough<ma>n." Ralph Hanna has asserted that the hand that wrote this note "is almost certainly that of Ralph Coppinger."[40] Coppinger is the man who lent Laud 581 to Nicholas Brigham. And Brigham, of course, is the source for Bale's ascription of *Piers Plowman* to Robert Langland. What we have, then, is quite literally a circle involving Coppinger, Brigham, Bale, and perhaps John Thynne. Though in many ways it is gratifying to find such antiquarian interest in *Piers Plowman* in the period prior to Crowley's editions, it does

make it a bit more difficult to identify where the idea for Robert Langland originated. We get some help from the manuscript that Coppinger lent to Brigham, as
in the upper margin of folio 1r is a note in Coppinger's hand that reads "Robart
langeland borne by malbovrne <hi>lles." We cannot be sure whether Coppinger
was the originator of this information, but Coppinger's note has the same peculiar spelling of "Malvern" as the information that Bale says he got from Brigham's
manuscript. It would appear that either Brigham or (by extension) Coppinger was
Bale's ultimate source for the ascription of the poem to Robert Langland. We know
that Laud 581 was in Brigham's collection for a time, so it is even possible that the
manuscript Bale categorizes in his notebook under *V* as *Visio Petri Ploughman* is
the Laud manuscript. Even if Bale would later turn Robert Langland's biography
to a specifically reformist agenda, at the outset reformers and conservatives seemed
to have been joined in a common goal of finding rather than inventing the author
of *Piers Plowman*. We have known for some time that, as Kane put it, "Catholics
and Protestants alike found contemporary application in the text," but the search
for the author of *Piers Plowman* seems to have been a collaborative project in which
religious differences were, for a time, subordinated to the search for knowledge.[41]

That they identified the wrong man as the author of *Piers Plowman* might
be seen as unfortunate, but it tells us something about the thought processes
that governed the search. Initially, at least, how they came to believe that Robert
instead of William Langland was the author of the poem seemed to be based on
internal evidence. Skeat pointed out long ago that the error could be accounted
for because of a reading of Passus 8, line 1 of the B text ("Thus yrobed in russet I
romed aboute"), had been corrupted to something like "thus I Robert in russet I
romed aboute." Skeat actually found such a corruption in Oxford, Corpus Christi
College, MS 201 that reads "and y Robert in rosset gan rome abowhte"; and Allen
Bright found a similar corruption in a copy of A in London, Society of Antiquaries, MS no. 687 "þus Roberd in Russet I Romyd abowtyn."[42] This, of course, does
not explain why William (who is actually named in the poem) should be rejected,
but George Kane suggested that

> It is possible to imagine how their deliberation went. Here was
> a poem in which the name Will occurred three times, and Rob-
> ert only once. Moreover on one occasion (B.15.148) the Dreamer
> unambiguously said *my name is longe wille*. But on two other occa-
> sions (B.5.62 and 8.124) he was referred to in the third person; and
> on all three he was engaged with imaginary characters. . . . This is
> not, the reasoning might have gone, how an author reports of his
> actual self. Whereas, in a passage between visions (B.7.139–8.67)
> distinguished from preceding matter by a marked changed of tone
> and concerned throughout with actualities, at 8.1 this new narra-
> tor Robert, referring to himself in the first person, recounted how

he disputed with a pair of friars, a very real and dangerous class of actual men. Thus Robert might have seemed to possess reality, and William therefore, to be his creation.[43]

Kane's suggestion seems perfectly plausible except that Crowley did not print the corruption that named Robert.[44] It is because of this that I think much of the group surrounding Crowley did not see the manuscripts that contained the mis-reading. In fact, it may be that Coppinger participated in the search only insofar as his note (which could have been based on the information in the two manuscripts) about Robert's authorship proved decisive. It is possible, of course, that Crowley saw or heard of the reading and suppressed it because it did not appear in many of the manuscripts that he had seen. But even then Crowley's rejection of the reading makes it clear that the group privileged what they thought was external evidence in order to identify the author of the poem.

The group's reliance on external instead of internal evidence seems a bit mysterious. After all, medieval dream visions frequently had the names of their authors inscribed within them.[45] But we might get a hint about why Crowley, at least, would have been uncomfortable with treating evidence within the poem as historical. In describing the work in his preface to the first edition, Crowley tells his readers that in *Piers Plowman* Langland reported "certayne visions and dreames, that he fayned hym selfe to have dreamed" (fol. A2r). Crowley would not have used the word "fayned" lightly; the word was used almost obsessively by reformers to describe and condemn relics, saints lives, and legendary histories.[46] The context of these condemnations was that Catholic histories and relics were seen as pretending to be that which they were not—true pieces of a saint's body, or true recountings of the past. In making clear that these visions and dreams were feigned, Crowley separates historical from poetic truth. The use of the poem, then, should be restricted to the ability of fiction (rather than history) to "enstruct the weake." At the same time, it remains important for Crowley to locate his poet in the period before the Reformation, and in order to do this he needs to make historical truth claims that can have nothing to do with feigning.

As I have suggested above, Crowley's adherence to what he believed was sound historical practice has not always been appreciated. Kane, for instance, feels the need to identify some more ideological Protestant reason for the error.

> And such a conclusion [that Robert Langland wrote the poem], attained by reasoning sound enough within its limits of available knowledge, would appear firm ground for correcting an ascription, from ancient, popish and therefore barbarous times, to William.[47]

Given the reformist leanings of Bale and Crowley, Kane's Protestant explanation seems very convincing in his assumption that they at least wished to "reform" the identity of the author of *Piers Plowman* by turning him from the popish Will to the reformist Robert. After all, Bale originally thought the work was by Wyclif and he may have wished to maintain a new ascription of the poem more congenial to his vigorous, even violent, reforming beliefs. Yet if Brigham or Coppinger were the source of Crowley's ascription, it is not clear that they would have been so quick to discount what Kane characterizes as the "popish" past. In fact, it is quite possible that even Bale or Crowley may have had a bit more respect for that past than Kane believes. It is unclear why Kane raises the spectre of what he calls "barbarous times" at all, unless he finds his initial explanation unconvincing. I think that what we have here is a kind of post-Reformation reformation of Robert Langland—reading the fictionality of Robert Langland back into the period of the Reformation. It is clear that even among reformers like Bale the relationship to the past was a bit more complicated and conflicted than the word "reform" makes it out to be. Indeed, as Simpson points out, the metaphor of light and darkness so apparent in sixteenth-century religious discourse breaks both ways. Those who have the true religion "see the light," and so bringing the darkened past into the present may be a matter of religious orthodoxy as well as a kind of ideal humanistic understanding.[48]

If, as L. O. Fradenburg has argued, the drive in late modern academic discourse is to get things "right"—i.e., to make sure that when we remember something, we remember it as it actually was—then it is also true that this drive is associated with an anxiety that we have lost the past.[49] Bale, as we have seen, gives voice to his anxiety that the reformation of England will lead to a loss of the past, and his collections of names in his various catalogs are an attempt to compensate for this loss. Brigham's enormous collection of books can also be seen as an attempt (as Pierre Bourdieu claims) "to master time."[50] Yet, as important as the cataloging and collecting impulses were to these two men, I would argue that the process by which this cataloging and collecting was carried out—the borrowing, lending of books, and the exchange of information—was at least as important to these men. In this way, perhaps, they are not so different from late modern medievalists. After all, as Paul Strohm put it, "rememorative reconstruction" is our job, and we value the method as much as what it produces.[51] For Bale and Brigham, the inscription into books of names such as Robert or William was linked to the inscription of their own names into these same books. The record that is left is that of a community of antiquarians who shared more than a few manuscripts.

Forged in Truth

Crowley's interpolation of Robert Langland's name into the *Index*'s text, then, might signal the existence of a humanistic impulse among these like-minded men that supersedes religious beliefs. At the same time, we must admit that if "Robert

Langland" is the result of this humanistic impulse, the biography attached to him in Crowley's edition seems just a step away from what Bale had originally claimed in his *Illustrium maioris Brytannie*: that Wyclif had written the work. Crowley famously proclaimed that the work was written in the time of Edward the third,

> In whose tyme it pleased God to open the eyes of many to se hys truth, geving them boldenes of herte, to open their mouthes and crye oute agaynste the workes of darckenes, as dyd John Wicklefe, who also in those dayes translated the holye Bible into the Englishe tonge, and this writer who in reportynge certaine visions and dreames, that he fayned him selfe to have dreamed, doth moste christianlye enstruct the weake, and sharply rebuke the obstinate blynde. There is no maner of vice, that reigneth in anye estate of men, whiche thys wryter hath not godly, learnedlye, and wittilye rebuked.
> (fol. 2r)

While it is clear that Crowley wished to represent "this writer" as someone who was sympathetic to Wyclif, he maintains a certain space between Wyclif and Langland. Not taking the position (as Bale would later) that Langland is a follower of Wyclif, Crowley only argues that his mission was similar. But why maintain this separation at all? In other words, if the motive is to insist that this work is in some sense a precursor to the Reformation, why engage in humanistic practices to identify the author? The answers to this question seem to reveal a space where reformist truth and humanistic truth overlap, especially as regards suspicions about the trustworthiness of "prophecy."

Much that has been written about the words Crowley uses to introduce *Piers Plowman* focuses on their prophetic qualities.[52] John N. King reads the section as "a prophecy of the English Reformation," and goes on to make the case that this sets the stage for presenting the work "as Protestant propaganda."[53] John Bowers essentially agrees with King about Crowley's motives but suggests that "Crowley remained suspicious of the poem's prophetic strains."[54] Specifically, Bowers cites Crowley's rejection of a prophecy at Passus 6, lines 327–31 of the B text: "And when you se the sunne amisse, & two monkes heades / And a mayde haue the maistrye, and multiplie it by eyght." Crowley asserts that "that whiche foloweth and geueth it the face of a prophecye: is lyke to be a thinge added of some other man than the fyrste autour" (fol. 2v). His ostensible reason is, as he famously says, "diuerse copies have it diuerslye." While his text has the above reading,

> some other haue.
> Thre shyppes and shefe, wyth an eight folowynge
> Shall brynge back bale and battell, on both halte the mone.
> (fol. 2v)

Crowley's problem with prophecy thus seems to be a textual one. Where there are different readings, one must be inauthentic, so the reasoning goes. Many critics point to this passage in order to indicate the care with which Crowley approached his text. I would not disagree. His adherence to a historical principle that admits the possibility of textual error actually makes his case for Robert Langland all the more believable.

But it is also clear that that Crowley's concern about prophecy, highlighted as it is, suggests something beyond mere interest in about the "rightness" of the text.[55] We know that later in the sixteenth century the genre of prophecy was in many ways suspect. As Alexandra Walsham has demonstrated, the genre often depended on some story about a text's "discovery" that indicated its genuineness. The prophecies were often found "in ancient houses, abbeys . . . behind altars . . . One was said to have been 'copied oute of a boke wherein was Wycliffes wourkes, lying in a Tailor's shop at Harlowe in Essex.'"[56] In this the genre imitated the medieval hagiographical topos of *inventio*, in which the lives of saints were themselves supposed to be discovered in hidden, antique places which ultimately were meant to give credence to the texts' representations of pious lives. These saints' lives were, for the most part, derided by early humanists. Erasmus claimed that they were "old wives' tales" and even Thomas More declared early in his career that there was scarcely one saint's life that was not corrupted by some pious fraud.[57] The topos, then, meant to give "false" saints' lives the air of authenticity by pre-reform religious writers, was a device that was appropriated by reformers to give their own prophetic "discoveries" some form of legitimacy. Predictably, such practices led conservatives to critique prophetic documents on the basis of the trumped-up stories of their finding. Both the Catholic nobleman Henry Howard and the physician John Harvey derided the genre of prophecy by attacking the means by which the texts were purportedly found. Harvey asks, are they not "craftily hidden in some old stonie wall, or under some altar, or in some ancient window . . . or in some like solemne place? And there forsooth casually found by some strange accident, unlooked for? First devised, and then laid up, and afterward divulged, or published, not bona fide, but dolo malo?"[58] Both Harvey's and Howard's critiques are later than Crowley's publication of *Piers*, but it is instructive to read backwards and uncover how they give a kind of template of what Crowley attempts to avoid. These prophecies are often found by "accident . . . unlooked for." The text of *Piers*, on the other hand, is manifest and actively sought—Crowley endeavors to gather together "such aunciente copies" as he could come by. The rhetoric here is less of finding, and thus by implication "inventing," and more of discovering. Howard accuses the publishers of these prophecies of using "moderne deceit" in order to "beget the colour and grace of venerable Antiquity."[59] Crowley, on the other hand, consults other men who "are more exercised in the studie of antiquities" than he was in order to uncover a name of a historical author and where he lived. Further, there is a careful consideration of the dating problem. Crowley spends almost half of his preface discussing the date of the poem. He claims to have used multiple manuscripts to determine a terminus a quo and terminus ad quem. In other words, Crowley goes out of his way to at least appear as if he is authenticating his text via time-honored humanistic methods. His manner of casting light upon the process of printing the text is meant to reflect the content of his work through which, as he tells us in his address to the reader, God opens "the eyes of many to se hys truth" (fol. 2r).

Why is Crowley so insistent on the dating of the poem? While I think it highly unlikely that anyone actually considered *Piers* a modern invention, the poem was printed in a moment when the charge of novelty was regarded as a serious threat to the legitimacy of the Protestant cause. As any number of critics have pointed out, it was important to these reformers to create a link with an earlier period in order to justify the reformed religion as having some priority over the Catholic Church. John Bale himself would resurrect the old story that Joseph of Arimithea came to England "and published there amonge them that Gospell of saluacion whiche Christe first of all and afterwardes hys Apostles had taught at Jerusalem. Untruly therefore are we reported of the Italyane writers and of the subtylle devysers of sanctes legendes that we shulde haue our first faythe from Rome and our cristen doctoryne from their unchristen byshoppes."[60] Bale's digs at the "subtylle devysers of sanctes legendes" and "Italyane writers" shape the evidence of the priority of the Catholic Church as a series of lies and dissimulations. He is attempting to reorder the authentic historical record more in line with a native legendary history.[61] This justification is merely the most blatant form of attempting to give the reformed religion priority. As suggested by an early sixteenth-century text (*The praier and complaynte of the ploweman vnto Christe*) that has connections with the Piers Plowman tradition, this attack on reformed religion

> ys no newe thinge
> but an olde practyce of oure prelates lerned of their fathers the
>   byschops phareses & prestes of the olde law
> to defame the doctrine of Christe with the name of new lerninge
> and the teachers thereof with the name of new masters.[62]

The writer of the preface obsessively returns, over half a dozen times in the space of three pages, to the notion that reformed religion is not "new learning." As Sarah Kelen suggests, the text at once dehistoricizes Protestantism and places it within a historical continuum. The text elides historical distance by analogizing Catholic prelates and biblical Pharisees and, at the same time, insists that the intervening historical period in which the suppression of the true faith occurs is absolutely central to understanding the present state of affairs.[63] Just as the attack on reformed religion is not new, the point is that the reformed religion is "no newe thyng" either, and what we have is a cyclic return to the early (read biblical) state of affairs with Protestants in the position of Christ.

By extension, the claim is that the texts that illustrate the existence of the new religion are not "new" either. They are printed versions of what was made out to be a rich manuscript tradition of work by protoreformers. The insistence on this on both the title page of the work and the preface to the second edition by one W. T. (perhaps William Tyndale) is expressed by the claim that it was "writte[n] nat longe after the yere of our Lorde. M. & thre hu[n]dred."[64] W. T. goes on to say,

> I haue put forth here in printe this prayer and complaynte of the
>   plowman which was written not longe after the yere of our
>   Lorde a thousande and thre hundred
> in his awne olde english
> chaingynge there in nothinge as ferforth as I could obserue it other
>   the english or ortographie
> addinge also there to a table of soch olde wordes as be nowe anti-
>   quate and worne out of knoulege by processe of tyme.[65]

The attempt, then, is to thrust the text back (probably too far back by at least seventy-five years) into the pre-Reformation in order to legitimate the text. In this calculus of authenticity, legitimacy is a product of antiquity, and the idea that forgeries might have happened in the past (as they did with the Catholic Church) needs not be dealt with because presumably, unlike saints' lives, old Lollard documents make no claims about signs and wonders *except* insofar as they exist as prophecies. Charges about "invention" then are always fundamentally charges about sixteenth-century "newness."

The context for these charges, at least before 1550, is a bit puzzling. It is not that editors or even humanists did not fall prey to the temptation to invent. Indeed, in the fifteenth century Domizo Calderni "flat-out 'invented a Roman writer, Marius Rusticus, from whom he claimed to derive disquieting information about the youth of Suetonius.'"[66] But for Protestants, inventing authors or texts would be to indulge in the "fantasticall dreames of those exiled Abbie-lubbers" that Thomas Nashe would later equate with the Catholic tendency to promote lying fictions.[67] And as Anne Hudson and others have argued, printings of old Lollard texts were, for the most part, what they claimed to be—authentic survivals of medieval texts.[68] But the chaotic larger context of printing in the early and mid-sixteenth century may have led to suspicions about the "authenticity" of such texts. Certainly the practices of printers at this time led to no great confidence in the claims on their title pages. Editors, attempting to circumvent regulations like those of 1529 that banned heretical books, often altered titles, omitted names, and falsified places of printing.[69] Even among like-minded reformers there was irritation expressed about how texts were interfered with. William Tyndale, annoyed with the Bible translator George Joye, remarks "But of this I challenge George Joye, that he did not put his own name thereto and call it rather his translation: and that he playeth boo peep, and in some of his books putteth in his name and title, and in some keepeth it out."[70] John Bale himself came under suspicion about the veracity of his version of *The Examinations of Anne Askew*. Stephen Gardiner claimed in a letter of May 21, 1547, to the Duke of Somerset that Bale's "untruth apereth evidently in setting forth the examination of Anne Askew which is utterly misreported."[71] Whether or not Gardiner (no friend to Bale) was being fair is not the point.[72] The suspicion was that Bale not only added "elucidations" to the narrative but that he materially altered the words of Askew, despite his own protestations that it was taken from a manuscript "sent abroade by her owne hande wrytinge."[73] These suspicions would have been enough to generate anxiety in reformist editors like Crowley, but it is clear that anxieties about alterations of even old reformist texts were not baseless.

Most notably, a text that was connected with *Piers Plowman*, *The Plowman's Tale* (sometimes titled *The Complaynte of the Plowman*), was altered to fit a sixteenth-century political context. Though *The Plowman's Tale* was perhaps originally an early fifteenth-century Wycliffite text, it was "improved" in the sixteenth century with a prologue that led it to be included in the *Canterbury Tales*. As Andrew Wawn has asserted, "the anonymous poem's doctrine was lent a cast of antiquity and hence respectability by its new association with England's most celebrated 'antient' poet."[74] Though there is evidence that the original text circulated among some readers without the sixteenth-century prologue, it remains unclear how many readers had suspicions about the attribution to Chaucer.[75] What is clear is that such forgeries created a confusing context for the recovery of medieval texts. The group of men surrounding Crowley only had to look as far as the work of John Leland to understand how error could render their own work suspect. Leland mistook *The Plowman's Tale* for *Piers Plowman* itself, listing the *Tale* as *Petri Aratori Fabula* and claiming that "the tale of Piers Plowman, which by the common consent of the learned is attributed to Chaucer as its true author, has been suppressed in each edition, because it vigorously inveighed against the bad morals of the priests."[76] Bale, of course, used Leland's work in the construction of the *Catalogus*, and while Bale perpetuated the erroneous belief that Chaucer wrote *The Plowman's Tale*, the ascription of *Piers Plowman* to Chaucer was obviously removed.[77] Crowley, Bale, and the others could appreciate, therefore, the need to create a verifiable medieval origin for the poem in the midst of such confusion.[78]

The conditions that made possible this community of those interested in antiquarian texts changed, I think, shortly after the printing of Crowley's editions in 1550, and had certainly altered by the advent of Elizabeth as queen in 1558. After Elizabeth took the throne, old books and antiquarianism came to be seen as dangerous, precisely because they not only called up the Catholic past of the Middle Ages but the past of Elizabeth's Catholic sister. There were those like Matthew Parker who, in the mode of John Bale, bewailed the loss of books and would borrow books such as Matthew Paris's *Chronica Majora* from religious conservatives like the antiquarian John Stow. But, as May McKisack tells us, "all too many of Parker's contemporaries . . . regarded the possession of medieval texts as indicative of leanings towards Popery."[79] Those antiquarians who did not fit into a "wicclevian" mold were in danger. John Stow, for instance, had his house ransacked and was in some danger for harboring "old written English Chronicles both in parchement and in paper . . . miscellanea of diverse sortes . . . many such also written in olde Englisshe on parchement"; these books, as Bishop Grindal wrote to Cecil and the Queen's Council, "declare him to be a great favourer of papistrye."[80] It is not, then, that there were not people to carry out the preservation and even publication of what Bale called "lively memorials" during the reign of Elizabeth, it is just that the conditions under which antiquarians operated became more fraught, and something like borrowing a book, even a book with a good reformist pedigree like *Piers Plowman*, might indicate an unhealthy and dangerous interest in the past. What made these old books so dangerous, ironically enough, was England's relapse into Catholicism. Religious conservatives like Brigham and reformers like Bale were less likely to work together to open up a small space of what might be called humanistic scholarly work because this space was itself seen as suspect—the temporal locus of the old religion that threatened for a time to become the future as well as the past.

So what is the work of Robert Langland? Despite the fact that he is in some sense the ultimate "nowhere man," I think we can recognize that he continues to do work in the field of medieval literary studies. For at least the past forty years he has labored to distance the sixteenth-century reception of *Piers Plowman* from its fourteenth-century origins. In terms of the larger atmosphere in the middle of the sixteenth century, this attribution has also had something of a corona effect, as it is often cited as one more piece of evidence that in this period the nature of *Piers Plowman* and *Piers*-like poetry is almost always insistently reformist. By being insistently reformist—"one of the first disciples of John Wycliff," as John Bale characterized him—Robert becomes the dark twin of William. Robert draws off the notion that the author of *Piers Plowman* was an ideologically driven reformer and authorizes our choice of William Langland as an author whose aesthetically complex verse rewards a nuanced approach, which not incidentally also rewards our own labors of scholarship.

What I have suggested here is that it is perhaps time for us to put Robert to work in a different way. His birth and fosterage in the minds of a group of like-minded antiquaries speaks less to the reforming nature of Robert and more to the desire to connect with a past that, although problematic for reformers like Bale and Crowley, was nonetheless recognized as the only heritage that England possessed. This is not to ignore the ways in which reformers saw in *Piers Plowman* a work that was congenial to their beliefs. Rather it is to recognize that even as some sixteenth-century readers of the poem created a false poetic presence, it was in the service of a past that was seen as anything but invented.

NOTES

1. Thomas Hardy, "The Three Strangers," in Hardy, *Wessex Tales*, 26.

2. For the various claimants to the title of "author of *Piers Plowman*" see Bloomfield, "Present State of *Piers Plowman* Studies," 224–225. See Kelen, *Langland's Early Modern Identities*, for a more recent treatment of the various ascriptions that in many respects mirrors my own work here, though to somewhat different conclusions.

3. Serious doubts have existed about "Robert Langland" ever since Walter Skeat discovered a reading that could explain the name in his 1869 edition of the B text; William Langland, *Vision of William*, xxviii, n. 3. However, it was George Kane's Piers Plowman: *The Evidence for Authorship* that more or less ended the authorship controversy. See Bloomfield, "Present State of *Piers Plowman* Studies" (225), and below for evidence that corroborated Skeat's initial finding. As we will see, it is difficult to pinpoint precisely when Robert Langland emerged, but it is worth remembering that until perhaps the middle of the twentieth century there were scholars who took very seriously the possibility that Robert Langland had written *Piers Plowman*. Morton W. Bloomfield said in 1939 that though William was the favored candidate (largely due to Walter Skeat's attribution in 1885) the authorship "question . . . will probably never be solved" (Bloomfield, "Present State of *Piers Plowman* Studies," 224). And in his 1965 work refuting the case for multiple authorship of *Piers Plowman*, George Kane spends a good deal of time disproving not only the possibility that Robert Langland wrote *Piers Plowman* but the possibility that Robert Langland ever existed.

4. There are minor differences between the addresses by the printer to the reader in Crowley's first, second, and third editions. This quotation is taken from the facsimile of Pepys's copy; see [Langland], *Vision of Pierce Plowman* (facsimile reprint), fol. 2r. Pepys's copy was a first edition, but it must have been one of those that remained initially unsold. As J. A. W. Bennett points out in the afterword to the facsimile, unsold copies of the first edition had title pages and addresses to the reader from the second edition inserted. This quotation is from the original title page to the first edition.

5. See note 16.

6. Cargill, "The Langland Myth," 42.

7. King, *English Reformation Literature*, 322.

8. Though Hailey makes it clear that "right" might mean something a bit different to us than to Crowley; see "Robert Crowley and the Editing of *Piers Plowman*," 146.

9. Scanlon, "Langland, Apocalypse," 55. I would not deny that ultimately Robert Langland was transformed into a reformer and that in Crowley's second and third editions the poem is gradually transformed into a reformist work. The first edition had fewer marginal notes to guide readers and may have been intended for a different audience than the following two editions. See Hailey, "Giving Light to the Reader," 63ff.

10. Hughes and Larkin, *Tudor Royal Proclamations*, 1:373–76.

11. See King, "Robert Crowley," 222. If, as King asserts, Richard Grafton (the King's printer) actually did the printing for Crowley, the need for an "authentic" author becomes even more evident. Hailey reports on a scholar who dissents from this view ("Giving Light to the Reader," 15n16).

12. For the production of this kind of propaganda in the form of "playes, songes and books," see James Simpson, *Reform and Cultural Revolution*, 528.

13. Machan, *Textual Criticism*, 17–22.

14. Woolfson, introduction to *Reassessing Tudor Humanism*, 11.

15. For a more measured assessment of Bale, see, for instance, James Simpson, *Reform and Cultural Revolution*.

16. The *Scriptorium Illustrium Maioris Brytannie Catalogus* (1550–59) was Bale's second published catalog. The text reads:

> Robertus Langelande, sacerdos, ut apparet, natus in comitatu Salopie, in uilla uulgo dicta Mortymers Clibery, in terra lutea, octauo a Maluernis montibus milliario fuit. Num tamen eo in loco, incondito & agresti, in bonis literis ad maturam aetatem usque informatus fuerit, cereto adfirmare non possum est. ut necqu, an Oxonii aut Cantabrigie illis insudauerit: quum apud eorum locorum magistros, studia praecipue uigerent. Illud ueruntamen liquido constat, eum fuisse ex primis Ionannis Vuicleui discipulis unum, atque in spiritus feruore, contra apertas Papistarum blasphemies aduersus Deum & eius Christum, sub amoenis coloribus & typis edidisse in sermone Anglico pium opus, ac bonorum virorum lectione dignum, quod uocabat
> *Visionem Petri Aratoris, Lib. 1.1 In aestivo temporare cum sol caleret*
> Nihil aliud ab ipso editum noui. In hoc erudito, praeter similitudines uarias & iucundas, prophetice plura predixit, que nostris diebus impleri uidimus. Comleuit suum opus anno Domini 1369, dum Ioannes Cicestrius Londini praetor esset.

Bale, *Scriptorvm illustriu[m] maioris Brytanni[a]e*, 474.

George Kane reports that London, Library of the Society of Antiquaries, MS no. 687 contains a late sixteenth- or early seventeenth-century note (clearly a translation of Bale) that reads "The author Robert Langland a cheife disciple of John Wickliffs" (*The Evidence of Authorship*, 43). Allan Bright, who once owned the manuscript, further reveals that this note is on the title page; see Bright, *New Light on "Piers Plowman,"* 42n1. And in a copy of Owen Rogers's 1561 "reprint" of Crowley's edition of *The Vision of Pierce Plowman* can be found an entry dated 1577 that virtually reinscribes Bale's entire biographical note from his 1559 work; Silverstone, "Vision of Pierce Plowman," 229–30.

17. Langland, *Vision of William*, 2:lxxiii. See also Hanna, *William Langland*, 27; Hudson, "Legacy of *Piers Plowman*," 261; Brewer, *Editing* Piers Plowman, 11.

18. Brewer, *Editing* Piers Plowman, 8.

19. In the *Illustrium maioris Brytannie Scriptorum* the name Langland does not occur, but the poem appears in a long list of works by Wyclif under the title *Petrum Agricolum*; see Bale, *Illustrium maioris Brytannie Scriptorum*, 157.

20. See also Moore, "Studies in '*Piers the Plowman*,'" 36. Kane, *The Evidence for Authorship*, 42n. Bale, *Index Brittaniae Scriptorum*, xixff.

21. See Poole's introduction to Bale, *Index Brittaniae Scriptorum*, viii–ix.

22. Fol. 204v:

> Robertus Langlande, natus in comitatu Salopie in villa Mortymers Clyberi in the Cleylande within viij. Myles of Malborne hylles, scripsit, Peer ploughman, Ii. i. 'In a somer sonday whan sote was ye sunne.'
> *Ex collectis Nicolai Brigan*

Fol. 186r:

Uisio Petri Ploughman, edita per Robertum Langlande, natum in comitatu Salopie, in villa Mortymers Clybery in the cley lande within viij. myles of Malborne hylles, Ii. i. 'In quodam estates die cum sol caleret,' etc.

Ex collectis Nicolai Brigam

Fol. 276r:

Robertus Langlonde, sacerdos (vt apparet) natus apud Clybery prope Maluernum Montem, scripsit Peers plowghman opus eruditum ac quodammodo propheticum. Claruit A. D.1369, dum Ioannes Chichestre pretor esse Londini.

Ex Ioanne Wysdome medico.

Fol. 277r:

Robertus Langlande, a Shropshyre man, borne in Claybery about viij. myles from Maluerne hylles, wrote Peers Ploughman, Ii. i. 'In a somer season whan set was the sunne,' etc.

Ex domo Guilhelmi Sparke.

23. Brigham has long been a suspect in the hunt for Bale's source, and it may be that the field is drawing close to scholarly consensus about Brigham's influence. See, for instance, Bowers, *Chaucer and Langland*, 63.

24. Skeat believes that Crowley simply misread the manuscript and that the word was altered later (presumably to agree with Crowley); see Langland, *Vision of William*, xxiin1. Kane, however, demonstrates that the reading was present quite early in the history of the manuscript (*The Evidence of Authorship*, 41n3).

25. The quotation of the first line of the poem in Crowley matches neither Bale's note nor the opening of Hm 128. Hm 128 reads "In a someres seysoun whan set was the sunne" (fol. 113r). Bale's notes get neither the reading of the first line of Hm 128 right nor the readings of any of the other incipits, which he apparently saw in other manuscripts.

26. Duggan and Hanna, *Oxford, Bodleian Library, Laud Misc. 581*, I.10.

27. Bale, *Scriptorvm illustriu[m] mairoris Brytanni[a]e*, 718. For the most up to date biography of Brigham, see Alsop, "Nicholas Brigham."

28. See Pearsall, "Chaucer's Tomb," 64. See also my *Chaucer's Dead Body*.

29. This connection between Brigham and Catholicism is supported by the fact that many of Brigham's friends were Catholic. Thomas Felton, for instance, writer of the tallies and Brigham's supervisor, was a religious conservative whose family supported Queen Mary against Lady Jane Grey. Brigham also attained his highest office (first teller of the exchequer) during Queen Mary's reign, so it is probable that he was sympathetic to the old religion.

30. Aston, "English Ruins and English History."

31. James Simpson, *Reform and Cultural Revolution*, 17.

32. Bale, address to the reader in *Laboryouse Journey and Serche*, fol. A7v, quoted in Aston, "Lollardy and the Reformation," 164.

33. Bale, *Laboryouse Journey and Serche*, fol. B8v, quoted in James Simpson, *Reform and Cultural Revolution*, 18. Bale's language here imitates the phrasing of Leland, which is itself discussed by Sarah A. Kelen in her introduction to this volume. See also Dan Breen's treatment of Leland, Bale, and the dissolution in his essay in this volume.

34. Levine, *Humanism and History*, 78. Indeed, in his essay in this volume, Dan Breen seems to take the strong position that Bale is "emphatically non-humanistic." Closer reading of his essay, however, reveals the more nuanced interpretation of Bale's career that has characterized more recent treatments of the sixteenth century.

35. Blodgett, "William Thynne," 36.

36. Chaucer, *Workes, newlye printed*, fol. A2v.

37. Davies, *Humanism*, 104.

38. Davies, *Humanism*, 76. For a treatment of the humanistic idea of friendship vis-à-vis Crowley, see Betteridge, *Literature and Politics*, 109.

39. See, for instance, what might be an attempt to reconcile the reading of "set" in the first line in HM 128 ("In a someres seson whan set was þe sonne") with the reading "softe" that was in other manuscripts Bale saw. Bale records the reading with a curiously ambivalent "sote" that has written above it "warm."

40. Duggan and Hanna, *Oxford, Bodleian Library, Laud Misc. 581*, I.10.

41. Kane, *The Evidence of Authorship*, 40.

42. Bright, *New Light on "Piers Plowman,"* 42. The quotation of the line is from fol. 29v and is quoted from Kane, *The Evidence of Authorship*, 42.

43. Kane, *The Evidence of Authorship*, 44–45.

44. There was, however, apparent confusion about the reading at B.8.1. Crowley's first edition has "throbed" while his second and third editions have "robed." HM 128 also has "robed" but this is written in a different hand in different ink over the erasure of a longer word. Kane believes that the confusion indicates "y Robert" must have been present "in an exclusive common ancestor" of HM 128 and Crowley's lost original (*The Evidence of Authorship*, 44). Kane is attempting to multiply possibilities for the group to see the misreading "Robert" but fails to explain why (if the appearance of the name in the manuscripts was decisive) Crowley would "correct" it.

45. R. W. Chambers not only gives a lucid treatment of the ascription of the poem to Robert, but demonstrates how widespread the convention was of "signing" one's poem. See Chambers, "Robert or William Longland?" 442–54.

46. The word was often used to characterize saints lives—especially Becket's. A set of royal injunctions in 1538 were specifically altered to justify the destruction of images and relics because they were "feigned." See Marshall, "Forgery and Miracles."

47. Kane, *The Evidence of Authorship*, 45.

48. See James Simpson, *Reform and Cultural Revolution*, 27.

49. Fradenburg, *Sacrifice Your Love*, 249.

50. Bourdieu, *Distinction*, 71–72.

51. Strohm, "Rememorative Reconstruction," 16.

52. Rebecca L. Schoff focuses on how Crowley makes "Langland's role while a living poet important to our own understanding of *Piers Plowman*." See Schoff, "Tudor Regulation of the Press," 97.

53. King, "Crowley's Editions of *Piers Plowman*," 348.

54. Bowers, *Chaucer and Langland*, 224.

55. Some of Crowley's reasons for wishing to distance his text from prophetic concerns have already been noted by Wendy Scase in her recent essay on *Dauy Dycars Dreame*. She notes that the twenty-eight-line poem (based on Langland's *Dawe þe dykere* at B.6.330) occasioned some political trouble for its author, Thomas Churchyard. She further argues that *Dauy Dycars Dreame*, often said to be published after Crowley's editions of *Piers Plowman* in 1550, was actually published before 1550. If true, then this would explain Crowley's rejection of the prophecy that is connected with *Dawe þe dykere* at 6.325–30: not only because prophecies differ in different manuscripts (and thus are apparently untrustworthy) but also because association with this prophecy recalls texts based upon *Piers Plowman* that ultimately have a subversive pedigree. Scase's discovery, then, goes a long way towards

explaining Crowley's curiously ambivalent attitude towards prophecy—unwilling to claim the genre for *Piers* at some junctures and seemingly willing to embrace it at others (as, for instance, in Crowley's claim that Langland predicted the suppression of the Abbeys). See Scase, "*Dauy Dycars Dreame.*" For a full discussion of Crowley's ambivalence about prophecy, see Kelen, *Langland's Early Modern Identities*, 32–38.

56. Walsham, "Inventing the Lollard Past."

57. Peter Marshall, "Forgery and Miracles," 45.

58. John Harvey, *A discoursive probleme*, 66, quoted by Walsham, "Inventing the Lollard Past," 649.

59. Henry Howard, *A defensative against the poyson of supposed prophecies*, 117r–v, quoted by Walsham, "Inventing the Lollard Past," 649.

60. Bale, *The Vocacyon of Johân Bale*, fol. B4v.

61. The first appearance of the story is in William of Malmsbury's *De antiquitate glastoniensis ecclesiae*, though it appears to postdate the original work by some hundred years.

62. *Praier and complaynte of the ploweman*, ed. Parker, 110.

63. Kelen, *Langland's Early Modern Identities*, 53.

64. See *Praier and complaynte of the ploweman*, ed. Parker, 41–47.

65. *Praier and complaynt of the Ploweman*, [London?], 1532, fol. A3v, quoted in Kelen, "Plowing the Past," 112.

66. Machan, *Textual Criticism*, 17, quoting Anthony Grafton, "On the Scholarship of Politian," 161.

67. Nashe, *Anatomie of Absurditie*, 11.

68. Hudson says, "It seems to me that it would be fair to say that, with very few exceptions, all the evidence points to a remarkable conservatism in the sixteenth-century handling of the medieval material" ("Legacy of *Piers Plowman*," 171). Alexandra Walsham more or less agrees, saying "there was nothing to suggest that they [lollard texts] were outrageous forgeries"; see Walsham, "Inventing the Lollard Past," 14. She makes the case, however, that the editors were not above putting a patina of age on a text.

69. Hughes and Larkin, *Tudor Royal Proclamations*, 181–86.

70. Tyndale, *Tyndale's New Testament*, 13–14. Tyndale's comment appears in the preface to his 1534 translation.

71. Foxe, *Actes and monuments*, 733.

72. But see Thomas S. Freeman and Sarah Elizabeth Wall, "Racking the Body, Shaping the Text.'"

73. Bale, *The first examinacyon of Anne Askewe*, fol. A5r.

74. Wawn, "Chaucer, *The Plowman's Tale* and Reformation Propaganda," 184.

75. See Wawn, "Chaucer, *The Plowman's Tale* and Reformation Propaganda," 184–92.

76. Leland, *Commentarii de scriptoribus Britannicis*, 420, 423.

77. Bale lists *arator narratio* as by Chaucer in the *Scriptorum illustrium Maioris Britanni[a]e*, 525.

78. In the context of these textual suspicions, texts within the *Piers Plowman* tradition might well take on a different meaning than is usually found there. The text *A proper dyaloge betwene a Gentilman and a Husbandman eche complaynynge to other their miserable calamite through the ambicion of the clergye* is a hybrid text, including a sixteenth-century introduction to a Lollard treatise that has the modern title *The clergy may not own property*. In the sixteenth-century postscript to the older text, the "gentleman" claims:

> Now I promyse the after my iudgement
> I haue not hard of soche an olde fragment

Better groundyd on reason with Scripture.
Yf soche auncyent thynges myght come to lyght
That noble men hadde ones of theym a syght
The world yet wolde chaunge perauenture
For here agaynst the clergye cannot bercke
Sayenge as they do thys is a newe wercke
Of heretykes contryued lately.
And by thys treatyse it apperyth playne
That before oure dayes men did compleyne
Agaynst clerkes ambycyon so stately.

The logic of this passage is a bit tortured. The gentleman refers to oral tradition in order to draw attention to its reasonableness. He then invokes the ancientness of the fragment in order to suggest that such a tradition could change the world. Most importantly, though, he attempts to absolve the work of being new and "contryued." It may well be that he is simply attempting to reinforce the age of the fragment and draw attention to the notion that contemporary reformers were not the only ones writing against the church. But it remains odd that the objection would even need to be raised. And one wonders how it would have been received in 1550. See [Roy?], *A proper dyaloge*.

79. McKisack, *Medieval History in the Tudor Age*, 72–73.

80. Quoted in Stow, *Survey of London*, xvii.

The Monkish Middle Ages:
Periodization and Polemic in
Foxe's *Acts and Monuments*

Jesse M. Lander

We cannot not periodize.—Frederic Jameson

Perhaps no book published in the sixteenth century had a greater impact on historical consciousness than John Foxe's *Acts and Monuments*.—D. R. Woolf[1]

Milton's Satan, journeying toward earth, alights on the outer sphere of the created universe, an empty place that will in time to come be known as the paradise of fools; in it will accumulate "all things vain and all who in vain things / Built their fond hopes."[2] The description that follows catalogs not only "painful superstition" and "blind zeal" but also "All the unaccomplished works of nature's hand, / Abortive, monstrous, or unkindly mixed," before concluding with a remarkable list of detritus:

> Cowls, hoods, and habits with their wearers tossed
> And fluttered into rags, then relics, beads,
> Indulgences, dispenses, pardons, bulls,
> The sport of winds; all these upwhirled aloft
> Fly o'er the backside of the world far off
> Into a limbo large and broad, since called
> The paradise of fools, to few unknown
> Long after, now unpeopled and untrod.
> (lines 490–97)

Milton's flight of fancy extends a long line of Protestant polemic aimed at Catholic devotional practices by proleptically consigning these practices to a zone outside the created world. Milton here creates in spatial and cosmological terms the sort of segregation achieved in historiography by positing a rupture between the medieval and the modern. Though the catalog is a common element in epic, this particular catalog is more indebted to the use of congeries or *accumulatio*—a rhetorical figure in which words are heaped up—in classical satire and, perhaps more importantly, in English anti-Catholic polemic. This polemical use of congeries or *accumulatio* is frequently accompanied by an implicit form of periodization that relegates Catholicism to a disorderly past, a past that has now been superseded, and John Foxe's influential *Actes and Monuments* offers what is perhaps the most significant and sophisticated articulation of this position. What makes *Actes and Monuments* especially interesting is the way in which the rhetorical figure of *accumulatio* is combined with an explicit and highly developed scheme of periodization. For Foxe, the figure of *accumulatio* is more than a device offering a satirical inventory of ridiculous particulars; instead, it replicates in rhetorical terms a historical process of accretion that has obscured the originally pristine truth of Christianity. Unsurprisingly, monasticism represents, in particularly acute form, a process of historical change which is viewed not as development driven by a recognizable internal logic but instead as an incoherent heaping up of regulations, doctrines, institutions, ceremonies, and superstitions. In Foxe's account, monasticism serves as an epitome of medieval religion. It is a discernible historical development with a beginning, middle, and, at least in late sixteenth-century England, an end, and paradoxically the strict regulation of monastic life becomes evidence of a disorderly multiplication of rules that is typical of the medieval church. For Foxe, then, the Middle Ages are themselves a congeries.

The notion that our modern schemes of periodization are driven by a polemical impulse is well established.[3] And yet despite our awareness that period concepts are tendentious and frequently misleading, they remain a regular part of our scholarly equipment. Indeed, despite having been recognized as polemical, periodization remains a prominent element in literary scholarship. "Periods are entities we love to hate," according to Marshall Brown, who immediately adds, "yet we cannot do without them."[4] Though Lee Patterson has suggested that periodization in the hands of some recent scholars of the Renaissance periodization has enabled an avoidance of history, Reinhart Koselleck insists that history "can only exist as a discipline if it develops a theory of periodization."[5] In what follows, I will examine the way in which *Actes and Monuments* responds to an experience of historical rupture by articulating a polemical vision of the Middle Ages. The polemical account of the Middle Ages offered by Foxe and other Protestant reformers promoted a perception of historical change that served to confirm their claim that the world was witnessing the dawn of a new age. While this vision was to be enormously influential, and it contributed to subsequent understandings of the medieval world that were emphatically secular in orientation, the book's initial appeal was to a particular variety of evangelical Protestant. What begins as a narrowly sectarian argument for epochal change will, however, in the course of time become a putatively neutral designation. But to understand this process in its full complexity, we must do more than simply deplore the deleterious effects of "the master narrative first put in place by the Renaissance."[6]

Patterson's critique is not ostensibly directed at periodization itself, a practice with a long medieval pedigree, but rather at the "crude binarism that locates modernity ("us") on one side and premodernity ("them") on the other, thus condemning the Middle Ages to the role of all-purpose alternative."[7] This would presumably allow for a sophisticated and pluralistic scheme of periodization, but it is difficult to see how the polemical aspect of periodization can be fully overcome. The procedure that divides history into segments or units and claims for these units an internal logic or identity is bound to produce or reproduce fundamental antagonisms. Rather than simply dismiss out of hand the disastrous consequences of a tendentious "master narrative," we need a better understanding of the way in which a variety of different historiographic traditions coalesced to form the grand scheme of periodization that has dominated modern Western scholarship. John Foxe's *Book of Martyrs* displays a particular sense of the Middle Ages that owes more to apocalyptic exegesis and anti-Catholic polemic than to humanist claims for the rebirth of the classical.

The importance of humanism for the development of modern historiography and its schemes of periodization would be difficult to exaggerate. The clarion calls of figures like Vasari, Alberti, and Machiavelli provide clear evidence of a new enthusiasm for the classical that was accompanied by an insistence that the classical legacy needed to be rescued from the depredations of time. Humanists ransacked archives in pursuit of "lost" manuscripts and produced editions that rejected the received textual tradition, with its accumulation of commentary and editorial interpolation, and claimed a new fidelity to the originals. The Italian humanists were, of course, relentless publicists who missed no opportunity to extol the *rinascita dell'arte*, and their story of cultural revival reaches its epitome in Jacob Burckhardt's famous work:

> In the Middle Ages both sides of human consciousness—that which was turned within as that which was turned without—lay dreaming or half awake beneath a common veil. The veil was woven of faith, illusion, and childish prepossession, through which the world and history were seen clad in strange hues. Man was conscious of himself only as a member of a race, people, party, family, or corporation—only through some general category. In Italy this veil first melted into air; an *objective* treatment and consideration of the State and of all the things of this world became possible. The *subjective* side at the same time asserted itself with corresponding emphasis; man became a spiritual *individual*, and recognized himself as such.[8]

According to Burckhardt, the Middle Ages was a time in which both objective and subjective reality alike were unrecognized.[9] Burckhardt's veil is not a blindfold, and his story should not be confused with common narratives of progressive enlightenment and emancipation; nonetheless, Burckhardt does suggest that the Renaissance achieves a cognitive gain. Objective reality comes into focus first as a result of new theorizing, associated with Machiavelli, about the state and history, and then as a consequence of an emergent science. Simultaneously, subjective reality emerges in the figure of the "spiritual *individual*," a development that entails the sloughing off of tribal and collective identities. Burckhardt's enormously influential account of the Renaissance was clearly shaped by the immediate social, cultural, and intellectual context of nineteenth-century Basel.[10] However, any historicization of Burckhardt must acknowledge that what he offers is a peculiar, even parochial, nineteenth-century articulation of a tradition that was itself initiated by the artists, poets, and scholars of fourteenth-century Italy.[11] Between defenders who argue that Burckhardt gives voice to the Renaissance's own self-understanding and detractors who insist that his "Renaissance" is a conservative reaction to the emergence of mass society and the bureaucratic state, what gets missed is the role played by the Reformation in Burckhardt's thinking.

It is conventional to argue that the Reformation merely continued and amplified the humanist polemic against the "Middle Ages," extending the argument from literature and the arts to also include religion. In this view, the Reformers publicized an image of the preceding age as monkish, friarly, and, most importantly, popish, but they did not contribute any conceptual novelty. The classic account of this process is given by Wallace K. Ferguson: "The theological scheme of universal history, to which all the reformers were addicted, prevented them from distinguishing the middle age as part of a formal system of periodization, but the whole tenor of their historical writing pointed to the existence of such a period and furnished it with a very definite character."[12] Certainly Ferguson is right to emphasize the way in which Protestant historiography invested the medieval past with "a very definite character." Unlike the humanists who were content to dismiss the "dark ages" as a time of ignorance and barbarism, Reformation polemic entailed a careful analysis of the cultural dysfunctions of the Middle Ages. While the humanists are limited by their narrow focus on artistic and literary culture, the Reformers are, according to Ferguson, "bound by the traditional scheme of the Four Monarchies" (74). To put this somewhat simplistically: the humanists have an appropriate form in their tripartite division of history but they lack appropriate content (i.e., they neglect the interstitial period and daily life); the Reformers have content in their thick descriptions of popish iniquity but lack an appropriate form. According to Ferguson, it is only in the late seventeenth century that a synthesis occurs, when the idea of a Middle Age is combined with the "invidious name . . . to form a practical periodization of history." This "practical periodization" serves as the backbone for the immensely popular late seventeenth-century handbooks of history written by Christoph Keller.

Ferguson's emphasis on the "practical use of the division of history into three periods" (75) carries an implicit criticism of prior historical schemes: they are, above all, impractical. Extravagant apocalyptic theologies of history have no purchase on the ground, and they certainly fail to meet the needs of "an indefatigable writer of textbooks, who understood the pedagogical value of a simple, precise method of organization."[13] And yet it is these very theologies of history that provide the driving force behind attempts at periodization in the West. Foxe was not "addicted to universal history"; indeed, his is at base an ecclesiastical history that begins with the establishment of the Christian church. Nor did the scheme of the four monarchies feature largely in his attempt to divide history into "five sundry diversities of times"—but he was committed to an apocalyptic interpretation of history. Influenced by his friend, John Bale, whose *Image of Both Churches* (1541) served as a model for the unification of scriptural exegesis and historical interpretation, Foxe worked strenuously at the numbers in an effort to get the known facts of history and the somewhat more labile terms of apocalyptic prophecy to coincide.

The first English edition of *Acts and Monuments*, published in 1563, has in its opening section "A cetaine brief description of the 4. ages of the Churche."[14] Despite the advertisement of four ages, which is preceded by an allusion to Daniel, what follows is divided into three ages, though the second age is itself divided between "the flourishing age" and the "midle age." In addition, Foxe deploys the vocabulary used in the traditional ages of man, in which the entirety of human history displays the same trajectory seen in an individual: "Thus the catholike church in her infancy, was innocent, in her childhode, she grew and multiplied, in her youthe she increased and gat strength. And in her middle age she wrestled with sundry sects, schisms and schismatickes" (8). The latter or "old age" of the church commences at the millennium, the year 1000. This also coincides with the beginning of the "third age": "To be shorte here came in the time, that the revelation speaketh of, whan Sathanas, the old serpent, beyng tied vp for a thousand yere, was losed for a certaine space" (11). Foxe here interprets the period immediately following the Passion according to Revelation 20:1–3:

> Then I saw an angel coming down from heaven, holding in his hand the key of the bottomless pit and a great chain. And he seized the dragon, that ancient serpent, who is the Devil and Satan, and bound him for a thousand years, and threw him into the pit, and shut it and sealed it over him, that he should deceive the nations no more, till the thousand years were ended. After that he must be loosed for a little while.[15]

"The view of history in *Acts and Monuments* 1563 is," according to Palle J. Olsen, "of unadulterated regression" (605). Christian history is bifurcated between a time of Christ and a time of Antichrist—with the present moment firmly on the wrong side of the boundary.

The limitations of this model were undoubtedly clear to Foxe even as he was writing; he allows that the decline of the church began earlier but insists that "those latter times, which times the Apostles prophecy of to be so pearylous and daungerous most of all began at the ful M. yeares and after" (11). There are two major difficulties that follow from this dichotomous view of history. It ascribes a beneficent unity to the church before the millennium—a position that was bound to be awkward from a Reformist perspective, since not all church abuses could be safely located as post-1000—and it fails to register the consequences of the Reformation, which gets swallowed up in the time of Antichrist. Both these difficulties are addressed by the five-fold time scheme that Foxe develops in the 1570 edition of *Acts and Monuments*.[16]

This five-fold periodization in the 1570 edition divides Christian history into three-hundred-year segments: "First to declare of the suffering time of the church, which conteyneth 300 yeares after Christ. Secondly, the florishying and growing tyme of the same: conteyning other 300 yeares. Thirdly, the declining tyme of the church, and of true religion, other 300 yeares. Fourthly, of the time of Antichrist, reigning and raging in the church, since the loosing out of Sathan. Lastly, of the reforming time of Christs church in these latter 300 years" (1570, 49). This new scheme allows for an earlier decline in the church (circa 600), and it also posits a "reforming time" that extends backward from the present three hundred years. The present persecution of the Protestants is thus prefigured by the Roman persecutions of the primitive church. However, this plan is not without its difficulties. The fourth period, the time of Antichrist, is not given a precise duration, though earlier Foxe specifies that it begins around the year 1000 and lasts four hundred years, which would seem to put the reforming time circa 1400. However, if the reforming time extends backwards three hundred years from the present, that would locate its start around 1270.

Despite his conviction that numbers were crucial for an adequate account of history, Foxe appears not to have had a very good head for figures. In the 1576 edition he includes an autobiographical note that explains how he arrived at his scheme. In writing his history he became increasingly perplexed by the cruelty of the ten persecutions of the primitive church, which appeared to him to have "no end determined, nor limitation set for their deliuerance."[17] Turning to Revelation, he finds mention of forty-two months—of a time, times, and half a time of 1260 days—but all of this "by computation coming but to three years and a half, came nothing near the long continuance of these persecutions, which lasted 300 yeares & a halfe" (1576, 101). "Vexed and turmoyled in spirite, about the reckenyng of these numbers and yeares," Foxe experiences an epiphany while lying in bed on a Sunday morning: "Sodenly it was answered to my mind, as with a maiestie, thus inwardly saying within me: Thou foole count these monethes by Sabbots as the Weekes of Daniell are counted by Sabbots." In the book of Daniel, the angel Gabriel speaks of weeks of years or units of seven years. Initially, Foxe attempted to calculate the period by "Sabbats . . . of monthes," but that does not work; next he tries "Sabbots of yeares wherein I began to feele some probable understanding" (102). In order to check his calculation, Foxe consults with some merchant friends who confirm that 42 sabbaths of years amounts to 294 years. That Foxe would need help with the elementary task of multiplication suggests a limited facility for arithmetic, and yet despite this lack of aptitude, Foxe clearly felt that these numbers were of enormous significance. The period of 294 years is "the full and iust tyme of these foresayd persecutions neither more nor lesse" (1576, 102).

Despite this precision, Foxe vacillates between the strict exactitude of 294 years and a looser period of three hundred. This more general figure becomes the basic temporal unit in the five diversities of times, and, despite the complications, Foxe offers a relatively clear punctuation of history: "For in these five diversities and alteracions of times, I suppose that the whole course and state of the Church may well be comprised" (1570, 1). Though the precision that he strove for eluded him, Foxe makes a strong case for dividing time, according each "diversity" its own identity and acknowledging the breaks or "alteracions" that separate one time from another. The fundamental dynamic in Foxe's scheme is differentiation, and it is, of course, to better distinguish between the true church and the false church that Foxe writes *Acts and Monuments*.

Seeing Foxe's entire project as an exercise in differentiation casts an interesting light on his description of the Middle Ages. It is common to see the Reformers' account of the preceding age as a systematic inversion, a projection backwards of the negation of every contemporary value—so that, for example, a premium on reading requires that the Middle Ages be seen as a time of illiteracy, and an obsession with enlightenment entails that the preceding age be understood as a time of darkness. While Foxe provides evidence for this rather mechanical operation, he also does something more subtle.

Foxe's "middle ages," the third and fourth periods of the five-fold scheme, run from approximately 600 to 1400, and he invests this span with a significant cultural homogeneity. Unlike the elite political history of the humanists and the haphazard inclusivity of the chronicle writers, Foxe is determined to assess the period's whole way of life. One of Foxe's most impressive and sustained accounts of the preceding age appears at the beginning of his treatment of John Wyclif. Wyclif emerges in a time of almost utter darkness: "all the world was in most desperate and vile estate, and . . . the lamentable ignorance and darkenes of God his truth had ouershadowed the hole earth" (1570, 544). Foxe describes Wyclif "as the mornyng starre beyng in the middest of a cloud," a figure that suggests not only the prevailing darkness but also the impending dawn of the Reformation. Foxe makes clear that the depravity of Wyclif's time was total—it included the whole world, secular and religious, elite and common. Foxe's critique of medieval culture reaches a climax with his indictment of ceremonialism:

> The world leauyng and forsakyng the liuely power of Gods spiri-
> tuall word and doctrine, was altogether led & blynded with out-
> ward ceremonies and humaine traditions, wherin the whole scope,
> in a maner of all Christian perfection did consiste and depende.
> In these was all the hope of obteynyng saluation fully fixed: here
> vnto all thynges were attributed. In so much, that scarsly any other
> thyng was seen in the temples or churches taught or spoken of in
> sermons, or finally intended or gone about in theyr whole life, but
> onely heaping vp of certain shadowed ceremonies vpon ceremonies,
> neither was ther any end of this theyr heapyng. (1570, 523)

Foxe's critique extends from the institutional practices of the church to what was "intended or gone about in theyr whole life"; the ceremonialism that Foxe detects is also the substance of everyday life. The centrality of ceremonialism to religious life in medieval England has recently been reaffirmed by Eamon Duffy: "Ceremonies which, to the reformers, were unchristian or idolatrous, were somewhere near the centre of things in the religious and communal instincts of the people."[18] Immediately after his account of medieval ceremonialism, Foxe asserts that "the people were taught to worshyp no other thyng but that whiche they did see, and did see almost nothyng whiche they did not worshyp" (1570, 523). The rhetorical figure of chiasmus insists on a central indistinction, a failure to differentiate between the visible and the sacred, the corporeal and the spiritual, seeing and worshiping. This tendency toward indiscriminant worship is, of course, a variety of idolatry, and idolatry was, for the Reformers, "the deadliest of sins."[19] Not only was the accusation of idolatry central in the Protestant attack on Catholicism, the same accusation also came to feature prominently in Protestant historiography, which, in the words of James Simpson, gave "forceful, violent, and enduring definition to the period from Henry II to Henry VIII as an era of idolatry, ruled by the imagination."[20]

Though the charge of idolatry is a constant refrain, Foxe here identifies the charge as the symptom of a more general confusion caused by "the heaping vp pf certain shadowed ceremonies vpon ceremonies" that is the exclusive focus of medieval life. Foxe's passage on the subject begins with "outward ceremonies and human traditions," but by the conclusion "tradition" has been transformed into "heaping up." Rather than the orderly handing on of what is best, tradition is here figured as disorderly accumulation: uninventoried piles, without logic or distinction, and, perhaps most frighteningly, without end. This suggestion that medieval culture operated according to a dynamic of heaping up finds expression in Foxe's use of the rhetorical figure of *accumulatio* to describe medieval conditions. As George Puttenham observes, "Arte and good pollicie moues vs many times to be earnest in our speach, and then we lay on such load and so go to it by heapes as if we would winne the game by multitude of words & speaches, not all of one but of diuers matter and sence, for which cause the Latines called it *Congeries* and we the heaping figure."[21] According to Puttenham, the figure allows for the rhetorical deployment of earnestness, a strategic enthusiasm that outruns syntax and subordination, and this certainly helps to explain the prominence of this figure in anti-Catholic polemic.

An English translation of Erasmus published around 1540 has a preface that commends the famous humanist for exposing and exhausting "the superiticyouse worshype and false honor gyuyn to bones, heddes, iawes, armes, stockes, stones, shyrtes, smokes, cotes, capes, hates, shoes, mytres, slyppers, sadles, rynges, bedes, girdles, bolles, belles, nokes, gloues, ropes, taperes, candelles, bootes, spores (my breath was almost past me) with many other soche dampnable allusyones of the deuylle."[22] Here the breathless inventory of Catholic superstition includes not only false relics but clerical vestments and the candles and bells that were an integral part of worship in the traditional church. William Tyndale, whose simple but lyrical cadences were to feature largely in the English translation of the Bible, makes frequent use of *accumulatio*. Criticizing the cost of church customs, Tyndale exploits the formal similarity between the figure and a bill of sale: "Offeringes at prestes first masses. Item no man is professed, of whatsoever religion it be, but he must bringe somme what. The halowinge or rather coniuringe of chirches, chapels, altars, superaltares, chalice vestimentes and belles. Then boke, bell, candelsticke, organes, chalice, vestimentes copes, altare clothes, syrpleses: towels basens, euars, shepe, senser and all maner ornamentes must be founde them freely."[23] In *An Answere unto Sir Thomas More* Tyndale exhorts his reader to "iudge their penaunce, pilgrimages, pardons, purgatory, prayinge to postes, domine blessings, dome absolucyons, their dome pateringe and howlinge, their dome disgysinges, their satisfaccions and iustefyinges."[24] In a passage that soon follows, Tyndale objects to the false totality invoked under the name of "holy church," a phrase which properly understood simply means: "the pope, cardenalles, legates, patriarckes, archbisshopes, bisshopes, abbots, priors, chauncelers, archdecons, commissaries, officials, prestes, monkes, freres, blacke, whit, pied, grey, & so forth, by (I trowe) a thousand names of blasphemy & of ypocrisie & as many sundrie facions of disgysinges" (A5v). As these examples suggest, within the context of Reformation polemic, the figure of *accumulatio* does more than simply convey an affective charge or the earnestness of a speaker whose words tumble vehemently forth—it also insists that the Catholic Church is not a unified whole but, in fact, a hopelessly confused congeries.

In an opening series of questions addressed to "The professed frendes and folowers of the popes procedynges," Foxe demands to know why Catholics remain committed to ceremonial observations:

> As your outward succession of Byshops, garmentes, vestures, gestures, coulours, choyse of meates, difference of dayes, tymes and places, hearyng, seyng, saying, touchyng, tastyng, numberyng of beades, gildyng and worshippyng Images, buildyng monasteries, risyng at mydnight, silence in cloysters, absteinyng from flesh and white meate, fastyng in Lent, kepyng Imberdayes, hearyng Masse and diuine seruice, seyng and adoryng the body in forme of bread, receauyng holy water, and holy bread, crepyng the crosse, caryng Palmes, takyng ashes, bearyng candels, pilgremage goyng, sensyng, kneelyng, knockyng, altares, superaltares, candlestickes, pardons: In orders crossyng, annoyntyng, shauyng, forsweryng Mariage: In baptisme, crossyng, saltyng, spattelyng, exorcisyng, washyng of handes: At Easter eareconfession, penaunce doyng, satisfaction: And in receauyng with beardes newshauen, to imagine a body, where they see no body: and though he were their present to be sene, yet the outward seyng and touchyng of hym, of it selfe, without faith, conduceth no more, then it dyd to the Iewes. (1570, C1r)

The point is clear enough: Foxe uses the "heaping figure" to define Catholicism as a formless accumulation of senseless corporeal practices. "All which thynges aboue recited," observes Foxe, "as they conteine the whole summary and effect of all the Popes Catholicke Religion: so are they all be corporall exercises, consistyng in the externe operation of man" (1570, C1r). This might be dismissed as a momentary burst of rhetorical enthusiasm if not for the fact that it happens again when Foxe comes to describe the advent of Luther and the beginning of the Reformation. Describing the corruption of the ancient and primitive church of Christ, Foxe identifies the doctrine of good works as the foundation of innumerable errors:

> And hereupon haue they planted all these their new deuises, so infinite that they can not well be numbred, as Masses, trecenares, diriges, obsequies, mattens and houres, singyng seruice, vigiles, mydnightrising, barefootegoyng, fishfastyng, lentfast, imberfast, stations, rogations, iubiles, aduocation of sainctes, praying to Images, pilgremage walking, workes of supererogation, application of merites, orders, rules, sectes of religion, vowes of chastitie, wilfull pouertie, pardons, relaxations, indulgences, penaunce and satisfaction, with auricular confession, foundyng of Abbays, building of chappels, geuyng to Churches: And who is able to recite all their laborious buildynges, falsely framed vpon a wrong grounde, and all for ignoraunce of the true foundation, whiche is the free iustification by fayth in Christ Iesus the sonne of God (1570, 966).

Foxe's use of an architectural metaphor here serves to bind all the disparate elements in his catalog: they are all heterogeneous parts of the monstrous edifice of the Roman Catholic Church. The rhetorical use of *accumulatio* has a counterpart in the iconography of *Actes and Monuments*. The woodcut depicting the departure of the papists at the outset of Edward VI's reign emphasizes the iconoclasm of the reformers and the enduring attachment of the papists to the objects of worship (see figure 1). This image shows "the papists packing away their paultrye," and, along with a priest carrying a monstrance, it also shows several figures hauling gigantic sacks presumably stuffed with rejected ecclesiastical furnishings. These distended sacks are the visual equivalent of Foxe's frequently deployed *accumulatio*: both insist that the medieval church has become massively swollen through the historical accretion of unwarranted traditions. This point is made even more emphatically in a woodcut that first appeared at the end of the 1576 edition's first volume. This image of Justice weighing the word of God against man's doctrines and traditions contrasts the simple unity of the single book with the multiplicity of objects associated with Catholic worship (see figure 2). Needless to say, the censer, crucifix, rosary beads, chalices, communion wafers, and books of decrees and decretals form a miscellaneous heap.

Foxe's *Acts and Monuments* and its five-fold scheme of periodization are designed to make sense of this jumble by paring away the extraneous accretions of history and thus restoring the church to her primitive and pristine condition. The third and fourth periods of Foxe's history are truly "just one damn thing after another," but they are not utterly devoid of truth. The true church is never entirely suppressed or extinguished: it constitutes a thin thread of continuity that runs down through history from the apostolic age. Of the true church, Foxe writes, "neither was it so inuisible or vnknowen, but, by the prouidence of the Lord, some remnaunt alwayes remayned, from tyme to tyme, which not onely shewed secret good affection to sincere doctrine, but also stode in open defence of truth agaynst the disordered Church of Rome" (1570, ☞3v) While Foxe is eager to tell the story of this heroic remnant, he is also determined to mark the gradual accumulation of doctrines and practices in the Roman church. Rather than being part of an immemorial tradition, sanctified by time itself, these things have a history. What Foxe attacks through his use of the heaping figure appears as a dense constellation of beliefs and practices, indeed, an entire way of life, but the point of the figure is to reveal through juxtaposition the entirely accidental nature of this historical accumulation.

According to Foxe, the Church of Rome is

> gone from the fayth that S. Paul taught, that if he were now a lyue, and saw these Decrees and Decretals of the Byshop of Rome, these heapes of ceremonies & traditions, these Masse bookes, these

The text visible within the illustration reads:

The ſhip of the Ro-
miſh Church.

Shoppe over your
trinkets and be pac-
king ye Papiſtes.

The Papiſtes packing away their
paultrye.

Burning of
Images.

The Temple
well purged.

Figure 1. "The papists packing away their paultrye." Detail. Foxe, *Actes and Monuments*, 2:1438. (Photo: By permission of the Folger Shakespeare Library.)

¶A liuely picture defcribyng the weight and fubftaunce of
Gods moft bleffed word, agaynft the doctrines and
vanities of mans traditions.

Figure 2. "A lively picture describing the weight and substance of Gods most blessed word agaynst the doctrines and vanities of mans traditions." Detail. Foxe, *Ecclesiastical History* (1576), copy 1, p. 771. (Photo: By permission of the Folger Shakespeare Library.)

portuses these festiuals and legendes, these processionals, hymnes and sequences, these beades and graduals, and maner of their inuocation, their canons, censures, and latter Councels, such swarmes of superstitious Monkes and Friers, such sectes of so many diuers religons, the Testament of S. Fraunces, the rule of S. Benedict, of S. Brigit, of S. Anthony. &c, the intricate subtletes and labyrinthes of the scholemen, the infinite cases and distinctions of the Canonistes, the Sermons in Churches, the assertions in scholes, the glory of the Pope, the pride of the Clergy, the cruelty of persecutyng Prelates with their officials & promotors: he would say this were not a defection, but rather a playne destruction and a ruine of fayth. (1570, 31)

Though each of the elements in this extensive catalog receives consideration, the multiplication of religious orders, both monastic and mendicant, receives particular attention because Foxe sees their emergence as an especially egregious case of the pluralizing of religion. Though Foxe gives considerable attention to the rise of the mendicant orders, the rise of monasticism is the subject of a more sustained analysis. In part this is because the longer history of monasticism makes it a harder case, since Foxe must make the argument that monasticism is not an ancient and apostolic practice. Of course, this longer history also allows Foxe to argue that the institutional development of monasticism is itself subject to periodization, and he divides monks of the early time from those of the middle time and the latter time. While Foxe considers the friars to be "more full of hypocrisy, blindnesse, Idolatry, and superstition" than the monks and goes out of his way to attack them, the longer history of monasticism offers a challenge and an opportunity.[25]

Along with the prospect of a specific narrative history detailing its rise and proliferation, monasticism presents a particularly appealing polemical target. Indeed, it was in sixteenth-century polemic that the pejorative adjective *monkish* emerged; the first instance of this word, as cited by the *OED*, appears in the *Original & Sprynge of all Sectes*, a 1537 translation of a text originally in High Dutch.[26] Perhaps the work of Miles Coverdale, this translation opened up a rich seam of polemic in English that focused on the profusion of orders within the Roman Catholic Church. Clearly designed to counter the charge that reformed religion was creating a proliferation of sects, this line of argument inevitably focused on the failures and corruptions of monastic life. While monasticism is, of course, held up as an example of superstition and hypocrisy, the feature of monastic life that most provokes Foxe is its regularity. The very aspect that attracted the attention of Max Weber, who saw in monastic regulation an important precursor to the forms of modern bureaucratic rationality, is for Foxe evidence of a lifeless and mechanical formality.

Monasticism, in Foxe's account, epitomizes the rigid ceremonialism of medieval religion, an association that allows him at one point to allude to the "fond ignorance of that monkish age" (1583, 1:126). Paradoxically, order here becomes a sign of disorder; monastic regulations are seen as yet another example of the accretion of human traditions that obscure the simple truth of the Gospel. In a lengthy digression found in the account of King Edgar, Foxe describes the history of monasticism. In order to enlighten "the simple Reader" who "in hearing the name of monkes in all histories of tymes" might falsely conclude that monks are "an ancient thing in Christian life," Foxe sets out to distinguish monks of the "primitiue tyme" from those of the "middle time" and the "latter age." He acknowledges that "the name and order of Monkes" is of "old continuance, during neare from the tyme of 300. yeares after Christ" (153), a date that places their emergence at the start of the "florishying and growing tyme" of the church. Though the harsh asceticism of the first monks is dismissed as superstition and their adherence to authority is taken as a servile dereliction of human reason and Christian liberty, the "Monkes of the middle age of the Church" are even worse. As the number and superstition of monks increased, they "began by little and little from their desolate dens in the vaste wilderness, to approach more neare to great towns, where they had solemn Monasteries founded." The progress of the monks continues, "from the cold field into warm townes and cloysters: from townes, then into cities, and at length from their close cellers and cities, vnto Cathedrall Churches . . . where, not only did they abound in wealth and riches (especially these Monkes of our latter tyme) but much more did swimme in superstition, and Pharisaicall hipocrisie." This description of institutional ascent is accompanied by a stinging critique of monastic rules that uses the familiar figure of *accumulatio*: "being yoked and tied in all their doings, to certain prescript rules and formal obseruances: in watching in sleeping, in eating, in rising, in praying, in walking, in talking, in looking, in tasting, in touching, in handling, in their gestures, in their vestures, euery man apparailed, not as the proper condition of other would require, nor as the season of the yeare did serue, but as the coacted rules & order of euery sect did inforce them" (1:154). Not only is monasticism an unbecoming form of bondage but it also manifests a fundamental indecorum, a refusal to recognize distinctions between persons and occasions.

Having catalogued the "infinitely diuers" sects that proliferated at this time, Foxe insists that despite their superficial variety, the disparate orders of monks are united in their hostility toward Christian liberty:

> So subiect were they to seruile rules, that no part of Christen liberty remained among them. So drowned and sunck in superstition: that not onely they had lost Christes religion, but also almost the sense and nature of men. For where men naturally are and ought to be ruled by the descrete gouernment of reason, in all outward doynges, wherein no one rule can serue for all men: the circumstaunce of tyme, place, person, and busines being so sundry and diuers. Contrary, among these, not reason but onely the knock of a bell, ruled all their doings: their rising, their sleeping, theyr praying, their eating, their comming in, their going out, their talking, their silence, & altogether like insensible people, either not hauing reason to rule themselues, or else as persons vngrateful to God, neyther enioyning the benefite of reason created in them, not yet vsing the grace of Christes libertie, whereunto he redeemed them. (1583, 154)

Foxe rejects a corporatist model of common life lived in obedience to a superior and instead espouses the "descrete gouernment of reason" and "Christen liberty." This autonomy allows the individual to observe decorum, suiting behavior to circumstances. Monastic discipline then represents the historical abandonment of Christian liberty, a perverse inversion in which bodily servitude, captured in the series of gerunds, replaces spiritual freedom.

While Foxe's attack on monasticism allows for the articulation of a number of familiar Protestant claims about the dismal quality of spiritual life before the Reformation, the approach also fulfills an important function in terms of his historiography. Foxe—who directly experienced Henry VIII's vacillations regarding religion, Edward VI's pursuit of reform, and Mary's restoration of Catholicism—was well aware that in a monarchical polity religion was vulnerable to sudden shifts as a result of changes of either personnel or policy at the top. However, he took the extirpation of monasticism in England to be final. Indeed, he justifies the destruction of the abbeys on the grounds that, had they not been destroyed, they might have been repopulated in the time of Mary.

The visible ruins of the monastic houses, then, served as a constant reminder that the present was indeed distinct from an earlier dispensation in which monks were held to embody the perfect Christian life. Moreover, while it is true that respectable Protestant opinion, especially in the seventeenth century and later, could express regret over the dissolution, it is also the case that the association between monks and the medieval formed a lively strand in subsequent English literature and historiography.[27] Margaret Aston has pointed out that monastic ruins "proved to be peculiarly fertile in stimulating consciousness of the past and in promoting historical activity."[28] Unlike the figures surveyed by Aston who were attracted to the ruins by a sense of loss and nostalgia, Foxe saw them as material evidence of a historical watershed. If, for Foxe, monkishness is characterized by a servile heaping up of rules, the ruined abbeys of the English countryside physically demonstrated that monasticism was no more. In the ruined abbeys Foxe's readers could see the edifying trace of a vast constellation of ritual practices that have now, along with the medieval past, vanished.

NOTES

1. The epigraphs are from Jameson, *A Singular Modernity*, 29; and Woolf, *Social Circulation of the Past*, 309

2. Milton, *Paradise Lost*, 3.448–49.

3. For an early account, see Falco, *La Polemica*. Controversy over the term Renaissance flourished in the mid-twentieth century (see especially Panofsky, "Renaissance and Renascences." Debate has recently turned to the relative merits of Renaissance and early modern as period designations. More generally, the debate about the postmodern (a period, a style, or a nonsense) focused attention on the question of periodization and the vexed terms modernity and modernism. See, for example, Jameson, *A Singular Modernity*.

4. Brown, "Periods and Resistances."

5. Lee Patterson, "On the Margin." Koselleck, *Practice of Conceptual History*, 4. Koselleck offers a compelling argument for the need for theoretical reflection in and on the disciplinary practice of history. Koselleck's entire body of work is a sustained and subtle meditation on the concept of modernity.

6. Lee Patterson, "On the Margin," 101. Patterson's intervention needs to be understood in a particular professional and institutional context; nonetheless, his suggestion that recent

work on the Renaissance has uncritically absorbed a nineteenth-century scheme of periodization (whether Burckhardtian or Marxian) overlooks the degree to which both Burckhardt and Marx were the inheritors of an earlier historiographic tradition that emerged in the wake of the Reformation. In other words, Patterson's emphasis on the influence of nineteenth-century thinkers, rather than their sixteenth-century precursors, enables him to suggest that the vision of periodization in circulation in the twentieth century is deeply anachronistic.

7. Lee Patterson, "On the Margin," 93. For medieval periodization see Cantor, "Interpretation of Medieval History"; and Funkenstein, "Periodization and Self-Understanding."

8. Burckhardt, *Civilization of the Renaissance in Italy*, 70.

9. Despite a professed antipathy toward Hegelian philosophy, Burckhardt's use of the subject-object dichotomy reveals the influence of Hegel, justifying Gombrich's assertion that *The Civilization of the Renaissance in Italy* "has been built, knowingly and unknowingly on Hegelian foundations which have crumbled"; see Gombrich, *In Search of Cultural History*. For an illuminating discussion of the way in which the terms "subject" and "object" have influenced accounts of the Renaissance, see the editors' introduction to De Grazia, Quilligan, and Stallybrass, *Subject and Object in Renaissance Culture*.

10. For an illuminating account of Burkhardt's engagement with the intellectual world of "pious Basel," see Thomas Albert Howard, *Religion and the Rise of Historicism*. For a nuanced treatment of *The Civilization of the Renaissance* that stresses Burckhardt's many hesitations about a period that he is often seen as naively celebrating, see Woolfson, "Burckhardt's Ambivalent Renaissance."

11. For an illuminating recuperation of Burckhardt, see Kerrigan and Braden, *Idea of the Renaissance*.

12. Ferguson, *The Renaissance in Historical Thought*, 73.

13. Ferguson, *The Renaissance in Historical Thought*, 75. Ferguson's admirable account of the emergence of the Renaissance within historical thought should be read alongside his earlier article, "Interpretation of the Renaissance." In that article he offers his own account of the Renaissance, proposing that it be understood as an age of transition spanning the period 1300–1600 and dividing the medieval and modern worlds. Ferguson is explicit here about his desire to define the period in a way that "will have practical value for the historian" (485).

14. Foxe, *Actes and Monuments*.

15. New Oxford Annotated Bible Revised Standard Edition. Olsen points out that Foxe's account of the binding of Satan is complex: "Satan, according to Foxe, was bound 'spiritually' at the Passion, i.e. at the Passion Satan lost power over the souls of men (in line with Augustine), but, he insists, Satan was not bound as regards 'the outward bodies of Christes poore saintes' until the persecution of the primitive Church ceased" ("Was John Foxe a Millenarian?" 608).

16. Foxe, *Ecclesiastical History* (1570).

17. Foxe, *Ecclesiastical History* (1576), 101.

18. Duffy, *Stripping of the Altars*, 532. Duffy, who obviously does not share Foxe's hostility toward ceremonialism, adds that "behind the repudiation of ceremonial by the reformers lay a radically different conceptual world, a world in which text was everything, sign nothing. The sacramental universe of late medieval Catholicism was, from this perspective, totally opaque, a bewildering and meaningless world of dumb objects and vapid gestures, hindering communication" (532).

19. Aston, *Laws Against Images*, 343.

20. James Simpson, "Rule of Medieval Imagination," 11. For the centrality of iconoclasm for Foxe's generation of reformers, see Collinson, *From Iconoclasm to Iconophobia*.

21. Puttenham, *Arte of English Poesie*, 300.

22. Erasmus, *Dialoge or Communication of Two Persons*, X3v–X4r.

23. Tyndale, *Obedience of a Christen Man*, fol. lxxviir.

24. Tyndale, *An Answere unto Sir Thomas Mores Dialoge*, sig. A4r.

25. Foxe, *Actes and Monumentes, newly revised*, line 1181. Thomas Freeman has suggested that Foxe considered the mendicant orders a continuing threat; certainly they are depicted as playing a prominent role in the Marian persecutions—"þe Fryers haue bene always the chief pillers & vpholders of þe popes church" (259)—and it must be remembered that the book was first shaped abroad as Foxe watched events unfold in England from his place of exile. See Freeman, "Offending God," 236.

26. *Original & Sprynge*, sig. A3r.

27. Francis Bacon's famous indictment of scholasticism exploits claustral imagery: "This kind of degenerate learning did chiefly reign amongst the schoolmen; who have sharp and strong wits, and abundance of leisure, and small variety of reading; but their wits being shut up in the cells of a few authors (chiefly Aristotle their dictator) as their persons were shut up in the cells of monasteries and colleges; and knowing little history, either of nature or time; did out of no great quantity of matter, and infinite agitation of wit, spin out unto us those laborious webs of learning which are extant in their books"; see *Francis Bacon*, 140.

28. Aston, "English Ruins and English History."

"That auntient authoritie": Old English Laws in the Writings of William Lambarde

Rebecca J. Brackmann

No one in Tudor England knew more about Anglo-Saxon law than William Lambarde. He edited the *Archaionomia*,[1] a facing-page edition of Old English laws and Latin translations, and authored several other influential legal handbooks and histories; the first history of an English county, the *Perambulation of Kent*, also came from his pen. A quick survey of the *Perambulation* shows that even when he was not writing a legal text, Lambarde regarded Anglo-Saxon law differently than he did other aspects of medieval history. The *Perambulation* must continually negotiate the need to use medieval (and hence Catholic) sources in order to learn about the past, and the need to reject them as flawed and inferior to "modern" (i.e., Protestant) thinking. Lambarde claims that only recently have "the late learned and yet best travailed in the histories of our countrey" spurned "the fonde dreames of doting monks and fabling friars."[2] Rejecting or demeaning monastic sources leaves a historian with little to work with, and Lambarde realizes this, but his Protestant agenda does not allow him much choice. However, when he draws on legal texts, his attitude alters from the apologetic and occasionally scornful tone he takes toward his other sources. Near the end of the *Perambulation*, Lambarde transcribes and translates an "English (or Saxon) antiquitie, which I have seene placed in divers old copies of the Saxon lawes."[3] This tract, which Felix Liebermann titled *Geþyncðu* (*Ranks*) in volume one of his *Gesetze* and which Lambarde copied from the *Textus Roffensis*, contains what Patrick Wormald observes are "among the best-known lines in Anglo-Saxon law" explaining how ceorls, merchants, or scholars can gain the status of thegns, and how thegns can become eorls.[4] Lambarde uses "English" and "Saxon" synonymously when he introduces the tract, giving the text more immediacy—it is an "English" document. Lambarde interprets the text as showing that "[vertue] ought by all reason to be rewarded with due enseignes of honour, to the end that vertue may be the more desirously embraced."[5] The Anglo-Saxon law

111

codes, described as "English," provide immediately applicable and unambiguously positive examples for Lambarde's readers, whereas other aspects of medieval history, embedded in and transmitted by monastic and clerical culture, must be carefully negotiated to separate "proper vanities" from "sincere veritie."[6]

This essay will explore why Lambarde thought differently about Old English law than he did about other areas of medieval culture by examining how his Anglo-Saxon research and his belief in English law's antiquity both shaped and were shaped by his conception of common law in his own day. Tudor antiquaries studied the Anglo-Saxon period with interests and emphases different from those of modern scholars; for instance, Theodore Leinbaugh and R. I. Page, among others, have documented the polemical uses to which Archbishop Matthew Parker put Old English homilies in the 1566 *A Testimonie of Antiquitie*.[7] Less work has been done on why the law codes of the Anglo-Saxons were of the first importance to Lambarde. The English legal system, however, mattered no less in early modern England than the Elizabethan religious settlement. J. G. A. Pocock contends, "[s]ince the common law unified so much in English social behaviour, it unified Englishmen's thoughts about the past, and gave them a set of beliefs about their national history more satisfying, because more relevant to their present social structure ... even than the myths of the original independence of the Anglican church."[8] Perhaps Pocock errs in attempting to claim pride of place for law over religion in English historical thought; both were crucial and, as I shall show, Lambarde felt they were mutually reinforcing. However, Pocock's statement underscores the Tudor exploration of English legal history, and Lambarde provides an excellent case study for how this research coincided with the dawn of Anglo-Saxon studies. Lambarde believed law was crucial to English identity because it not only enforced perceived differences between English and foreign but itself stood as one of those differences, in its non-Roman origin and its long-standing force. The common law's development from Anglo-Saxon law meant that both law and Protestantism could be traced back to England's past, and could support each other as focal points for English identity.[9] In fact, in Lambarde's view, Anglo-Saxon laws were so fundamental that by examining them he was studying the very principles of the common law that endowed it with its particularly English qualities.

The *Archaionomia*'s first sentence establishes the themes that run through many of Lambarde's later discussions. Lambarde's preface, dedicating the book to William Cordell, Master of the Chancery Rolls, begins with a paraphrase of Heraclitus: "Praeclare mea quidem Sententia Heraclitus (vir praestantissime) leges ciuitatis murum atque uti moenia defendendas affirmauit" (in my opinion [most superior man], Heraclitus excellently declared that the laws are the wall of the city, and are to be defended as the fortifications). Lambarde further elaborates the philosopher's spare dictum: if the walls are solid, society is safe from hostile forces, but if they are breached or trampled down, it spells disaster ("maximam calamitatem") for the citizens.[10] Like walls, laws must be avidly defended. Walls not only defend cities, however, but define their borders, a function that Lambarde also, by implication, assigns to the law. Lambarde's text asserts the importance of law, specifically of ancient law, and although it was the first of Lambarde's books, the *Archaionomia* was not the last to make such a claim. Lambarde believed that English common law's theoretical underpinnings could be found in Anglo-Saxon laws, and that obedience to the common law not only protected the English but also set up the boundaries that distinguished them from foreigners and aliens. This defining, exclusionary capacity that the laws bring to the concept of Englishness explains why they were the ideological battleground for many of the later debates in England, as the sixteenth century drew to a close and the early decades of the seventeenth century unfolded. It also makes clear that Lambarde's retrospection was no disinterested survey, but rather embodied his ideas about Englishness in the Anglo-Saxon past.

J. G. A. Pocock, in his influential discussion of legal historians, followed S. Kliger in identifying two schools of thought on the common law: the "immemorialists" and the "Gothicists."[11] Immemorialists believed the common law was literally immemorial—predating all written history. Gothicists believed the law was Germanic in origin and stemmed mainly from the ancestors of the Anglo-Saxons.[12] The early modern theorists themselves were not always consistent, as Pocock also points out: "Contemporaries intent only on asserting the antiquity of the law might combine the two."[13] Where does this leave Lambarde? He does not claim that the common law is immemorial—the adjective he most often uses is "ancient," which could imply that he was a Gothicist or an immemorialist. His examination of Anglo-Saxon law uncovers the premises behind the law codes, which could mean that he felt the theories of Anglo-Saxon lawgivers were hints to the themes of "immemorial law" or that the Germanic Anglo-Saxons held the origin of the law. I suspect that he was a Gothicist—he was, after all, an Anglo-Saxonist, and his studies led him to emphasize Old English law. The modishly Greek title of his edition suggests Gothicism as well; he usually refers to the original English law as "the ancient law," and the Greek *Archaionomia* translates to "ancient laws." I do not think, however, that we must look for complete consistency in "Gothicism" or "immemorialism" among his documents, written as they were over a period of thirty years and for widely varying audiences. His statements about Anglo-Saxon law could support either view, and probably did both when later common lawyers used them. What does remain consistent is his use of Anglo-Saxon law as his ultimate test of legal validity.

The Ancient Roots of the Common Law

Lambarde never lost sight of the antiquity of the common law, even when he wrote technical treatises that would seem to have little to do with it. In the *Eirenarcha*, Lambarde's handbook for justices of the peace, he notes that the duties of a JP are based on common law precedent: "That auntient authoritie . . . uppon which thys latter power is (as it were upon a Stocke) set and engraffed."[14] Such grafting suggests that old laws and precedents, though not always identical to the current system, are necessary for its survival; without such roots, the upper portion of the tree would die. Lambarde not only wanted the justices of the peace to appreciate the antiquity of their tradition but wished that the juries of the Sessions of the Peace might understand their place in the history of common law. In an address to a session of the peace jury in 1591, he gave a mini-lesson in English legal history:

> The law or policy of this realm of England, as it is a peculiar gov-
> ernment, not borrowed of the imperial or Roman law (as be the
> laws of the most part of other Christian nations) but standing upon
> the highest reason, selected even for itself; so doth it in one special
> thing above any other most apparently vary from the usage of other
> countries: I mean in the manner of proceeding that we have by
> jurors, which our law calleth the judgment by peers or equals, and
> that as well in civil questions that do arise privately between man
> and man as also in criminal causes that lift up the head against the
> commonwealth, in the latter of which we are not, as other nations,
> to be accused or indicted at the pleasure or for the gain or malice
> of any one or a few men but by the oaths and consciences of the
> twelve at the least, and in either of which we enjoy this singular
> freedom and prerogative that we are not to be peremptorily sen-
> tenced by the mouth of the judge, as other people are, but by the
> oath and verdict of jurors that be our equals, and the same not
> strangers born but our own countrymen, not far dwelling but of the
> nearest neighborhood that we have.[15]

For Lambarde, the history and non-Roman origin of English law give it particular nationalistic force and set it apart from that of "other Christian nations." Lambarde repeatedly uses the first person plural possessive ("our law," "our own countrymen") to highlight juries as a specifically English institution. The jury system bases itself not on Roman law but on a separate tradition, which Lambarde describes as "standing up on the highest reason"—as opposed to the "Roman law," which he implies is less reasonable.

It is worth a brief digression to examine how Lambarde and his contemporaries viewed Roman law, and what he knew of it. Civil law (the legal system based on the Roman codes, particularly the *Institutes* of Justinian) was the basis for some of the episcopal courts and for legal proceedings in the Court of the Admiralty.[16] Lambarde owned and annotated Conrad Lagus's *Methodica iuris vtriusque traditio* (1556), a book detailing the textual basis of and procedures for civil law; he also indexed and annotated a copy of Justinian's *Institvtiones ivris civilis*, which he had inherited from his acquaintance Laurence Nowell, so he was certainly not ignorant of civil law.[17] However, civil law was based on the laws of ancient Rome, and Rome, of course, was in Lambarde contemporary times the seat of the Catholic Church. As F. J. Levy observes in *Tudor Historical Thought*, "the Reformation put a premium on the independence of England from Rome—not, to be sure, the Rome of Cicero but that of the popes. Still, it was clear that the two visions of Rome were connected."[18] John Curran's *Roman Invasions* explores this conflation in early modern England of imperial Rome with the Roman Catholic Church, and discusses how lawyers wanted to claim common law's independence from civil law "guilty by association with popery," although he focuses mainly on later legal scholars such as Edward Coke.[19] Curran also examines "the central figure of the entire competition with Rome," King Arthur.[20] Tudor historians wanted to see Arthur's defeat of the emperor of the Romans, described by Geoffrey of Monmouth, as prefiguring the triumph of Protestantism over Catholicism, a portent of England's ecclesiastic independence. The survival of this desire to prove Arthur's historicity and the truth of his "Roman victory" in the face of strong evidence to the contrary only shows how appealing the story was, and how strong the tendency was to equate Roman imperialism with "popery."[21] Lambarde's 1591 statement to the jury, contrasting English law with Roman law, implicitly figures English law as Protestant, an opposition present throughout the law's history all the way back to the early medieval past.

Such approaches were consonant with other areas of Renaissance retrospection on the Middle Ages. Like English common law, Protestantism had to be shown to extend continuously through England's history. Protestant polemicists claimed that Lollardy and other forms of anticlericalism were proto-Protestant; Matthew Parker cited Anglo-Saxon evidence in his argument that priests should marry.[22] Lambarde, anticipating a preoccupation of the Stuart common lawyers, tried to show a similarly unbroken history for the law, as he claimed the Norman Conquest did not interrupt the English legal traditions. He foregrounded the ancient origins of English common law particularly in *Archeion*, a 1591 treatise on the courts of equity and the prerogative courts. Lambarde never printed this work, but sent it in manuscript form to Robert Cecil, privy councilor and William Cecil's capable younger son; manuscript copies also circulated among legal practitioners in Lambarde's lifetime and after his death.[23] An authorized edition was produced by his heirs in 1635, prompted by an unauthorized edition earlier that year.[24] The *Archeion* argues that prerogative courts have a traditional (and therefore legitimate) place in the English legal system. Lambarde maintains that since all monarchs take an oath to provide their people with justice, they must have an apparatus with which to do it—even when justice is not possible under statutory law. Lambarde traces this right and duty of the king to administer justice to his subjects, at times separately from the courts, back to the most foundational legal writings he can find—the laws of the Anglo-Saxons: "And that this was no new-made *Law*, or first brought in by the *Norman Conquest*, I must put you in mind of that which I have vouched before, out of the *Saxon Lawes* of King *Edgar . . . Nemo in lite Regem appellato, nisi quando domi jus consequi non poterit, sin juris summi onere domi prematur, ad Regem ut is id oneris allevet, provocato*, Let no man in *Suit* appeale to the King, unlesse he may not get *right* at home" (58). Lambarde refers to the Norman laws and traditions, some of which he has been discussing at great length, as "new-made." The real law, the authentic piece of evidence, comes from the Anglo-Saxon codes—or rather from Lambarde's translation of them, for the Latin in this passage is a condensed form of his translation in *Archaionomia*. Even though later Norman rulers modified the system (producing the various courts, rather than having the king himself hear all cases), the ultimate principle arises from the Anglo-Saxons. Therefore, the common law allows for the royal courts and lawyers have no grounds to criticize their existence, as all courts stem from the same ancient authority and are part of the same basic system. Lambarde recognizes that the higher courts have changed quite a bit, but since Old English law allows them to exist in some form, the royal courts are legally valid. The Anglo-Saxon laws are his final arbiter for the courts' legitimacy.

Lambarde does admit, however, to some brief periods of interruption in the *practice* of the ancient laws. After the conquest, particularly, things were unsettled: "And after this order, and in those two sorts of *Courts* [i.e., local and the king's] was all *Iustice* administred, untill the time of *King William the Conquerour*. During whose Reigne (as also under the Government of *King Rufus* his Sonne) it is to be thought, that the ordinarie course of *Iustice* was greatly disturbed, as well by reason of the intestine and forraine *Warres*, as also because that these two *Princes* governed by a meere and absolute power, as in a Realme obtained by *Conquest*" (17). Lambarde takes a line similar to one Archbishop Parker used with respect to religion: the Anglo-Saxons had excellent laws but the Conqueror failed to keep them. However, unlike religion, the "course of Iustice" is only disrupted—the execution of the law stops, but its foundation is not destroyed: "But yet it was so farre off, that any of them did utterly abolish these *Courts* that the same did not only remaine during all their times (howsoever put to silence for a season;) but also had continuance afterwards, and doe yet (as they may) beare life amongst us" (17). The link to the definitive period in their legal history, Anglo-Saxon England, was never broken; Lambarde admits that the courts were not used for a time, but this interruption does not, for him, render them invalid. The principle behind royal courts remained, and so their antiquity and common law validity were not damaged by the conquest; neither was the continuity of the English legal system disrupted. The royal courts, like the rest of the common law, go back to ancient history and are represented in the Anglo-Saxon laws; the courts were also too impressive for the Normans to abolish (although they might not at first have made best use of them), and therefore should be maintained as part of the current English legal system.

Lambarde insists further in *Archeion* that the maintenance of the common law is a basic requirement for a good monarch: "And so I conclude, that not onely during the time of the *Conqueror* himselfe, of *William* his Sonne, and of his other Sonne *Henry* (which was a peaceable Prince, and a maintainer of ancient *Lawes*, and learned in them; whereof he had the name *Beauclarke*) but also under the government of King *Stephen*, and of this *Henry* the second, there was one *High Court* following the King, which was the place of soveraigne *Iustice* both for matter of *Law* and *Conscience*; and one other standing *Court*, which was governesse onely of the *Land* and *Revenues* of the Crowne" (25). Lambarde presents "Peaceable Prince" and "maintainer of ancient Lawes" as if the two roles are inextricable. A sovereign who upholds the ancient (i.e., Anglo-Saxon) law will bring prosperity to the land and glory to himself; the right to royal courts is one that the prince (to use Lambarde's usual term for a reigning monarch) must maintain. However, even the prince must abide by the proper divisions of jurisdiction, and for this Lambarde cites Magna Carta and its function. Magna Carta came about because the later Norman rulers abused the royal courts and extended their authority into areas where the common law courts were competent to render judgment. It was a back-to-the-origins treatise, which Lambarde calls "that *Great Charter* of the *Liberties* of *England* (which I may call the first *Letters* of *Manumission* of the people of this *Realme* out of the *Norman* servitude)" (62). He makes clear that to leave Norman servitude was to return to the more "original" law, the Anglo-Saxon one: "By pretence of which *Grant*, the common *Subject* thought himselfe free from that irregular *Power* which the former Kings and the Councell of Estate had exercised upon him; and phantasied, that he ought not thenceforth to be drawne to answer in any *Case*, except it were by way of *Indictment*, or by tryall of good and lawfull men (being his Peeres) onely after the course of the *Common Law*: Whereas indeed, these words of the Statute ought to be understood of the restitution then made of the ordinarie *Iurisdiction* in common *Controversie*" (62). The phrases "thought himself" and "phantasied" imply that Magna Carta did not quite fulfill its promises and did not always effect the changes it supposedly mandated.[25] However, these changes themselves were to free subjects from "irregular power" and to effect a "restitution." The Normans had veered from the proper course of law and had thus placed their subjects in "servitude," but Magna Carta (in theory at least) restored the true, Anglo-Saxon law. Individual kings may have hampered its execution, but at no point was the line to the ancient past broken.

In a 1595 jury address, Lambarde suggests that such legal continuity coincided with racial continuity:

> The tenure of the prince, with all the incidents thereto, as rents, oaths, reliefs, wardships, primer seisin, livery, and the rest, is no new imposition but a most ancient right; no exaction by absolute authority but a settled duty by ordinary law, as well common as statute, <a not> unreasonable demand in itself but grounded upon just cause and most reasonable consideration. . . . [T]he right of tenure is of equal antiquity in this land with any law that we have, not only since the Conquest but long before, even with the first government of the Germans here, from whom both we and the Norman conquerors are descended and who be the first authors of the laws *de feodis*, or of tenures, altogether unknown to the ancient Romans or civil lawyers. (177)

This is Lambarde's most Gothicizing moment, as he claims that land tenure comes from Germanic tribes and, since tenure is "of equal antiquity" with other laws, thus implies that the entire common law stemmed from them (and therefore not the Roman laws). Even the Norman Conquest did not disrupt the English common law, since the Normans were of the same people. Lambarde makes a racial argument, although a brief one, for English purity. The common Germanic ancestry of the Normans and Anglo-Saxons means that their legal system can lay an even stronger claim to constancy, unsullied by Roman (and Roman Catholic) influences.

Law and Society

Lambarde's discussions of common law repeat the themes of its ancient origin, its steadfast endurance throughout English history, and its role as the "roots" of the Tudor legal system. His ideas about the common law's permanence and its origin affected his views on the place of that law in English society. Although Lambarde at no point wrote a theoretical treatise on the social ramifications of English law, his conception of the law's civic function can be inferred from moments in his texts that hint at larger structures of thought. It should be noted that such an analysis is at heart a literary one, and it makes no claims about how accurate Lambarde's descriptions were or how relevant to the practice of the courts in his day. Lambarde's texts articulate his related conceptions of English law's social function: as a determiner of the true English subjects, as a medicine for the body politic of the English nation, and finally as the sine qua non for English society.

In Lambarde's writings, the idea that English people have a truly English legal system transforms into a claim that the English legal system protects the truly English people. As in Lambarde's borrowed metaphor of the laws as city walls, the law defines who is and is not an English subject. When Lambarde discusses resident aliens in *Eirenarcha*, he states that they may not ask for surety, since the law makes no provision for it unless they are specifically under the Queen's protection:

"the Commission it self seemeth to authorize the Justice of Peace, no further than to prouide for the Queenes people, of whiche number no Alien seemeth to be."[26] However, "why an Alein [*sic*] may not be bound to the Peace, I do not see."[27] Aliens must obey the law, but they cannot seek protection under it. The law discriminates between true English citizens ("the Queenes People") and other people who live in the kingdom. A short step from refusing the protection of the law to aliens is the recasting of offenders themselves as "aliens." Good English subjects obey the law; offenders are therefore not good English subjects and, as such, their nationality becomes suspect. Lambarde more than once suggests that breaking the law marks a criminal as "foreign": "And have not our countrymen, think you, by their continual travel abroad transported unto us the evils of those nations with whom they have been conversant? Have not our most obstinate recusants and unnatural conspirators fetched their popish treason from beyond the seas?" (95). Lawlessness is external to the body of the English people. In the same address Lambarde assigns specific social ills to certain European countries—Catholicism and sedition to Italy and France, drunkenness and pilfering to the Low Countries (95–96). Laws, therefore, both define and chasten the "foreign" elements.

Lambarde again equates illegal behavior with foreign status in an address to a Quarter Session Court in 1596. He claims that the English imported their bad habits from contact with foreign peoples during the recent wars, so that now "what Frenchman so garish and light in apparel, what Dutchman so daily drunken and given to the pot, what Irish more idle and thievishly disposed, what Scot more cowardly, sudden, and ready to stab, what Spaniard more insolent, fleshly, or blasphemous than be a many of our own English, who have not only learned and transported hither all these vices of those other men, but are grown so perniciously cunning therein that they excel their teachers and teach it to others at home!" (129–30). Vices such as these originate abroad, Lambarde suggests; the practitioners, though English, have been polluted by international experience. Even though the English offenders "excel their teachers" (a claim which is itself perhaps a perverted expression of national pride) the root of their vices lies in their contact with the non-English nations. A pure Englishman would not be a drunkard, thief, coward, murderer, adulterer, or blasphemer. Lambarde obviously knows that these offenses were committed in England before the most recent wars, but he still claims that they are not "English" in origin.

The problem with claiming that legal offenders are not really English returns us to the metaphor that Lambarde used in the preface to *Archaionomia*—the laws as city walls in need of defense. Lambarde made use of similar tropes twice in his charges to juries. In 1598, in his usual exhortation that the juries must report equally all misdeeds of which they know, Lambarde tells them they are guards, "placed for the present in the watchtower of the commonwealth and that you be, as it were, so many scouts and espies, drawn together for intelligence out of diverse and dispersed dwellings, and then, if you shall not ring the alarm nor make sign when offenders, (the enemies of the commonwealth) do approach to invade, what do you less than betray your country, which you profess to defend and maintain?" (134). Lambarde makes the upholding of the law the defense of the nation; violators are then "invaders," an external threat. However, in reality these offenders are local—they are Kentish residents. In 1600, when Lambarde tries this metaphor again, the inconsistency surfaces quickly: "Assured we are that if laws be duly administered they be the very walls of our country and commonwealth. But what walls, though of brass itself, be not expugnable if there be not men to defend them? Understand ye also that offenses (the intestine, and therefore also the most dangerous enemies) cannot without discovery and presentment be heard and tried" (142).

Lambarde's metaphor seems to be slipping here, as he admits that the worst enemies are "intestine"—within the walls, so to speak, or even within the "body" of the nation. Lambarde separates himself from this confusing image by making clear that it comes from another source: "Assured we are." But by whom? The walls fail to keep the enemy out, it would seem, or at least are not a perfect method for exclusion and inclusion. The difficulties with this metaphor do not entirely stem from inability on Lambarde's part but also from the slippery nature of the concepts "English" and "foreign."

A description of evildoers as "intestine" presents the realm as having a bodily existence. The body politic metaphor, with the monarch as the head of the national "body," has been well documented.[28] Descriptions of the nation as a body by no means originated in the early modern period, but at no other time are they more widespread. Lambarde makes frequent use of somatic metaphors in discussing laws, and his favorite is of law as the medicine for the national body. He was not alone in this; as Jonathan Gil Harris has demonstrated, "Throughout the Tudor and Stuart period, an unprecedented and sustained series of exchanges took place between medical and political institutions and their discourses."[29] Lambarde found this interchange particularly fruitful, and one cannot go far in his writings without finding comparisons of the legal system to medicine. In *Archeion*, the discussion of the high courts of England, he describes local courts and royal courts as herbal remedies: "And therefore even as two *herbes* being in extremitie of heat, or cold, bee by themselves so many poysons, and if they bee skilfully contempered, will make a wholesome *Medicine*: So also would it come to passe, if either this *Arithmeticall Govermement* (as they call it) by rigour of *Law* onely, or this *Geometricall Iudgement* at the pleasure of the *Chancellour* or *Prætor* onely should bee admitted; and yet if they bee well compounded together, a most sweete and harmonicall *Iustice* will follow of them" (44). Describing justice as medicine allows Lambarde the perfect scope to express why both the royal courts and the local courts must exist. Either of them without the other is "poyson" to the body of the nation; together they bring about justice.

Lambarde at times juxtaposes the idea that the monarchy's atemporal existence is the source of the law's authority (an early modern commonplace) with the description of the law as the medicine of the body politic. In a charge to a Session of the Peace in 1582, Lambarde exhorts his jury to remember that

> Our good Queen is the supreme executioner of all her laws. Between her Highness and you, in this part of the law, stand we that are justices of her peace. Between us and the offenders are you set chiefly that be sworn to inquire of offenses. Her Majesty, as a good physician of the disease of her country and people, doth continually for her part offer remedy and medicine for the same: sometimes in her leets, lawdays, and turns, sometimes in her commissions of oyer and determiner and gaol delivery; and many times by us in this her commission of the peace. (69)

The commission of the peace is one small part of the staying of the "disease of her country and people." In this example, however, the queen is external to the diseased body—she is the physician, the source of the medicine, not (in this quotation) the head of the body politic. To place her in her usual role as the head would be to implicate her in the illness of the nation, which is unthinkable, since her safety and physical integrity are crucial for national identity; one cannot be an English subject if one has no monarch to subject oneself to.

Since describing England as a diseased body rests uneasily with referring to the queen as its head, Lambarde does not explicitly mention her in a 1583 address, but does have the personified nation itself asking for help: "Consider that you [the commission of the peace] represent the body of your natural country, which lieth now afflicted with many griefs and putteth you in trust to seek help for her" (75). The afflicted nation looks to its officers for succor. It needs law to be put into use: "But now again, no more than medicines can avail the body if they be not received into the body . . . no more, I say, can these laws, though never so politicly devised, bring unto us any good at all whilst they lie shut up in our books only as dumb letters and dead elements, unless they shall be drawn forth and carefully put into continual ure and practice, which are the only means by which their sweet and wholesome juice, power, and virtue may be drawn and had from them" (117–18).

The somatic representation of the nation is so widespread that it might seem easy to dismiss Lambarde's metaphors or to imagine that the image of law healing the body politic is entirely benevolent. However, the process by which early modern physicians believed remedies to work can also apply to this representation of law:

> For if a man would, on the one side, call to remembrance how many most godly, politic, and wholesome laws be at every session

published, with earnest exhortation and desire to have the same embraced and put in execution, and should also, on the other side, consider and behold how transgressions against those statutes do daily grow from evil to worse and are now mounted to an heaped and overflowing measure, so as, like evil humors, they threaten at the least some extreme sickness if not the utter decay and death of the body of this commonwealth, he shall be forced to think and confess that howsoever there be some at the bench that proclaim good laws, yet there come none to the bar that do give ear and willingly mark them. (94–95)

The nation's disease is described as "evil humors." Contemporary medical theory held that illness stemmed from a surfeit of one of the bodily humors, and treatment often involved attempting to purge the excess. Bleeding was common in sixteenth-century medicine as a way to remove the surfeit of a humor (blood was believed to contain all four humors and, depending where it was drawn, to be able to remove an abundance of any one); emetics and laxatives were also "prized because they removed superfluities or bad humors."[30] By implication, the role of the law is also to remove these overabundant or bad humors, logically, those who break the laws. The laws again define what does and does not belong within English society. Although describing law as the nation's medicine might seem a far cry from describing it as the nation's walls, in both tropes the laws serve an exclusionary purpose—to divide those who belong within the body/city from those who do not.

Lambarde makes this point even more expressly in a 1595 charge to a jury:

That it is the very drift, mark, and end of all good laws and policies to cherish virtue and to chastise vice it doth well appear, not only to the mind by discourse of inward reason and conceit, but also to all outward show and proof indeed by continual practice and experience. For even as within the natural body of man medicine doth both sensibly purge and cast out the evil humors that they be no longer noisome, and doth therewithal confirm the vital parts that they may be enabled to do their best offices; so likewise in the politic body of the commonwealth laws have their apparent worth and effect, not only as curative medicines against wicked doers that either by their act or example or both do breed the dishonor of God and distemper of the country, but also as preservatives from all those and the like evils. (94–95)

Lambarde directly correlates law's medicinal value with its purging powers. In some ways, the law could literally remove bad elements from society—for instance, by imprisoning or executing them—and this is likely what Lambarde means by "curative measures." "Preservatives" would more likely be corporal punishments that served as a deterrent but did not remove the offender from English society. The depiction of law as medicine emphasizes that it excludes from the English body anyone who does not properly belong to it, whether because they are foreign or because, like ill humors, they threaten it from within.

We have seen that for Lambarde, the law serves both an inclusionary and an exclusionary function: it casts English subjects as specially Protestant throughout their history; it distinguishes "foreign" elements who threaten the purity of the commonwealth; and it expels any person, originally internal to the realm, who seems a risk to its security. Identity politics are based on such a dynamic of inclusion and rejection. Certainly English law was not the only point around which national identity was constructed, but Lambarde realized that the law provided both a potent source of identity in its Anglo-Saxon (and non-Roman) origin and a means of enforcing the integrity of the perceived English realm. By 1596 he begins to allow law a higher status in the body politic than simply its medicine:

> It is an ancient truth, confirmed as well by the judgment of the learned that have written concerning the government of countries and commonwealths as also by the continual practice of all societies and nations, that even as no man can live comfortably without the fellowship of men, so no fellowship can stand without law and discipline; and that even as the body of man and all the parts and members thereof derive their life, sense, and moving from the soul or spirit of man, so the laws of each country and kingdom be the very soul and life thereof, by whose continuance they do joy, grow, and flourish, and by the neglect and want wherof they fall to jar, poverty, ruin, and desolation in the end. (128)

Lambarde has raised the stakes: law is no longer just the medicine by which the bad humors are purged, but instead has become the very soul of human society. Law is the sine qua non for any commonwealth; it not only regulates but also animates the nation. Lambarde probably knows that he cedes to law a place that, in John of Salisbury's *Policraticus*, is held by religion. In the *Policraticus*, religion must be the soul of any nation.[31] Given the crucial role of Protestantism in Elizabethan identity politics, we might expect Lambarde to follow this traditional assignment, but he does not. As Lambarde continues, "such and so great is the use and necessity of law as that without it neither any private family nor town nor city nor nation nor the universality of mankind nor the nature of things created nor this mighty mass of the world itself is able to stand and continue, and that to take from men the exercise of law were to draw the benefit of the sun from the world, whereof palpable darkness, confusion, and horror of all things would immediately follow and fall upon it" (128). Lambarde was not the first to see the law as the soul of the body politic—Thomas Starkey had done so in 1535—but that should not obscure the importance that he decides to give to law here.[32] Lambarde's depiction of law as the key element of human existence stems in part from a fear of anarchy, but it is also, as I have argued, based on his recognition of law's ability to define society. Without law there can be no society, because without law society cannot enforce its self-definitions, particularly in England, which worked to conceive of itself as a Protestant state separate from the laws of the Roman Catholic Church. Law worked in tandem with religion to separate an "English" identity, since Lambarde believed it, like Protestantism, stemmed from before the conquest. The medieval origins of English law, as well as its contemporary function, led Lambarde to assign it the highest place in the constitution of English identity. All this is why a "Saxon" legal document, in his view, was an "English" one, as he claimed in the *Perambulation of Kent*.

Later common lawyers such as Edward Coke valued Lambarde and his writings for his emphasis on ancient authority and the need to maintain it, as well as for his meticulous research; R. J. Schoeck observes that "the defense of the common-law tradition and the people was possible only after the early work of Elizabethan legal scholars like Lambarde."[33] Lambarde's *Eirenarcha* was an instant classic—Coke used it in his law courses at the Inns of Court—and it remained a standard how-to manual for justices of the peace for almost a century.[34] The common lawyers also used his historical studies as fuel for their arguments. Lambarde's *Archaionomia* was the only printed book that gave lawyers direct access to the Old English laws, and common lawyers needed to search out the oldest examples of the law to sort out what the common law traditions were. Coke, especially, seems to have held Lambarde in highest esteem—the two knew each other slightly; Lambarde, as one of the masters of Chancery, was present at Coke's debut as Speaker of the lower house. In 1628 Coke was imprisoned for seven months and his study was removed and searched. As he later told Parliament in a speech, three items were not returned: "Lambard's abreviat of the Tower Records, his abreviat of the ancient orders of Chancery, and a treatise on the government and laws of Ireland."[35] Coke wistfully added that he would "give three hundred pounds" for the return of the missing books.[36] Doubtless the historical subject matter explains why Coke so keenly felt the loss of Lambarde's two books, but he would hardly lament their absence if he had no regard for Lambarde as a scholar. Lambarde's influence and his opinions about the common law stretched forth into what were, arguably, some of the most crucial decades in Anglo-American constitutional history. Lambarde's research on Anglo-Saxon law, led by his understanding of the common law in his own day, may have done more than any other Renaissance view of the past to guide the shape of future discourses, as his ideas influenced Coke, Blackstone, and through them nearly everyone else who worked on Old English laws for centuries after the Renaissance itself was a matter for retrospection.

NOTES

Some of the material in Rebecca Brackmann's essay appears as well in Brackmann, *The Elizabethan Invention of Anglo-Saxon England: Laurence Nowell, William Lambarde, and the Study of Old English* (Woodbridge: D. S. Brewer, 2012).

1. Lambarde, *Archaionomia*. I follow the standard critical practice of transliterating Lambarde's Greek titles into English characters.

2. Lambarde, *Perambulation of Kent*, 9.

3. Lambarde, *Perambulation of Kent*, 450.

4. Liebermann, *Die Gesetze Der Angelsachsen*, 1:456–58; Wormald, *Making of English Law*, 393. Wormald describes the *Textus Roffensis* on 244–53.

5. Lambarde, *Perambulation of Kent*, 454.

6. Lambarde, *Perambulation of Kent*, 70.

7. Parker, *Testimonie of Antiquitie*; Page, *Matthew Parker and His Books*; Leinbaugh, "Aelfric's *Sermo De Sacrificio*." The most recent collection of essays on the topic of Old English studies in the Renaissance is Graham, *Recovery of Old English*.

8. Pocock, "Origins of the Study of the Past," 232.

9. For an overview of Lambarde's and others' views of the role of Anglo-Saxon law in English common law, see Wormald, *Making of English Law*, 4–15. The most influential discussion of early English nationalism is Helgerson, *Forms of Nationhood*; see also Shrank, *Writing the Nation in Reformation England*.

10. Lambarde, *Archaionomia* [sig. A2r].

11. Pocock, *Ancient Constitution and the Feudal Law*, 56–57. J. W. Tubbs challenges the view that all common lawyers were fixated on the law's antiquity; see Tubbs, *Common Law Mind*.

12. Pocock, *Ancient Constitution and the Feudal Law*, 57. Janelle Greenberg, however, argues that "immemorial" sometimes only meant predating 1189, the start of legal record; see Greenberg, *Radical Face of the Ancient Constitution*, 20–30.

13. Pocock, *Ancient Constitution*, 58.

14. Lambarde, *Eirenarcha*, 11.

15. Lambarde, *William Lambarde and Local Government*, 104–5. Subsequent citations will be parenthetical in the text.

16. In *An Introduction to English Legal History*, J. H. Baker discusses the post-Reformation use of civil law in the ecclesiastical courts (150–52) and in the Courts of Admiralty (141–43).

17. Lambarde's copy of Lagus is in the Folger Shakespeare Library; his annotated copy of Justinian is in the University of Virginia Library.

18. Levy, *Tudor Historical Thought*, 65.

19. Curran, *Roman Invasions*, 130.

20. Curran, *Roman Invasions*, 225.

21. Curran, *Roman Invasions*, 225–50. Andrew Escobedo also discusses the importance of Arthur; see Escobedo, *Nationalism and Historical Loss*, 47.

22. Parker, *Defence of Priestes Mariages*. For Parker's use of Anglo-Saxon sources, see Kleist, "Matthew Parker."

23. Paul Ward discusses manuscripts of the text in his appendix to his edition of *Archeion*; see Lambarde, *Archeion*, 145–76.

24. Ward's appendix to his edition of *Archeion* points out that the Star Chamber section was probably added to the manuscript later, as it was being printed, for Lambarde wrote it

as a separate treatise; see, Lambarde, *Archeion*, 150–51. Nevertheless, for ease of reference, I will refer to any text appearing in the modern edition as *Archeion*. Subsequent citations to *Archeion* will be parenthetical in the text.

25. It is worth noting that Lambade's word "phantasied" had none of the derogatory implications of willful or irrational belief now associated with that word. For him, "fantasy" had a more neutral meaning of "belief"; c.f. Lambarde, *Archeion*, 37: "I speak of the Court of *Equitie*; which, in my fantasie, is not altogether so ancient as the other. . . ." This meaning was not uncommon in the Renaissance.

26. Lambarde, *Eirenarcha*, 89.

27. Lambarde, *Eirenarcha*, 89.

28. Kantorowicz, *King's Two Bodies*, focuses on the Middle Ages, but his work is often cited by scholars of the early modern period as well.

29. Harris, *Foreign Bodies*, 19.

30. Siraisi, *Medieval and Early Renaissance Medicine*, 148. For the use of bleeding in purging bad humors, see 139–40.

31. "By all means, that which institutes and moulds the practice of religion in us and which transmits the worship of God . . . acquires the position of the soul in the body of the republic." John of Salisbury, *Policraticus*, 66–67.

32. Harris discusses Starkey's use of the body politic metaphor at some length; see Harris, *Foreign Bodies*, 19–47.

33. Schoeck, "Early Anglo-Saxon Studies," 106.

34. Bowen, *Lion and the Throne*, 17.

35. Quoted in Bowen, *Lion and the Throne*, 491.

36. Quoted in Bowen, *Lion and the Throne*, 491.

The Rebel Kiss: Jack Cade, Shakespeare, and the Chroniclers

Kellie Robertson

In the summer of 1450 the rebel leader Jack Cade camped on Blackheath and demanded governmental reform. Chief among his rebels' complaints were the regular extortions practiced by local and royal officials, a lack of free elections for knights of the shire, and the increasingly onerous labor laws that were felt to impinge on long-standing tenant rights. But their grievances also went beyond the merely local: they charged that the king's advisors had mismanaged affairs in France and that the king himself had excluded from his counsel lords of hereditary right. The list of grievances sent to the king emphasized that Cade and his followers were loyal to the king and that they saw themselves as petitioners engaged in a political process rather than rebels intent on the overthrow of their sovereign.

Over one hundred years later, the grand project of Tudor revisionist history passed a less kind judgment on Cade and his comrades. Memorialized by Shakespeare in *2 Henry VI*, the Elizabethan Cade is characterized by his bloodthirsty desire to murder all the gentry and their betters. When the decapitated heads of Cade's political enemies are brought before him, the rebel leader proposes that they be used as props in a rogue "pageant":

> CADE: But is this not braver? Let them kiss one another, for they
> loved well when they were alive. Now part them again, lest they
> consult about the giving up of some more towns in France. Sol-
> diers, defer the spoil of the city until night; for with these borne
> before us instead of maces will we ride through the streets, and at
> every corner have them kiss. Away!
> (*2 Henry VI*, 4.7.122–28)[1]

Shakespeare's portrayal of this posthumous kiss is part of a protracted genealogy of rebel representation that bridges the medieval and early modern periods.

While this kiss exists in only a single contemporary chronicle account, its presence becomes ubiquitous in later, sixteenth-century chronicle accounts and literary retellings of the rising.

Analyzing the portrayal of Cade has also become something of a cottage industry in Shakespearean criticism: for Annabel Patterson, Cade is part of a continuum of radical protest across the medieval and early modern periods, an instance of genuine "peasant ideology" and an embodiment of the play's wish to privilege authentic manual labor even as this ethos gets corrupted by the hypocritical Cade. On the other hand, critics like Richard Helgerson and Richard Wilson see in Shakespeare's Cade a desire to tar the vox populi as degraded at best and delusional at worst; and in these readings, Cade cannot be a locus for realizable social change.[2]

This essay sidesteps the New Historicist debate over Shakespeare's "intention" in representing Cade in order to explore instead the ways in which chronicle accounts refashioned the rebel kiss for their own historiographical ends, and, subsequently, how these accounts were transformed by Shakespeare into a metatheatrical moment that addressed the problem of acting itself. The chronicles represent the kiss as a type of "political street theater," wherein the dead mouths were effectively made to speak the rebel transcript. In early modern chroniclers such as Edward Hall and Raphael Holinshed, we see how the mechanics of gesture inscribes meaning in the medieval Cade in ways that language alone cannot. Their accounts demonstrate not only how the social meaning of nonconformity gets produced over the *longue durée* but also the necessary iterability of rebel gesture that authorizes a legible, transhistorical text like a chronicle. Thus, insofar as the act of historical writing reanimates dead bodies, the posthumous kiss in both chronicles and *2 Henry VI* is essentially metahistorical, an emblem of the history tellers' own larger project of refashioning the body politic.

Chronicling the Posthumous Kiss

Shakespeare's primary chronicle sources for *2 Henry VI*, Hall and Holinshed, provide virtually identical accounts of Cade's Rebellion. They follow the mid-fifteenth-century chronicles in setting out the context for the rebels' murder of Lord Saye, Henry VI's treasurer, and Saye's son-in-law, William Crowmer, sheriff of Kent. Henry had reluctantly imprisoned Saye in the Tower before exiting London himself, despite pleas (and bribes) from its citizens. Saye was an obvious target for the Kentish rebels, both because Saye had been the former, corrupt sheriff of Kent, and was also a partisan of the unpopular Duke of Suffolk, notorious for his mishandling of foreign policy in France.[3] Unsurprisingly, Saye was taken to the guildhall, charged with treason, then summarily dragged to the Standard in Chepe and beheaded; Saye's son-in-law Crowmer had met the same fate earlier in the day. Holinshed recounts Cade's quasi-ceremonial reentry into the city with the heads of Saye and Crowmer mounted on pikes: "And with these two heads this bloudie wretch entred into the citie againe, and as it were in a spite caused them in euerie street to kisse togither, to the great detestation of all the beholders."[4] Holinshed's account makes clear that the onlookers were appropriately horrified by this rebel dumb show.

While Holinshed imagines the audience's response, his likely source—a medieval chronicle—significantly makes no such attempt. Holinshed's account seems to take its details from an account of the rebellion such as that found in London, British Library, MS Cotton Vitellius A.XVI, the most complete and detailed eyewitness account of the rebellion and the only extant chronicle that mentions the posthumous kiss.[5] The Vitellius chronicler describes that kiss in the following manner: "they browgth the hedis of the lord Say and of Crowmer vpon ij stakis, or polis, and in dyvers placis of the Cite putte theym togidir cawsyng that oon to kysse that other" (161). The kiss episode reappears, somewhat surprisingly, again at the end of the Vitellius manuscript. There, amidst a laundry list of the names of "diverse lords, knights and gentlemen" killed in England since the Duke of Gloucester's death in 1446, the rebellion gets renarrated in miniature:

> Jack Cade of Kente come vnto London, and rode vnto Myle ende: the whiche Cade was the Kentissh mens Capteyn at that tyme. And there he toke Crowmer, Shiriff of Kente, and smote of his hede. The whiche Crowmer had wedded the lorde Saies Doughter. And so the saide Capteyn retourned ageyn vnto London, bryngyng the said Crowmours hede vpon a billys poynt. And the said Cade rode to the Towre, and toke out the lord Say, and had hym forth into Chepesyde of London a litell aboue the Standard; *and there he gan smyte of the said Sayes hede, and there he made bothe hedes kisse to gider:* And after, made the said lord Sayes body to be drawen with cordis vnto Newgate and so to be brought in at Ludgate.
> (emphasis mine, 276)

There were, of course, many other "lords, knights and gentlemen" killed in Cade's rebellion, but none are mentioned, and the chronicler passes quickly on to events later in the decade. In both places the Vitellius chronicler reports the deed neutrally, omitting the crowd's reaction, an omission that may suggest either Yorkist leanings or merely a lack of indignation over the deaths of men considered, in many quarters, to be oppressive partisans. The second narration of the kiss in the Vitellius manuscript makes this point even clearer than the first, since the bloody spectacle was there placed in the context of the misrule of Henry's reign. The rebels' violent treatment of Saye and Crowmer is juxtaposed with such recent events as the suspicious death of Humphrey, Duke of Gloucester, an event attributed—in the common perception at least—to the political machinations of his enemies, the Duke of Suffolk and his client Lord Saye. In this context the kiss looks less like the work of a bloody-minded renegade and more like political policy.

The sixteenth-century view of onlookers finding the posthumous kiss "detestable" may reflect more than just the later chronicler's own aversion to such bloody retaliation. In Holinshed the Cade kiss was more than just a singular (if particularly gruesome) episode in the upheaval that marked the middle years of Henry VI's reign. It was an identifiable episode in a longer narrative of insurgent gesture that can be seen to inform a rebel "vocabulary of the body" that spans the fourteenth, fifteenth, and sixteenth centuries. The condemnatory tone of Holinshed's recitation of the events in 1450 recalls the same tone he had previously used to describe the events of the Rising of 1381. This is unsurprising given that the two rebellions shared similar aims, tactics, and rebel appropriations of official ritual. In Holinshed's account, however, there is also a shared rhetoric of gesture that includes the rebel kiss among its bodily enactments.

For a reader of Holinshed's *Chronicles*, the 1450 kiss explicitly recalls the earlier posthumous kiss organized by the 1381 rebels. This earlier kiss was allegedly orchestrated by John Wrawe, the leader of the revolt in East Anglia. One of the East Anglian rebels' first victims was John Cavendish, chief justice of the King's Bench and a substantial Suffolk landowner. Cavendish was chased down and executed, after which his head was set on the pillory in the market square of Bury St. Edmunds. The prior of Bury St. Edmunds, John Cambridge, had also attempted to flee the rebels but was caught the next day and beheaded. His head was likewise set upon a pole, "the which coming to Burie, and entring the towne in maner of a procession, when they came into the market place where the pillorie stood, as it were in token of the old friendship betwixt the lord chiefe iustice, and the said prior, they made sport with their heads, making them sometime as it were to kisse, other whiles to sound in either others eare. After they had taken their pastime inough herewith, they set both the heads againe aloft vpon the pillorie."[6] Holinshed here quite literally echoes his medieval source, the chronicler Thomas Walsingham, who describes the rebels' activities in similar terms. According to Walsingham, the rebels

> bore the head of the prior high on the end of a lance in full view of
> the townspeople, as if they were going round in a procession, until
> they reached the pillory. When they arrived there, to signify the
> friendship that had existed previously between the prior and John
> Cavendish, and to deride each of these persons, they most shame-
> fully brought the heads together in turn at the tops of the lances,
> first as if they were whispering to each other, then as though kiss-
> ing. Finally, when they had had their fill of poking fun at them in
> this way, they again placed both heads upon the pillory.[7]

Walsingham condemns the rebel actions as degraded, considering them to have been performed shamefully ("cum maxima inepcia"). This judgment on the earlier kiss seems to color Holinshed's portrayal of the later, 1450 kiss. No medieval chronicles would have contained both the 1381 and the 1450 kisses; thus, an early modern reader of Holinshed would have a unique perspective on the iterative nature of the rebels' bodily lexicon. The 1450 kiss seems more the fulfillment of a typological imperative for Holinshed, the necessity of a historiographical "emplotment"—to use Hayden White's term—that demanded that rebels always behaved this way and that, consequently, onlookers would always find such gestures detestable.[8]

Both accounts of rebel-orchestrated "kissing" emphasize the ways in which the rebels have appropriated what James Scott calls the "official transcript" of recognizable social practice.[9] David Aers, in his discussion of the representation of the popular voice in chronicle accounts of the 1381 rising, rightly argues that the kiss orchestrated by Wrawe and his band becomes an "inversion of the structures of power, manipulation and silencing acted out against the representatives of royal and ecclesiastical power."[10] Just like the 1381 kiss, the 1450 kiss was a type of political inversion that recognized how power travels through society in avenues both acknowledged and disavowed.

However, it is also important to note the medium rather than just the message in both of these episodes, since the kiss is "acted" on the stage of civic space. The medieval and early modern chronicles agree that the rebels were sophisticated readers of the city's spatial syntax as well as its ritual dramatic gestures. It is no coincidence that both rebellions began during the festival of Corpus Christi and hence make use of the popular theatrical conventions associated with it.[11] Rebellion is, of course, innately theatrical; it demands that the rebel imaginatively occupy a position of legal and social power that he does not occupy in everyday life.[12] Yet "rebellion as theater" is more than mere analogy in these chronicle accounts, since the rebel leaders are conspicuously shown to convert preexisting civic ritual into an avenue of political agency. In his account of Wrawe in 1381, Holinshed claims that the rebels carried their victims' heads "in maner of a procession."[13] The idea of the rebels as "players" in a civic pageant is also implicit in the contemporary medieval chronicles, one of which refers to the rebels as *illudentes*.[14] In his account of the 1450 rebellion, Holinshed notes that Cade makes the heads kiss not just once but "in euerie street to kisse togither"; this account seems to echo the mid-fifteenth-century Vitellius chronicler who has them kissing "in dyvers placis of the Cite."[15] This detail suggests that, like a mystery play or other civic pageant, the dumb show was performed at several dramatic "stations." Just as the Corpus Christi festival used the capacious body of Christ to knit together the disparate spaces and business interests of the city, so too the rebels are shown to have used—through a kind of corporeal alchemy—the dead bodies of hated political partisans to link together the interests of a diverse group of disgruntled citizens.

Kissing in the City

In both rebellions the kissing of decapitated heads demonstrated a similar ventriloquization of ritual space—first in Bury, then in London—that depended on the legibility of the kiss as a signifier of social and political power. The kiss's plasticity within the rebel vocabulary of representation can be attributed to the diverse ways in which public kissing organized both late medieval and early modern urban spaces. Not fifty years after Cade's rebellion, London was famously described by Erasmus as a "world of osculation."[16] Erasmus's proleptically Jamesian comment reflected the English habit of kissing upon greeting and farewell, a custom familiar to the modern reader from medieval romances, where the ostensibly public, ritual kisses between Guinevere and Lancelot take on a more personal, private meaning. A Bohemian visitor to London in the 1460s relates a situation similar to the one described by Erasmus a few decades later, telling of a city where a guest arriving at an inn was expected to kiss his hostess along with each member of her household rather than shaking hands.[17] The gesture of the kiss also played a role in organizing the city's guild structures. Londoners received into religious guilds like those dedicated to St. Katharine or Sts. Fabian and Sebastian were expected upon entering to kiss all the other members of the guild as a sign of the love they bore to their brothers.[18]

The feudal kiss of vassalage was probably the best known kiss of the Middle Ages: the ceremony of homage involved the vassal kneeling in front of his lord and placing his joined hands in the lord's hands as a sign of his fidelity, whereupon the lord would promise him protection and maintenance. The lord then sealed this exchange by kissing the vassal on the mouth.[19] Even though feudalism was technically waning by the fifteenth century, this particular custom was still very much in use, as is evidenced by an English law passed to allow for its temporary suspension. In 1439 the Commons successfully petitioned Henry VI that, on account of the plague, knights owing him allegiance could omit the kiss from the act of homage, but that the act would still have the same force despite the omission of this gesture.[20] In addition to the kiss demonstrating homage and fealty, there was also the kiss of reconciliation enacted on so-called "pax days" or "luve daies." It can be assumed that such days were enacted with varying degrees of actual love, as in the case of Richard II who, in the wake of the Appellant Crisis, had to agree to kiss Bolingbroke and Woodstock in a public ceremony of reconciliation at Westminster.

As a symbol of a more generalized reconciliation among Christians, the kiss of peace—taken before communion—was once a central part of the Christian liturgy. By the end of the thirteenth century, however, this practice had been replaced by kissing a plaque with a picture of Jesus or one of the saints on it.[21] The kiss of peace had thus been replaced by kissing the "pax-borde." While J. Russell Major documents the decline of the gesture between people in the public sphere toward the end of the Middle Ages, the kissing of objects was still much in fashion. The kissing of relics at churches was a common and well-documented practice; Lollard polemics frequently objected to the behavior of pilgrims at saints' shrines, where (it was alleged) the pilgrims would "cleuen sadly stokande and kyssand these olde stones and stokkis."[22] Whatever a given member of society thought in private about the public act of kissing, all of these diverse kisses had the same goal: they were designed to insure the smooth integration of the individual into the community—whether of the lord's affinity, the guild, a larger political grouping, or the circle of the saved.

In a world where the act of kissing was a conduit for feudal, mercantile, and religious power, the posthumous kisses orchestrated by the 1381 and the 1450 rebels were more than just kisses. They were a display of bastardized fealty that allowed the rebels to occupy public space and to broadcast their message without ever having to say a word. That bodies could speak, even when silent, was a cause of some concern throughout the medieval and early modern periods. Hugh of St. Victor's treatise, *De institutione novitiorum*, perhaps the best known of all discussions of medieval gesture, complained that each bodily member should perform its own singular function, and he urged that all of these should be regulated in what he calls the *respublica* of the body.[23] If the body is a republic, the decapitated heads in these rebel plays have certainly become "public things"—but things in a dangerous sense, animated merely by some debased feudal energy rather than guided by living intent. This use of dead bodies is thus more than merely carnivalesque inversion (a cog in a New Historicist ideological "containment" argument); instead, the public gesture of the kiss points to abused fealty, an abuse that the rebel "ritual" makes manifest.

The rebels would have taken their bodily lexicon of spectacular play not only from civic ritual but also from the surprisingly plastic lexicon of posthumous punishment common in the medieval period. Such a widely known postmortem "show" was enacted in the wake of the murder of Charles the Good in Flanders in 1127. According to the chronicler Galbert of Bruges, two of the conspirators were hanged and then displayed to public view in the town square, "so that just as they had been equals in treachery, so they should die as equals in torment." Galbert's description then continues: "After this they placed the bodies of both men on the wheel of a cart, fastened to a high tree, and exposed them to the gaze of all the passers-by; bending their arms around each other's necks as if in a mutual embrace, they made those dead men look as if they were plotting and conspiring for the death of their lord, the most glorious and pious Charles, even after they had been dead for three days."[24] These *tableaux non-vivants* are a type of bodily clamor with social consequences, a nonverbal pointing that substitutes for utterance in a socially resonant way.

The posthumous kiss also made an occasional appearance in medieval ceremonial executions and their aftermath. In Paris in 1407, two clerks were unlawfully hanged by secular authorities. The University of Paris faculty threatened to leave the city unless an "unhanging" ritual was enacted: they demanded that the *prévot* responsible for the deaths personally cut the bodies down, kiss them on the lips, and return them to the appropriate ecclesiastical authorities for proper burial. The bodies were duly cut down, but, as they had been hanging for five months, the *prévot* was not ultimately forced to kiss them.[25] This example shows the central role that even a posthumous kiss could play in the reintegration of an accused criminal into society. In her study of public executions, Esther Cohen asserts that in the medieval period "justice was synonymous with political lordship, and doing justice meant putting to death."[26] Cade's assumption of this power in 1450 is a clear marker of his assumption of feudal lordship. The 1381 and 1450 rebels had each used these posthumous spectacles to restage the Judas kiss of betrayal, a misgovernment that was seen to inhere in the bodies of these corrupt individuals and thus to corrupt the body politic.

The 1381 and 1450 kisses shared a similar rebel vocabulary of the body, a somatic spectacle borrowed from the liturgical and political realms. The fact that the gesture is repeated in both rebellions points to the necessary iterability of rebel gesture, not just the repetition of rebel language or rebel tactics. It was not just the rebel voice but the rebel body that had to be reproduced in each instance of rebellion. If, according to Hugh of St. Victor, gestures were supposed to bind inner intentions together with exterior actions—and, in a well-regulated body, no slippage was experienced between the two—the justices and the rebels saw themselves as restoring not only political balance but also a corporeal balance to a gestural economy that had gone awry. As Jean-Claude Schmitt has noted, gestures did not just transmit religious and political power, they also "bound together human wills and human bodies."[27] In this respect both the feudal kiss and the kiss of peace were integral to the establishment and maintenance of medieval structures of feeling. The rebel appropriation of the kiss gesture suggests that it was understood to be an action that completed an almost quasi-mechanical "circuit" of social power. The 1381 and 1450 kisses possessed both semiotic and instrumental meanings: they communicated a specific message about the abrogation of feudal power, while, at the same time, they completed the circuit of rebellion by incorporating the humiliated bodies of oppressive partisans into a powerful spectacle that appropriated its symbolism from secular ceremonial as well as liturgical models. The embodied nature of this spectacle is significant, because rebel words alone would not have accomplished the same message in a society where the power of the gesture was more than supplemental to the written or spoken word. In the rebel kiss gesture exceeds speech, conveying both facts and feelings that enunciation alone could not convey. Rebel gesture, as portrayed by the chroniclers, is irreducible to, and more powerful than, rebel speech.

The medieval and early modern chroniclers, as transmitters of these extra-linguistic spectacles, served to make dead bodies speak again, even when they could utter no more political speeches (and give away no more towns in France). More than just a kind of corporeal *contrapasso*, the chronicle representations of these kisses allow these spectacular bodies to remain pedagogically useful long after their deaths.[28] Annabel Patterson has argued that Holinshed's account of popular unrest was (like his views on religion) "less committed to social polarization than to social mediation and negotiation."[29] This judgment seems less compelling with regard to his representation of rebellion than his representation of religious difference. Instead, Holinshed repeatedly offers a transhistorically unified set of rebel voices and practices, portraying them as dangerous episodes of social unrest, episodes which should only and always be met with "detestation." Similarly, while Holinshed's concept of what we might call a national history may allow for religious plurality (particularly in its past), it does not allow for the inversion of official religious rites by rebels, even if these old rites are no longer considered viable by a contemporary audience.

The Rebel Kiss on the Early Modern Stage

The reception of the posthumous kiss on the early modern stage speaks to an increasingly troubled attitude toward the spectacle of corporeal transformation. In Shakespeare's *2 Henry VI* (ca. 1591), early modern theatergoers were treated to a reenactment of the bloody scene that medieval street audiences would have witnessed firsthand. Critics attempting to imagine how early modern audiences would have reacted to this spectacle of public punishment have usually approached the representation of Cade (with its conscious anachronism that turns 1450 into 1381) as a window onto Shakespeare's "own" views about recent political agitations such as the Hacket Rising, Kett's Rebellion, or the unruly revelry of London cloth workers.[30] Some critics have argued that the representation of Cade shows Shakespeare's sympathy (to varying extents) with an egalitarian culture of popular protest that resisted aristocratic monopolies on good-faith dealing and political common sense; other critics have viewed Cade's bloodthirstiness (much exaggerated from the chronicles) as a conservative, "law-and-order" response to *any* episode of social unrest; finally, one critic has even argued that the play somehow expresses both these contradictory sentiments simultaneously.[31] The fact that the Cade episode can be read antithetically to support both populist and antipopulist readings of Shakespeare seems to suggest that we should perhaps look elsewhere for the episode's lessons. All these interpretations of Shakespeare's Cade treat Shakespeare as if he were a chronicler—a writer who is most interested in the "truth" of a given historical event, inflected through contemporary circumstances—rather than a playwright who may be more interested in the episode's metadramatic rather than historiographical possibilities.

The textual and Stationer's Register evidence suggests that *2 Henry VI* was one of Shakespeare's earliest plays and, most likely, his first attempt at writing a history play. In it we find him working out problems about what it means to perform history rather than merely to record it (as the chroniclers do).[32] Shakespeare's version of Cade in *2 Henry VI* highlights not only the theatrical nature of rebellion as we have seen in the chronicle accounts but positions Cade himself as the epitome of the "bad" actor. On the other hand, Shakespeare's chronicle sources, Hall and Holinshed, portray Cade as the consummate impersonator: Cade's easy assumption of the Yorkist alias "John Mortimer" is an effective piece of playacting that, combined with his rhetorical "perswasions," gain him ready adherents.[33] Similarly, the early modern chroniclers document Cade's unimpeded progress through the city: he dresses himself in the noble clothing of the slain Stafford and enacts the civic ritual—"strikyng his sworde on London stone"—that had long signified symbolic possession of the city and its inhabitants. For Shakespeare, however, Cade's theatrical impersonation of civic authority is always hindered by an onstage "audience" who immediately take the measure of Cade's "bad" acting:

> CADE: My father was a Mortimer—
> BUTCHER: [*aside*] He was an honest man, and a good bricklayer.
> CADE: My mother a Plantagenet—
> BUTCHER [*aside*]: I knew her well, she was a midwife.
> CADE: My wife descended of the Lacies—
> BUTCHER [*aside*]: She was indeed a pedlar's daughter and sold
>   many laces.
> WEAVER [*aside*]: But now of late, not able to travel with her furred
>   pack, she washes bucks here at home.
> CADE: Therefore am I of an honourable house.
> (*2 Henry VI*, 4.2.35–45)

Cade's genealogical masquerade gets him heckled by a less-than-appreciative audience of tradesmen. Unlike the authors of medieval and early modern chronicles, who tend to emphasize how successful Cade's social playacting was (at least initially), Shakespeare presents Cade as an embodiment of the dramatic problems that arise when acting is revealed as burlesque, playing mere pantomime. Similarly, the chronicles' emphasis on the dangers of social climbing is in Shakespeare transformed into a meditation on the actor-audience relationship.

If the play highlights Cade's bad acting—rather than just his inept aping of his social betters—the posthumous kiss scene manifests more serious charges frequently leveled against the stage in antitheatrical polemic. To show two decapitated heads interacting onstage was to remind audiences that living actors in history plays were really making dead mouths speak again. Antitheatrical polemic had long stigmatized acting as mere "dead stuff": a grotesque reanimation that could lead an unwary audience into vice and even possibly idolatry. This antitheatrical prejudice had a long genealogy: from medieval Lollard writings such as the *Tretise of Miraclis Pleyinge* (ca. 1380–1425) to the early modern polemics of Rankins, Gosson, Stubbes, and Prynne, among others.[34] In *Th' Overthrow of Stage-Playes* (1599) John Rainolds claims that the danger of the theater, like the danger inherent in relics, is that men "may be ravished with loue of stones, of dead stuffe."[35] If Puritan antitheatrical discourse demanded that the "sign" match the thing, the spectacle of the posthumous kiss is an emblematic moment in Shakespeare's plays: a moment, like acting itself, where a conspicuously dead mouth gives voice to a living script.

In its combination of antitheatricality and metatheatricality, the posthumous kiss scene enacts what Jonas Barish and Houston Diehl have described as a self-conscious unmasking of theatricality, an early modern playwright's seeming mistrust of his own *modus operandi*.[36] For Shakespeare, acknowledgment of the danger of playing is linked, quite materially, to the dangers involved in bodily gesture. Such dangers, familiar from the fear of bodily riot that we have already seen in the writings of Hugh of St. Victor, are given new voice in early modern antitheatrical polemic. In *A Second and Third Blast of Retreat from Plays and Theaters* (1580) Anthony Munday marvels at how "the gesturing of a plaier, which Tullie termeth the eloquence of the bodie, is of force to move, and prepare a man to that which is il."[37] Such fears about the inappropriateness of theatrical gesture—its ability to change the ontological state of the viewer—overlapped with Protestant fears about spectacular bodies performing "wild" gestures during mass. Tyndale objects to the elaborate vesture and gestures of priests who "with signs and proffers, with nodding, becking and mowing, as it were jackanapes . . . it bringeth them [i.e., the congregation] into such superstition, that they think they have done abundantly enough for God . . . if they be present once in a day at such mumming."[38] The gestural bodily spectacle of the mass is a kind of playacting that has the potential to "infect" its viewers with unreformed religion. So, too, rebel gesture could potentially contaminate the commons with ideas of revolt, as it was alleged with regard to the notorious 1601 performance of *Richard II*, orchestrated as part of the Earl of Essex's failed rebellion. Ungoverned gestures of the body—whether performed by a priest, a rebel, an actor, or (one must suppose) an actor playing a rebel—would have conveyed the dual threats of contaminated theatrical gesture and the bodily spectacles enacted in the sacramental culture of unreformed religion. The kiss scene orchestrated by Cade appears to be just such a moment of somatic antitheatricality "built into" Shakespeare's play. As such, it raises the question not of "who was right" but of what it means to act history without becoming an idolater of the past. If the chronicles did not have to address this particular aspect of historical representation, they bequeathed to Shakespeare the emblematic gesture with which to do so.

Some Shakespearean critics have assumed that historical rebellion is logically prior to theatrical rebellion; others (influenced by cases like the Essex Rebellion) have suggested that theatrical rebellion was necessarily prior to actual rebellion. I have been arguing that in the specific case of Shakespeare's Cade, theatrical rebellion may actually tell us more about theater than it does about rebellion. The Cade episode, particularly the posthumous kiss, should be seen as a symptom of social unease about theatrical spectacles of incorporation and the reanimation of dead bodies in public rituals. The diverse representations of the kiss across the medieval and early modern periods tells us more about the common ground between chronicle accounts and history plays as vehicles for making dead mouths speak than it does about what Shakespeare's "own" views about social unrest may have been. Lurking somewhere below the obvious anxieties about the social consequences of rebellion, then, were perhaps more powerful concerns about the social reality of gesture (reformed or otherwise) as well as the empty actions of bodies that were now being given the power to animate historic fact on a new London stage.

NOTES

This essay had its origins in a paper presented at the International Congress on Medieval Studies in Kalamazoo, where I received very useful suggestions from Matthew Giancarlo and Steven Kruger. I am also grateful to Eric Jager, who suggested an example of a posthumous dumb show. Above all, my thanks to Sarah Kelen, sympathetic reader and patient editor.

1. All references to Shakespeare's *2 Henry VI* are taken from *The Arden Shakespeare*.

2. See Annabel Patterson, *Shakespeare and the Popular Voice*, chaps. 1–3; Helgerson, *Forms of Nationhood*, 235, 240; and Wilson, "'A Mingled Yarn.'"

3. The most complete work on these events is I. M. W. Harvey, *Jack Cade's Rebellion*. The rebel petitions are reproduced as appendix A, 186–91. Also informative is McLaren, *London Chronicles of the Fifteenth Century*, 67–72.

4. Holinshed, *Holinshed's Chronicles*, 3:225. All subsequent references to Holinshed refer to *Holinshed's Chronicles*. According to the Arden editor, Ronald Knowles, Shakespeare's primary source for the Cade rising was Holinshed's 1587 *Chronicle*. The accounts of Cade's Rebellion in the 1577 and 1587 versions of Holinshed differ slightly, since the 1587 version includes the rebel petitions. The account in Shakespeare's other chronicle source, Edward Hall, is virtually identical: "And this cruell tryraunt not content with the murder of the lorde Say, wente to Myle end, and there apprehended syr Iames Cromer, then shreue of Kent, and sonne in law to the sayd lord Say, & hym without confession or excuse heard, caused there likewyse to be hedded, and his head to be fixed on a poole, and with these two heddes, this blody butcher ntered into the citie agayn, and in despyte caused them in euery strete, kysse together, to the great detestacion of all the beholders" (221). All references to Edward Hall refer to Ellis, *Hall's Chronicle*.

5. The Vitellius manuscript has been edited by Kingsford in *Chronicles of London*. Further references are to this edition.

6. The description of the 1381 kiss appears in Holinshed 2:744. The 1381 kiss appears in

neither the Vitellius chronicle (which concentrates mainly on London events) nor in *Hall's Chronicle* (since Hall's account only begins with Henry IV).

7. See Walsingham, *Historia Anglicana*, vol. 2, p. 4. Walsingham's account echoes that of the abbey's almoner, John Gosforth, who himself narrowly escaped the rebels, but Walsingham ups the outrage ante by adding a substantial description of the saintly character of Prior Cambridge; thus, his death is transformed into a martydom. Gosforth's account is edited in Powell, *Rising in East Anglia*, 139–43.

8. On ideas about "truth and fiction" in medieval chronicles, see Spiegel, "Theory into Practice"; Robert Stein, *Reality Fictions*; and Lauryn Mayer, *Worlds Made Flesh*. On "emplotment," see Hayden White, *Metahistory*.

9. Scott, *Domination and the Arts of Resistance*.

10. Aers, "*Vox Populi*," 435.

11. Holinshed mentions that John Wrawe began his attack in Suffolk "the self same saturdaie after Corpus Christi day" (2:744). On the significance of Corpus Christi more generally, see Rubin, *Corpus Christi*.

12. Rebellion relies on contingent tactics, since the rebel does not have a place of his own. It is, in Michel de Certeau's words, the domain of "guileful ruses," wherein the rebel turns the language of power against itself, exploiting ambiguities and the "problematics of enunciation." See Certeau, *Practice of Everyday Life*, 36–40.

13. This detail echoes Walsingham almost exactly: "tamquam processionaliter circumeundo" (*Historia Anglicana*, vol. 2, p. 4).

14. Powell, *Rising in East Anglia*, 140.

15. See Holinshed 3:225; and for the Vitellius chronicler, Kingsford, *Chronicles of London*, 161.

16. See Erasmus, *Correspondence*, letter no. 103, to Fausto Andrelini, 193.

17. This episode is recounted in J. A. Burrow, *Gestures and Looks in Medieval Narrative*, 32.

18. For a general history of the public kiss in the Middle Ages, see Perella, *The Kiss Sacred and Profane*.

19. On the history of the feudal kiss, see Major, "'Bastard Feudalism' and the Kiss"; Carré, *Le baiser sur la bouche*; and Frijhoff, "Kiss Sacred and Profane."

20. The statute is quoted in Major, "'Bastard Feudalism' and the Kiss," 526.

21. See Petkov, *Kiss of Peace*.

22. From a Lollard treatise on images and pilgrimage edited by Hudson, *Selections from English Wycliffite Writings*, 87.

23. For Hugh of St. Victor, see the twelfth chapter of *De institutione novitiorum*, "De disciplina servanda in gestu." On gesture more generally, see Schmitt, *La raison des gestes*.

24. Galbert of Bruges, *Murder of Charles the Good*, 213.

25. This episode is recounted in Esther Cohen, *Crossroads of Justice*, 197.

26. Esther Cohen, *Crossroads of Justice*, 181.

27. Schmitt, "The Rationale of Gestures," 60.

28. On the spectacle of punishment in the medieval period, see Enders, *Medieval Theater of Cruelty*, who describes a shift from "intellectual to bodily hermeneutics" where "the inquiry into a legal subject and its parts becomes an inquiry into the body and its parts, a bodily invention" (38). This observation also applies to a posthumous subject: what begins as a rhetorical inquiry (a legal investigation into the victim's alleged misdoings) becomes a bodily parsing. On representations of medieval punishment more generally, see Merback, *The Thief, the Cross, and the Wheel*.

29. See Annabel Patterson, "Populism," in *Reading Holinshed's Chronicles*, esp. 190. This reading is typical of the way in which Patterson allows those she admires (Shakespeare, Holinshed) a more modern view of the causation behind lower-class political unrest. For her attempts to do this with Shakespeare, see Annabel Patterson, *Shakespeare and the Popular Voice*, chaps. 1–3.

30. On Hacket's Rising and Kett's Rebellion, see Fitter, "'Your Captain Is Brave'"; on the feltmaker's revolt in Southwark, see Wilson, "Mingled Yarn."

31. For those who believe that Shakespeare was sympathetic, see Annabel Patterson, *Shakespeare and the Popular Voice*; Fitter, "Your Captain Is Brave"; and Hattaway, "Rebellion." For the law-and-order Shakespeare, see Wilson, "Mingled Yarn"; and Helgerson, *Forms of Nationhood*. Paolo Pugliatti says the play can be read as simultaneously sympathetic and unsympathetic to popular unrest; see "'More than history can pattern.'" Other treatments of the Cade episode include Cartelli, "Jack Cade in the Garden"; Andy Wood, *Riot, Rebellion, and Popular Politics*; and Longstaffe, "'A Short Report and Not Otherwise.'" For thinking about the relation between rebellion and theatricality, see Mervyn James, "Crossroads of the Political Culture"; and Greenblatt, "Murdering Peasants."

32. On the dating of *2 Henry VI*, see the introduction to the play (entitled, as in the quarto, "The First Part of the Contention of the Two Famous Houses of York and Lancaster") in *The Norton Shakespeare*, 203–12.

33. See Ellis, *Hall's Chronicle*, 220.

34. On this aspect of medieval antitheatricality, see *Tretise of Miraculis Pleyinge*, 98–99. The writer here condemns plays as "signs without deeds"—that is, the outer expressions of the actors did not fully match their inner intentions.

35. Rainolds, *Th'overthrow of Stage-Plays*, 34.

36. See Diehl, *Staging Reform*, 64; and Barish, *Antitheatrical Prejudice*, esp. chap. 4, "Puritans and Proteans."

37. Anthony Munday, *Second and Third Blast of Retreat*, 95.

38. Tyndale and Frith, *Works*, 2:260. Similar complaints are found in Stubbes, *Anatomy of Abuses*, 141–45.

At Hector's Tomb: Fifteenth-Century Literary History and Shakespeare's *Troilus and Cressida*

William Kuskin

A number of recent monographs have argued for the importance of the fifteenth century in the development of authorship, humanism, and the formation of the English literary book.[1] These studies have complicated the easy division between medieval and early modern literary cultures. It remains difficult, however, to point to discrete examples of the ways fifteenth-century writing shapes early modern literature. As a result, the major literary historians of the late Middle Ages hew to period, bracketing the fifteenth-century literary culture as heterodox and decentralized, distinct from the poetics of modernity.[2] Yet to conceive of literary history as defined by period is to subordinate our disciplinary charge to the grand narratives of monarchical and ecclesiastical fortunes.[3] Certainly literature is politically inflected, but it is also formally structured, and it is to the history of these forms that writers of all ages turn. Such formal structure is at least twofold: rhetorical, in the received tropes and schemes of literary expression, and material, in the documentary modes that physically articulate and archive literature. I term such a double structure textual formalism, and suggest that because the fifteenth century introduced significant and enduring changes to the material form of literature—witness the refinement of the vernacular literary manuscript and the introduction of the printed book—we should not be surprised to find their modifications to the rhetorical axis lasting as well. Because this physical nexus is so important to literature, conceiving of this dual formalism in terms of temporality has less to do with a transition from one period to the next than with understanding how the material intrusion of chronologically older items into later points in time constitutes a powerful intellectual effect. The book, no less than the literature contained with its covers, possesses an imaginative relationship to time, and in what follows I hope to demonstrate how this transcends historical period. Thus I propose a literary history not of period and progress but of contingency and

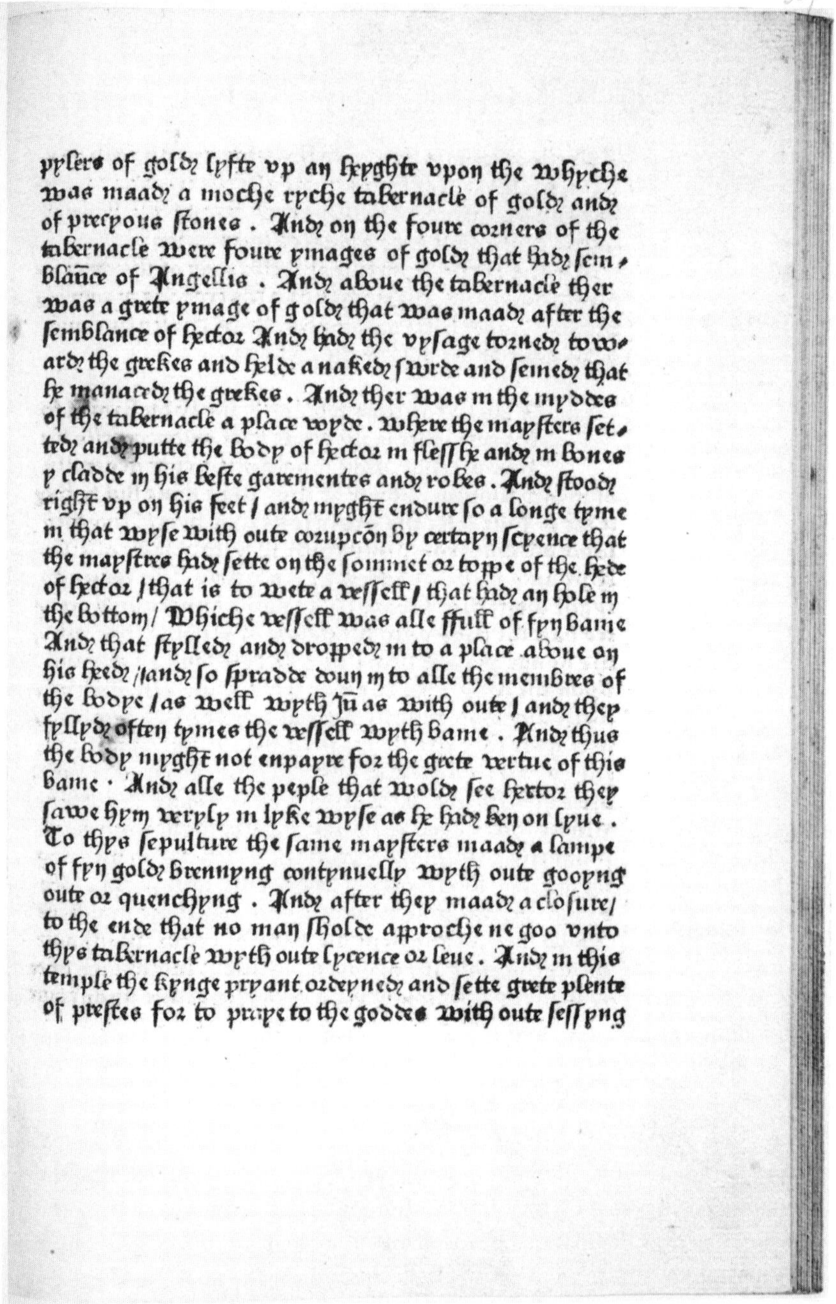

pplers of golde lyfte vp an heyghte vpon the whyche
was maade a moche ryche tabernacle of golde and
of precyous stones . And on the foure corners of the
tabernacle were foure ymages of golde that had sem‑
blaunce of Angellis . And aboue the tabernacle ther
was a grete ymage of golde that was maade after the
semblance of hector And had the vysage torned towe‑
arde the grekes and helde a naked swrde and semed that
he manaced the grekes . And ther was in the myddes
of the tabernacle a place wyde . where the maysters set‑
tede and putte the body of hector in flesshe and in bones
y cladde in his beste garementes and robes . And stode
right vp on his feet / and myght endure so a longe tyme
in that wyse with oute corupcon by certayn scyence that
the maystres had sette on the sommet or toppe of the hede
of hector / that is to wete a vessell / that had an hole in
the bottom / Whiche vessell was alle ffull of fyn bame
And that styllede and droppede in to a place aboue on
his hede / and so spradde doun in to alle the membres of
the bodye / as well wyth in as with oute / and they
fyllyd often tymes the vessell wyth bame . And thus
the body myght not enpayre for the grete vertue of this
bame . And alle the peple that wolde see hector they
sawe hym veryly in lyke wyse as he had ben on lyue .
To thys sepulture the same maysters maade a lampe
of fyn golde brennyng contynuelly wyth oute goyng
oute or quenchyng . And after they maade a closure /
to the ende that no man sholde approche ne goo vnto
thys tabernacle wyth oute lycence or leue . And in this
temple the kynge pryant ordeyned and sette grete plente
of prestes for to praye to the goddes with oute sessyng

Figure 1. Raoul Lefèvre. *Recuyell of the Histories of Troye* (Bruges: William Caxton, 1473/74), bk. 3, p. [308]r. *STC* 15375 RB 62222 (Photo: Reproduced by permission of The Huntington Library, San Marino, CA.)

continuity mediated by the book, of texts circulated against the grain of chronology and read in spite of their moments of origin.

Fifteenth-century writers and printers were well aware of the implications of such a textual formalism. One powerful example exists in book 3, chapter 18 of William Caxton's *Recuyell of the Histories of Troye*, the section in which Caxton translates Guido delle Colonne's ekphrasis of Hector's tomb (figure 1). Ornately crafted, the tomb features four golden pillars supporting a golden tabernacle encrusted with precious stones and images of angels. Above this is set "a grete ymage of gold that was maad after the semblance of hector" brandishing a naked sword at the Grecian encampment. "In the myddes of the tabernacle [in] a place voyde," Caxton continues, "the maysters setted and putte the body of hector in flesshe and in bones y cladde in his beste garementes and robes. And stood right vp on his feet . . . veryly in lyke wyse as he had ben on lyue." The tomb thus presents a double image: here is the semblance of Hector; here is Hector. Which is the more daunting, it asks, the golden statue or the standing body? Yet Hector's body is not presented as simply the natural original set out for comparison, innocent of human contrivance; rather, it is itself preserved so that it "myght endure so a longe tyme in that wyse with oute corupoun by certayn science," not embalming but simply a vessel placed on "the sommet or toppe of the hede of hector" that drips fluid "doun in to alle the membres of the bodye." Plasticity in representation is ekphrasis's governing theme, and so this passage gives us artifice as a hall of mirrors, for here there is no natural world to contrast human construction, only repeated forms of representation: the saturated body, the golden effigy, and the literary description.

In his epilogue to book 3 of *Recuyell*, Caxton makes a similar distinction between assumed naturalness and fabrication for the printed page, remarking that he has "practysed 7 lerned at my grete charge and dispense to ordeyne this said book in prynte after the maner 7 forme as ye may here see / and is not wreton with penne and ynke as other bokes ben." The *Recuyell* is printed in Caxton's Type 1, a typeface cut for him by the master type designer of the Low Countries, Johannes Veldener, to echo a Burgundian scribal book hand. By commenting on this echo, Caxton draws it to the reader's attention, underscoring that the page is not a transparent vehicle for literary meaning but a contrivance, a figuration evoking a prior form, a representation no more natural than Hector's tomb. If the ekphrasis of Hector's tomb sets the reader on notice regarding any presumption of naturalism in the story's evocation of the Trojan heroes, Caxton's epilogue turns this on the page itself, casting its typographical metallurgy as an ekphrasis of literary writing. Bruce Holsinger writes, "ekphrasitic poetics elaborate a kind of literary hall of mirrors: a recursive self-reflexivity that is also a self-reflectivity, a mode in and by which literary language gazes at the visual as a lens upon the beauty of its own performance."[4] Representation is everywhere—in the doubling figures, the evocation of the Trojan past, the page's letters—and nowhere is it to be taken for granted: troping in the *Recuyell* cuts across any easy division between literary content and printed form. Caxton's version of Hector's tomb achieves mimesis through a reproduction process that is jointly material and rhetorical, and that insists on the verisimilitude of its recreation of preexisting forms while underscoring its own artificiality.

My guiding question, then, is what does it mean to stand at Hector's tomb? On one level such a question asks after local literary history: what does it mean to follow out the Troy story in the wake of fifteenth-century writers? On another level, it asks after the story we tell of literary influence. That is, as we come across the ruins of Hector's tomb in the manuscripts and printed books that constitute our entryway into the past, what do we see? The traditional report has been of a chasm at the exact point of the fifteenth century, a rupture in the panorama of authority and inheritance that forces us to look backward to Chaucer's Middle Ages and forward to Shakespeare's Renaissance. Thus, when Shakespeare returns to the literary past in *Troilus and Cressida*, he is understood as engaging in a long look back, not to the fifteenth century he thought and wrote so much about but to Chaucer.[5] Accordingly, our view of Hector's tomb from the Renaissance cannot help but be retrospective, and this is of a piece with our understanding of Shakespeare's age, one sealed off from fifteenth-century tellings of Troy by milestones such as John Bale's 1548 literary history, Gavin Douglas's 1553 *Eneados*, and Chapman's 1598 translations—*Achilles Shield* and the *Seauen Bookes of Iliades*.[6] Still, there can be no doubt: Shakespeare's main source for *Troilus and Cressida* is chapters 12–17 of book 3 of William Caxton's *Recuyell of the Histories of Troye*.[7] The *Recuyell* has manifold import for literary history. As Caxton's first independent production, it initiates English printing. Reprinted no less than sixteen times, it appears to have had continuous readership through the eighteenth century.[8] In the prologue to the *Recuyell* Caxton announces that his text comes from three books chronicling the three falls of Troy, all of which were written by Burgundian court writer Raoul Lefèvre. Lefèvre developed the first two of these from Giovanni Boccaccio's *Genealogia deorum gentilium* and based the third on Guido delle Colonne's 1287 *Historia destructionis troiae*, itself a silent revision of Benoit de Sainte-Maure's twelfth-century *Roman de Troie*. Caxton offers his version of this final destruction of Troy, the *Recuyell's* third book, as a prose alternative to John Lydgate's *Troy Book*, and this association is carried into the sixteenth century, even as Caxton's persona as the first English printer is subordinated to his role as a translator, his language adjusted to fit contemporary standards. Read as merely a source for Shakespeare, the *Recuyell* is no more than a mumble from the caesura separating the medieval and the modern. Read as part of an ongoing exploration of English form that reproduces a network of texts dating from the thirteenth through the fifteenth centuries, the *Recuyell* significantly complicates the clear boundaries of period to argue for a notion of literary history as an ongoing process of inheritance, revision, and reproduction.

Thus, I suggest that we possess more elegant tools for reading literary history than periodization. In her introduction to the *PMLA*'s special issue on the history of the book, Leah Marcus points out "when critics speak of 'formalism,' they usually mean verbal form; in contrast, book historians keep redrawing the boundary separating the words themselves from extrinsic features such as spelling, spacing, and typeface. Far from replacing hermeneutics by pedantry, book history insists that every aspect of a literary work bears interpretation—even, or especially, those that look most contingent."[9] Medievalists, so long intimate with the history of the book through manuscript and early print studies, have been surprisingly slow to assert their role in the larger book history Marcus writes of here, and as Jessica Brantley discusses in a more recent *PMLA*, "Medieval studies can benefit enormously from helping to write this more capacious history of the material text."[10] In some sympathy with notions of New Formalism, I propose a return to formalism and note that English formalism is *textual*—the major authors are consistently mediated by scribes and printers, their meter counted out to a more exacting standard and their genres regularized; England, as opposed to the Continent, encountered printing as a specifically vernacular event.[11] English formalism is also *persistent*: witness the continual problems of authorial intention and canonicity in the Chaucerian manuscripts and Shakespearian quartos. This double investment explains the failure of either rhetorical formalism or historicity alone to account for literary history as the assertion of ideal categories over the literary object. I argue that in adapting a view of textual formalism we needn't subscribe to a firm line between form—whether derived from critical theory or literary formalism—and history. Both aspects are contained within the text, which is durable and reproduces its meaning in different temporalities.

The center of my argument is that the issue of representation so alive in the ekphrasis of Hector's tomb is a fundamental theme of Shakespeare's *Troilus and Cressida*, not by accident but by design. For Shakespeare followed fifteenth-century writers in the course of his play, and the trace of this engagement remains to us not merely in the quartos and folios labeled with this name but in the sixteenth-century witnesses to Caxton's and Lydgate's works such as William Copland's 1553 *Recuile of the Histories of Troie . . . Translated out of Frenche in to English by Wyllyam Caxton*, and Thomas Marshe's 1555 version of the *Troy Book*.[12] Speaking through the technology of the book, these texts all share a thematic interest in textual formalism; that is, they imagine literature as achieving its representative force by intertwining rhetorical and bookish forms. So I argue that because Shakespeare's *Troilus and Cressida* relies first and foremost upon William Caxton's *Recuyell of the Histories of Troy*, we should be cautious about broad and commonplace distinctions between medieval and modern literature, and instead should be willing to imagine how textual formalism sustains literature long after its inception. In such a conception of literary history, the descriptors "medieval" and "modern" become less important than the local organization of the rhetorical and the material literary forms that produce the individual pieces. My thesis, then, is threefold: first, literary history needs to account for the dynamic relationship between rhetorical and material forms. I term this textual formalism. Second, such a category for analysis reveals a persistent grouping of problems concerning authorship and this expanded sense of form for vernacular literature across the fifteenth, sixteenth, and seventeenth centuries. This essay explores form in Lydgate's, Caxton's, and Shakespeare's tellings of the Troy story. Finally, and more broadly, when folded over into temporality, textual formalism suggests an alterative mode of reading literary history, one that describes not medieval otherness and early modern origins but the structural problems of representation implicit in vernacular literary production.

For *Troilus and Cressida* is a problem, and its problems are inseparable from its material form.[13] These problems coalesce in the prefatory pieces that front the quarto and folio versions of the play. Both are qualifications of sorts, second thoughts to first attempts inserted after the printing process had begun. The first occupies two leaves asserted onto the initial version of the 1609 quarto, printed by George Eld for Richard Bonian and Henry Walley, and comprises a new title page and an epistle to the reader. This new title page reproduces the earlier title page's format—its engraved design and printer's identification are identical with the first version, which was apparently left standing in the *forme*—but renames the play from *The Historie of Troylus and Cresseida* to *The Famous Historie of Troylus and Cresseid* (figure 2).[14] The new page also replaces the original title's performance history ("*As it was acted by the Kings Maiesties / seruants at the Globe*") with plot synopsis ("*Excellently expressing the beginning / of their loues, with the conceited wooing / of Pandarus* Prince of *Licia*"). This is followed by the epistle (¶2r-v), which Leslie A. Fiedler terms "the earliest extended response to Shakespeare as a writer of comedy."[15] Titled "A neuer writer, to an euer reader. Newes," the epistle contradicts the February 7, 1603, permission to James Roberts in the Stationers' Register that reports "The booke of Troilus and Cresseda as yt is acted by my lord Chamberlens Men," as well as the original title page's production history, by announcing "Eternall reader, you haue heere a new play, neuer stal'd with the Stage, neuer clapper-clawd with the palmes of the vulger, and yet passing full of the palme comicall."[16] Hence the problems with *Troylus*: the play is "famous" yet claims never to have been acted; it is a history full of the "palme comicall"; and its original state occurs not once but twice.[17] The epistle attempts to consolidate these problems by connecting the play's literary kind (history or comedy) to its material form (theatrical record or freestanding commodity) and offering up a single generic entity—the published, but not played, quarto comedy—but the connection is difficult at best, undercut by the print history surrounding it and the labored explanation within it.

THE
Famous Hiſtorie of
Troylus *and* Creſſeid.

Excellently expreſſing the beginning
of their loues, with the conceited wooing
of *Pandarus* Prince of *Licia.*

Written by William Shakeſpeare.

LONDON
Imprinted by *G.Eld* for *R. Bonian* and *H. Walley*, and
are to be ſold at the ſpred Eagle in Paules
Church-yeard, ouer againſt the
great North doore.
1609.

Figure 2. *The Famous Historie of Troylus and Cresseid* (London: George Eld for Richard Bonian and Henry Walley, 1609), title page. *STC* 22332. (Photo: By permission of the Folger Shakespeare Library.)

These problems are obviated in the First Folio, which rigorously defines the plays within according to author and genre in the authoritative folio-book format. The fit is not quite so seamless in quarto: cheap, dispensable, and unbound, the quartos grasp at formal descriptions to articulate what they are; so their title pages gesticulate broadly with literary terms before resorting to plot summary while alternately claiming, ignoring, or feinting at authorial identity. We can parse these problems into discrete instances and understand them as the specific confusions of individual printers, but collectively they speak of the difficulty of matching rhetorical and material literary categories. So the quartos exist in a transformational state somewhere between ephemera—the playwright's imagination, the company's improvisation, the live performance, the pirate's recreation, the foul papers—and the definitive single-author book. As a result, they possess the indeterminate literary authority of "bad," memorial, or draft texts. Thus the *Troylus and Cresseid* epistle takes up a problem central to the quartos overall: literary form, or of how to classify—materially as a book and rhetorically as an artwork—the play's representational status.

If genre is the epistle's theme, transformation is its mode. "And were but the vaine names of commedies changde for the titles of Commodities, or of Playes for Pleas," it imagines, "you should see all those grand censors, that now stile them such vanities, flock to them for the maine grace of their grauities: especially this authors Commedies, that are so fram'd to the life, that they serue for the most common Commentaries, of all the actions of our liues" (¶2r). Changing the title from comedy to commodity or fixing it in legal terms as a plea, the Never Writer tells us, makes the play's benefits so obvious that even the vain censor would see them.[18] This is just what printer George Eld's revision has done to the title page: it has transformed the play into a commodity through the techniques at his disposal. The new title page revises the play's name and erases its performance history to make it an autonomous textual object; accordingly, the epistle helps this transformation along by moving the contents from history to comedy and then to commodity. The point is that the epistle is not naive to the complexities of form; however hyperbolically, it presents a transformation of rhetorical and material genres to articulate whatever coherency it can for the quarto as a unified object.

The possibility of transformation is within the epistle in other ways as well. For example, the epistle stakes out a number of finite subject positions—it is written by the "neuer writer," who later assumes the first person, "I"; we are the "euer" or "Eternall" reader, later "you"; there is also the theatre-going audience, the censors, and the author. The "never writer" initially casts distinctions between these groups—writers write and readers read, the audience is vulgar, the censors are obtuse—which he soon clouds through the very notion of commodity circulation. Thus, if the censors flock to the author's comedies when they are renamed, the "never writer" hypothosizes, "when he is gone, and his Commedies out of sale, you will scramble for them, and set up a new English Inquisition" (¶2v). Both censor and reader not only jostle for texts, they do so in a strangely clerical mode: the censors apparently suppress them and the readers set up an English Inquisition. As much as this inquisition is specifically English, the readers are vulgar clerics at that. Reader, censor, and audience member are all ultimately connected through their mutual consumption and regulation of English texts. In its slippery way, then, the epistle suggests that textual transformation organizes individuals— reader, writer, author, censor, audience—into a collectivity. Indeed, all these subject positions come together in the play, which comments on "our liues." Thus in delivering the work from "the smoaky breath of the multitude" (¶2v), the epistle effectively recreates the disparate collective of a theatre-going audience as a textual audience, looking ahead to the constellations of identification between insular community and anonymous commerce, between private and public, that Pandarus makes overt in his closing address to the "Brethren and sisters of the hold-ore trade."[19] The epistle argues that the latent power of comedy to unify—a power capable of moving from audience to reader in the transformational process of its own construction—is made palpable as the work becomes a textual commodity. This recognition is essential to the play's authority, for it is the engagement with the author's wit through the text that changes people so that they "haue found that witte there, that they neuer found in them-selues" (¶2r). If genre is the epistle's theme and transformation its mode, literary authority is its product.

Transformation is also a theme in the preface to the First Folio's version of *Troylus and Cressida*, albeit in a different register. Unlisted in the opening catalog, *The Tragedie of Troylus and Cressida* is a late addition to the folio, one only announced on the first page to the play itself, which is wedged between *The Life of King Henry the Eight* and *The Tragedy of Coriolanus*. Again, this late addition grapples with issues of genre. On the one hand, it summons up yet a third literary genre to describe the text, "tragedie"; on the other, it reinscribes the play in a supremely literary material genre, the single-author edition. And again, the modification is essentially an afterthought, for there are a number of variations of the play's initial page. The play seems to have first been placed after *Romeo and Juliet* (a version of the First Folio remains with the last page of *Romeo* on its opening recto) and later inserted after *Henry the Eight* with an entirely blank opening recto.[20] The final version includes a prologue on this recto (figure 3). Like the epistle it replaces, the prologue enacts a formal reading of the play. Ostensibly, this reading is entirely concerned with narrative: "IN Troy there lyes the Scene: From Iles of Greece," the prologue opens, continuing,

> The Princes Orgillous, their high blood chaf'd
> Haue to the Port of Athens sent their shippes
> Fraught with the ministers and instruments
> Of cruell Warre.

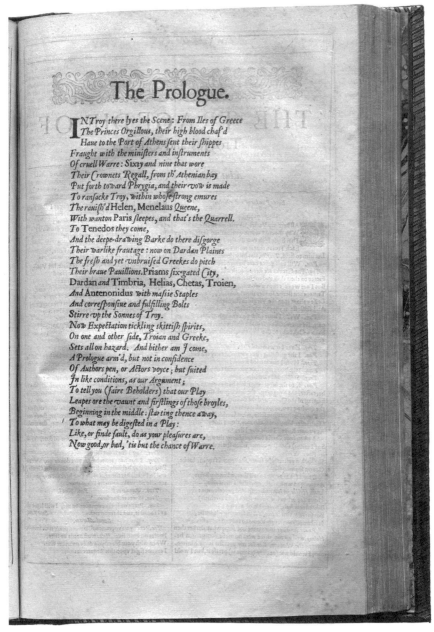

On this level the prologue orients the reader to the plot, necessary because, as it points out, the play itself "Leapes ore the vaunt and firstlings of those broyles, / Beginning in the middle: starting thence away." Plot leads directly to genre, however; on a second level the prologue's epic troping and heroic tone position it on the high ground between history and tragedy, paralleling its physical place in the Folio's collection of plays. On a third level the prologue's scene setting is self-consciously theatrical, even as it is textual: addressing the readers as "faire Beholders," it announces that "our Play" jumps into the middle of things, so as to cover only "what may be digested in a Play." Just as the epistle constructs shifting categories of transformations—from history to comedy to commodity, from individual reader to textual community, from ephemera to literature—the prologue transforms the play once again. Underscoring its gravity and theatricality to produce the play as a textual experience of drama, the prologue retrofits *Troylus and Cresseid* to the context of the folio collection of stage plays. Overall, then, both prologue and epistle are formal pieces designed to work in conjunction with the material format of the individual text. Their dynamic interaction is imbricated in specific questions of genre—of the literary genres of history, tragedy, and comedy, and the print genres of the quarto play text and the single-author folio edition. It cannot be otherwise. As the text is produced through jointly rhetorical and material forms, the two are inseparable for a written document to perform successfully the authority we accord literature.

Like the epistle before it, then, the prologue is caught up in a transformation of genre from an ephemeral action—a play that leaps and vaunts—to a textual thing:

> And hither am J come,
> A Prologue arm'd, but not in confidence
> Of Authors pen, or Actors voyce; but suited
> Jn like conditions, as our Argument.

As opposed to the quartos, which teeter on the brink of incoherence as they attempt to produce literary authority in a textual form, the Folio is so confident in the efficacy of its generic classifications that any loosening in its hold, any reminder that these once were performance pieces, any suggestion that the plays leap and vault of their own imaginative accord, appears a mere feint and ultimately underscores the Folio's definitive nature as a record of Shakespeare's work. As neither author's pen nor actor's voice, this prologue is fundamentally different from, say, that of *Pericles*, where Gower enters as an author from the past. For this is a textual voice, an overview of "our Argument," a reading. Specifically, the prologue reads the first eleven chapters of the *Recuyell*'s book 3, presenting a montage of essential moments. It sketches the *Recuyell*'s plot, and turning to Copland's 1553 edition we can read of the "sixty & nine . . . [that] assembled at the porte of Athenes," of their arrival at "the porte of Thenedon," of the encounter on "a greate playne . . . out of the gate named Dardan," and, finally, of the "sixe principal gates: of Whome that one was named Dardane, ye seco*n*de Timbria, the thirde Helyas, the fourthe Chetas, the fifte Troyen, and the sixt Antenorides."[21] The prologue picks out lexical details from the *Recuyell* as well, such as Priam's definition of the Greeks as "orguyllous and proude," that they are "chauffyd," that the Grecian "qua-rel" is specifically that Helen is "rauysshed," and that their tents are "pauyllon[s]."[22]

These details locate the prologue's reading almost exactly. Caxton first printed the *Recuyell* in Bruges in 1473 or 1474; it was then revised and reissued in London by his successor, Wynkyn de Worde, in 1502 as the *Recuyles*. In 1553 William Copland collated these two editions into a third, the *Recuile*—closer to Caxton's original but following de Worde's double-column format and indexing conveniences while adding chapter headings in roman type. This text was, in turn, "Newly corrected, and the English much amended, by *William Fiston*" for Thomas Creede and Valentine Simmes's 1596/7 *Destruction of Troy . . . Translated out of French into English, by W. Caxton*. De Worde's edition names the last of the six gates of Troy "ammorydes," not "Antenorides" as in all the other editions.[23] When the prologue cites the six gates, then, it reveals the particularities of its reading, eliminating de Worde's edition as a possible reference. Similarly, Phiston mod-ernized Caxton's language for the 1596/7 version, substituting "pride," "insolent," "high minded," and "hautinesse" for "orgulous" at every turn.[24] The prologue's lan-guage thus also rules out Phiston's edition, and points specifically to either Cop-land's 1553 *Recuile* or, more speculatively, to Caxton's original.

The prologue sets the scene, therefore, in both literal and figural terms. Lit-erally, it provides a context for the play's plot by formulating a review of Caxton's Troy story, indeed an explicit reading of Caxton or Copland that hangs on the gates of Troy and the word "orgulous." Figuratively, the prologue defines the text's genre as a play within a definitive collection and, cuing the reader to the upcom-ing "orgulous" tone as high and somewhat old fashioned, suggests its subgenre as a tragedy, though its physical location in the Folio's organizational framework hedges this definition by placing it in a liminal zone between genres.

Appearing neither in Chaucer's *Troilus and Criseyde* nor in Lydgate's *Troy Book*, this term, "orgulous," is not Chaucerian. For Phiston, it is archaic and thor-oughly negative, a synonym for excessive pride. Caxton uses it in this manner as well, especially as a doublet with "proud." For instance, in his 1474 *The Game and Play of Chess* he writes, "For hit happeth ofetyme that the ministris by theyr pryde and orgueyll subuerte Iustice and do no ryght," and in the 1477 *Historie of Iason* translates "Men saye / that the most orguilloust & proudest creature that is / is the deuill."[25] Like the *Recuyell*, both of these texts come from Caxton's experience of Burgundian literary culture: printed in Bruges immediately after the *Recuyell*,

The Game and Play of Chess is Caxton's second English text, and though he prints *Iason* in England, it is also by Lefèvre. "Orgulous" appears in a text authored by an Englishman as well, and it appears throughout the *Le Morte Darthur*, which features, among other instances, the "castel Orgulous" in chapter 3 and the names "Sire Bellangere le orgulous" in chapter 11 and "Belliau*n*ce le orgulus" in chapter 41. King Arthur comments on it as an attribute of his character about which he is circumspect: "Thenne arose Arthur / and wente to syr Vwayn and said to sire Tristram we haue as we haue deserued / For thurgh our orgulyte we demaunded bataille of you."[26] One is not always so self-reflective. For example, the first book of the *Recuyell* recounts "orguyllous serpentes," and Bellephon and Persus come upon "beastes [that] were cruell and full of orgueyll"—these creatures are no doubt mighty and proud but inchoately so, not in the sense implied by Arthur's self-criticism.[27] The *OED* traces the word's origins to "an unattested West Germanic noun with the sense 'excellence, pride' (compare the corresponding adjective represented by Old High German *urguol*, 'famous, renowned')," and this root meaning describes Caxton's use well: orgulous is a sense of excellence; perhaps justified, perhaps inarticulate, it is nevertheless so extreme as to be dangerous, to be Satanic.[28]

    Book 3 of the *Recuyell* is the most orgulous of all. Where Caxton uses the word four times in books 1 and 2, he uses it five times in book 3 alone—all before the second battle scene and therefore in the portion mapped out by the First Folio's prologue. This is concentrated orgulty. In book 3, chapter 8, Agamemnon addresses the Grecian host at Thenedon "as a good captaine ought," announcing "that it please the gods that it be wythout pryde and felonnye. For it is so that of the sine of pride growe all other vyces, and that ye goddes resist and wythstonde the orgulous and proude people. And therfore we ought to put away pride fro our werkes."[29] Agamemnon names orgulous pride a sin and suggests that the Grecian mission be without it, a dispassionate act of martial justice. He continues, "kynge Pryant dyd dooe requyre vs by hys specyal messangers that we should rendre to him hys Syster Eione: that by our Orguyell and Pryde we woulde not delyuer her agayne, and yf we had delyueryd and sente her home agayne: these euelles had neuer happened."[30] Here Agamemnon voices Priam's accusation from book 3, chapter 1: "for so litle a cause or trespasse as ye know how the grekes by theyr orguyel ben comen in to thys countrey. . . . And for these thynges me semeth that it shoulde be well reason that by the helpe of ye goddes that resist the orguyl-lous and proude."[31] Yet Agamemnon delivers this observation flatly, not to contest Priam's point so much as to affirm it. Thus, he continues, "And there is none of vs that knoweth what shal happen to hym good or euyl." Agamemnon goes on to insist on the rightness of the Grecian claim, to predict the destruction of Troy, and to announce that posterity will favor the Greeks, but ultimately he offers no greater guarantee than this series of observations: the gods resist the orgulous and proud, we could have avoided war, we did not, and none of us now knows his fate. Through our orgulty we demanded battle of you, laments Arthur to Sir Tristram, but reflecting upon this truth, however profoundly, hardly mitigates its consequences. *Orgulous* defines the third destruction of Troy not simply as of pride but of a pride that, although self-knowing, plunges headlong into self-destruction.

"Now good, or bad, 'tis but the chance of Warre," closes the prologue to the Folio's *Troylus*, and Caxton's Agamemnon would agree, for both stories write war as the unavoidable and unpredictable consequence of self-proclaimed excellence. The characters in both stories recognize this fact, but are far too orgulous to stop themselves. Indeed, in the Folio version of *Troylus and Cressida*, Ulysses thinks through exactly this problem with Nestor ("I haue a young conception in my braine, / Be you my time to bring it to some shape").[32] "This 'tis," he reflects,

> Blunt wedges riue hard knots: the seeded Pride
> That hath to this maturity blowne vp
> In ranke *Achilles*, must or now be cropt,
> Or shedding breede a Nursery of like euil
> To ouer-bulke vs all.

According to Ulysses, Achilles's pride is a wedge in the Grecian alliance and undoes the knot that binds their union. Such is Ulysses's thinking earlier in the act, when he announces "This Chaos, when Degree is suffocate, / Followes the choaking," which is to say that such pride will overwhelm the collectivity.[33] Ulysses mulls the metaphor over with Nestor, and by turns Achilles's pride is a wedge loosening a knot of rope and, simultaneously, a chisel splitting a knot in a plank of wood. From woodworking to horticulture, Achilles's "seeded pride" is growing, and growing recklessly, becoming bloated and blocking the sun from the rest of the plants in the nursery—as Ulysses said earlier, so follows the choking. This subtlety with metaphor marks a powerful difference between *Troilus and Cressida* and the *Recuyell*, which is far less delicate with language. Regardless, both are concerned with the proper representation of heroic excellence.

Given this overriding theme, Ulysses has less interest in eradicating orgulty than in managing it. He asserts that the Greeks are disorganized, but this assertion provides no brake, no caution against self-inflation. In fact, he implies that perhaps the Greeks are not orgulous enough ("Degree being vizarded"). Thus the conception in Ulysses's brain ages, and the metaphor (pride is a wedge, pride is a chisel) changes to pride as a pruning knife, transforming its destructive force into a tool for Grecian victory, exactly the turn Ulysses takes later in the play when he maneuvers Achilles into meeting Hector in combat. In this, the entire speech on degree never attains the introspection or regret of Arthur's one-sentence remark to Sir Tristan. Indeed, just the opposite is true: rapacious self-promotion is exactly as necessary in the public sphere as Achilles is to the Grecian cause. For Ulysses, therefore, Achilles's greatest offense is not his orgulty but his willingness to indulge in misrepresentation: "He Pageants vs," Ulysses complains, "He acts thy Greatnessse in."[34] The utility of pageantry is a given in the *Recuyell* and *Troylus* alike, one Ulysses can hardly object to: strutting and posturing are both stories' means of introducing heroes. Rather, Ulysses lays a specific problem of genre at Achilles's tent. For according to Ulysses, Achilles's orgulty makes the Grecian heroes ridiculous:

> From his deepe Chest, laughes out a lowd applause,
> Cries excellent, 'tis *Agamemnon* iust.
> Now play me *Nestor*; hum, and stroke thy Beard . . .
> Tis *Nestor* right . . .
> Or, giue me ribs of Steele.

Ulysses cannot even summon up Achilles's rendition of him, only comment obliquely that Achilles calls his kind of strategizing "Bed-worke, Mapp'ry, Closset-Warre." Achilles mixes genres, transforming the heroic into farce: "As stuffe for these two, to make paradoxes"; he characterizes the Grecian princes not as the stuff of history or tragedy but of a subgenre of theatrical entertainment at the Inns at Court.[35] Ulysses names this kind of pageantry "pale, and bloodlesse Emulation," and this defines his objection overall: the representation is not robust and full blooded. It borders on sickly. "What is mesmerizing about the idea of emulation," writes Eric Mallen, is that it brings together competition and representation, "For, as a mimetic act, emulation is always to some degree an aesthetic one as well. It is a poetics of success through imitative conduct."[36] This sense of emulation is exactly at issue in Hector's tomb, for, following Guido, Caxton describes art as appearing to emulate nature—the golden statue mimicking the real body, the typeface indistinguishable from pen and ink—when in fact it competes with layers of contrivance in the preserved corpse and the technology of writing. So the threat of sickness: Hector's tomb epitomizes the attempt to represent adequately heroic excellence and the equivalent risk that such an attempt will miss its mark to become bloated and appear merely gaudy, or, worse, distended. This is a worry that thoroughly permeates *Troilus*: Ulysses observes that the "enterprize is sicke," Thersites ruminates on the "botchy core" at the heart of things, and the undertow of prostitution, with its hazy connection to disease and plague, taints any possibility for straightforward romantic love in the play.[37] In both Caxton and Shakespeare, representation walks the line between veneration and corruption, a truth for fifteenth- as well as sixteenth-century writing.

The Shakespearian version of the Troy story nuances the existing interest in orgulty by bringing to the story a sophistication in language that frames every passage, and not just a highlighted ekphrasis, as a meditation on the limits of trope. With this, it intertwines material and rhetorical formalism in the characters' very lines. For example, Hector finds himself read by Achilles, and blusters at the book simile, arguing that it specifically fails to account for the depth he would claim for himself: "O like a Booke of sport thou'lt reade me ore: / But there's more in me then thou vnderstand'st."[38] Similarly Troilus, Cressida, and Pandarus are all too aware that posterity will flatten them out, will reduce them to words, characters as letters on a page rather than as people: "Let all constant men be *Troylusses*, all false women *Cressids*, and all brokers betweene, Panders," Pandarus proclaims with a bravado that cloaks the truth that they are already booked, already read over by generations of readers, already flattened into icons.[39] In this respect, it strikes me as somewhat disingenuous to read Shakespeare's Cressida in comparison to Chaucer's Criseyde, because to do so is to imagine that the thousands of editions of the *Recuyell* and the *Troy Book* that stand between them had never been published, to pretend that reader and writer come to this character in a vacuum, as if she had no intervening figuration in English literature other than Chaucer's. The obvious truth is that Achilles, Hector, Troilus, Pandarus, Cressida, and the rest are already entombed, already representations of a prior figuration speaking about the very process that simultaneously constitutes and limits their evocation. So, though they may not possess the emotional depth of Malory's and Caxton's Arthur, these characters betray a sophistication about the very status of representations that eludes the *Recuyell*'s blocky personages. "Words, words, meere words," moans Troilus, "no matter from the heart," and to say this is to reflect on how Shakespeare's characters are like Hector's corpse—representations with the semblance of life but lacking internal depth.[40] In this they are indeed self aware, but obliquely so, as Holsinger's self-reflexive and thus self-reflective commentary on literary form, rather than as psychologically real.

"Orgulous" is thus a powerful sign at the head of the *Tragedie of Troylus and Cressida*, though at our first encounter we may not know how to read it. Upon reflection, it guides the reader in a number of ways. Literally, it marks the prologue's reading matter. On this level the prologue's opening lines, "IN Troy there lyes the Scene: From Iles of Greece," amount to much the same as the first line of Caxton's third book, "For to entre tha*n* into ye mater," in that they both invite the reader to lay aside much of the story and concentrate on the war over Helen.[41] So the prologue signals its reading of Caxton's *Recuyell*, or more likely Copland's *Recuile*, and indeed much of *Troilus and Cressida* draws from the eleven chapters it covers: for example, the Trojan women at the city walls; Hector's caution about, and Paris's endorsement of war; and Ulysses's description of Troilus as "a second hope, as fairely built as *Hector*," forecast by Caxton's description that "he resembled moche to Hector, and was the seconde after hym of prowesse."[42] The action of Shakespeare's play occurs from chapter 11's "second battle" through Hector's death in chapter 17, and here too we find much of the play adumbrated by Caxton's prose. Act 4 uses Hector's recognition of Ajax (picking up the specific term, "cosyn germayne") and the interview in Achilles's tent ("Achilles behelde hym gladlye for asmuche as he had neuer seen hym vnarmed").[43] The rush of act 5 draws out the Trojan attempt to dissuade Hector from combat as he and Troilus arm, and also lifts the name of Hector's horse ("Galathe"), Diomedes's capture and delivery of Troilus's horse to Cressida, Hector's penchant for taking armor, his encounter with Achilles in which Achilles is forced to retire, and Achilles' questionable victory.[44] The burning misogyny that underwrites the play overall is a set piece in the *Recuyell*, one its narrative voice often pauses to mitigate or explain away.[45] In fact, the play's somewhat abrupt ending stops just before chapter 18 of the *Recuile*, the chapter describing "the ryche sepulture of Hector." More broadly, the prologue's use of "orgulous" stakes out *Troylus and Cressida*'s overriding genre and theme. Generically, it marks a transformation of narrative material from the category of *recueil* (*OED*, n., "A literary compilation or collection") into a textual drama leaning from history to tragedy.[46] Thematically, the prologue concentrates this drama on the way self-approbation leads to self-destruction. In this, it folds the physical problems of genre into the play itself. That is, just as the quarto's title page and epistle focus on the movement from ephemeral production to commodity, denying the one in order to emphasize the other, the Folio's prologue positions the play as about literary genre and heroic representation. Indeed, it wraps plot, genre, and theme together to suggest a number of relationships between fifteenth-century prose story and seventeenth-century dramatic text.

It is worth pausing over what these relationships imply for the print history of Shakespeare's plays. The version of the *Recuyell* printed chronologically closest to Eld's 1609 quarto of *Troylus* is Creede and Simmes's 1596/7 *Destruction of Troy*, modernized by Phiston. Creede and Simmes were far and away the most ambitious printers of Shakespeare's quartos, printing for publishers such as Thomas Millington, Andrew Wise, Thomas Pavier, and Nathaniel Butter.[47] The closeness between Eld's quarto of *Troylus* and their version of the *Recuyell* suggests that that the products connect across various generic boundaries. That is, finding in the quarto format a certain generic looseness, Creede, Simmes, Eld, Bonian, and Walley exploit it, bringing to market products that are associated in plot and theme. Indeed, Creede and Simmes produce the *Destruction* so as to separate out the final book, printed by Simmes in 1597. This third book has a unique title page (figure 4), suggesting its autonomy as a product, and with grill-work identical to that Eld used on his versions of *Troylus*. The two texts make a matched set. The strategy of matching prose and drama is not unheard of in Shakespearean publications: witness interconnections between the 1609 quarto of *Pericles* printed by William White for Henry Gosson, and George Wilkins's 1608 *The Painfull Aduentures of Pericles Prince of Tyre as it was lately presented by the worthy and ancient poet Iohn*

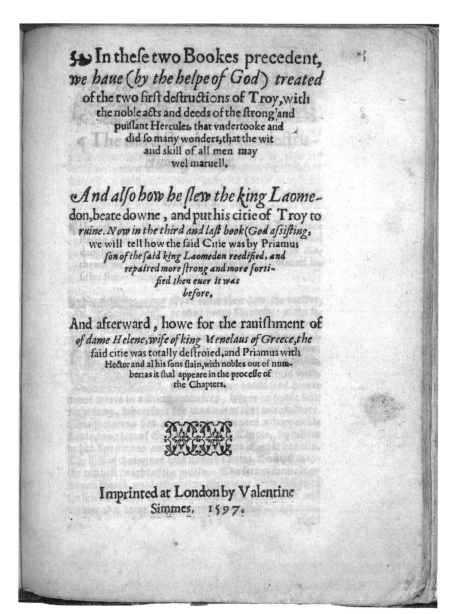

In these two Bookes precedent,
we haue (by the helpe of God) treated
of the two first destructions of Troy, with
the noble acts and deeds of the strong and
puissant Hercules, that vndertooke and
did so many wonders, that the wit
and skill of all men may
wel maruell.

And also how he slew the king Laome-
don, beate downe, and put his citie of Troy to
ruine. Now in the third and last book (God assisting,
we will tell how the said Citie was by Priamus
son of the said king Laomedon reedified, and
repaired more strong and more forti-
fied then euer it was
before.

And afterward, howe for the rauishment of
of dame Helene, wife of king Menelaus of Greece, the
said citie was totally destroied, and Priamus with
Hector and al his sons slain, with nobles out of number: as it shal appeare in the processe of
the Chapters.

Imprinted at London by Valentine
Simmes. 1597.

Figure 4. Raoul Lefèvre. *The Auncient Historie of the Destruction of Troy* (London: Thomas Creede, 1596/97), title page. *STC* 15379. (Photo: By permission of the Folger Shakespeare Library.)

Gower, printed by Thomas Purfoot for Butter.[48] In fact, there are a number of similarities between these two pairs, *Pericles* and *The Painfull Aduentures*, and *Troylus* and the *Recuyell*: both *Pericles* and *Troilus and Cressida* have a strong English literary history, the one stemming from Gower, the other from Caxton; both, too, have an awkward relationship to the Folio, the one eliminated entirely, the other a late addition. From the vantage point of an established literary history the First Folio is a print masterstroke, yet it is only one material articulation of the possible ways of collating Shakespearean authority, one not necessarily exclusive of other connections. For by 1623 Creede and Simmes had not only printed Phiston's 1596/7 version of the *Destruction of Troy* but Creede had gone on to print another edition in 1607, as had Barnard Alsop in 1617. The Folio was, of course, reprinted in 1632, 1663, and 1664; the *Recuyell*, too, was reprinted across this period, in 1636, and after that in 1663, 1670, 1676, 1680, and 1684.[49] The significant dates here—the 1597 *Destruction of Troy*, the Stationer's report that the play was acted in 1603, Creede's 1607 solo edition of the *Destruction*, Eld's 1609 quartos of *Troylus*, and the seventeenth-century reprinting of Shakespeare's and Caxton's editions—point to a complex intertwining of literary-commercial interests in which prose and play versions appear as complementary products. *Troilus and Cressida* and the *Recuyell* are dynamic partners in print, articulating two literary genres against one another in the symbolic production of literature in a material form.

Such dynamism is at the heart of Caxton's own observations. In his epilogue to book 2 of the *Recuyell*, an epilogue that survives Phiston's modernization, Caxton explains his rationale for translating the third book: "And as for the thyrd booke whiche treateth of the generall and laste dystruccion of Troye," he observes, "It nedeth not to translate it in to Englishe, for asmuche as that worshypfull and religious man dan Iohn lydgate monke of Burye dyd translate it but late, after whose worke I feare to take vpon me that am not worthy to beare his penner & ynke horne after hym, to meddle me in that werke."[50] The problem is one of literary precedence: Lefèvre's third book duplicates Lydgate's *Troy Book*; both are translations of Guido delle Colonne's *Historia destructionis troiae*. Caxton presents this issue of literary history as one of humility (his unworthiness to carry Lydgate's pen and ink horn), and this has tended to overwhelm the significance of his discussion for recent scholarship. Witness James Simpson's argument that "the works of Leland and Bale . . . are, however, the first attempts to shape a British, or even English, tradition as an identifiable national tradition of letters."[51] Simpson's claim for the originality of sixteenth-century writers denies exactly Caxton's point—Caxton premises his authority on his ability to articulate English literary history, to comprehend Lydgate's biography ("dan Iohn lydgate monke of Burye"), to assess the texts' circulation in English ("as ferre as I knowe it is not had in prose in our tonge"), and to account for their transmission ("he translated after some other Auctor"). He does this repeatedly in his prologues and epilogues when he praises Chaucer by weaving his encomium from lines of Lydgate, when he frames his romances in terms of the array of vernacular languages, and when he links multiple texts in series.[52] As Caxton's epilogue to book 2 of the *Recuyell* continues, it is his implicit control of the categories of authorship and literary history that ground his introduction of a new literary genre—the printed English prose *receuil*—as related to, but different from, the preexisting genre of the English verse manuscript. According to Caxton, the introduction of this new form depends upon the different aesthetic appeal inherent in different generic forms, as he says, "dyuerse menne ben of dyuerse desyres. Some to rede in ryme and metre, and some in prose." Rather than some sort of instability in authorship or murkiness about literary history—all to be sorted out in the sixteenth century—by the fifteenth century the material text is understood to embody a process of reproduction of vernacular literary history in its relationship to generic form.

What is amazing about the technology of the book is that, because Caxton's *Recuyell* is continually reprinted, this dynamic reproduction process is never fixed at a single chronological point in time and so never stops articulating a relationship between genres, never stops seeking out new relationships, and never stops transforming the text. Books endure: whether we imagine the First Folio's prologue an intrinsic part of the original play or an afterthought added in the final production process—a passage intruded from the lost prompt book, a notation added by Shakespeare in some final authorial revision, a contrivance of one of the Folio's editors—it announces that Copland's 1553 edition (if not Caxton's original) remained in use even as Phiston was revising Caxton's orgulous language and his work was being reprinted by Creede, Alsop, and others. So the quarto and folio versions of *Troilus* are involved in the very process of generic negotiation that is articulated in terms of verse and prose by Caxton, *simply because Caxton's text was still being read.* Indeed, the project is adumbrated *not* by Caxton's relationship to Lydgate in the fifteenth century but by his relationship to Lydgate in the sixteenth and seventeenth centuries. For example, the connection Caxton casts between his 1473/4 printed *Recuyell* and some unidentified manuscript of Lydgate's *Troy Book* is recast for the sixteenth-century reader as between the *Recuyell* and, perhaps, Richard Pynson's 1513 *Troy Book*,[53] or between Copland's 1553 *Recuile* and Thomas Marshe's 1555 *Troy Book*, or between any combination of these editions. For example, in the "the pistle to the reader" that begins Marshe's edition, Robert Braham discusses "Caxtons recueil" (which he terms "but a longe tedious and brayneles bablyng, tendyng to no end"), and in this way recreates the tension Caxton himself perceived in the fifteenth century—but does so by triumphing Lydgate for the sixteenth.[54] For the seventeenth-century reader, this network of associations is expanded even more by the ensuing editions of the *Recuyell* and by Thomas Purfoot's 1614 *The Life and Death of Hector . . . Written by Iohn Lidgate monke of Bery.*[55] These texts did not go unread. John Tatlock sources to Caxton's *Recuyell* and Lydgate's *Troy Book* Robert Greene's 1587 *Euphues his censure to Philautus*, George Peele's 1589 *Tale of Troy*, Thomas Heywood's 1609 *Troia Britanica*, 1611 *Golden Age*, 1613 *Brazen Age* and *Siluer Age*, and 1632 *Iron Age*, as well as the plays listed in the "Admiral Fragment" (BL, MS Additional 10449).[56] The central point, and to my mind even more important than the print strategies of marketing Troy in various formats, is this durability: the physical nature of the book ensures that it reproduces its contents as immediate. My point is not merely that literature is produced through textual formalism but that this textual formalism is *persistent*, reproducing chronologically older texts not as dormant fossils of an earlier literary period suitable only to antiquarian interests but as speaking to the reader and therefore actively shaping contemporary writing.

Moreover, the physical page, not the edition or the idea, is the primary instrument of such literary reproduction. For instance, Copland's rendition of the *Recuyell* expresses temporality not as an abstract chronological progression in time but as a dimensional movement through space (figure 5). Here de Worde's double columns of text are juxtaposed with roman chapter headings. The effect is to manage the reader, to carry him or her from medieval blackletter text to modern editorial voice and back.[57] Typographically these are graphic tropes for temporality, and if literary language is defined by troping, I argue that this is true for the material text as well. Further, within this very page, Caxton is intent on managing the readers' relationship to the past. In figure 5, six lines down the left hand column, Caxton folds Chaucer's *Troilus and Criseyde* into Guido's *Historia destructionis troiae*, writing, "There was neuer seen so mouche sorowe made betwene two louers at their departynge, who that lyste to here of all theyr loue: let hym rede the booke of Troyllus that Chaucer made, wherein he shall fynde ye storye whole, whyche were to longe to write here."[58] When William Shakespeare moved through this page, as he most likely did, his perception of the relationship between the past and the present is truly involute: managed by the typography, the page continually reminds him that he is reading a narrative located in the blackletter past but mediated by the roman present; he is no less managed by Caxton's voice from this past, one that reminds him not to forget literary history, not to pass over Chaucer's place in this history, and not to neglect the two stories being told here—one of an arrogant war and one of a betrayed love; finally, it is also managed by his own voice, a voice that, like any reader's, hears Diomedes's requests, Criseyde's delay, and her speech to Calcus in the right-hand column that he too shall be reduced to a mere representation ("ye shalt not onli be blamed in thi life: but ye shalt also after thy death"). The physical book operates in the same way as its contents: both attempt to represent the fullness of life in a textual form but depend upon the reader's engagement—in this particular case, Shakespeare's—to give them life. Mimesis in the face of corruption: the book is an orgulous technology. Its potency lies in its excellence in the representation of literary material, and so it transcends its period of origination to communicate its contents forowe,for she was his fouerayne lady of loue,and in sembiable wise Breseyda loued stronglye Tropilus.and she made also the greatest sorowe of the worlde for to leaue her foueraine lorde in loue. There was neuer seen so mouche sorowe made betwene two louers at their departynge,who that liste to here of all theyr loue: let hym rede the booke of Troyllus that Chaucer made,wherein he shall fynde þ storye whole,whyche were to longe to wryte here, but finalye Breseyda was led vnto the Grekes whome they recepued honourably. Among them was Diomedes that anon was enflamed wyth the loue of Bryseyda, whan he sawe her so fayre,and in tidinge by her side: he shewed to her all his corage,and made to her many promysses and speeyally desired her loue, and thã whan she knew the corage of Dyo medes:she excused her sayinge that she woulde not agree to him ne re fuse him at þ time,for her hert was not disposed at þ tyme to answer other wyse. Of thys answer Dyo medes had greate ioye,for asmuch as he was not refused vtterly,and he accompanyed her vnto the tente of her father,and halpe her downe of her horse, and tooke fro her one of her gloues that she helde in her handes,and she suffred hym swe tely. Calcas recepued her wt great ioye,and whan they were in priuetie betwene hem bothe: Breseyda sayde to her father these and sem blable wordes.

Na, my father how is thy wytte fayled that were wote to be so wise and the moste honou red and beloupd in the citie of troy,

& gouernedst al þ was win,and had dest so manye richesses and posse ssions,and hast ben traytour thou that oughtest to haue kepte thy ri chesses and defended thy countrey vnto the death:but thou louest bet ter to lyue in pouerty and in exyle amonge the mortal enemies of thy countrey. O how shall this turne to the greate bilonpe: certes thou shalt neuer get so muche honoure: as thou hast goten bilonpe, and þ shalt not onli be blamed in thi life: but þ shalt also after thy death & be dampned in hel. And me semeth yet it had ben better to haue dwelled out of the people vpon some yle of the Sea,than to dwell here in thys dishonour and bilony,wenest thou that the grekes holde the for trewe and faythful,that art openly fals & vntrewe to thy people: Certes it was not onli the god Appollo that thus abused thee: but it was a compa ny of deuils. And as she thy⁹ spake her father:she wepte strongly for þ displeasur that she had. &c.

Na,my doughter sayd Cal cas,than wenest thou it is a sure thinge to despyre the answer of the goddes,and specially in that thinge that toucheth my health: I know certaynly by their answers that this warre shal not dure loge that the Citie ne shalbe destroyed, and the nobles also and the burgei ses,and therfore it is better for vs to be here safe, than to be slayne wyth thẽ:and than finisshed they their parlament. The compnge of Breseyda pleased muche to all the Grekes,and they cam thether and feasted her,and demaũded of her ti dynges of Troy and of the kynge

Priant

Pryst,and of them that were with
in,& she said vnto hem as much as
she knew curtoysly.Thã al ÿ greatest that were ther:prompsed her to
kepe her and holde her as dere as
her doughter ,and than eche man
wente into hys owne Tente,and
there was none of hem but that
gaue to her a iewell at the departynge,and than it pleased her wel
to abide and dwell wyth the Grekes,and forgat anon the noble citie of Troy,and the loue of the noble Troyllus.O how sone is the
purpose of a woman chaunged &
turned:certes more sooner than a
man can saye or thynke , now late
had Breseyda blamed her Father
of the vyce of trayso , which the her
selfe excersised in forgettynge her
countrey and her truce frende troy
lus.&c.

¶How the Grekes and troyans begã
the sixt batayle that dured by the
space of thirty dayes in whiche were
many kinges and prices dead of that
one syde and of that other,and how
diomedes smote downe Troyllus of
his horse & sente it to Breseyda hys
loue that receyued it gladly.&c.

After the thre monthes of
truce passed: on the morne
betymes the Troyans apparayled
them to batayle.And whan Hector
had ordeyned all hys batayles : he
issued out first and tooke with him
syftene thousande fightynge men
and troyllus folowed him with tẽ
thousãde knyghtes,after hym cam
Paris wyth thre thousande fygh-
tynge men and good archers and
well horsed . After came Deyphe-
bus wyth thre thousand fyghters,
after hym came Eneas and the o-
ther all in ordre so mani that there
were this daye of the partye of the

Troyans:more than an hondred
thousande good fyghtyng men and
hardy.Of the party of the Grekes
came al there fyrst Menclaus with
seuen thousande knightes, and after hym Dyomedes with as many,
and than achilles that lad also te-
uen thousande,the kynge Pampitus with a great multytude of knightes , and the other after lyke as
they were ordeyned. The kynge
Philes adtaunced him ayther first,
and Hector came agaynste hym so
stronglye that he slewe hym wyth
hys spere.Thã there arose a great
crye of his death amonge the Grekes,and the occysion and slaughter began so greate:that it was an
horrible sight to se as well of that
one syde as of that other.The king
Pampitus slewe manye Troyans
for to venge the death of his vncle
& assayled Hector,but Hector gaue
hym so greate a stroke wyth hys
swerde that he slewe him also,and
for to auége his death the Grekes
slewe manye of the Troyans .A-
chilles slewe manye noble men, a-
monge the whiche he slewe the duke
Braon,and Euforbe that was a
moche noble man : Hector was
this daye sore hurte in the visage
and bledde greate plentye of bloud
and wyste not who had douen it,
and therefore the Troyans reculed
vnto the walles,and whan hector
behelde and sawe vpon the walles
the quene Hecuba his mother and
hys systers:he had greate shame,&
by greate pre assayled the king Me-
non cosyn of Achilles,& gaue him
so manye strokes wyth his swerde
vpon his helme:that he slewe hym
seinge Achilles ,that wende for to
haue enraged and tooke a stronge
spere

beyond their invention. But this excellence comes with no promise. The book moves through time, simultaneously dated and decrepit, a relic of the past, and urgent, alive in its reader's hands. Energized by the press, the book's orgulty represents literature as paradoxical, contained within time and immediate.

Because of this immediacy in relation to time, I argue, fifteenth-century writing is important to early modern poetics. For example, Lydgate, author of courtly and mercantile mummings, was himself a dramatist and in the *Troy Book* dilates on tragedy and comedy as specifically dramatic genres.[59] Like Guido before him and Caxton after him, Lydgate initially describes Troy as a place of artifice by emphasizing the tremendous craftsmanship that goes into Priam's rebuilding of the city. In contrast to both Guido and Caxton, Lydgate introduces an ekphrasis of a dramatic performance during this preliminary section, opening with an excurses on the dramatic forms of tragedy and comedy. Of course, Chaucer famously defines "de casibus" or "Gothic" tragedy in his translation of Boethius's *Consolation of Philosophy* and in the prologue to the Monk's Tale. He also cites both tragedy and comedy in *Troilus and Cresyede*.[60] Though Chaucer never articulates a definition of comedy, most scholarship proceeds as if Lydgate's discussion in the *Troy Book* is entirely derivative of this earlier work.[61] As a result, Lydgate's dramatic sensibility is perceived as having nothing to contribute to Shakespearean themes. But this is a tautological proof, dependent entirely on eliding the fifteenth century into a long English Middle Ages that finds its significance in Chaucer's initial formulation of courtly writing. In truth, both Chaucer's and Lydgate's understanding of tragedy are derivative.[62] Liberated from this predetermined historical structure and recognized as available in sixteenth-century editions, indeed as embedded in publishing schemes and drawn upon as a source for a number of plays, Lydgate's *Troy Book* takes on greater importance for literary history. If we turn to an edition of Lydgate contemporary to Copland's *Recuyell*—for example, Marshe's 1555 edition of the *Troy Book*—we find that Lydgate is interested in exactly the problems surrounding *Troilus and Cressida*: the relationship between the Troy story and genre, and how one genre can transform into the next.

Lydgate expands upon Chaucerian tragedy by defining it in relation to comedy. The two have this "fynall difference" he tells us:

> ¶ A comedye hath in his gynnynge,
> A pryme face a maner complaynynge,
> And afterwarde endeth in gladnesse

but tragedy,

> begynneth in prosperitie,
> And endeth lykewyse by aduersytie.[63]

Lydgate's conception of tragedy is deeply Boethian—it is centered on a fall—but it is also complementary to comedy, the subsequent rotation of Fortune's wheel that reverses adversity, bringing it to gladness. For Chaucer, tragedy is entirely unidirectional: it is a singular fall from grace epitomized by Adam's choice, and ceaselessly reenacted across human history. As a result, Chaucerian tragedy is relentlessly ahistorical, and so Chaucer applies the definition to pagan, Hebrew, and Christian exempla. By defining tragedy in relation to comedy, Lydgate implies that one form might ever be transformed into the next and that the fall might also be a redemption. Lydgate's tragedy is not universal but dependent upon history, not a closed form but open to the contingency of events. This is part of Lydgate's definition in that tragedy alone

> doth also of the conquest treate,
> Of ryche kynges and of lordes great.
> Of mighty men and olde conquerours.[64]

In this vein, the entire discussion is merely a prelude for the ekphrasis, which gives a historical account of Trojan performance. Lydgate subsequently depicts the semicircular Trojan theatre upon which an altar and pulpit sit, and he visualizes the "auncient poete" who mounts the stage. As this poet sings, Lydgate reports, blood leaves his face ("With deadly face all deuoyde of blode") and a chorus of masked players emerge from a tented section of the theatre.[65] The song continues, cycling from joy to heaviness, from comedy to tragedy, and with this the blood ebbs and flows from the poet's face. The action is paralleled by a transfiguration of the chorus's masks, "So that there was no maner discordaunce, / Atwen his ditees and their contenaunce." Lydgate's emphasis on blood is one with the economy of representation we see in Caxton and Shakespeare, in which the ability to manipulate the presence and absence of blood is no less than the ability to achieve the illusion of representation.

In the *Troy Book* this first ekphrasis operates as a balance to that of Hector's tomb, the one introduces Trojan art before the war and the other brings it to its height at the truce just after Hector's death. Lydgate substantially amplifies upon Guido delle Colonne in this second passage, exaggerating both the techniques of preserving Hector's body and its results. "By subtyll crafte as it were lyuynge," Lydgate begins, granting Hector virtual life,

> Of face and cheare and of quicke lokinge,
> And of colour southly and of hewe,
> Beynge as freshe as any rose newe.

Rather than simply a vase that uses the force of gravity to carry fluid through Hector's body, Lydgate's Hector is permeated by

> pipes artyfyciall
> Through necke and head into many place,
> Penetrable by vaynes of the face.

Sweetening the colors and heightening the contrivance, Lydgate immerses the reader in both formal technique and its results. So we are implicitly invited to imagine the labor of making, of threading these tiny rods through Hector's face, breast, arms, hands, and feet, and tempted to read this labor of making into Lydgate's own tropes—for example, his use of simile and amplification to construct the passage overall. This rhetorical amplification has the material result that Hector is, if not sentient, then otherwise alive,

> Comparisoned as it were semblable,
> To a soule that were vegetable,
> The whych without sensybelyte,
> Ministreth life in herbe, floure, and tre.[66]

Caxton's version presents mimesis through reproduction; fitting a printer, his notion of artistic production relies on techniques of material duplication to represent—indeed, to replace—the natural world. For Lydgate, the poet, the passage is similarly about reproduction but is focused on the way formal artifice—similes and small pipes—narrows the distance between fabricated representation and original life, making a living art that lacks only consciousness. In both cases Hector's tomb is a metonym for literary formalism that combines rhetorical and material making into a single vernacular statement.

Again, Simpson's reading in *Reform and Cultural Revolution* affords a useful contrast to my argument. There he reads Hector's tomb as it is rendered in John Whalley's *Destruction of Troy*, a fourteenth- or early fifteenth-century descendant of Guido's *Historia*. Simpson argues that "the poet's description of the tomb places so much emphasis on the very ingeniousness of the craftsmen who constructed it that heroism is displaced by admiration for macabre engineering. There is nothing here of the divine technology of the *Aeneid* . . . there is, certainly, no stellification of dead heroes."[67] Simpson's reading limits the scene to admiration of the gruesome literal, surely a lesser intellectual interest than the divine figuration he finds in the *Aeneid*. Remaining in only one manuscript and never printed, Whalley's telling is minor for literary history, yet as Simpson parallels it with Lydgate's *Troy Book* and does not explore the *Recuyell*, his conclusion must stand for all: "In the fifteenth century the 'tragic' is the preserve of clerics, who certainly address the interests of secular warriors, but who speak from a distinct and partly oppositional discursive position."[68] Without literary history, uninterested in the deeper issues of heroism, insulated by clerical authors, and defined by totalizing genres, Simpson's fifteenth-century literary culture is contained by period. Yet Caxton is no cleric, and Lydgate writes of a fluid sense of tragedy and comedy. Indeed, these blurred distinctions—the mercantile nature of literature, and the slippage between genres—define the English editorial problems of *Troylus* well into the seventeenth century. And is it not exactly the issue of stellification that so interests Lydgate, Caxton, and Shakespeare in the notion of orgulousness? Is it not exactly the problem of artistic mimesis—the possibility that human labor might figure life from pale and bloodless technology—that Lydgate broaches with his similes and tiny rods? As a metonym for art, Hector's tomb demonstrates how the tomb, the book, the performance, the trope, and the typeface are jointly rhetorical and material. Hence my point in insisting upon a textual formalism: literary history is a story of imitative conduct, one in which each author—Lydgate, Caxton, or Shakespeare—is first a reader who returns to the past through the text, and then a writer who engages and thereby continues that past. Readership, literary culture, and transformation; literary history differs from political history in that it has the ability to circumscribe temporality to tell not of linearity but of recursion, not of historical period but of transcendence.

What does it mean, then, to stand at Hector's tomb? We should look to Achilles. For the task facing Lydgate—and Caxton and Shakespeare as well—is to tell a story that has been told before, to represent in the wake of prior writing. Thus Lydgate's *Troy Book* is filled with commentary on previous writers: on Guido, Homer, Ovid, but above all, on Chaucer. Yet, Lydgate's most involved engagement with Chaucer—when Achilles stands at Hector's tomb—is unmarked. In book 4, Lydgate writes of Achilles's visit to Hector's tomb in terms strikingly reminiscent of Troilus's encounter with Criseyde in the Palladium in Chaucer's book 1. The scenes are parallel: gazing on Criseyde, Troilus is struck through his eyes by her beauty; so too does Achilles gaze on Polyxena. Now hot, now cold, both heroes retreat to their beds.[69] Both scenes are overtly about representation. Chaucer's Troilus makes a mirror of his mind in which to view Criseyde;[70] standing before Hector's tomb Achilles and Polyxena exist in a world of aesthetic contrivance. If Hector's tomb is a metonym for artistic rendering, Achilles comes to it as a representation given life by a silent appropriation from an earlier text, as an emulation of Guido's Achilles filtered through Chaucer's Troilus. And thus Achilles, that most orgulous of heroes, is humbled: in Lydgate, as in Guido and Caxton, it is this scene, and not his love for Patroclus, that motivates his refusal to fight. But strangely, Lydgate and Chaucer betray an inverted history at this moment. As Larry Benson points out, Lydgate draws his version of Achilles through Chaucer's own appropriation of an early telling of Achilles: "Boccaccio apparently drew suggestions for his account of Troilus's enamorment from an episode in Benoît (17489ff) telling of Achilles's love for Polyxena, and from his own Filocolo."[71] Lydgate thus performs a sort of double appropriation of Benoît's *Roman de Troie*, once in his translation of Guido's *Historia destructionis Troiae* and again in his interpolation of Chaucer's *Troilus and Criseyde*, which returns the figuration of Achilles from Troilus back to Achilles. In this Achilles's experience at Hector's tomb parallels Lydgate's in all his major works by embodying what it means to be constituted by prior writing. At Hector's tomb: Achilles sets out the parameters of this English formalism, neither as a break into originality nor a return to a more classical sense of figuration, but as a ceaseless and ongoing process of literary reproduction in which the literary past is never sealed off by historical period but is continually reread and rewritten, reproduced across time through the medium of the book.

NOTES

I thank Sarah Kelen, David Glimp, and Richelle Munkhoff for reading earlier drafts of this essay. Their insightful commentary allowed me to revise it substantially. This chapter appears in a much revised form as chapter four in Kuskin, *Recursive Origins: Writing at the Transition to Modernity* (Notre Dame, IN: University of Notre Dame Press, 2013).

1. See, for example, Meyer-Lee, *Poets and Power*; Wakelin, *Humanism, Reading, and English Literature*; and Gillespie, *Print Culture and the Medieval Author*.

2. The literary histories from Oxford and Cambridge emphasize a clear medieval–early modern boundary line. For example, see James Simpson's conclusion that "the dissolution of the boundary line [between medieval and Renaissance] would be a misrepresentation of history," in *Reform and Cultural Revolution*, 558. Though David Wallace's *Cambridge History of English Literature* chases its story well into the sixteenth-century, its essays on fifteenth-century poetry return to the familiar themes of inhibition and limitation: both Paul Strohm ("Hoccleve, Lydgate and the Lancastrian Court," 640–61) and Colin Burrow ("Experience of Exclusion," 793–820) describe a fifteenth century in which political rivalry overwhelms literary production; as Wallace sums up, the major poets appear "frustrated or unnerved by the dangers of employing" humanist eloquence (638). In turn, Lowenstein and Mueller, *The Cambridge History of Early Modern English Literature*, remain comfortable trumpeting the "triumph of the book" and "the emergence of the author" as modern events (88 and 108). In each case the fifteenth century is conceived of as facilitating a clear division of period.

3. See Simpson's insistence on reformation politics as defining English literary history in "Making History Whole," where he writes, "the break in England was not restricted to a given discursive area, such as, say, ecclesiology or education. State-driven as the cultural revolution was in England, it affected the entire discursive landscape," in McMullen and Matthews, *Reading the Medieval*, 17.

4. Holsinger, "Lollard Ekphrasis," 75.

5. For discussion of Chaucer and Shakespeare, see, for example, Thompson, *Shakespeare's Chaucer*; Donaldson, *Swan at the Well*; and Mann, "Shakespeare and Chaucer." There is an older tradition of source study represented by Rollins, "The Troilus-Cressida Story," and Bradbrook, "What Shakespeare Did," that sees Shakespeare as not fully understanding the dividing line between Chaucer and Henryson; this interpretation was effectively refuted by Donaldson, *Swan at the Well*, 76–78.

6. Simpson emphasizes the importance of John Bale's literary history (*STC* 1295) and Gavin Douglas's *Eneados* (*STC* 24797) in chapter one of *Reform and Cultural Revolution*, 7–33. Chapman's 1598 translations, *Achilles Shield* (*STC* 13635) and *Seauen Bookes of Iliades*

(*STC* 13632), are widely cited in the literature on *Troilus and Cressida*, and with the *Eneados* are discussed as significant markers of period by Boffey and Edwards, "Literary Texts," 575.

7. Caxton's *Recuyell of the Historyes of Troye* has long been recognized as a major source for Shakespeare's play on grounds of plot similarity. See Tatlock, "Siege of Troy in Elizabethan Literature"; Bullough, *Narrative and Dramatic Sources of Shakespeare*, 83–111, with sample texts on 112–221; Muir, *Sources of Shakespeare's Plays*, 141–57; and Bevington, "'Instructed by the antiquary times.'" Robert K. Besson provides a useful review of the early scholarship in *Shakespeare's Troilus and Cressida & The Legends of Troy*, though he weighs Chapman's Homer as the primary source. The consensus is that Shakespeare did not rely on Lydgate's *Troy Book*; see Elizabeth Stein, "Caxton's *Recuyell* and Shakespeare's *Troilus*."

Troilus and Cressida is often read as a local allegory, either for the political life of the Earl of Essex or for the Wars of the Theatres. See, for example, E. A. J. Honigmann's argument for dating the play at 1601 through the Essex rebellion in "Date and Revision of Troilus and Cressida"; and more recently, Mallen, "Emulous Factions"; and "'Tricks we play on the dead,'" chapter 3 of Heather James, *Shakespeare's Troy*. See Robert Kimbrough's similar conclusion for the War of the Theatres, in "Origins of *Troilus and Cressida*," 195–96. Because Chapman's work can be connected to these twin themes through issues of patronage and allusion, it has been regarded as source of overwhelming importance. Few critics have explored the *Recuyell* thematically, however; and I argue that if we open up the *Recuyell*, we find a much broader connection to *Troilus* around the issue of literary representation than has been recognized.

8. There are seventeen English editions of the *Recuyell*, listed here chronologically, by printer:

1. William Caxton, *Recuyell of the Historyes of Troye*, folio, *STC* 15375 (Bruges, 1473/4). Caxton also produced a French edition of this text in 1474 with Colard Mansion, entitled *Recueil des histories de Troie*, which I do not number here.

2. Wynkyn de Worde, *The Recuyles or Gaderinge to Gyder of the Hystoryes of Troye*, folio, *STC* 15376 (London, 1502), with a variant edition: *STC* 15377 (London, 1503).

3. William Copland, *The Recuile of the Histories of Troie*, folio, *STC* 15378 (London, 1553). This is a conflation of *STC* 15375 and 15376/7.

4. Thomas Creede and Valentine Simmes, *The Auncient Historie of the Destruction of Troy*, quarto, *STC* 15379 (London, 1596/7). Revised by William Phiston. Books 1 and 2 are printed by Creede with title pages indicating 1596; book 3 by Simmes has a title page labeled 1597. This is the basis for all of the following editions to William Morris's version.

5. Thomas Creede, *The Ancient Historie, of the Destruction of Troy*, quarto, *STC* 15380 (London, 1607).

6. Barnard Alsop, *The Ancient Historie of the Destruction of Troy*, entitled the "Fifth Edition," quarto, *STC* 15381 (London, 1617).

7. Barnard Alsop and Thomas Fawcett, *The Ancient Historie of the Destruction of Troy*, "Sixth Edition," quarto, *STC* 15382 (London, 1636).

8. Samuel Speed, *The Destruction of Troy*, "Seventh Edition," quarto, book 1, Wing L929; book 2, Wing L934; book 3, Wing L938 (London, 1663). Here and following, Caxton's name is eliminated from the title page.

9. Thomas Passenger, *The Destruction of Troy in three books*, "Eighth Edition," quarto, Wing L930 (London, 1670). Additionally, Wing L935 is book 2, printed by Speed; and Wing L939 is book 3, printed by Passenger.

10. ——, *The Destruction of Troy*, "Ninth Edition," quarto, Wing L931, L936, L940 (London, 1676).

11. ——, *The Destruction of Troy*, "Tenth Edition," quarto, Wing L932, L937, L941 (London, 1680).

12. ——, *The Destruction of Troy*, "Eleventh Edition," quarto, Wing L933, L937A, L941A (London, 1684).

13. Eben Tracey, *The Destruction of Troy*, "Twelfth Edition," quarto (London, 1702).

14. ——, *The Destruction of Troy*, "Thirteenth Edition," quarto (London, 1708).

15. Thomas Browne, *The Destruction of Troy*, "Eighteenth Edition," quarto (Dublin, 1738).

16. William Morris, *The Recuyell of the Historyes of Troye* (Hammersmith, 1892).

17. Ballantyne, Hanson & Co, *The Recuyell of the Historyes of Troye*, edited by H. Oskar Sommer for The Early English Text Society (London, 1894).

In the bibliography all editions of the *Recuyell*, as well as all other works edited by Caxton, are alphabetized under Caxton's name.

9. Marcus, "Reading Matter," 11.

10. Brantley, "Prehistory of the Book." Two recent monographs that follow out such a capacious history of books are Jennifer Summit's *Memory's Library* and Siân Echard's *Printing the Middle Ages*.

11. New Formalism has recently been discussed by Marjorie Levinson in "What is New Formalism?," and to some extent by Marjorie Perloff in her "Presidential Address 2006," as well as by Stephen Cohen in his introduction to *Shakespeare and Historical Formalism*, 1–27.

12. Lydgate, *Auncient Historie*.

13. Following convention, I use the titles *Troilus and Cressida* to refer to Shakespeare's play and *Troilus and Criseyde* to refer to Chaucer's long poem in the abstract. When I discuss or cite the play, I refer to a specific printed title. In all cases, I have modernized long *s* and expanded abbreviations with italics.

The criticism on *Troilus and Cressida* as a problem play is usefully summarized in Bevington's introduction to the Arden edition, "'Instructed by the antiquary times,'" 1–19. See also: Elton, *Shakespeare's Troilus and Cressida*, 1–17.

14. These are listed in the *STC* as *The Historie of Troylus and Cresseida* ("Qa," STC 22331) and *The Famous Historie of Troylus and Cresseid* ("Qb," STC 22332). They were entered into the Stationers' Register by Richard Bonian and Henry Walley on January 28, 1603. For publication details, see Philip Williams Jr., "'Second Issue' of Shakespeare's *Troilus and Cressida*." The 1623 First Folio is *STC* 22273.

15. Fielder, "Shakespeare's Commodity-Comedy," 50.

16. For the Stationers' Register, see Wells and Taylor, *Textual Companion*, 424.

17. Gary Taylor suggests that the epistle was a late discovery in the printing process, some sort of remaindered essay from the play's early circulation at the Inns of Court only realized by the printer, George Eld, after production had begun; see Taylor, "*Troilus and Cressida*," and Wells and Taylor, *Textual Companion*, 424–26. For a strong caution against Taylor's editorial conclusions, see Jensen, "Textual Politics of *Troilus and Cressida*."

Taylor dates the composition of the play at 1602 (Wells and Taylor, *Textual Companion*, 123), though Honigmann and others date it at 1601 (see Honigmann, "Date and Revision," 43; and Kimbrough, "Origins," 196). Current views hold the quarto text as coming from an authorial manuscript. Isaac Jaggard apparently possessed an unmarked version of this text from which he set four pages of the play, placing it after *Romeo and Juliet*, but then stopped, moving the entire piece to after *Henry the Eight* and switching to an annotated version.

"It is generally assumed," Taylor writes, "that the initial setting of *Troilus* was abandoned because of difficulties over copyright" (Wells and Taylor, *Textual Companion*, 425). In any case, the Folio's final version represents the quarto with annotations from a manuscript, perhaps a promptbook from a Globe production. The differences between the quarto and Folio versions concern the prefatory material and a number of repeated lines, listed on 426–43.

18. See Elton, "Appendix II: Troilus and Legal Terms," in *Shakespeare's Troilus and Cressida*, 175.

19. *The Famous Historie of Troylus and Cresseid*, M^v. The First Folio presents this line as "hold-dore trade" (signed ¶¶¶); cf. Shakespeare, *Arden Shakespeare: Troilus and Cressida*, 5.11.51.

20. Wells and Taylor, *Textual Companion*, 425.

21. The first eleven chapters are reprinted in Copland's 1553 edition of the *The Recuile*, bk. 3, fol. i recto–fol. xxiiii verso. These particular examples appear as follows: the sixty and nine at the port of Athens (fol. xii recto), the port of Thenedon (fol. xiiii recto), the Dardan plains (fol. xix verso), and the gates of Troy (fol. ii recto).

22. In Copland's 1553 edition of the *Recuile*, bk. 3, "orguyllous and proude" (fol. ii verso), "chauffyd" (fol. iii recto), "rauysshed" (fol. vii recto), "quarel" (fol. xii verso), and "pauyllon" (fol. xvii recto).

23. Caxton, *Recuyles or Gaderinge to Gyder*, Aa.vi recto.

24. In Caxton, *Recuyell*, STC 15379, "pride" (p. 438), "insolent" (pp. 439 and 480), "high minded" (p. 466), and "hautinesse" (p. 480).

25. Jacobus de Cessalis, *The Game and Play of Chess*, chap. 5, pages unsigned and unnumbered; Raoul Lefèvre, *Historie of Iason*, pages unsigned and unnumbered. Caxton uses the term in a number of editions, such as *Godefrey of Boloyne*, i2 verso and i3 recto; the 1483 *Curial*, i verso; Geoffroy de la Toure Landry, *Knyght of the Toure*, aviii recto; and Christine de Pizan, *The Boke of the Fayt of Armes and of Chyualrye*, Aiiii verso.

26. Thomas Malory, *Le Morte Darthur*, zvi recto.

27. Caxton, *Recuile*, STC 15378, bk. 1, fol. iii recto and fol. li verso, respectively.

28. *OED*, s.v. "orgel." Orgulous appears across the sixteenth century in instances such as the triangular heading "Odyous / orgulyous / and flyblowen opinions" of John Skelton's *Replycacion*, and William Wyrley's 1592 *The True Use of Armorie*: "I discontent for orgule that he did / Refuse: dischargd, and back to Poycters rid" (p. 91), and

> Which seen the English orgulous words did say
> Gainst Lord *Cowcie*, which English houerd still,
> Who was in Austrige warring at his will. (p. 150)

29. Caxton, *Recuile*, STC 15378, bk. 3, fol. xiiii verso.

30. Caxton, *Recuile*, STC 15378, bk. 3, fol. xv recto.

31. Caxton, *Recuile*, STC 15378, bk. 3, fol. ii verso.

32. The pages of *Troylus and Cressida* in the First Folio are signed out of sequence with the volume overall. Ulysses's discussion with Nestor occurs on pages ¶2r–¶2v; cf. Shakespeare, *Arden Shakespeare: Troilus and Cressida*, 1.3.310–92.

33. First Folio, ¶v; cf. Shakespeare, *Arden Shakespeare: Troilus and Cressida*, 1.3.125–26.

34. First Folio, ¶v; cf. Shakespeare, *Arden Shakespeare: Troilus and Cressida*, 1.3.150–58.

35. Elton, *Shakespeare's Troilus and Cressida*, 6.

36. Mallen, "Emulous Factions," 152.

37. Respectively, First Folio, ¶v; cf. Shakespeare, *Arden Shakespeare: Troilus and Cressida*, 1.3.103, and First Folio, ¶2v; cf. Shakespeare, *Arden Shakespeare: Troilus and Cressida*, 2.1.6.

38. First Folio, ¶¶4r; cf. Shakespeare, *Arden Shakespeare: Troilus and Cressida*, 4.5.239–40.

39. First Folio, ¶6v; cf. Shakespeare, *Arden Shakespeare: Troilus and Cressida*, 3.2.197–99. On this point, see Charnes, "'So Unsecret to Ourselves.'"

40. First Folio, ¶¶6r; cf. Shakespeare, *Arden Shakespeare: Troilus and Cressida*, 5.3.107.

41. Caxton, *Recuile*, STC 15378, bk. 3, fol. i verso.

42. In Caxton, *Recuile*, STC 15378, bk. 3, fol. xx verso, fol. iiii recto, and fol. x[i] recto, respectively. For Ulysses's line, see Folio, ¶¶3v ; cf. Shakespeare, *Arden Shakespeare: Troilus and Cressida*, 4.5.110.

43. Caxton, *Recuile*, STC 15378, bk. 3, fol. xxiii verso and fol. xxvii recto.

44. In Caxton, *Recuile*, STC 15378, bk. 3: the women's lament and Hector's response occur from fol. xxiiii recto fol. xxix recto; "Galathe" is mentioned five times, on fols. xx verso, xxi recto, xxii recto, and twice on fol. xxvi verso; Diomedes's taking of Troilus's horse is on fol. xx[vi]ii verso (signed "fol. xx ii verso"); Hector takes armor and captives on fols. xxi recto, xxiii recto, and xxx recto; Hector defeats Achilles on fol. xxiiii recto; and Achilles slays him on fol. xxx recto: "[Hector] had caste hys sheelde behinde him at his backe, & had lefte his breste discouerte and as he was in thys poynte & tooke none hede of Achilles that came pryueyly unto hym and put thys spere with in his body, and Hector fell downe dead, to the grounde."

45. See, for example, the discussions in book 3 of "Helayne incontinent" (Caxton, *Recuile*, STC 15378, fol. viii recto), and of Breseyda (Cressida), fol. xx[vi]ii recto (signed "fol. xx ii recto").

46. Also defined by Derek Pearsall in "The English Romance in the Fifteenth Century," 78.

47. Creede printed the first play attributable to Shakespeare for Millington, a 1594 variant of *Henry VI, Part 2*, known as *The First Part of the Contention* (*STC* 26099); Simmes printed the first edition of *Hamlet* in 1603 (*STC* 22275) for Nicholas Ling and John Trundell. They continued to print quartos through the turn of the century, and though by 1610 they seem to have been superceded by Eld and Jaggard (Eld printed the quarto versions of *Troilus and Cressida* as well as *Shake-speares Sonnets* in 1609 for Thomas Thorpe, *STC* 22353a, and Jaggard printed the Pavier collection before going onto the Folio), both resurfaced in the beginning of the second decade with some final Shakespearean quartos. In 1611 Simmes printed an edition of *The Troublesome Raigne of Iohn King* for John Helme, flirtatiously attributed to "W. Sh." on its title page (*STC* 14646), and, more conjecturally, had some involvement in Eld's 1611 edition of *Hamlet* for John Smethwick (*STC* 22277), as noted by Andrew Murphy in *Shakespeare in Print*, 298. Creede printed the 1612 editions of the *Merry Deuill of Edmonton* as it was acted by "his Majesties seruants, at the Globe" for Arthur Johnson *(STC* 7494) and *The Tragedie of King Richard the third* (*STC* 22318).

48. *Pericles* (*STC* 22334) and *The Painful Aduentures of Pericles* (STC 25638.5) are discussed in Wells and Taylor, *Textual Companion*, 557.

49. 1632 (by Cotes, *STC* 22274/with variants a–e), 1663 (by Roger Daniel, Alice Warren, and another, Wing S2913), and 1664 (Wing S2914). See note 8 above for the editions of the *Recuyell*.

50. Caxton, *Recuile*, STC 15378, bk. 2, fol. lii[i] verso.

51. Simpson, *Reform and Cultural Revolution*, 11.

52. See my discussion of these issues in *Symbolic Caxton*.

53. Lydgate, *Hystorye, Sege and Dystruccyon of Troye*.

54. Lydgate, *Auncient Historie*, π.

55. Lydgate, *Life and Death of Hector*.

56. Tatlock, "Siege of Troy in Elizabethan Literature," 676–77. Greene, *Euphues his censure to Philautus*; Peele, *A Tale of Troy*; Heywood, *Troia Britanica*; Heywood, *Golden Age*; Heywood, *Brazen Age*; Heywood, *Siluer Age*; Heywood, *Iron Age*.

57. We would be mistaken to assume that this process of management is somehow new; the roman typeface is based just as thoroughly on scribal practice as Caxton's bastarda. The history of the roman style is excellently reviewed by Stanley Morrison in "Early Humanistic Script"; see also Echard, *Printing the Middle Ages*, 12, 34–35.

58. Caxton, *Recuile*, *STC* 15378, bk. 3. fol. xxvii verso.

59. See Nolan, "Social forms, literary contents: Lydgate's Mummings," chap. 2 in *John Lydgate*, 71–119.

60. See *The Riverside Chaucer*: Boethius's *Consolation of Philosophy*, bk. 2, prose 2, line 70, pp. 409–10; the Prologue of the Monk's Tale, lines 1973–77, p. 241; and *Troilus and Criseyde*, lines 1786–88, p. 584.

61. For example, Lydgate's modern editors are somewhat dismissive of his work here. Henry Bergen comments that "throughout almost this entire passage he has drawn on his own reading," in *Lydgate's Troy Book*, 121; Robert R. Edwards, Lydgate's most recent editor, writes "the generic descriptions of comedy and tragedy are commonplaces," see Lydgate, *Troy Book Selections*, 368.

62. M. H. Marshall points to Isidore of Seville's *Etymologies* as a likely source for Chaucer and Lydgate in "Theatre in the Middle Ages," 9; Paul Strohm suggest that "a definition of tragedy of the sort Vincent [of Beauvais] and other medieaval scholars would have known is that of the thirteenth century Catholicon of Johannes Januensis, in which he distinguishes between tragedy and comedy on the basis of the persons they treat, the levels of their styles, and the upward or downward moments of their plots," in "Storie, Spelle, Geste, Romaunce, Tragedie," 356.

63. Lydgate, *Auncient Historie*, F.vi recto–verso; cf. Lydgate, *Troy Book Selections*, 2.842–914.

64. C. David Benson suggests that Lydgate's *Troy Book* reveals "a genuine sense of historical perspective that is not found in any of the other Middle English histories of Troy," in *History of Troy*, 106–8.

65. Marshall identifies this as the "main error" of medieval understandings of classical drama; see "Theatre in the Middle Ages," 375. Nonetheless, this should not distract us from the fundamentally historical nature of Lydgate's attempt.

66. Lydgate, *Auncient Historie*, S.iv recto; cf. Lydgate, *Troy Book Selections*, 3.5575–764.

67. Simpson, *Reform and Cultural Revolution*, 89.

68. Simpson, *Reform and Cultural Revolution*, 103.

69. Compare Lydgate, *Troy Book Selections*, bk. 4, lines 603–7 and 649–52, with Chaucer, *Troilus and Criseyde*, in *Riverside Chaucer*, bk. 1, lines 266–73, 358–64, and 420.

70. Chaucer, *Troilus and Criseyde*, in *Riverside Chaucer*, line 365.

71. Chaucer, explanatory notes to *Riverside Chaucer*, 1026.

Owning the Middle Ages:
History, Trauma, and English Identity

Nancy Bradley Warren

The Traumatic Middle Ages

In the Tudor period history was a hot commodity, and the history of the medieval past proved to be an especially valuable tool for asserting political legitimacy. Occasions calling for such assertion arose repeatedly throughout the Tudor era, appearing with particular frequency during Elizabeth I's rule. The beginning of her reign and the succession crisis that marked its end were especially fraught times in which rival factions strove mightily to own medieval history, to produce definitive versions of it, and to turn it to partisan purposes. As political assets go, however, history was hardly trouble free. Early modern engagements with medieval history call for a modification of George Santayana's much-quoted remark: those who *did* know history not only desired to repeat it (in that they wished to write it in ways favorable to a particular cause at a moment of cultural rupture) but they were also condemned to repeat it (in that they were compelled to reexperience its crises as and because they retold it).

For early modern writers who turned to medieval history at moments of instability, the good news and the bad news were in effect one and the same: the past and the present were seen to resemble each other. Medieval history could provide answers to questions in the present because it provided precedents, but the medieval past could also raise questions in the present because it was itself so replete with the unresolved. Indeed, the same anxieties about religion, lineage, monarchical legitimacy, and gender so prevalent in the Tudor era fundamentally shaped and animated the very medieval history to which early modern politicians and propagandists so readily turned. In particular, coming to terms with female bodies and the roles those bodies play in legitimating or delegitimating dynastic lineages is of primary concern in the early modern texts under consideration here as well as in the medieval histories to which the early modern writers turn. In

174

these early modern texts, and in the political difficulties prompting their production, we see, in effect, reemergences of medieval trauma that are constitutive of distinctively English modes of negotiating competing versions of national identity at the interface between past and present.[1]

The Lancastrian Line and the Lancastrian Repressed: Elizabeth I, Robert Parsons, and the Claims of the Past

The Lancastrian era began with a deposition, with the triumph of Henry Bolingbroke over Richard II, and, when Edward IV triumphed over Henry VI for the second time in 1471, it also ended, at least temporarily, in one. Lancastrian revival, however, came thanks to another act of deposition when Henry Tudor defeated Richard III at Bosworth Field in 1485. Originating with an episode so closely recalling the earlier Henry's dethroning of the earlier Richard, the new Tudor dynasty found itself contending with an all-too-familiar crisis of legitimacy. Remedies were, somewhat paradoxically, sought through what John N. King has called the "incessant Tudor claim to Lancastrian descent."[2]

In his account of the last days of Richard III's reign, Polydore Vergil—no stranger to Tudor Lancastrianism—presents a series of encounters that highlights both the desirability and the ambivalent status of the Lancastrian inheritance at the moment the Tudor dynasty was being born. Leading up to his discussion of Henry Tudor's arrival in England from France, Vergil discusses the conflict between Richard III and Henry, Duke of Buckingham, who in Vergil's version of events appears as a key agent in engineering Henry Tudor's return. Vergil first traces Buckingham's own connections to the Lancastrian line. The duke was the son of Humphrey, the first Duke of Buckingham; Humphrey's father was Edmund of Stafford, and his mother Anne was the daughter of Thomas of Woodstock and Alienor of Hereford. Anne had been heir to her mother's inheritance after Richard II executed Woodstock and confiscated his possessions. Alienor's sister Mary had married Henry of Derby (who became Henry IV). As Vergil reports, "And so by the maryage of Anne and Mary was therle of Herefords inherytance devydyd, thone moytie to thowse of Lancaster, thother to the bloode of Staffords, from whome the dukes of Buckingham deryve ther pedygre."[3] Since the line of Henry IV ended with the death of Henry VI and his son Edward, Prince of Wales, "Henry of Buckingham thowght that he might by good right demand that part of therle of Herefords patrimony which in the right of Mary had coommyd to the howse of Lancaster, which whan King Richard held the right of the crown, with thother possessions of the howse of Lancaster" (193). Buckingham thus demanded what he perceived as his rightful inheritance from Richard III, who, according to Vergil, did not respond favorably: "To this king Richard . . . ys reportyd to have answered furthwith in great rage: 'What now, duke Henry, will yow chalenge unto you that right of Henry the Fourth wherby he wyckedly usurpid the crowne, and so make open for yourself the way therunto?'" (193). The Lancastrian inheritance, which for Buckingham was something of great value worth claiming, is for Richard III a legacy of usurpation and illegitimacy.

The royal response to Buckingham's demand almost prophetically envisions a recurrence of Lancastrian trauma in positioning Richard III as a potential new Richard II. The monarch's retort indeed suggested precisely such an association between the two Ricardian monarchs to Buckingham, who reportedly was motivated by Richard III's scornful answer to seek the king's deposition and the triumph of the house of Lancaster by means of Henry Tudor. Vergil says, "Which king Richards answer settlyd depe into the dukes breste, who from that time furth, movyd muche with ire and indignation, began to devyse by what meane he might thrust owt that ungratefull man from the royall seat. . . . Than the duke unfoldyd all thynges to the bisshop of Ely, and dyscoveryd himself wholy, shewing how he had devysyd the meane wherby both the bloode of king Edward and of Henry the Sixth that yeat was remaining, being conjoignyd by affynytie, might be restoryd to the domynion dew unto both their progenyes" (193–94). The plan, of course, is that "Henry erle of Richemond . . . might be sent for in all hast possyble . . . so that he wold promyse before by solemne othe, that after he had once obtaynyd the kingdom he wold take to wyfe Elyzabeth, king Edwards eldest dawghter" (194).

Vergil's partisan account throws into sharp relief, albeit perhaps unwittingly, the paradox inherent in the fact that the first monarch of the Tudor dynasty would invoke Lancastrian heritage—a heritage that, considering its origins in an act of deposition, was replete with anxieties about legitimacy—to legitimate a reign also founded on deposition. Furthermore, the paradox of Tudor Lancastrianism as inaugurated by Henry VII is heightened by the fact that Henry's connection to the Lancastrian line is so fragile and relies on female descent. The questionable legitimacy of female descent, like the problem of usurpation, persistently troubled earlier generations of Lancastrians. The medieval Lancastrian kings depended on descent through the female line for their claim to the French throne, which they pursued so avidly through the later fourteenth and fifteenth centuries. However, the necessity that the English royal line be an exclusively masculine one uncontaminated by a feminine presence was something upon which the Lancastrians insisted quite forcefully, an insistence that only intensified once the Yorkist faction began to advance its claim.[4]

Buckingham's involvement of the Bishop of Ely in his plans to enable the return of Henry Tudor, offspring of the Lancastrian line, echoes a strategy characteristic of earlier Lancastrians, especially Henry V—that is, turning to the realm of religion to enhance the credibility of reigning monarchs and causes. Though this strategy would prove to be a favorite of early modern kings and queens— as throughout much of the sixteenth and seventeenth centuries Catholic and

Protestant rivals struggled mightily to assert that they enjoyed the right to the throne by divine mandate as well as by Lancastrian blood—spiritual assets had, like the Lancastrian inheritance, their own paradoxical political dimensions. For example, as Henry V consolidated the Lancastrian hold on the throne of England and pressed the English claim to France in the early fifteenth century, he worked to maintain a delicate balance between forms of holy kingship at odds with each other as he also negotiated the aforementioned contradictory stances on women in the line of succession. On the one hand, Henry claimed to be descended from a holy line of English priest kings, a sacerdotal model of kingship that excluded women from the royal succession. On the other hand, he embraced "incarnational kingship"—a model that granted women a legitimate place in the royal line by pointing to the example of the Virgin Mary and Jesus as a case in which a virtuous woman transmitted a divine inheritance to a male heir. The inherent trickiness of managing spiritual assets was intensified when those assets were combined with the Lancastrian inheritance; for instance, as I shall discuss shortly, Protestant propagandists wrestled with the awkward fact of their Lancastrian ancestors' Catholicism while early modern Catholics partisans strived to cope with the presence of Henry VIII among the descendants of the house of Lancaster.

The benefits of the Lancastrian inheritance were thus forever complicated by mutually reinforcing anxieties concerning gender, religion, legitimacy, and lineage. The glories of the Lancastrian past brought with them traumas only ever partially repressed and incompletely resolved. Since repression is, as Freud instructs us, "the precondition for the construction of symptoms," it is not surprising that the return of the Lancastrian dynasty in the person and propaganda of Henry VII was accompanied by another sort of return—the return of the Lancastrian repressed.[5]

Henry VII's granddaughter Elizabeth faced challenges to her reign on multiple grounds—the legitimacy of her birth, her Protestant religion, and her gender. The Lancastrian inheritance offered virtually irresistible material to use in holding these challenges at bay, providing a means of foregrounding both Elizabeth's dynastic and divinely-ordained rights to the throne. Accordingly, the pageants staged to mark Elizabeth's entry into London preceding her coronation in 1558 prominently exploited her Lancastrian ties. An anonymous account of the processions and pageants, entitled *The royall passage of her Maiesty from the Tower of London, to her palace of White-hall with all the speaches and deuices*, reports that early in the ceremonies, in "Gracious street . . . at the upper end, before the signe of the Eagle," a stage was erected consisting of "three Parts; and over the middlemost was aduaunced three severall stages in degrees."[6] The pageant bore a wreath inscribed with its title, "The vniting of the two houses of Lancaster and Yorke" (fol. A4r), and it displayed a classic version of Elizabethan Lancastrianism, the oft-used imagery of the Tudor rose tree. Invoking the iconography of the tree of Jesse, as well as the elaborate Lancastrian genealogical propaganda that circulated during the reign of Henry VI, the Tudor rose tree had been used by Elizabeth's father, Henry VIII, to proclaim his own legitimacy.[7]

In the version of the image incorporated into the pageants, on the lowest of the three stages, Henry VII and his wife, Elizabeth, appear. Henry is enclosed in the red rose of Lancaster, Elizabeth in the white rose of York, and the figures' hands are joined. The author reports, "Out of the which two Roses, sprang two branches gathered into one, which were directed upward to the second stage or degree: wherein was placed one, representing the valiant & noble Prince King Henry the eight" (fol. A3v). He is accompanied by a figure representing Anne Boleyn, and from the two of them a single branch extends to a representation of Elizabeth I on the uppermost stage. The interpretation given for this pageant seeks to minimize the problematic dimensions of the Lancastrian past by underlining, and thereby uniting, the concord of past and present. Noting that the reigning queen shares the name Elizabeth with the one whose marriage to Henry VII ended "the long warre between the two houses of Yorke and Lancaster," the author declares: "So since that the Queenes Maiesties name was Elizabeth, and forsomuch as she is the onely heire of Henry the eight, which came of both houses, as the knitting up of concord, it was deuised, that like as Elizabeth was the first occasion of concord, so shee another Elizabeth might maintaine the same among her Subiects; so that vnitte was the end where at the whole deuise shot, as the Queenes Maiesties names moued the first ground" (fol. A4r). Elizabeth is heir not only to the Lancastrian heritage, a heritage that is embraced even as its traumas are elided in its representation by the red rose surrounding Henry VII, but also to a Tudor legacy of peace and unity.

A particularly interesting example of Elizabethan Lancastrianism appears in Richard Grafton's discussions of the aforementioned precoronation pageant series in his *Abridgement of the Chronicles of England*.[8] Grafton's description, like that in the anonymous pamphlet *The royall passage*, emphasizes Queen Elizabeth's connection to the Lancastrian line; like the pamphlet author, Grafton engages in a sort of typological reading. In this case, it is not Elizabeth I's reign of concord that is prefigured by the earlier Elizabeth who unified warring factions. Instead, confounding those who deny Elizabeth's right to rule on grounds of faith, Grafton imaginatively posits that the Lancastrian line enjoys a sort of retroactive Protestantism. Grafton had been appointed king's printer under Edward VI and imprisoned under Mary I, so this stance is not unexpected. Grafton glosses the nuptial union of Henry VII and Elizabeth of York as a symbol of "the coniunction and coupling together of our soueraigne Lady with the Gospell and veritie of Goddes holy woord, for the peaceable gouvernement of all her good subiectes" (fol. 178v). Henry VII's place in relation to Elizabeth of York is thus occupied by the Gospel and Word of God, which are coupled with Elizabeth I. Elizabeth I's representation as the bride of the Gospel and the Word of God—a significant modification, on behalf of the "Virgin Queen," of the nuptial role of bride of Christ, the Word made Flesh, central to the identity of Catholic nuns—confirms Elizabeth's divine mandate to reign.[9] Furthermore, the description of Elizabeth I united with the Word of God suggests that Elizabeth, succeeding the Catholic Mary I, caused true religion to displace a false ecclesiastical regime in the same way that Henry VII displaced the false reign of Richard III with Henry's true one.

Elizabeth's Catholic opponents saw her complex construction of an identity, dependent in some respects on transforming the incarnational piety on the cult of the Virgin Mary, quite differently than her supporters did. So, too, did these opponents remember Henry VIII differently. While the author of *The royall passage* declares that "this Realme doth hold" Henry VIII "so worthy of memory" and expresses hopes that Elizabeth I will reiterate her father's "doings" (fol. D3r), English Catholic writers opposed to Elizabeth's reign and concerned with restoring a Catholic monarch to the throne interpreted Henry VIII's break with Rome (rather than Henry Bolingbroke's deposition of Richard II) as the moment of rupture that constituted cultural crisis. Similarities, however, underlie the divergent understandings of what constituted a critical break. For Catholics, as for Protestants, the results of rupture were deep concerns about the interplay of religion, lineage, legitimacy, and gender, all of which shaped their perspectives on Elizabeth's rule and the question of who should succeed her.

The Jesuit Robert Parsons, writing as R. Doleman, directly addresses this knotty complex of issues directly in *A Conference About the Next Succession to the Crowne of England*, published in 1594.[10] This work might equally be titled "A Revisionist History of the House of Lancaster," and it makes abundantly clear how valuable the Lancastrian inheritance is. Parsons faces a daunting task in staking his claim, however. He finds it necessary to argue that authentic Englishness resides outside of Protestant England, and, like the fifteenth-century Lancastrian monarchs laying claim to the throne of France, he needs to make a persuasive case for the rightful place of women in dynastic lineages while at the same time anticipating the anxiety-provoking scenario of a female monarch ruling independently.

The *Conference* "is in the form of discourses by a civilian and a temporal lawyer respectively," and is divided into two sections. The first section, in the voice of the civilian lawyer, treats political philosophy; the second section (the one with which I am concerned) is "the discourse of the temporal lawyer" and "deals with the claims of various pretenders to the succession."[11] From Parsons's perspective, Henry VIII represents the real problem point in Lancastrian history, while the originary trauma of Richard II's deposition becomes an asset rather than a liability. Parsons argues that "both by reason authority and examples of all nations Christian" it is lawful that a monarch "vppon iust causes . . . may be deposed" (*Conference*, 61). He then goes on to present the arguments of the Lancastrian and Yorkist factions concerning whether or not the deposition of Richard II was done by just cause. Parsons concludes that the usurpation was a justified, and in fact a divinely approved, political action. One might be led to believe that such a line of argument would in fact aid the cause of pro-Elizabethan Lancastrianism, since an obvious point to be drawn is that the Lancastrians need suffer no loss of legitimacy as a result of the deposition that established their dynasty. It is, however, in Parsons's account of the deposition of Richard II that Elizabethan versions of medieval history, and Elizabeth's representational strategies that rely on such versions of history, come to be troubled by the legacies of Lancastrian trauma. Parsons first argues that Richard never should have reigned; rather, John of Gaunt should have succeeded Edward III (77–78). Accordingly, Gaunt's descendents should bear no taint of usurpation because Henry IV had simply reclaimed what should always have been his rightful inheritance.

Parsons also argues that *real* Lancastrian ancestry can only be claimed by those who descend from John of Gaunt's first marriage, to Blanche of Lancaster. He observes that "Iohn of Gaunt third sonne of king Edward being duke of Lancaster by his wife . . . had three wiues in al, and by euery one of them had issue"; however, he goes on to note that since "only the first wife was daughter and heyre of the house of Lancaster and iohn of Gaunt duke thereof by her, it followeth that the children only that were borne of her can pretend properly to the inheritance of that house" (41). The line descended from John of Gaunt and his first wife, and the right to legitimate inheritance of the English throne that goes with it, ended in England in the aftermath of Henry VI's deposition.[12] In Parsons's version of Lancastrian history one must look outside of England to find *true* Lancastrians descended from John of Gaunt and Blanche of Lancaster in the sixteenth century. Hence, Parsons deals with the problem of Henry VIII's presence in the Lancastrian line by removing him and his descendents, including Elizabeth I, from that line.

In Parsons's view the only royal legacy Henry VIII and Elizabeth I can claim is that of the house of York, which was joined to the "pseudo-Lancastrian" line when Henry VII married Elizabeth, daughter of Edward IV. Far from being a moment of union that prefigures the harmony to be solidified by Elizabeth's reign, this marriage is the impetus for the perpetuation of a false Lancastrian line and a nefarious Yorkist one. The Yorkist line, in which Henry VIII is firmly placed, emerges as a conduit of trouble and misrule as Parsons sets up a comparison between the monarchs he deems to be authentically Lancastrian and those "that have bin of the house of York, to wit Edward the fourth, Richard the third, *Henry the eight*, and Edward the sixt" (97, my emphasis). He calls attention to "al their acts both at home & abroade, what quitnes or troobles haue passed, and what the common wealth of Ingland hath gotten or lost under each of them" (97), concluding that "we shal finde, that God hath seemed to prosper and allow much more of those of Lancaster than of those of Yorke, for that under those of Lancaster the realme hath enioyed much more peace, and gayned far greater honor, and enlarged more the dominions of the crowne then under those of Yorke" (97–98).

Although Parsons never states it directly, the intended conclusion the reader is to draw is obvious: Elizabeth I is heir to a legacy of misrule, misrule is grounds for justified deposition, and Elizabeth should be deposed. This perspective is strengthened by the list of rightly-deposed monarchs Parsons musters to support his argument that Richard II was rightfully dethroned. The last two in the list are not kings but queens—Jezebel and Athalia. If it is true that Parsons was directly involved in a plot to kill Elizabeth, as John Bossy argues, the Jesuit's account of Athalia's fate is especially sinister:

> And in the same booke of kings within two chapters after, there is other example how God moued Ioïada high priest of Ierusalem to persuade the Captaines and Coronels of that cittye to conspire against Athalia the Queene that had reigned six years, and to arme them selues with the armor of the temple, for that purpose, and to besiege the pallace wher she lay, and to kill al them that should offer or goe about to defend her, & do they did, and hauing taken her aliue, she was put to death also by sentence of the said high priest, and the fact was allowed by God, and highly commended in the Scripture.[13]

Immediately upon concluding this account, Parsons declares summarily, "And this seemeth sufficient proofe to these men, that king Richard of Ingland might be remoued by force of armes, his life and gouerment being so euel and pernitious as before hath bin shewed" (72).

In Parsons's exposition of Lancastrian history, Elizabeth I is not a Henry IV or Henry V—she is a Jezebel, Athalia, or, indeed, Richard II. That possible parallels might be drawn between Elizabeth and Richard II did not escape Elizabeth herself; in an often-quoted conversation with the historian William Lambarde she purportedly remarked, "I am Richard II, know ye not that?"[14] Interestingly, the title page of the *Conference* declares that the work is "Directed to the Right Honorable the earl of Essex of her Maiesties priuy councell, & of the noble order of the Garter." As Ronald Corthell notes, with this direction "Parsons boldly politicizes his own excursion into English history."[15] At the time of publication this mention caused Robert Devereux, Earl of Essex, certain trouble and embarrassment.[16] In time, though, he perhaps took some of Parsons's arguments to heart, much as Vergil reports the Duke of Buckingham took up the inadvertant hint dropped by Richard III. Famously, on the eve of his rebellion Essex announced his dissent from both Elizabeth's rule and pro-Elizabethan historiography, asserting her connections with Richard II as a monarch ripe for deposition by sponsoring a performance of Shakespeare's *Richard II* at the Globe Theater.

It is not only in the Lancastrian histories produced by Elizabeth's opponents that the traumatic aspects of the past resurface when that past is harnessed
for present ends. Even in presentations of medieval Lancastrian history designed
to advance Elizabeth's legitimacy as queen, such elements ultimately prove inescapable. The woodcut border of the title page of John Stow's *The Annales of England* (figure 1), published in 1592 and reissued during Elizabeth's reign in 1600
and 1601 with the same title page, bears witness to the truth of Paul Strohm's
remark that "those texts which try hardest to ignore or exclude an event—to 'forget' history—tend to be the very places where the absent event stages its most
interesting and complicated return."[17] The border is another use of the image of
the Tudor rose tree, revising one included in Edward Hall's 1550 *Vnion of the two
noble and illustre famelies of Lancastre & Yorke*.[18] In the woodcut in the *Annales*,
twining branches springing from the recumbent form of Edward III depict the
Lancastrian line on the left and the Yorkist line on the right; these join in a
crowned circle bearing the name of Henry VIII. At the top, connected to that
circle, are pictures of his three children who wore the crown: Edward VI on the
left; Mary I on the right; and Elizabeth I in the center, directly above Henry VIII.
Her picture is flanked by the words "VIVAT REGINA."

Clearly, the message of this image is that Elizabeth is the rightful heir of
the combined Lancastrian and Yorkist lines, as was her father before her. By placing her image directly above Henry VIII's name, the artist indicates her closeness
or likeness to her father, echoing the representational strategies discussed earlier;
she is "another himself." However, the strong vertical axis of the tree, in which the
text's title is centered in a rectangular frame, runs from Elizabeth to Henry VIII
directly to Richard II. The full title of the book—*The Annales of England, faithfully
collected out of the most autenticall Authors, Records, and other Monuments of Antiquitie, from the first inhabitation untill this present yeere 1592*—which both names
the history at hand and makes reference to historical sources, is placed between
Henry VIII and Richard II, standing in the place of rupture (that is, the deposition of Richard II). In the very act of naming itself as history, the history recalls
trauma into being. The image links Elizabeth directly with the traumatic past and
foregrounds the possibility that she will reenact that past. An image designed
to assert Elizabeth's Lancastrian inheritance ends up also asserting that she is,
at least potentially, another Richard II, another victim of Lancastrian trauma,
another manipulator of the past claimed by history.

Parsons equally cannot escape the claims of history, and in the *Conference*
he cannot ultimately assign all of the inconvenient baggage of the past to the Protestants. Just as the woodcut on the title page of the *Annales* casts into sharp relief
that which it would likely rather conceal, the *Conference*, though it often seems
at pains to deny it, is troubled by some of the very issues that bedeviled Lancastrian monarchs in their struggles for legitimacy. As I indicated earlier, Parsons

Figure 1. John Stow, *Annales of England*, 1592. Title page with genealogy of Elizabeth I. (Photo: Reproduced by permission of The Huntington Library, San Marino, CA. Call number: RB 69560.)

holds that to find *true* Lancastrians in the sixteenth century one must look outside England, specifically in Spain and Portugal. He describes the authentic Lancastrian line—that of the offspring of John of Gaunt's first marriage, to Blanche of Lancaster—immediately moving into Portugal with John and Blanche's daughter Philippa's marriage to John I of Portugal; the line then continues through Edward I of Portugal, Alfonsus V of Portugal, and on to Parson's present time.[19] Weighing evidence, Parsons presents the cases of other claimants to the Lancastrian inheritance as well, but he ultimately concludes that the Iberian claim is the best.

Parsons similarly outlines the pros and cons of the possible successors for Elizabeth, but he never makes an absolutely definitive statement in favor of any one candidate.[20] There is no doubt, though, that he sees the best claim to be that of the potential successor who is most authentically Lancastrian; accordingly, one can readily discern his preference for the Infanta Isabel (eldest daughter of Philip II) as that successor. Parsons's preference for a Spanish successor is made all the more clear by the fact that "[e]ven before the news of the execution of Mary, Queen of Scots, reached Rome in March 1587, Parsons had begun researching the descent of the House of Lancaster with the intent of supporting Philip II's claim to the English throne."[21] Parsons insists that the infanta "is of the ancient blood royal of Ingland, even from the conquest" (*Conference*, 150); he also claims that her father, King Philip of Spain, who is "at this day king also of Portugal" is "the cheife titler of that house vnto Ingland" (161).[22] He underlines the fact that the heir to the throne of Portugal is also heir to the throne of England, saying, "I haue byn the longer in setting downe this contention about the succession to the crowne of Portugal, for that it includeth also the very same pretence and contention for the crowne of Ingland" (186). In the years after the 1588 Armada, arguments for Philip himself as the right monarch of England would have been unpalatable even to many who might otherwise have been sympathetic to Parsons's arguments; choosing Philip's daughter as the successor undoubtedly seemed a politic compromise. The infanta presented the further advantage of a "French connection," bearing the royal blood of France on her mother's side, since she descended "as wel from Queene Blanch as from Lewys" (24).[23]

It is in making his case for the infanta that Parsons is in his own turn troubled by unresolved issues from the Lancastrian past—namely, the anxieties raised by the presence of women in the line of succession. Legitimating women's transmissive abilities requires for Parsons, as it did for the earlier Lancastrian monarchs, dealing with the troubling possibility of independent female rule. Parsons thus finds himself in precisely the same dilemma the fifteenth-century Lancastrians had to face in balancing contradictory approaches to women in the line of succession in relation to their English and French claims. Like the fifteenth-century Lancastrians, Parsons wishes in effect to have it both ways—he wants a woman to be a legitimate heir, but he does not want her fully to possess that inheritance.

Uneasiness about female rule and about including women in the line of succession surfaces even as Parsons puts forward a female candidate for succession whose claim depends on descent through the female line. For instance, in making his case for the greater legitimacy of those of true Lancastrian descent, he denigrates the Yorkist title because it is "by a woman" (75), seemingly forgetting that what he purports to be the *real* Lancastrian line also enjoys that title "by a woman."[24] Furthermore, in presenting the deficiencies of Arabella Stuart as a successor to Elizabeth, he includes a fairly lengthy diatribe against female rule, even though he ultimately holds up another woman as the best candidate to occupy the English throne. Parsons says, "It should be hurtful to the realme to admit this lady Arbella for Queene, as first of al for that she is a woman, who ought not to be preferred, before so many men as at this tyme do or may stand for the crowne: and that it were much to haue three women to reigne in Ingland one after the other, wher-as in the space of a-boue a thousaid [sic] yeares before them, there hath not reigned so may of that sexe, nether together nor a sunder" (128). He goes on to point out that between the time of "king Cerdrick first king of the west Saxons" and the reign of "Egbright the first monarch of the Inglish name and nation," a period of more than three hundred years, no woman reigned. Then, from the time of Egbright until the coming of William the Conqueror, another period of approximately three hundred years, no woman occupied the throne. Furthermore, in the five hundred years after the conquest, "one only woman was admitted for inheritrix, which was Maude the Empresse," and she was a special case since "she neuer receaued by the realme, vntil her sonne Henry the second was of age to gouerne himselfe, and then he was receaued with expresse condition, that he should be crowned, and gouerne by himself, and not his mother" (128).

In facing the quintessentially Lancastrian dilemma of negotiating the place of women in royal lineages, Parsons borrows a page from the Lancastrians' book. As did the genealogical propaganda of Henry VI's reign, Parsons stresses women's subordination to men.[25] To mitigate the consequences of arguing a case that might well enable ongoing female rule in England, he emphasizes that in Spain, where the Lancastrian line has devolved, women who are the heirs in a royal line are, like the English Empress Maude, merely placeholders for a male who will *actually* rule. Parsons follows his discussion of Maude quoted above by remarking that this "very condition was put also by the spaniards not long after, at their admitting of the lady Berenguela yonger sister of lady Blauch neese to king Henry the second, wherof before often mention hath bin made, to wit the condition was, that her sonne Fernando should gouerne, and not she, though his title came by her" (128–29). He suggests that the infanta will follow this same pattern, and stresses her desirability as a wife, suggesting that should she succeed Elizabeth, a husband will be brought into the picture with all due haste. Indeed, he turns the infanta's marriageability into an asset that strengthens the case for her as a successor to Elizabeth. Parsons writes, "My reasons for the former part, about the Lady Infanta, are, that she is a woman, and may easely ioyne (if her father will) the titles of Britany and Portugal together, she is also vnmarried, and by her marriage may make some other composition, either at home or abroade, that may facilitate the matter, she is a great Princesse and fit for some great state, and other Princes perhapps of Christendome would more willingly yeald and concurr to such a composition" (263).

Working to emphasize that a woman's role, while necessary, is necessarily subordinate to male authority is not the only Lancastrian-style move that Parsons makes in legitimating a line of succession that depends on women. As did Henry V, he turns to female spirituality, especially to Brigittine spirituality, to lend support to his cause. Henry V found St. Birgitta and the Brigittine Order to be especially useful in constructing his self-representational strategy centering on "incarnational kingship," because not only did Birgitta's revelations suggest that God was on the English side in the dispute over who should rule France, but the Brigittine Order's particular form of monastic life also emphasized the role of the Virgin Mary in salvation history, placing particular stress on her role in the incarnation.[26] In his account of the foundation, history, and exile of the English Brigittine community of Syon, Parsons repeats his argument that the true heirs to the house of Lancaster, and so to the English throne, are to be found on the Iberian Peninsula in what might, if one were not aware of the significance of the Brigittine Order to the Lancastrian dynasty, initially seem a rather unlikely place.

Syon, having left England after the Dissolution of the Monasteries and having repeatedly fled Protestant forces in the Low Countries and France, settled in Lisbon in 1594. The Spanish monarchs who held sovereignty over Lisbon at that time were important financial supporters of the exiled English monastic community. One obvious motive for Parsons to incorporate in his history of Syon his argument that the heirs of Lancaster were to be found in Spain and had the right to claim the English throne might be to thus curry favor with the king who had for so long trained his gaze on England. However, that Parsons rehearses the argument of the *Conference* in miniature in a Brigittine text that is precisely contemporaneous with the *Conference* suggests that his discussion in this particular context has greater significance than flattering the Spanish monarch. As he does in the *Conference*, Parsons here insists on the Catholic orthodoxy of the Lancastrian line, stressing that Syon's founder, Henry V, was renowned "for matters of religion and piety."[27] More pointedly, he writes, "And now, considering the circumstances of these Religious, it certainly seems not to be without a mystery that by the particular Providence of God they have been brought through so many travels and banishment to the kingdom of Portugal, there to repose themselves securely within the protection of the descendants of the House of Lancaster and the blood royal of their founder King Henry the Fifth: for the kings of Portugal descend in a right line from the royal house of Lancaster."[28] In this passage Parsons's reference to Henry V as founder of Syon helps us to see that Parsons is himself using a representational tactic that the fifteenth-century ruler mobilized to great effect. As Henry V did by founding Syon, Parsons draws on the symbolic resources of Brigittine spirituality to enhance the legitimacy of a genealogy that depends on descent through the female line. In his day Edward IV made generous grants to Syon, becoming the house's "second founder" and tapping into the symbolic benefits of Syon's distinctive brand of female spirituality, something every bit as useful to the Yorkists in bolstering their claim to the English crown as it was to the Lancastrians in representing their French claim.[29] In his history of Syon, Parsons positions the king of Spain not only as the heir of Syon's first founder—Henry V, "descend[ed] in a right line"—but also in effect the house's third founder, thanks to his role as protector of the community. Philip is thus the rightful inheritor of both the throne of England and the symbolic benefits of Brigittine spirituality that had aided his Lancastrian ancestors nearly two centuries earlier.

However, St. Birgitta and Brigittine spirituality were also, unlikely though it might seem, a symbolic resource to which Protestant propagandists and supporters of Elizabeth I turned, as we find in the writings of John Foxe and Edmund Spenser. In 1570, in the disturbed aftermath of the 1569 rebellion of the northern earls and at the precise moment that Pius V promulgated the bull *Regnans in Excelsis*, which excommunicated Elizabeth I and encouraged her deposition, John Foxe published a revised and expanded edition of the *Actes and Monuments*, which had appeared initially in 1563. In the 1570 edition Foxe is especially interested in combating the charge of Protestant novelty and in countering "Roman Catholic allegations that Protestants were innovators who departed from tenets of early Christianity."[30] The work is an important contribution to the intense, long-lived struggle between Catholics and Protestants to embrace the past of the early church as their own, and, accordingly, Foxe added to the 1570 edition "hundreds of pages of documentation concerning the first millenium of the Christian era. . . . [T]he first volume of the 1570 version begins at a chronological point much earlier than the era when the 1563 version had effectively begun" (113–14).

In the 1570 edition Foxe is also interested in history more recent than that of the early church. Lancastrian history and medieval female saints play important roles in Foxe's project, much as they do in Parsons's *Conference* and his history of Syon. In book 5 Foxe includes a discussion of the law of praemunire, recounting that Edward III "[n]ot onely reuiued the sayd statute made by Edward the first his graundfather, but also inlarged the same" (517). Foxe immediately follows the discussion of Edward III's expansion of this statute with something rather unexpected, given his general hostility toward saints other than those whose lives have scriptural warrant. Whereas Parsons mobilizes the life, revelations, and monastic order of St. Birgitta to support his Catholic revision of Lancastrian history and his argument for a Spanish claimant to the English throne, Foxe joins Edward III, the monarch to whom the competing Lancastrian dynastic arguments all look for the source of their ultimate legitimacy, with St. Birgitta of Sweden. Foxe then makes this saint, who was passionately committed to the cause of the Roman papacy, serve the Protestant aim of undermining papal authority and bolstering English monarchical independence.

Foxe says, "About thys tyme, being þe yeare of our Lord. 1370. lyued holy Brigit, whom the churche Rome hath canonised not onely for a saynt, but also for a prophetis: who notwithstanding in her booke of reuelations, which hath bene oft times imprinted, was a great rebuker of the Pope, and of the filth of his clergy, calling hym a murtherer of soules, a spyller, and pyller of the flocke of Christ" (517). He proceeds to incorporate various elements of her critiques of clerical and papal corruption (which are admittedly plentiful in her revelations, though they are never targeted at denying the authority of the papacy or the priesthood as offices). Then, stating, "It were long and tedious to declare" all that she writes against the clergy, he concludes, "Among the rest which I omit, let this suffice for all, where as the sayd Brigit affirmeth in her reuelations, that when the holye virgine should say to her sonne, how Rome was a fruitfull and fertile field: yea, sayd he, but of weedes only & cockle.&c" (517). Foxe pits Brigittine incarnational piety and the characteristic dual focus on the Virgin Mary and the incarnate Christ against the church, which claims to be Christ's true body, and against its head, who claims to be Christ's earthly representative.

Another pro-Elizabethan invocation of St. Birgitta in response to a moment of dynastic anxiety occurs in the "July" eclogue of Edmund Spenser's *Sheaperdes Calendar*, a text much engaged with contemporary political debates, particularly those concerned with religious controversy and with the related matter of Elizabeth I's potential marriage. In this eclogue Morrell says to Thomalin:

> Syker, thous but a laesie loord,
> and rekes much of thy swinck,
> That with fond termes, and weetlesse words
> to blere myne eyes doest thinke.
> In euill houre thou hentest in hond
> thus holy hylles to blame,
> For sacred vnto saints they stond,
> and of them han theyr name.
> S. Michels mount who does not know,
> that wardes the Westerne coste?
> *And of S. Brigets bowre I trow,*
> *all Kent can rightly boaste:*
> And they that con of Muses skill,
> sayne most what, that they dwell
> (As goteheards wont) vpon a hill,
> beside a learned well.[31]

Josephine Waters Bennett argues that the reference to "S. Brigets bowre" likely refers to Greenwich, saying that "Spenser had reason to believe that Greenwich and all the surrounding countryside had formerly belonged to a famous nunnery dedicated to St. Bridget"—that is, Syon.[32]

Bennett argues that Spenser's reference to Greenwich as "S. Brigets bowre" has multilayered significance. Not only was Greenwich Palace Elizabeth's "birthplace and a favorite residence in the summer" but "there was another, and to Queen Elizabeth a most unwelcome, association with the royal Pleasance at Greenwich which the poet may have been attempting to supplant." In anti-Elizabethan propaganda designed to stir up scandal about the queen's relationship with the Earl of Leicester, Greenwich is associated with the castle of Miraflores in the romance *Amadis of Gaul*; at this castle "Amadis carries on a clandestine love-affair with the English princess Oriana." Oriana bears an illegitimate child with Amadis, and "allusion to Oriana had been used to libel the Queen."[33] If, as Bennett allows is possible, Spenser thought St. Birgitta of Sweden was a virgin, as most female saints were, linking St. Birgitta with Elizabeth's birthplace reinforces the queen's virginal identity in the face of sexual slander. On the other hand, if Spenser knew the biographical details of St. Birgitta's marriage and maternity, which Bennett finds "quite probable," then Spenser, as a supporter of the marriage of Elizabeth I and the earl of Leicester (rather than the duc d'Alençon), may have called Greenwich "S. Brigets bowre" because "he wished to suggest a parallel between St. Bridget, the Swedish princess who had married and borne children and yet been a saintly reformed of the church, and Queen Elizabeth."[34] Either way, the life of a medieval Catholic holy woman serves as a political asset for a Protestant queen in an environment in which the legitimacy of her reign and her dynastic legacy are under attack.

Tudor Legacies and Medieval Afterlives: Protestant Propaganda and the "Spanish Match"

Parsons's efforts to mobilize the symbolic capital available from the English Brigittines in exile to advance the case for a Spanish succession to the English throne came back to cause difficulties for the English Catholic cause a generation later, in the era of the controversial Spanish marriage. The Protestant James VI of Scotland had, of course, succeeded Elizabeth as James I of England, but the hopes of English Catholics were raised when the proposal emerged for his son Charles to marry the Infanta Maria of Spain (daughter of Philip III). Although the Protestant partisans Foxe and Spenser found St. Birgitta to be a useful figure, the Brigittine community of Syon had never been anything but hostile to Protestant rule in England, and they strongly supported the Spanish match. The nuns and abbess directed a petition to the infanta in which they address her as the Princess of Wales ("La Altissima Señora Prinçesa de Walia") in advance of the marriage and in which they set out a view of the Lancastrian descent that harmonizes precisely with Parsons's.[35] Indicating their belief that the Catholic, Spanish monarchs are the true Lancastrian heirs and, accordingly, the heirs to the throne of England, they thank the Spanish kings for their financial support. Expressing their gratitude to Philip III, they say, "driven out from their royal foundation, *founded and endowed by Your Majesty's predecessors the Kings of England*, these servants of Our Lord did not lack protection, for he touched and inspired the royal hearts of Your Majesty and of Your Most Zealous father, King Philip II, *true descendants of their founders the English Kings*, to take them to your charge and sustain them."[36] The nuns likewise declare their hopes that the Infanta Maria, like Mary Tudor before her, will prove to be a savior for the community in exile and "resettle it a second time from the foreign kingdoms to which it had again been exiled."[37]

For English Protestants opposed to the Spanish marriage, this tie between the infanta and English women in Iberia who embodied the "old religion" was at once anxiety provoking and useful. Gender and religion once again combined with anxieties about lineage and legitimacy to emerge as a locus of crisis. Cristina Malcolmson argues that during the period in which the Spanish marriage looked likely, there was a strong association "of women with Spanish infiltration."[38] Among English Protestants "a powerful fear" existed "about . . . the Spanish princess, who as queen would be mother to the future English king. . . . [T]he Spanish Infanta was seen as the avenue through which the Catholic Church and the Spanish Empire would enter the English state and rob it of its national strength."[39]

Thomas Robinson's *The Anatomie of the English Nunnery in Portugal* (1622) represents the Protestants' strategy for turning the troubling nexus of fears raised by the Spanish marriage to their advantage.[40] Robinson claimed to have been forcibly detained by the confessor general Seth Foster and put to work as a copyist.[41] Hence he was, at least purportedly, in the position to tell all the scurrilous secrets of convent life. In the *Anatomie*, medieval female spirituality and medieval history taint, rather than support, the cause of the infanta and her English Catholic supporters. Playing off the widespread Protestant representation of the Catholic Church as the "whore of Rome" or the "whore of Babylon," Robinson portrays the exiled Brigittine community of Syon as a nest of sexual vice. The explanation of the title Robinson gives in his address "To the indifferent Reader" makes immediately evident his interest in female bodies—the actual bodies of the nuns and the symbolic, feminized body of the Catholic Church—as well as in these bodies' corrupt excesses. He first warns that the reader should not expect the sort of medical work possibly signaled by his title, saying, "Reader, if the Title of this booke, being The Anatomie of the English Nunnery at Lisbon, doo make the expect some Chyryrgicall mysteries, or profound Lecture upon a dissected body, let me satisfie thee, and saue thee a labour in reading it." He goes on to indicate that bodies are, however, in fact a central topic of discussion in the text, claiming that the treatise "hath truly anatomized this handmaid of the Whore of Babylon; laying open her principall veins and sinews."

The image included on the title page, which is accompanied by an explanatory poem, further indicates Robinson's concern with female bodies. The title page bears a series of pictures (conveniently labeled with letters keyed to corresponding passages in the explanatory verses) in which a nun enters a cleric's chamber through the grate where he hears her confession. Subsequent images unflinchingly reveal their debauched activities within the chamber. As the poem gleefully explains:

> So on a bed they wanton clippe and kisse,
> There's nothing in a Nunnery amisse.
> Then doth a banquet on a Table stand,
> And from the bed he leads her by the hand;
> Whereat they eate, carouse, and kisse againe;
> And, in a word, doe no delight refraine.

The rampant vice in a nunnery where "nothing [is] amisse" is manifested by the bodily delights of the nun and cleric: hugging, kissing, banqueting, carousing.

Robinson's interest in female bodies extends to an interest in lineage. He notes that although Syon was founded by women of royal blood and was previously populated by women from well-born families, the women in the house now are personally corrupt and derived from undistinguished backgrounds. He says, "at this present it is not of any extraordinary repute; neither are the people of it for birth and parentage equall to their predecessors, who were wont to be of good descent: whereas now (saue only a few) they are Recusants daughters of the meaner sort" (7). Furthermore, he claims that many of the postulants flee to the Continent because they have "ministered to their spirituall fathers in all things: and by such means having gotten a clap, diuers of them become Nunnes" (7). In a marginal note on this passage, Robinson bitingly observes, "It is no great miracle for a whore to become a Nunne; nor for a Nunne to become a whore" (7nb). Therefore the only lineage to be found at Syon is fundamentally illegitimate in every sense of the term; in fact, Robinson makes unmistakably clear that Syon is characterized by female carnality, sexual corruption, and a tainted inheritance when he reports his discovery of the bones of nuns' illegitimate children enclosed within the nunnery walls.[42]

Robinson strikingly suggests that Syon's present sexual corruption is rooted in the Brigittine Order's medieval past. Indeed, the nuns' vice appears to be the direct result of their continual employment of the practices of that age. Again directing attention to lineage and origins, Robinson notes that "in the Catholique

Romane Church, amongst all the disordered Orders of swarming Locusts . . . there is none but take their beginning from one supposed Saint or another" (4). Robinson then turns to a central figure in Parsons's, and indeed in Henry V's, symbolic programs—St. Birgitta herself. The Brigittines, Robinson notes, "take their beginning from their holy Mothers Saint *Bridget*, and her daughter Saint *Katherine*" (6). He admits that these women were of royal blood and that Birgitta was "a woman (questionlesse) of a good vnderstanding and singular memory" (6). However, far from being a visionary who founded a monastic order on God's command and who received that order's rule from Christ, she was "miserably seduced and led away by the subtil allurements of her ghostly Father, by whose perswasions and counsell she went to *Rome* as a Pilgrime, and coming before the Pope, she pretended to haue diuers reuelations from God; amongst which, one was for the founding of this Order of Nunnes" (6).

The sexual connotations of the language in this passage (in particular, the references of seduction and subtle allurements) make St. Birgitta appear to be much the same as the postulants who come to Lisbon after being seduced by seminary priests, or, indeed, like the nuns who dally with their confessors (as in the opening image), only to bear illegitimate children. Her status as a married woman who bore children, though not overtly condemned, seems to lurk in the background, playing a symbolic role precisely counter to the role her married maternity potentially has in Spenser's *Shepeardes Calendar*. The idea emerges that the legacy to be had at Syon is not one of a distinctive form of medieval female spirituality but rather one of stereotypical feminine sexual corruption reaching back to the house's fifteenth-century foundation. Robinson strengthens this negative portrait by stressing that Syon, unlike other English monastic communities in exile, has an unbroken connection to the (corrupt) medieval past. He points out that English nunneries exist in Bruxelles, Gravelines, and Lisbon, "but none that haue continued euer since the suppression of Abbeys in England, saue only that at Lisbon" (8nb).

In Robinson's *Anatomie*, St. Birgitta, the medieval past, and the nuns of Syon do not lend symbolic support to a case for the legitimate place of women in a line of succession. Rather, they model a tainted female lineage and demonstrate that medieval female spirituality is simply a guise for feminine carnality. The *Anatomie* seems to make, at least indirectly, a claim like that of William Prynne, who writes that the Spanish hoped to cause England's downfall through the "project of marrying us to the whore of Rome by matching the heire of the crownse of England to a *Romanist*."[43] For Robinson, the saintly founder of the Brigittine order, the English nuns of Syon living in Lisbon, the Infanta Maria with whom they are closely tied, and the Roman Catholic Church to which all these women belong are all, in effect, whores.

Robinson thus categorically denies to the supporters of the Spanish marriage all symbolic value deriving from female purity and holiness. He similarly denies the Catholic cause the benefits to be obtained through Syon's strong links to Lancastrian royalty. Indeed, while he cannot dismiss the house's foundation by the Lancastrian Henry V "at his returne from his famous Conquest in France" (2), he portrays the dissolution as being a more glorious Lancastrian triumph. He writes, "[I]t pleased the lord of his infinit mercy to disperse and scatter those thick cloud of ignorance and superstition, which had long time bedimmed the eyes, and darkend the vnderstanding of our forefathers, and that the glorious light of the Gospell began to be more and more resplendent in the latter end of the reigne of King Henry the 8" (3). Whereas Parsons seeks to give the Spanish monarch legitimating symbolic capital by positioning him, like Henry V, as a patron of Syon, Robinson inverts this strategy, making dissolution, rather than foundation, a source of symbolic value. As we have seen, Grafton imaginatively crafts on Elizabeth I's behalf a Protestant Lancastrian line, and Parsons emphasizes on the infanta's behalf the *true* Lancastrian line's Catholic orthodoxy. Robinson, on behalf of those opposed to the Spanish marriage, in turn creates a Lancastrian line cleansed of Catholic taint by exalting Henry VIII's heroic action in doing God's work of banishing "ignorance and superstition."

Coda: Parsons's Return

In the era of the English Civil Wars, anxieties about religion, monarchical legitimacy, lineage, and gender dramatically emerged front and center. England was thrown into tumult by yet another act of deposition when, in 1649, Charles I was executed and his French Catholic wife Henrietta Maria fled to the Continent with their children. In an act demonstrating that the medieval past was still very much worth appropriating, those in favor of ending monarchical rule in England turned to a most surprising resource—Robert Parsons's *Conference*. The first part of Parsons's text was "plagiarized and . . . reappear[ed] unexpectedly in 1648 in a pirated version under the pen of Oliver Cromwell's own publicist, Henry Walker."[44] The *Conference* obviously appealed to Republicans for its pro-deposition arguments. Indeed, they clearly want to suggest that Charles is yet another Richard II.[45] It is difficult to imagine, however, anything more incongruous than a Jesuit work committed to making a case for the divine legitimacy of a Catholic monarch being turned to Republican ends. The republication of the *Conference* casts into sharp relief not only that it remained impossible, well after the Tudor era, to escape the legacies of the medieval past by rejecting them, but also that the unresolved traumas of the past would never cease to reemerge to unsettle present invocations of it.

NOTES

A different version of Nancy Bradley Warren's essay appears as part of chapter five in Warren, *The Embodied Word: Female Spiritualities, Contested Orthodoxies, and English Religious Cultures, 1350–1700* (Notre Dame, IN: University of Notre Dame Press, 2010).

1. Paul Strohm, writing about Edward IV's return to England in 1471 to reclaim the throne from the recently reinstated Henry VI, describes a dynamic similar to the one upon which I focus, pointing out the inseparability of desired and undesirable effects that result from mobilizing history for political ends. Strohm notes that the account of Edward's return in the *Historie of the Arrivall of Edward IV* deliberately connects Edward's landing in England with the return to England of Henry IV after his banishment by Richard; he then observes, "Representational, and ultimately political, capital is to be had from invocation of so influential a precedent . . . . But an adherence to pattern also carries a downside risk for an imitator who wants to capitalize upon some, but not all, of a pattern's previous implications. Here, the risk for Edward involves the difficulty of establishing a difference between his own reassertion of legitimate sovereign claims and the stark fact of Henry's original usurpation" (*Politique*, 24). Strohm continues, "The problem with a recognized pattern, and precedent, rests in the difficulty of using it for some things and not for others. In this case the affirmative and negative elements of Henry's previous pattern will finally turn out to be inextricable" (25).

2. King, *Tudor Royal Iconography*, 216.

3. Vergil, *Anglica Historia*, 193; hereafter cited parenthetically.

4. The Yorkist claim through Lionel, Duke of Clarence—a son of Edward III older than the Lancastrian progenitor John of Gaunt, Duke of Lancaster—depended at two points on succession through women: Lionel's daughter Philippa and great-granddaughter Anne Mortimer. On these Lancastrian representational strategies, see chapter 5 of Warren, *Spiritual Economies*. Henry Tudor's Lancastrian connection came through his mother, Margaret Beaufort, a descendant of John of Gaunt and his third wife, Katherine Swinford. The Tudor claim to Lancastrian descent was further complicated by the fact that Margaret descended from one of John and Katherine's children born prior to their marriage but later made legitimate.

5. Freud, *Introductory Lectures on Psycho-Analysis*, 364.

6. *The royall passage of her Maiesty*, p. A3v. This text, although printed in 1604, is based on one printed only nine days after the events in question: *The Quenes maiesties Passage through the Citie of London to Westminster the Day before her coronacion.* Hereafter I cite *The royall passage of her Maiesty* parenthetically.

7. For an example of such genealogical propaganda, see the elaborate frontispiece illumination in London, British Library, MS Royal 15 E VI, depicting Henry VI's claims to the thrones of England and France.

8. Richard Grafton, *Graftons Abridgement*, fol. 178v, hereafter cited parenthetically. I include a briefer discussion of the precoronation pageants in chapter 6 of *Women of God and Arms*.

9. On Elizabeth's engagement with medieval female spirituality, especially the cult of the Virgin Mary, see Hackett, *Virgin Mother, Maiden Queen*, and Yates, *Astraea*; see also chapter 6 of Warren, *Women of God and Arms*.

10. L. Hicks believes Parsons was a contributor to the *Conference*, not its sole author or even its main contributor; see "Robert Parsons," 126–28. I tend to agree with Victor Houliston's perspective that "although Allen and Englefield, and possibly others, provided

material for the book, Parsons compiled and wrote the final version"; Houliston, "Hare and the drum," 237. In addition to the evidence Houliston marshals, I would add that Parsons's rehearsal in his history of Syon of virtually the same argument about the Lancastrian line that he presents in the *Conference*, and that the works were produced at the same time, gives further weight to the case for his authorship. On Parsons's history of Syon and the Lancastrian line, see below.

11. Hicks, "Robert Parsons," 105; for a detailed description and summary, see 104–6.

12. Parsons declares "in this king Henry the 6 and his sonne prince Edward, ended all the blood royal male of the house of Lancaster, by Blanch the first wife of Iohn of Gaunt" (*Conference*, 44).

13. Parsons, *Conference*, 71. On Parsons's possible involvement in a plot to kill Elizabeth, see John Bossy, "Heart of Robert Parsons," esp. 144–50.

14. Quoted in volume 3 of Nichols, *Progresses and Public Processions*, 232.

15. Corthell, "Robert Persons and the Writer's Mission," 46.

16. For accounts of Elizabeth's reaction to the work and Essex's response, see Hicks, "Robert Parsons," 123. Hicks notes that it may have been Lord Burghley or his son Sir Robert Cecil who gave a copy of the *Conference* to the queen; as relations between Essex and the Cecils were at this time "very strained," they may have given Elizabeth the book "for the very purpose of causing a rift in the Earl's relations with the Queen" (123).

17. Strohm, *Theory and the Premodern Text*, xii–xiii. Stow's *Annales* were printed several more times after Elizabeth's reign, but beginning with the first edition after her death, that of 1605, the title page was changed and no longer contained a genealogical component. Stow, *Annales of England*.

18. Hall, *Union of the two noble and illustre famelies*.

19. Parsons writes, "so by this marriage of lady Phillip, to the first king Iohn, these princes of the house of Portugal that liue at this day, do pretende that the inheritance of Lancaster is only in them, by this lady Phillip, for that the succession of her elder brother king Henry the fourth, is expired long ago" (*Conference*, 161).

20. Houliston writes, "The treatise can be said to promote, not simply one candidature, but a certain frame of mind in the reader" ("Hare and the drum," 242). Drawing on Annabel Patterson's work on Holinshed's *Chronicles*, Houliston suggests that an application of her version of the concept of "indifference" can be made to Parsons's text. He says that Patterson "argues that indifference is central to the entire Holinshed project: what appears to be shapeless or incoherent in the *Chronicles* derives from a deliberate attempt to allow the reader to confront the past indifferently in all its multivocal diversity and self-contradiction. In an obvious sense, this applies to part 2 of the *Book of Succession*, where each claim is allowed to speak for itself" ("Hare and the drum," 243). Patterson's analysis of Holinshed is from *Reading Holinshed's Chronicles*.

21. Jean-Christophe Mayer, "'This Papist and His Poet,'" 123.

22. Philip II ruled Spain 1556–98; he was ruler of Portugal (as Philip I) 1580–98. His son succeeded him upon his death, ruling Spain and Portugal (the latter as Philip II) 1598–1621.

23. Cardinal William Allen's interpretation of the *Conference*, outlined in "The opinion and iudgment of C. A. before his deathe," bolsters the assertion that Parsons's text has a clear pro-infanta message. Allen's text also suggests that this position was not an idiosyncratic one confined to Parsons. The author Roger Baines (Allen's secretary), who signs himself "Yors euer to command B.S." (fol. 10v), declares that "Towching . . . the Ladye Infanta of Spaine, the opinion of C. A. was that . . . all thinges considered . . . he did see no other person in the worlde so fytt to accommodate all matters and to end all controuersyes

to breake all difficulties and to avoyde all dangers on euery syde, as yf this Ladye should be agreed on of all handes to haue hir tytle preferred & established" (5r–v). On the authorship of this text, see Hicks, "Robert Parsons," 128; and Houliston, "Hare and the drum," 237 and 237n9.

24. In asserting Lancastrian superiority to the Yorkists, Parsons says, "Moreouer it is alleaged for Henry that his title came by a man, and the others by a woman, which is not so much fauoured either by nature law or reason" (*Conference*, 75). However, as he notes in an earlier passage, upon the death of Henry VI and Prince Edward, "the inheritance of the said lady Blanch returned by right of succession . . . vnto the heyres of lady Phillip her eldest daughter, married into Portugal, whose nephew named Alfonsus the fift kinge of Portugal liued at that day when king Henry the 6 and his heyre were made away" (*Conference*, 44). To accomplish the necessary but daunting representational tasks before him in legitimating a female successor whose claim depends on descent through the female line, Parsons spends some time explaining that the French prohibition of succession through the female line does not apply in England, where Salic Law has never been in force. Cardinal William Allen reinforces this point regarding Salic Law. In "Opinion and iudgment," he reports that in his view, "England . . . regardeth no law Salique as all the worlde knoweth" (5r). However, given Parsons's denigration of the English Yorkist claim as a lesser one since it relies on the female line, this argument about Salic Law is not entirely persuasive.

25. See, for instance, the elaborate genealogical frontispiece in MS Royal 15 EVI; for an insightful discussion of this image, see Michel-André Bossy, "Arms and the Bride."

26. For Birgitta's revelation regarding England's right to rule France, see *Liber celestas*, book 4, chaps. 104–5 (St. Bridget, *Liber celestis of St. Bridget of Sweden*). See also Vauchez, "St. Birgitta's Revelations," 180–81. I discuss St. Birgitta's importance for Lancastrian political strategies at greater length in chapter 5 of *Spiritual Economies*. For instances of the importance of Mary's maternal transmission of salvation in Brigittine divine service, see Blunt, *Myroure of Our Ladye*, 104, 141, 194.

27. Hamilton, *Angel of Syon*, 97–98.

28. Quoted in Hamilton, *Angel of Syon*, 111.

29. In order to claim descent from Lionel, Duke of Clarence, an elder son of Edward III than John of Gaunt, Duke of Lancaster, the Yorkist faction had to rely on descent through the female line at two junctures.

30. King, *Foxe's "Book of Martyrs,"* 113; hereafter cited parenthetically.

31. Emphasis added. Spenser, *Shepheardes Calendar*, fol 26v.

32. Bennett, "St. Bridget, Queen Elizabeth, and *Amadis of Gaul*," 27. Bennett explains that Greenwich actually belonged to the Carthusian charterhouse of Sheen, but she points out, "There is adequate record that the two institutions were confused" in Spenser's day (28).

33. Bennett, "St. Bridget, Queen Elizabeth, and *Amadis of Gaul*," 31.

34. Bennett, "St. Bridget, Queen Elizabeth, and *Amadis of Gaul*," 32–33

35. "Petition a La Altissima Señora Prinçesa de Walia," in de Hamel and Robinson, *Syon Abbey*; henceforth I quote the English translations given in this volume and include page references for both the English and the Spanish. I discuss the "Petition," including the passages mentioned here, in greater detail in chapter 6 of *Women of God and Arms*.

36. English translation of the "Petition," in de Hamel and Robinson, *Syon Abbey*, 33; for the Spanish text, see 22.

37. De Hamel and Robinson, *Syon Abbey*, 24; for the Spanish text, see 12.

38. Malcolmson, "'As Tame as the Ladies,'" 333.

39. Malcolmson, "'As Tame as the Ladies,'" 333–34.

40. An earlier, briefer discussion of *The Anatomie* and the Spanish marriage appears in chapter 6 of *Women of God and Arms*.

41. Robinson, *Anatomie of the English nunnery at Lisbon*, 1; hereafter cited parenthetically.

42. Robinson asserts that he "did chance to make a hole in a hollow place in a wall . . . out of which hole I pul'd sundry bones of some dead children, and left many more remaining behind" (*Anatomie of the English nunnery at Lisbon*, 27). By emphasizing feminine corruption and the nuns' undistinguished parentage, Robinson is himself embracing a strategy with a long medieval—indeed, a long Lancastrian—history. Robinson does to the Brigittine nuns, whose spirituality has the potential to aid the cause of his Catholic enemies, the very thing that the Lancastrians did to Joan of Arc during her trial and Tudor propagandists did to her in the pages of chronicles after her death. Henry VIII's "reformers" too adopted this strategy in the course of the Dissolution of the Monasteries.

43. Quoted in Malcolmson, "'As Tame as the Ladies,'" 334; emphasis in original.

44. Mayer, "'That Papist and His Poet,'" 127.

45. For instance, witness the argument that "King Richard the second . . . forgetting the miserable end of his great Grandfather for evil government, as also the felicity, and vertue of his Father and Grandfather for the contrary, suffered himselfe to be abused and misled by evill councellours, to the great hurt and disquietnesse of the Realme. For which cause after he had reigned 22 yeares, he was deposed by act of Parliament holden in *London*, and condemned to perpetuall prison in the Castle of *Pomfret*. . . . [A]nd in this man's place by free election was chosen for King the noble Knight *Henry* Duke of *Lancaster*, who proved afterwards a notable King"; see *Severall Speeches Delivered at a Conference concerning the Power of Parliament, to proceed against their King for Misgovernment*, Wing P573A (London, 1648), 20.

Bibliography

Aers, David. "*Vox Populi* and the Literature of 1381." In Wallace, *Cambridge History of Medieval English Literature*, 423–53.

Allen, William. "The opinion and iudgment of C. A. before his deathe concernyng the late printed Booke of the succession of England, and certayne poyntes therunto apperteyning." Valladolid, Colegio San Albano, Serie II, Legajo 12, document 9 version 3.

Alsop, James. "Nicholas Brigham (d. 1558), Scholar, Antiquary, and Crown Servant." *Sixteenth Century Journal* 12, no. 1 (1981): 49–67.

Aston, Margaret. "English Ruins and English History: The Dissolution and the Sense of the Past." *JWCI* 36 (1973): 231–55. Reprinted in *Lollards and Reformers*, 1984.

———. *Laws against Images*. Vol. 1 of *England's Iconoclasts*. Clarendon Press, 1988.

———. *Lollards and Reformers: Images and Literacy in Late Medieval Religion*. London: Hambledon Press, 1984.

———. "Lollardy and the Reformation: Survival or Revival?" *History* 49 (1964): 149–70

Bacon, Francis. *Francis Bacon: A Critical Edition of the Major Works*. Edited by Brian Vickers. Oxford: Oxford University Press, 1996.

Baker, J. H. *An Introduction to English Legal History*. 3rd ed. London: Butterworths, 1990.

[Baldwin, William, et al.] *A Myrroure for Magistrates*. STC 1247. London: Thomas Marshe, 1559.

Bale, John. *The Complete Plays of John Bale*. Edited by Peter Happé. 2 vols. Cambridge: D. S. Brewer, 1985.

———. *The first examinacyon of Anne Askewe, lately martyred in Smythfelde, by the Romysh popes upholders, with the Elucydacyon of Johan Bale*. STC 848. Marpurg [Wesel], 1546.

———. *Illustrium maioris Brytanniae scriptorum, hoc est, Angliae, Cambriae ac Scotiae, summarium. . . .* STC 1295. Ipswitch [Wesel]: [John Overton], 1548.

———. *Index Britanniae Scriptorum*. Edited by Reginald Lane Poole and Mary Bateson. Oxford: Oxford University Press, 1902. Reprint, Bury St. Edmunds: D. S. Brewer, 1990.

———. *King Johan*. Edited by Barry B. Adams. San Marino, CA: Huntington Library, 1969.

———. *The Laboryouse Journey and Serche of Johan Leyland*. STC 15445. London, 1549.

———. *Select Works of John Bale*. Edited by Rev. Henry Christmas. Cambridge, 1849.

————. *Scriptorvm illustriu[m] maioris Brytanni[a]e, quam nunce Angliam & Scotiam uocant: Catalogus. . . .* Basel, 1557–59. Reprint, Farnborough: Gregg, 1971.

————. *The Vocacyon of Johân Bale.* STC 1307. Rome [Wesel], 1553.

Barish, Jonas. *The Antitheatrical Prejudice.* Berkeley: University of California Press, 1981.

Barr, Helen. *The Piers Plowman Tradition.* London: J. M. Dent, 1993.

Bennett, Josephine Waters. "St. Bridget, Queen Elizabeth, and *Amadis of Gaul.*" *English Literary History* 10, no. 1 (1993): 26–34.

Benson, C. David. *The History of Troy in Middle English Literature: Gudio delle Colonne's Historia Destructionis Troiae in Medieval England.* Woodbridge, Suffolk: D. S. Brewer, 1980.

Bernard, G. W. "The Tyranny of Henry VIII." In *Authority and Consent in Tudor England: Essays Presented to C. S. L. Davies,* edited by G. W. Bernard and S. J. Gunn, 113–29. Burlington, VT: Ashgate, 2002.

Besson, Robert K. *Shakespeare's "Troilus and Cressida" and "The Legends of Troy."* Madison: University of Wisconsin Press, 1953.

Betteridge, Thomas. *Literature and Politics in the English Reformation.* Manchester: Manchester University Press, 2004.

————. "Staging Reformation Authority: John Bale's *King Johan* and Nicholas Udall's *Respublica.*" *Reformation & Renaissance Review* 3 (2000): 34–58.

————. *Tudor Histories of the English Reformations, 1530–83.* Brookfield, VT: Ashgate Publishing, 1999.

Bevington, David. "'Instructed by the antiquary times': Shakespeare's Sources." In Shakespeare, *Arden Shakespeare: Troilus and Cressida,* 375–97.

Blodgett, James. "William Thynne." In *Editing Chaucer: The Great Tradition,* edited by Paul Ruggiers, 35–52. Norman, OK: Pilgrim Books, 1984.

Bloom, Harold. *The Anxiety of Influence: Theory of Poetry.* 2nd ed. New York: Oxford University Press, 1997.

Bloomfield, Morton. "Present State of *Piers Plowman* Studies." *Speculum* 14 (1939): 215–32.

Blundeville, Thomas. *The true order and Methode of wryting and reading Hystories. . . .* STC 3161. London, 1574.

Blunt, John Henry. *The Myroure of Our Ladye.* Early English Text Society, e.s., 19. London: Kegan Paul, 1873.

Boffey, Julia, and A. S. G. Edwards. "Literary Texts." In *The Cambridge History of the Book in Britain,* vol. 3, *1400–1557,* edited by Lotte Hellinga and J. B. Trapp, 555–75. Cambridge: Cambridge University Press, 1999.

Bossy, John. "The Heart of Robert Parsons." In *The Reckoned Expense: Edmund Campion and the Early English Jesuits,* edited by Thomas M McCoog, 141–58. Woodbridge, Suffolk: Boydell, 1996.

Bossy, Michel-André. "Arms and the Bride: Christine de Pizan's Military Treatise as a Wedding Gift for Margaret of Anjou." In *Christine de Pizan and the Categories of Difference,* edited by Marilynn Desmond, 236–56. Minneapolis: University of Minnesota Press, 1998.

Bourdieu, Pierre. *Distinction: A Social Critique of the Judgement of Taste.* Translated by Richard Nice. Cambridge, MA: Harvard University Press, 1984.

Bowen, Catherine Drinker. *The Lion and the Throne: The Life and Times of Sir Edward Coke.* Boston: Little, Brown and Company, 1957.

Bowers, John M. *Chaucer and Langland: The Antagonistic Tradition.* Notre Dame, IN: University of Notre Dame Press, 2007.

———. "Piers Plowman and the Police: Notes toward a History of the Wycliffite Langland." *Yearbook of Langland Studies* 6 (1992): 1–50.

Bradbrook, M. C. "What Shakespeare Did to Chaucer's Troilus and Criseyde." *Shakespeare Quarterly* 9 (1958): 311–19.

Brantley, Jessica. "The Prehistory of the Book." *PMLA* 124 (2009): 632–39.

Brett, Caroline, and James P. Carley. Introduction to *Index Britanniae Scriptorum*, by John Bale. Edited by Reginald Lane Poole and Mary Bateson. Bury St. Edmunds: D. S. Brewer, 1990. Pp. xi–xviii.

Brewer, Charlotte. *Editing "Piers Plowman": The Evolution of the Text.* Cambridge: Cambridge University Press, 1996.

[Bridget of Sweden]. *The liber celestis of St. Bridget of Sweden.* Edited by Roger Ellis. Early English Text Society, o.s, 291. Oxford: Oxford University Press, 1987.

Bright, Allan H. *New Light on "Piers Plowman."* London: Oxford University Press, 1928.

Brown, Marshall. "Periods and Resistances." *Modern Language Quarterly* 62 (2001): 309–16.

Bullough, Geoffrey. *Narrative and Dramatic Sources of Shakespeare.* Vol. 6. New York: Columbia University Press, 1966.

Burckhardt, Jacob. *The Civilization of the Renaissance in Italy.* Translated by S. G. C. Middlemore. Vienna: Phaidon Press, 1937.

Burrow, Colin. "The Experience of Exclusion: Literature and Politics in the Reigns of Henry VII and Henry VIII." In Wallace, *Cambridge History of Medieval English Literature*, 793–820.

Burrow, J. A. *Gestures and Looks in Medieval Narrative.* Cambridge: Cambridge University Press, 2002.

Campbell, Emma. "Sexual Poetics and the Politics of Translation in the Tale of Griselda." *Comparative Literature* 55 (2003): 191–216.

Campbell, Lily B., ed. *The Mirror for Magistrates.* Cambridge: Cambridge University Press, 1938.

Canning, R., ed. *The principal charters which have been granted to the corporation of Ipswich in Suffolk.* London, 1754.

Cantor, Norman F. "The Interpretation of Medieval History." In *Essays on the Reconstruction of Medieval History*, edited by Vaclav Murdoch, 1–18. Montreal: McGill-Queen's University Press, 1974.

Cargill, Oscar. "The Langland Myth." *PMLA* 50 (1935): 36–56.

Carré, Yannick. *Le baiser sur la bouche au Moyen Age.* Paris: Le Léopard d'Or, 1992.

Cartelli, Thomas. "Jack Cade in the Garden: Class Consciousness and Class Conflict in *2 Henry VI.*" In *Enclosure Acts: Sexuality, Property, and Culture in Early Modern England*, edited by R. Burt and J. M. Archer, 48–67. Ithaca, NY: Cornell University Press, 1994.

Cavanagh, Dermot. *Language and Politics in the Sixteenth-Century History Play.* New York: Palgrave Macmillan, 2003.

———. "The Paradox of Sedition in John Bale's *King Johan,*" *English Literary Renaissance* 31 (2001): 175–79.

Cavendish, George. *Life and Death of Cardinal Wolsey.* Edited by Richard S. Sylvester. Early English Text Society, o.s., 243. London: Oxford University Press, 1959.

———. *Metrical Visions.* Edited by A. S. G. Edwards. Columbia: University of South Carolina Press, 1980.

Cawsey, Kathy. "'I Playne Piers' and the Protestant Plowman Prints: The Transformation of a Medieval Figure." In *Transmission and Transformation in the Middle Ages: Texts and*

Contexts, edited by Kathy Cawsey and Jason Harris, 189–206. Dublin: Four Courts Press, 2007.

———. "Tutivillus and the 'Kyrkchaterars': Strategies of Control in the Middle Ages." *Studies in Philology* 102 (2005): 434–51.

Caxton, William. *Recuyell of the Historyes of Troye.* STC 15375. Bruges, 1473.

———. *The Recuyles or Gaderinge to Gyder of the Hystoryes of Troye.* STC 15376. London: Wynkyn de Worde, 1502. Variant *STC* 15377. London: Wynkyn de Worde, 1503.

———. *The Recuile of the Histories of Troie.* STC 15378. London: William Copland, 1553.

———. [*Recuyell*, variant title] *The Auncient Historie of the Destruction of Troy.* Revised by William Phiston. *STC* 15379. London: Thomas Creed and Valentine Simmes, 1597.

———. [*Recuyell*, variant title] *The Auncient Historie, of the Destruction of Troy.* STC 15380. London: Thomas Creede, 1607.

———. [*Recuyell*, variant title] *The Ancient Historie of the Destruction of Troy.* Titled the "Fifth Edition." *STC* 15381. London: Barnard Alsop, 1617.

———. [*Recuyell*, variant title] *The Ancient Historie of the Destruction of Troy.* "Sixth Edition." *STC* 15382. London: Barnard Alsop and Thomas Fawcett, 1636.

———. [*Recuyell*, variant title] *The Destruction of Troy.* "Seventh Edition." Book 1, Wing L929; book 2, Wing L934; book 3, Wing L938. London: Samuel Speed, 1663.

———. [*Recuyell*, variant title] *The Destruction of Troy.* "Eight Edition." Wing L930, L935, L939. London: Thomas Passenger, 1670.

———. [*Recuyell*, variant title] *The Destruction of Troy.* "Ninth Edition." Wing L931, L936, L940. London: Thomas Passenger, 1676.

———. [*Recuyell*, variant title] *The Destruction of Troy.* "Tenth Edition." Wing L932, L937, L941. London: Thomas Passenger, 1680.

———. [*Recuyell*, variant title] *The Destruction of Troy.* "Eleventh Edition." Wing L933, L937A, L941A. London: Thomas Passenger, 1684.

———. [*Recuyell*, variant title] *The Destruction of Troy.* "Twelfth Edition." London: Eben Tracy, 1702.

———. [*Recuyell*, variant title] *The Destruction of Troy.* "Thirteenth Edition." London: Eben Tracy, 1708.

———. [*Recuyell*, variant title] *The Destruction of Troy.* "Eighteenth Edition." Dublin: Thomas Browne, 1738.

———. *The Recuyell of the Historyes of Troye.* Hammersmith: William Morris, 1892.

———. *The Recuyell of the Historyes of Troye.* Edited by H. Oskar Sommer. Early English Text Society. London: Early English Text Society, 1894.

Certeau, Michel de. *The Practice of Everyday Life.* Translated by Steven Rendall. Berkeley: University of California Press, 1984.

Chambers, R. W. "Robert or William Longland?" *London Mediaeval Studies* 1, pt. 3 (1948 for 1939): 43–462.

Chapman, George. *Achilles shield. Translated as the other seuen bookes of Homer, out of his eighteenth booke of Iliades.* STC 13635. London, 1598.

———. *Seaven bookes of the Iliades of Homere, prince of poets.* STC 13632. London, 1598.

Charnes, Linda. "'So Unsecret to Ourselves': Notorious Identity and the Material Subject in Shakespeare's *Troilus and Cressida.*" *Shakespeare Quarterly* 40 (1989): 413–40.

Chartier, Alain. *The Curial. STC* 5057. Westminster: William Caxton, 1483.

Chaucer, Geoffrey. *The Riverside Chaucer.* Edited by Larry D. Benson. 3rd ed. Boston: Houghton Mifflin Company, 1987.

[Chaucer, Geoffrey]. *[The Plowman's Tale]. STC* 5099.5. London, 1535.

————. *The workes, newlye printed, wyth dyuers workes whych were neuer in print before.* Edited by William Thynne. *STC* 5069. London, 1542.

Cohen, Esther. *The Crossroads of Justice: Law and Culture in Late Medieval France.* Leiden: Brill, 1992.

Cohen, Stephen. *Shakespeare and Historical Formalism.* Burlington, VT: Ashgate, 2007.

Collinson, Patrick. *From Iconoclasm to Iconophobia: The Cultural Impact of the Second English Reformation.* Reading: University of Reading, 1986.

Corthell, Ronald. "Robert Persons and the Writer's Mission." In *Catholicism and Anti-Catholicism in Early Modern English Texts,* edited by Arthur F. Marotti, 35–62. New York: St. Martin's, 1999.

Curran, John E. *Roman Invasions: The British History, Protestant Anti-Romanism, and the Historical Imagination in England, 1530–1660.* Newark: University of Delaware Press, 2002.

Dane, Joseph A. "Bibliographical History versus Bibliographical Evidence: The Plowman's Tale and Early Chaucer Editions." *Bulletin of the John Rylands University Library of Manchester* 78 (1996): 47–61.

Davies, Tony. *Humanism.* New York: Routledge, 1997.

de Cessalis, Jacobus. *The Game and Play of Chess. STC* 4920. Bruges: William Caxton, 1474.

De Grazia, Margreta, Maureen Quilligan, and Peter Stallybrass, eds. *Subject and Object in Renaissance Culture.* Cambridge: Cambridge University Press, 1996.

de Hamel, Christopher, and John Martin Robinson. *Syon Abbey: The Library of the Bridgettine Nuns and Their Peregrinations after the Reformation.* London: Roxburghe Club, 1991.

de Pizan, Christine. *The Boke of the Fayt of Armes and of Chyualrye. STC* 7269. Westminster: William Caxton, 1484.

Diehl, Houston. *Staging Reform, Reforming the Stage.* Ithaca, NY: Cornell University Press, 1997.

Dillon, Janette. *Language and Stage in Medieval and Renaissance England.* Cambridge: Cambridge University Press, 1998.

Dinshaw, Carolyn. *Chaucer's Sexual Poetics.* Madison: University of Wisconsin Press, 1989.

Dodds, Madeleine Hope, and Ruth Dodds. *The Pilgrimage of Grace and the Exeter Conspiracy.* 2 vols. Cambridge: Cambridge University Press, 1915.

Donaldson, E. Talbot. *The Swan at the Well: Shakespeare Reading Chaucer.* New Haven: Yale University Press, 1985.

Douglas, Gavin. *The xiii. bukes of Eneados of the famose poete Virgill. STC* 24797. London, 1553.

Duffy, Eamon. *The Stripping of the Altars.* New Haven, CT: Yale University Press, 1992.

Duggan, Hoyt N., and Ralph Hanna, eds. *Oxford, Bodleian Library, Laud Misc. 581.* Vol. 4 of *The Piers Plowman Electronic Archive.* Woodbridge, Suffolk: Boydell and Brewer for the Medieval Academy of America and SEENET, 2004.

Echard, Siân. *Printing the Middle Ages.* Philadelphia: University of Pennsylvania Press, 2008.

Edwards, A. S. G. "The Early Reception of Chaucer and Langland." *Florilegium* 15 (1998): 1–23.

An Elegy on the Truly Honourable, and Most Virtuous, Charitable, and Pious Lady, Countesse of Devonshire, Who lately Departed this Life, being a hundred and odd Years of Age, whose Corps now Lies in Deserved State in Holbourn. London, 1675.

Ellis, Henry, ed. *Hall's Chronicle: Containing the History of England . . . carefully collated with the editions of 1548 and 1550.* London: J. Johnson, F. C. and J. Rivington, et al., 1809.

Elton, W. R. *Shakespeare's Troilus and Cressida and the Inns of Court Revels.* Brookfield, VT: Ashgate, 2000.

Enders, Jody. *The Medieval Theater of Cruelty: Rhetoric, Memory, Violence.* Ithaca, NY: Cornell University Press, 1999.

Erasmus, Desiderius. *The Correspondence, Letters 1 to 141.* Trans. R. A. B. Mynors and D. F. S. Thomson. Toronto: University of Toronto Press, 1974.

————. *A Dialoge or Communication of Two Persons, deuysyd and set forth in the laten tonge, by the noble and famose clarke. Desiderius Erasmus.* STC 10454. London, [1540?].

Escobedo, Andrew. *Nationalism and Historical Loss in Renaissance England: Foxe, Dee, Spenser, Milton.* Ithaca, NY: Cornell University Press, 2004.

Fairfield, Leslie P. *John Bale: Mythmaker for the English Reformation.* West Lafayette, IN: Purdue University Press, 1976.

Falco, Giorgio. *La Polemica Sul Medio Evo.* Turin: Biblioteca Della Societa Storica Subalpina, 1933.

Ferguson, Wallace K. "The Interpretation of the Renaissance: Suggestions for a Synthesis." *Journal of the History of Ideas* 12 (1951): 483–95

————. *The Renaissance in Historical Thought: Five Centuries of Interpretation.* Cambridge, MA: Houghton Mifflin Company, 1948.

Fiedler, Leslie A. "Shakespeare's Commodity-Comedy: A Meditation on the Preface to the 1609 Quarto of *Troilus and Cressida.*" In *Shakespeare's "Rough Magic": Renaissance Essays in Honor of C. L. Barber*, edited by Peter Erickson and Coppélia Kahn, 50–60. Newark, NJ: University of Delaware Press, 1985.

Fielde, John. *A Caueat for Parsons Howlet. . . .* London, 1581.

Fitter, Chris. "'Your Captain Is Brave and Vows Reformation': Jack Cade, the Hacket Rising, and Shakespeare's Vision of Popular Rebellion in *2 Henry VI.*" *Shakepeare Studies* 32 (2004): 173–219.

Fletcher, Angus. *Evolving Hamlet: Seventeenth-Century Tragedy and the Ethics of Natural Selection.* New York: Palgrave Macmillan, 2011.

Fletcher, John Rory. *The Story of the English Bridgettines of Syon Abbey.* Devon: Syon Abbey, 1933.

Forest-Hill, Lynn. *Transgressive Language in Medieval English Drama.* Burlington, VT: Ashgate, 2000.

Fowler, Edward. *A friendly conference between a minister and a parishioner of his, inclining to Quakerism.* London, 1676.

Foxe, John. *Actes and monuments of these latter and perillous dayes. . . . STC* 11222. London, 1563.

————. *Acts and Monuments.* Edited by Rev. Steven Reed Cattley and Rev. George Townsend. 8 vols. London, 1837–43.

————. *Actes and monuments, newly revised.* 2 vols. [4th ed.] *STC* 11225. London, 1583.

————. *Ecclesiastical History.* 2 vols. [2nd edition of the *Acts and Monuments.*] *STC* 11223. London, 1570.

————. *The Ecclesiastical History.* 2 vols. [3rd edition of the *Acts and Monuments.*] *STC* 11224. London, 1576.

Fradenburg, L. O. Aranye. *Sacrifice Your Love.* Minneapolis: University of Minnesota Press, 2002.

Freeman, Thomas S. "Offending God: John Foxe and English Protestant Reactions to the Cult of the Virgin Mary." In *The Church and Mary*, edited by R. N. Swanson, 228–38. Studies in Church History 39. Woodbridge, Suffolk: Boydell Press, 2004.

Freeman, Thomas S., and Sarah Elizabeth Wall. "Racking the Body, Shaping the Text: The Account of Anne Askew in Foxe's 'Book of Martyrs.'" *Renaissance Quarterly* 54 (2001): 1165–96.

Freud, Sigmund. *Introductory Lectures on Psycho-Analysis*. Edited and translated by James Strachey. New York: Norton, 1933.

Frijhoff, Willem. "The Kiss Sacred and Profane: Reflections on a Cross-Cultural Confrontation." In *A Cultural History of Gesture*, edited by Jan Bremmer and Herman Roodenburgh, 210–36. Ithaca, NY: Cornell University Press, 1992.

Funkenstein, Amos. "Periodization and Self-Understanding in the Middle Ages and Early Modern Times." *Medievalia et Huministica*, n.s., 5 (1974): 3–23.

Galbert of Bruges. *The Murder of Charles the Good*. Translated by James Bruce Ross. New York: Columbia University Press, 2005.

Gerhardt, Ernst. "'No quyckar merchaundyce than lybrary bokes': John Bale's Commodification of Manuscript Culture." *Renaissance Quarterly* 60 (2007): 408–33.

Gillespie, Alexandra. *Print Culture and the Medieval Author: Chaucer, Lydgate, and Their Books 1473–1557*. Oxford: Oxford University Press, 2006.

Godefrey of Boloyne. STC 13175. Westminster: William Caxton, 1481.

A godly dyalogue & dysputacyon betwene Pyers plowman, and a popysh pryest. . . . STC 19903. [London], [ca. 1550].

Gombrich, E. H. *In Search of Cultural History*. Oxford: Clarendon Press, 1969.

Gower, John. *The Painfull Aduentures of Pericles Prince of Tyre*. STC 25638.5. London: Thomas Purfoot, 1608.

Gradon, Pamela. "Langland and the Ideology of Dissent." *Proceedings of the British Academy* 66 (1980): 179–205.

Grafton, Anthony. "On the Scholarship of Politian and Its Context." *Journal of the Warburg and Courtauld Institutes* 40 (1977): 150–88.

Grafton, Richard. *Graftons Abridgement of the Chronicles of Englande*. STC 12151. [London], 1570.

Graham, Timothy, ed. *The Recovery of Old English: Anglo-Saxon Studies in the Sixteenth and Seventeenth Centuries*. Kalamazoo, MI: Medieval Institute Publications, 2000.

Great Britain, Public Records Office. *Letters and Papers, Foreign and Domestic, of the Reign of Henry VIII*. Edited by J. S. Brewer and J. Gairdner et al. Vol. 6. London: H. M. Stationery Office: 1862–1932.

Greenberg, Janelle. *The Radical Face of the Ancient Constitution: St. Edward's "Laws" in Early Modern Political Thought*. Cambridge: Cambridge University Press, 2001.

Greenblatt, Stephen. "Murdering Peasants: Status, Genre, and the Representation of Rebellion." *Representations* 1 (1983): 1–29.

Greene, Robert. *Euphues his censure to Philautus*. STC 12239. London, 1587.

Griffin, Benjamin. "The Birth of the History Play: Saint, Sacrifice, and Reformation." *Studies in English Literature* 39 (1999): 217–32.

Guild, William. *Anti-Christ pointed and painted out. . . .* London, 1655.

Guy, John. *Tudor England*. Oxford: Oxford University Press, 1988.

Hackett, Helen. *Virgin Mother, Maiden Queen: Elizabeth I and the Cult of the Virgin Mary*. New York: St. Martin's, 1995.

Hadfield, Andrew. *Literature, Politics, and National Identity*. New York: Cambridge University Press, 1994.

Hailey, R. Carter. "'Geuying light to the reader': Robert Crowley's Editions of *Piers Plowman* (1550)." *Papers of the Bibliographical Society of America* 95 (2001): 483–502.

———. "Giving Light to the Reader: Robert Crowley's Editions of *Piers Plowman* (1550)." PhD diss., University of Virginia, 2001.

———. "Robert Crowley and the Editing of *Piers Plowman* (1550)." *Yearbook of Langland Studies* 21 (2007): 143–70.

Hall, Edward. *Hall's Chronicle: The Union of the Two Noble and Illustre Famelies of Lancastre & Yorke....* New York: AMS Press, 1965.

———. *The Union of the two noble and illustre famelies of Lancastre & Yorke....* London: Richard Grafton, 1550.

Hamilton, Adam. *Angel of Syon: The Life and Martyrdom of Blessed Richard Reynolds, Bridgettine Monk of Syon, Martyred at Tyburn, May 5, 1535.* London: Sands & Co., 1905.

Hanna, Ralph, III. *William Langland.* Aldershot, Hamp.: Ashgate Publishing, 1993.

Happé, Peter. "Dramatic Images of Kingship in Heywood and Bale." *Studies in English Literature* 39 (1999): 239–54.

———. *John Bale.* Twayne's English Authors Series. New York: Twayne Publishing, 1996.

Hardy, Thomas. *Wessex Tales.* Vol. 9 of *The Writings of Thomas Hardy in Prose and Verse.* London: Harper and Brothers, 1903.

Harper-Bill, Christopher, ed. *Charters of the Medieval Hospitals of Bury-St. Edmunds.* Suffolk Charters Series 14 (Woodbridge, Suffolk: Boydell Press, 1994), nos. 168, 176.

Harris, Jonathan Gil. *Foreign Bodies and the Body Politic: Discourses of Social Pathology in Early Modern England* (Cambridge: Cambridge University Press, 1998).

Harvey, I. M. W. *Jack Cade's Rebellion of 1450.* Oxford: Clarendon Press, 1991.

Harvey, John. *A discoursive probleme concerning prophesies....* STC 12908. London, 1588.

Hattaway, Michael. "Rebellion, Class Consciousness, and Shakespeare's *2 Henry VI.*" *Cahiers Elisabethans* 33 (1988): 13–22.

Helgerson, Richard. *Forms of Nationhood: The Elizabethan Writing of England.* Chicago: University of Chicago Press, 1992.

Hellinga, Lotte, and J. B. Trapp. *Cambridge History of the Book in Britain.* Vol. 3, *1400–1557.* Cambridge: Cambridge University Press, 1999.

Here begynneth a lytell geste how the plowman lerned his pater noster. STC 20034. London, 1510.

Heywood, Thomas. *The Brazen Age.* STC 13310. London: Nicholas Okes, 1613.

———. *The Golden Age.* STC 13325. London: [Nicholas Okes] for William Barrenger, 1611.

———. *The Iron Age.* STC 13340.5. London: Nicholas Okes, 1632.

———. *The Siluer Age.* STC 13365. London: Nicholas Okes, 1613.

———. *Troia Britanica.* STC 13366. London, 1609.

Hicks, L. "Father Robert Parsons S.J. and *The Book of Succession.*" *Recusant History* 4 (1957): 114–37.

Holinshed, Raphael. *Holinshed's Chronicles of England, Scotland, and Ireland.* Ed. Henry Ellis. 6 vols. London, 1807–8.

———. *The Laste volume of the Chronicles of England, Scotlande, and Irelande, with their descriptions....* STC 13568.5. London, 1577.

Holsinger, Bruce. "Lollard Ekphrasis: Situated Aesthetics and Literary History." *Journal of Medieval and Early Modern Studies* 35 (2005): 67–89.

Honigmann, E. A. J. "The Date and Revision of Troilus and Cressida." In *Textual Criticism and Literary Interpretation*, edited by Jerome McGann, 38–54. Chicago: University of Chicago Press, 1985.

Houliston, Victor. "The Hare and the Drum: Robert Persons's Writings on the English Succession, 1593–6." *Renaissance Studies* 14 (2000): 235–50.

Howard, Henry. *A defensative against the poyson of supposed prophecies. . . . STC* 13859. London, 1583.

Howard, Thomas Albert. *Religion and the Rise of Historicism: W. M. L. De Wette, Jacob Burckhardt, and the Theological Origins of Nineteenth-Century Historical Consciousness.* Cambridge: Cambridge University Press, 2000.

Howe, Nicholas. "From Bede's World to 'Bede's World.'" In *Reading Medieval Culture: Essays in Honor of Robert W. Hanning*, edited by Robert M. Stein and Sandra Pierson Prior, 21–44. Notre Dame, IN: University of Notre Dame Press, 2005.

Hudson, Anne. "Epilogue: The Legacy of *Piers Plowman*." In *A Companion to "Piers Plowman*," edited by John A. Alford, 251–66. Berkeley: University of California Press, 1988.

———. "Lollard Book Production." In *Book Production and Publishing in Britain 1375–1475*, edited by Jeremy Griffiths and Derek Pearsall, 125–42. Cambridge: Cambridge University Press, 1989.

———. "'No newe thyng': The Printing of Medieval Texts in the Early Reformation Period." In *Middle English Studies Presented to Norman Davis in Honour of His Seventieth Birthday*, edited by Douglas Gray and E. G. Stanley, 153–74. Oxford: Clarendon, 1983.

———. *Selections from English Wycliffite Writings.* Toronto: University of Toronto Press, 1997.

———. "*Visio Baleii*: An Early Literary Historian." In *The Long Fifteenth Century: Essays for Douglas Gray*, edited by Helen Cooper and Sally Mapstone, 313–29. Oxford: Clarendon Press, 1997.

Hugh of St. Victor. *De institutione novitiorum.* PL 176: cols. 938–43.

Hughes, Paul L., and James F. Larkin, eds. *Tudor Royal Proclamations.* 3 vols. New Haven, CT: Yale University Press, 1964.

Hunt, Alice. *The Drama of Coronation: Medieval Ceremony in Early Modern England* Cambridge: Cambridge University Press, 2008.

I Playne Piers which can not flatter . . . 1st ed. *STC* 19903a. [London?], [1550?].

James, Heather. *Shakespeare's Troy: Drama, Politics, and the Translation of Empire.* Cambridge: Cambridge University Press 1997.

James, Mervyn. "At the Crossroads of the Political Culture: The Essex Revolt, 1601." In *Society, Politics and Culture: Studies in Early Modern England*, edited by Mervyn James, 416–66. Cambridge: Cambridge University Press, 1986.

Jameson, Fredric. *A Singular Modernity: Essay on the Ontology of the Present.* London: Verso, 2002.

Jensen, Phebe. "The Textual Politics of *Troilus and Cressida*." *Shakespeare Quarterly* 46 (1995): 414–23.

John of Salisbury. *Policraticus: Of the Frivolities of Courtiers and the Footprints of Philosophers.* Edited and translated by Cary J. Nederman. Cambridge Texts in the History of Political Thought. Cambridge: Cambridge University Press, 1990.

Johns, Adrian. *The Nature of the Book: Print and Knowledge in the Making.* Chicago: University of Chicago Press, 1998.

Johnson, Barbara. *Reading "Piers Plowman" and "The Pilgrim's Progress": Reception and the Protestant Reader.* Carbondale: Southern Illinois University Press, 1992.

Jotischky, Andrew. *The Carmelites and Antiquity.* Oxford: Oxford University Press, 2002.

Kane, George. *"Piers Plowman": The Evidence for Authorship.* London: Athlone Press, 1965.

Kantorowicz, Ernst. *The King's Two Bodies: A Study in Mediaeval Political Theology.* 1957. Reprint, Princeton: Princeton University Press, 1997.

Kastan, David Scott. "'Holy Wurdes' and 'Slypper Wit': John Bale's *Kynge Johan* and the Poetics of Propaganda." In *Rethinking the Henrician Era*, edited by Peter C. Herman, 267–82. Urbana: University of Illinois Press, 1994.

———. *Shakespeare after Theory.* New York: Routledge, 1999.

Kelen, Sarah A. "'It is dangerous (gentle reader)': Censorship, Holinshed's *Chronicles*, and the Politics of Control." *Sixteenth Century Journal* 27 (1996): 705–20.

———. *Langland's Early Modern Identities.* New York: Palgrave Macmillan, 2007.

———. "Plowing the Past: 'Piers Protestant' and the Authority of Medieval Literary History." *Yearbook of Langland Studies* 13 (1999): 101–36.

Kelley, Donald R. "Humanism and History." In *Renaissance Humanism*, edited by Albert Rabil Jr., 3:236–70. Philadelphia: University of Pennsylvania Press, 1988.

Kerrigan, William, and Gordon Braden. *The Idea of the Renaissance.* Baltimore: Johns Hopkins University Press, 1989.

Kimbrough, Robert. "The Origins of *Troilus and Cressida*: Stage, Quarto, and Folio." *PMLA* 77 (1962): 194–99.

King, John N. *English Reformation Literature.* Princeton, NJ: Princeton University Press, 1982.

———. *Foxe's "Book of Martyrs" and Early Modern Print Culture.* Cambridge: Cambridge University Press, 2006.

———. "Robert Crowley: A Tudor Gospelling Poet." *Yearbook of English Studies* 8 (1978): 220–37.

———. "Robert Crowley's Editions of *Piers Plowman*: A Tudor Apocalypse." *Modern Philology* 73 (1976): 342–52.

———. *Tudor Royal Iconography: Literature and Art in an Age of Religious Crisis.* Princeton, NJ: Princeton University Press, 1989.

Kingsford, C. L. *Chronicles of London.* Oxford: Clarendon Press, 1905.

Kleist, Aaron J. "Matthew Parker, Old English, and the Defense of Priestly Marriage." In *Anglo-Saxon Books and Their Readers: Essays in Celebration of Helmut Gneuss's "Handlist of Anglo-Saxon Manuscripts,"* edited by Thomas N. Hall and Donald Scragg, 106–33. Kalamazoo, MI: Medieval Institute Publications, 2008.

Koselleck, Reinhart. *The Practice of Conceptual History: Timing, History, Spacing Concepts.* Translated by Todd Samuel Presner, Kerstin Behnke, and Jobst Welge. Stanford, CA: Stanford University Press, 2002.

Kuskin, William. *Symbolic Caxton: Literary Culture and Print Capitalism.* Notre Dame, IN: University of Notre Dame Press, 2008.

Lambarde, William. *Archaionomia.* London: John Day, 1568.

———. *Archeion, or a Discourse Upon the High Courts of Justice in England.* Edited by Charles H. McIlwain and Paul L. Ward. Cambridge, MA: Harvard University Press, 1957.

———. *Eirenarcha.* English Experience, Its Record in Early Printed Books Published in Facsimile 273. New York: Da Capo, 1970.

———. *A Perambulation of Kent.* London: W. Burrill, 1826.

———. *William Lambarde and Local Government: His "Ephemeris" and Twenty-Nine Charges to Juries and Commissions.* Edited by Conyers Read. Ithaca, NY: Cornell University Press, 1962.

Langland, William, *The Vision of William concerning Piers the Plowman.* Edited by Walter W. Skeat. 2 vols. Oxford: Oxford University Press, 1924.

———. *The Vision of William Concerning Piers the Plowman together with Vita de Dowel, Dobet, et Dobest.* Edited by Rev. Walter Skeat. 4 vols. London: N. Trübner, 1869.

[Langland, William]. *The Vision of Pierce Plowman, now fyrst imprinted by Robert Crowley....* STC 19906. London, 1550.

———. *The Vision of Pierce Plowman, now fyrst imprinted by Robert Crowley....* London: 1550. Facsimile reprint, David Paradine Developments, 1976.

La Toure Landry, Geoffroy de. *Knyght of the Toure.* STC 15296. Westminster: William Caxton, 1484.

Lawton, David. "Dullness and the Fifteenth Century." *English Literary History* 54 (1987): 761–99.

Lefèvre, Raoul. *Historie of Iason.* STC 15383. Westminster: William Caxton, 1477.

Leinbaugh, Theodore. "Aelfric's *Sermo De Sacrificio in Die Pascae*: Anglican Polemic in the Sixteenth and Seventeenth Centuries." In *Anglo-Saxon Scholarship: The First Three Centuries*, edited by Carl Berkhout and Milton McCormick Gatch, 51–68. Boston: G. K. Hall, 1982.

Leland, John. *Commentarii de scriptoribus Britannicis.* Edited by Anthony Hall. Oxford: Sheldonian Theatre, 1709.

Lerer, Seth. *Chaucer and His Readers: Imagining the Author in Late-Medieval England.* Princeton: Princeton University Press, 1993.

———. *Courtly Letters in the Age of Henry VIII: Literary Culture and the Arts of Deceit.* Cambridge: Cambridge University Press, 1997.

Levine, Joseph. *Humanism and History: Origins of Modern English Historiography.* Ithaca, NY: Cornell University Press, 1987.

Levinson, Marjorie. "What Is New Formalism?" *PMLA* 122 (2007): 558–68.

Levy, F. J. *Tudor Historical Thought.* San Marino, CA: Huntington Library, 1967. Reprint, Toronto: University of Toronto Press, 2004.

Liebermann, Felix, ed. *Die Gesetze Der Angelsachsen.* 3 vols. Halle: Max Niemeyer, 1903.

Liedl, Janice. "The Penitent Pilgrim: William Calverley and the Pilgrimage of Grace." *Sixteenth Century Journal* 25 (1994): 585–94.

Longstaffe, Stephen. "'A Short Report and Not Otherwise': Jack Cade in *2 Henry VI*." In *Shakespeare and Carnival: After Bakhtin*, edited by Ronald Knowles, 13–35. London: Macmillan, 1998.

Lowenstein, David, and Janel Mueller, eds. *The Cambridge History of Early Modern English Literature.* Cambridge: Cambridge University Press, 2002.

Lydgate, John. *The Auncient Historie and Onely Trewe and Syncere Cronicle of the Warres Betwixte the Grecians and the Troyans ... translated in to englyshe verse by Iohn Lydgate moncke of Burye.* STC 5580. London: Thomas Marshe, 1555.

———. *The Hystorye, Sege and Dystruccyon of Troye [The Troy Book].* STC 5579. London: Richard Pynson, 1513.

———. *The Life and Death of Hector [The Troy Book].* STC 5581.5. London: Thomas Purfoot, 1614.

———. *Lydgate's Troy Book.* Part 4. Edited by Henry Bergen. Early English Texts Society 126. London: Oxford University Press, 1935.

———. *Troy Book: Selections.* Edited by Robert R. Edwards. Kalamazoo, MI: Medieval Institute Publications, 1998.

MacCulloch, Diarmaid. "The English Reformation, 1500–1640: One or Many?" Folger Institute Seminar, Washington, DC, Summer 2004.

———. *Thomas Cranmer: A Life.* New Haven, CT: Yale University Press, 1996.

Machan, Tim William. *Textual Criticism and Middle English Texts.* Charlottesville: University Press of Virginia, 1994.

Major, J. Russell. "'Bastard Feudalism' and the Kiss: Changing Social Mores in Late Medieval and Early Modern France." *Journal of Interdisciplinary History* 17 (1987): 509–35.

Malcolmson, Cristina. "'As Tame as the Ladies': Politics and Gender in *The Changeling.*" *English Literary Renaissance* 20, no. 2 (1990): 142–62.

Mallen, Eric. "Emulous Factions and the Collapse of Chivalry: *Troilus and Cressida.*" *Representations* 29 (1990): 145–79.

Malory, Thomas. *Le Morte Darthur. STC* 801. Westminster: William Caxton, 1485.

Manly, John M. and Edith Rickert, eds. *The Text of the "Canterbury Tales" Studied on the Basis of All Known Manuscripts.* 6 vols. Chicago: University of Chicago Press, 1940.

Mann, Jill. "Shakespeare and Chaucer: 'What is Criseyde worth?'" In *The European Tragedy of Troilus*, edited by Piero Boitani, 219–42. Oxford: Clarendon Press, 1989.

Marcus, Leah. "Reading Matter." *PMLA* 121 (2006): 9–16.

Marshall, M. H. "Theatre in the Middle Ages: Evidence from Dictionaries and Glosses." *Symposium* 4 (1950): 1–39, 366–89.

Marshall, Peter. "Forgery and Miracles in the Reign of Henry VIII." *Past and Present* 178 (2003): 39–73.

Matthews, David. "From Mediaeval to Mediaevalism: A New Semantic History." *Review of English Studies* 62, no. 257 (2011): 695–715.

Mayer, Jean-Christophe. "'This Papist and His Poet': Shakespeare's Lancastrian Kings and Robert Parsons's *Conference About the Next Succession.*" In *Theatre and Religion: Lancastrian Shakespeare*, edited by Richard Dutton, Alison Findlay, and Richard Wilson, 116–29. Manchester: Manchester University Press, 2003.

Mayer, Lauryn. *Worlds Made Flesh: Reading Medieval Manuscript Culture.* New York: Routledge, 2004.

McCarl, Mary Rhinelander. *The Plowman's Tale: The c. 1532 and 1606 Editions of a Spurious Canterbury Tale.* New York: Garland, 1997.

McLaren, Mary-Rose. *The London Chronicles of the Fifteenth Century.* Cambridge: D. S. Brewer, 2002.

McKisack, May. *Medieval History in the Tudor Age.* Oxford: Clarendon Press, 1971.

McMullan, Gordon, and David Matthews, eds. *Reading the Medieval in Early Modern England.* Cambridge: Cambridge University Press, 2007.

Merback, Mitchell B. *The Thief, the Cross, and the Wheel: Pain and the Spectacle of Punishment in Medieval and Renaissance Europe.* Chicago: University of Chicago Press, 1999.

The merry deuill of Edmonton. STC 7494. London: Thomas Creede, for Arthur Iohnson, 1612.

Meyer-Lee, Robert J. *Poets and Power From Chaucer to Wyatt.* Cambridge and New York: Cambridge University Press, 2007.

Middleton, Anne. "William Langland's 'Kynde Name': Authorial Signature and Social Identity in Late Fourteenth-Century England." In *Literary Practice and Social Change in Britain 1380–1530*, edited by Lee Patterson, 18–82. Berkeley: University of California Press, 1990.

Milton, John. *Paradise Lost.* Edited by David Scott Kastan. Indianapolis: Hackett, 2005.

Moore, Samuel. "Studies in *Piers the Plowman.*" *Modern Philology* 12 (1914): 19–50.

Morrison, Stanley. "Early Humanistic Script and the First Roman Type." *The Library*, 4th ser., 24 (1943): 1–29.

Muir, Kenneth. *The Sources of Shakespeare's Plays.* New Haven, CT: Yale University Press, 1978.

Munday, Anthony. *A Second and Third Blast of Retreat from Plays and Theaters*. New York: Johnson Reprint Corporation, 1972.

Murphy, Andrew. *Shakespeare in Print: A History and Chronology of Shakespeare Publishing*. Cambridge: Cambridge University Press, 2003.

Nashe, Thomas. *The Anatomie of Absurditie. . . . STC* 18364. London, 1589.

Nichols, John. *The Progresses and Public Processions of Queen Elizabeth*. 2nd ed. London, 1823.

Nolan, Maura. *John Lydgate and the Making of Public Culture*. Cambridge: Cambridge University Press, 2005.

O read me for I am of great antiquitie. I playne Piers which can not flatter . . . . 2nd ed. *STC* 19903a.5. [London?], [1589?].

Olsen, Palle J. "Was John Foxe a Millenarian?" *Journal of Ecclesiastical History* 45 (1994): 600–24.

The original & Sprynge of all Sectes & Orders. London, 1537.

Page, R. I. *Matthew Parker and His Books*. Kalamazoo, MI: Medieval Institute Publications, 1993.

Panofsky, Erwin "Renaissance and Renascences." *Kenyon Review* 6 (1944): 201–36.

Parker, Matthew. *A Defence of Priestes Mariages*. London: John Kingston, 1567.

———. *A Testimonie of Antiquitie Shewing the Auncient Fayth in the Church of England*. London: John Day, 1566.

Parsons, Robert [R. Doleman, pseud.]. *A Conference About the Next Succession to the Crowne of Inglond. . . .* 1594. The English Experience: Its Record in Early Printed Books Published in Facsimile 481. Amsterdam: Theatrum Orbis Terrarum; New York: Da Capo, 1972.

Patterson, Annabel. *Reading Holinshed's Chronicles*. Chicago: University of Chicago Press, 1994.

———. *Shakespeare and the Popular Voice*. Oxford: Basil Blackwell, 1989.

Patterson, Lee. "Chaucer's Pardoner on the Couch: Psyche and Clio in Medieval Literary Studies." *Speculum* 76 (2001): 638–56.

———. "On the Margin: Postmodernism, Ironic History, and Medieval Studies." *Speculum* 65 (1990): 87–108.

Pearsall, Derek. "Chaucer's Tomb: The Politics of Reburial." *Medium Aevum* 64 (1995): 51–73.

———. "The English Romance in the Fifteenth Century." *Essays and Studies*, n.s., 29 (1976): 56–83.

Peele, George. *A Farewell . . . VVhereunto is annexed: a Tale of Troy. STC* 19537. London, 1589.

Perella, Nicolas. *The Kiss Sacred and Profane*. Berkeley: University of California Press, 1969.

Perloff, Marjorie. "Presidential Address 2006: It Must Change." *PMLA* 122 (2007): 652–62.

Perry, Curtis, and John Watkins, eds. *Shakespeare in the Middle Ages*. New York: Oxford University Press, 2009.

Petkov, Kiril. *The Kiss of Peace: Ritual, Self and Society in the High and Late Medieval West*. Leiden: Brill, 2003.

Pineas, Rainer. "The Polemical Drama of John Bale." In *Shakespeare and Dramatic Tradition: Essays in Honor of S. F. Johnson*, edited by W. R. Elton and William B. Long, 194–208. Newark: University of Delaware Press, 1989.

Pocock, J. G. A. *The Ancient Constitution and the Feudal Law: A Study of English Historical Thought in the Seventeenth Century*. Cambridge: Cambridge University Press, 1957.

———. "The Origins of the Study of the Past: A Comparative Approach." *Comparative Studies in Society and History* 4 (1962): 209–46.

Pollard, A. W., and G. R. Redgrave, compilers. Revised by W. A. Jackson and F. S. Ferguson, completed by Katherine F. Parker. *A Short-Title Catalogue of Books Printed in England, Scotland, and Ireland, and of English Books Printed Abroad, 1475–1640.* 2nd ed. 3 vols. London: Bibliographical Society, 1976–91. [Cited throughout as *STC*]

Powell, Edgar. *The Rising in East Anglia in 1381.* Cambridge: Cambridge University Press, 1896.

The praier and complaynte of the ploweman vnto Christe. [London?], 1532. Reprint, edited by Douglas H. Parker. Toronto: University of Toronto Press, 1997.

Prendergast, Thomas A. *Chaucer's Dead Body: From Corpse to Corpus.* New York: Routledge, 2004.

Pugliatti, Paola. "'More than history can pattern': The Jack Cade Rebellion in Shakespeare's *Henry VI, 2.*" *Journal of Medieval and Renaissance Studies* 22 (1992): 451–78.

Puttenham, George. *Arte of English Poesie.* Edited by G. D. Willcock and Alice Walker. Cambridge: Cambridge University Press, 1936.

Pyers plowmans exhortation, vnto the lordes, knightes and burgoysses of the Parlyamenthouse. *STC* 19905. London, 1550.

Rainolds, John. *Th'overthrow of Stage-Playes.* Middleburgh: R. Schilders, 1599.

Rex, Richard. *Henry VIII and the English Reformation.* New York: St. Martin's Press, 1993.

Robinson, Thomas. *The Anatomie of the English nunnery at Lisbon in Portugall Dissected and laid open by one that was sometime a younger brother of the conuent.* *STC* 21123. London, 1622.

Rollins, Hyder E. "The Troilus-Cressida Story from Chaucer to Shakespeare." *PMLA* 32 (1917): 383–429.

Ross, Trevor. *The Making of the English Literary Canon.* Montreal: McGill-Queen's University Press, 1998.

[Roy, William?]. *A proper dyaloge betwene a gentillman and an husbandma[n] . . . .* [Antwerp], 1529.

The royall passage of her Maiesty from the Tower of London, to her palace of White-hall with all the speaches and deuices. *STC* 7593. London, 1604.

Rubin, Miri. *Corpus Christi: The Eucharist in Late Medieval Culture.* Cambridge: Cambridge University Press, 1991.

Ryrie, Alec. *The Gospel and Henry VIII.* Cambridge: Cambridge University Press, 2008.

Scala, Elizabeth. Review of *Shakespeare in the Middle Ages*, edited by Curtis Perry and John Watkins. *The Medieval Review*, 10.05.21.

Scanlon, Larry. "Langland, Apocalypse and the Early Modern Editor." In McMullen and Matthews, *Reading the Medieval*, 51–73.

Scase, Wendy. "*Dauy Dycars Dreame* and Robert Crowley's Prints of *Piers Plowman.*" *Yearbook of Langland Studies* 21 (2007): 171–98.

———. *Literature and Complaint in England, 1272–1553.* Oxford: Oxford University Press, 2007.

Schmitt, Jean-Claude. *La raison des gestes dans l'Occident médiévale.* Paris: Gallimard, 1990.

———. "The Rationale of Gestures in the West: Third to Thirteenth Centuries." In *A Cultural History of Gesture*, edited by Jan Bremmer and Herman Roodenburgh, 59–70. Ithaca, NY: Cornell University Press, 1991.

Schoeck, R. "Early Anglo-Saxon Studies and Legal Scholarship in the Renaissance." *Studies in the Renaissance* 5 (1958): 102–10.

Schoff, Rebecca L. "*Piers Plowman* and Tudor Regulation of the Press." *Yearbook of Langland Studies* 20 (2006): 93–114.

Schwyzer, Philip. *Archaeologies of English Renaissance Literature*. Oxford: Oxford University Press, 2007.

———. "The Beauties of the Land: Bale's Books, Aske's Abbeys, and the Aesthetics of Nationhood." *Renaissance Quarterly* 57 (2004): 108–22.

Scott, James. *Domination and the Arts of Resistance: Hidden Transcripts*. New Haven, CT: Yale University Press, 1990.

Severall Speeches Delivered at a Conference concerning the Power of Parliament, to proceed against their King for Misgovernment. Wing P573A. London, 1648.

Shakespeare, William. *The Arden Shakespeare: King Henry VI, Part 2*. Edited by Ronald Knowles. Walton-on-Thames, Surrey: Thomas Nelson and Sons, 1999.

———. *The Arden Shakespeare: Troilus and Cressida*. Edited by David Bevington. 1998. Reprint, London: Thomson Learning, 2001.

———. *Comedies, Histories & Tragedies: Published according to the true originall copies*. Edited by John Hemming and Henry Condell. *STC* 22273. London: W. Jaggard, I. Blount, 1623. 2nd ed., *STC* 22274. London: Tho. Cotes for Robert Allot, 1632. 3rd ed., Wing S2913. London: Roger Daniel, Alice Warren and another for Philip Chetwinde, 1663. 4th ed., Wing S2914. London: for P. C, 1664.

———. *The Famous Historie of Troylus and Cresseid*. "Qb," *STC* 22332. London: R. Bonian and H. Walley, 1609.

———. *The First and Second Part of the Troublesome Raigne of Iohn King by W. Sh. STC* 14646. London: Valentine Simmes for Iohn Helme, 1611.

———. *The First Part of the Contention Betwixt the Two Famous Houses of Yorke and Lancaster. . . . STC* 26099. London, 1594.

———. *Hamlet*. [First Quarto.] London: Nicholas Ling and John Trundell, 1603.

———. *The Historie of Troylus and Cresseida*. "Qa," *STC* 22331. London: R. Bonian and H. Walley, 1609.

———. *The Norton Shakespeare*. Edited by Stephen Greenblatt et al. New York: Norton, 1997.

———. *Pericles*. *STC* 22334. London: William White for Henry Gosson, 1609.

———. *The Tragedie of King Richard the Third*. *STC* 22318. London: Thomas Creede, 1612.

———. *The Tragedy of Hamlet Prince of Denmark*. *STC* 22277. London: [G. Eld] for Iohn Smethwicke, 1611.

———. *William Shake-speares Sonnets*. *STC* 22353. London: G. Eld for T. T., 1609.

Shrank, Cathy. "John Bale and Reconfiguring the 'Medieval' in Reformation England." In McMullan and Matthews, *Reading the Medieval*, 179–92.

———. *Writing the Nation in Reformation England 1530–1580*. 2004. Reprint, Oxford: Oxford University Press, 2006.

Sidney, Philip. *The Major Works*. Edited by Katherine Duncan-Jones. Oxford: Oxford University Press, 1989. Revised paperback edition, 2002.

Silverstone. "The Vision of Pierce Plowman." *Notes and Queries*. 2nd ser., 6 (1858): 229–30.

Simpson, J. A., and E. S. C. Weiner, eds. *The Oxford English Dictionary*. 2nd ed. 20 vols. Oxford: Clarendon Press, 1989.

Simpson, James. *1350–1547: Reform and Cultural Revolution*. Vol. 2 of *The Oxford English Literary History*. Oxford: Oxford University Press, 2002.

———. "Making History Whole: Diachronic History and the Shortcomings of Medieval Studies." In McMullen and Matthews, *Reading the Medieval*, 17–30.

―――. "The Rule of Medieval Imagination." In *Images, Idolatry, and Iconoclasm in Late Medieval England: Textuality and the Visual Image*, edited by Jeremy Dimmick, James Simpson, and Nicolette Zeeman, 4–24. Oxford University Press, 2002.

―――. *The Vision of William concerning Piers the Plowman.* Oxford: Oxford University Press, 1924.

Siraisi, Nancy. *Medieval and Early Renaissance Medicine: An Introduction to Knowledge and Practice.* Chicago: University of Chicago Press, 1990.

Skelton, John. *A Replycacion Against Certayne Yong Scolers Abiured of Late. STC* 22609. London, 1528.

Smith, Lucy Toulmin, ed., *The Itinerary of John Leland in or about the Years 1535–1543.* 5 vols. London: George Bell and Sons, 1907. Reprint, Carbondale: Southern Illinois University Press, 1964.

Spenser, Edmund. *Shepheardes Calendar (1579): A Facsimile Reproduction.* Edited by S. K. Heininger Jr. Delmar, NY: Scholars' Facsimiles and Reprints, 1979.

Spiegel, Gabrielle. "Theory into Practice: Reading Medieval Chronicles." In *The Medieval Chronicle*, edited by Erik Kooper, 1–12. Amsterdam: Rodopi, 1999.

Stein, Elizabeth. "Caxton's *Recuyell* and Shakespeare's *Troilus*." *Modern Language Notes* 45 (1930): 144–46.

Stein, Robert. *Reality Fictions: Romance, History, and Governmental Authority, 1025–1180.* Notre Dame, IN: University of Notre Dame Press, 2006.

Stow, John. *The Annales of England: faithfully collected out of the most autenticall authors, records, and other monuments of antiquitie from the first inhabitaton vntill this present yeere 1592. STC* 23334. London, 1592.

―――. *Survey of London.* Edited by C. L Kingsford. Oxford: Oxford University Press, 1908.

Strohm, Paul. "Hoccleve, Lydgate and the Lancastrian Court." In Wallace, *Cambridge History of Medieval English Literature*, 640–61.

―――. "The *Mirror* Syndicate Reads Lydgate, 1553." Paper presented at the International Congress on Medieval Studies, Kalamazoo, MI, May 2004.

―――. *Politique: Language of Statecraft between Chaucer and Shakespeare.* Notre Dame, IN: University of Notre Dame Press, 2005.

―――. "Rememorative Reconstruction." *Studies in the Age of Chaucer* 23 (2001): 3–16.

―――. "Storie, Spelle, Geste, Romaunce, Tragedie: Generic Distinctions in the Middle English Troy Narratives." *Speculum* 46 (1971): 348–59.

―――. *Theory and the Premodern Text.* Minneapolis: University of Minnesota Press, 2000.

Stubbes, Phillip. *Anatomy of Abuses.* 1583. Reprint, London: Johnson Reprint, 1972.

Summit, Jennifer. *Memory's Library: Medieval Books in Early Modern England.* Chicago: The University of Chicago Press, 2008.

―――. "Monuments and Ruins: Spenser and the Problem of the English Library." *English Literary History* 70 (2003): 1–34.

Tatlock, John S. P. "The Siege of Troy in Elizabethan Literature, Especially in Shakespeare and Heywood." *PMLA* 30 (1915): 673–770.

Taylor, Gary. "*Troilus and Cressida*: Bibliography, Performance, and Interpretation," *Shakespeare Studies* 15 (1982): 118–21.

Thompson, Ann. *Shakespeare's Chaucer: A Study in Literary Origins.* New York: Barnes & Noble, 1978.

Tinkle, Theresa. "The Wife of Bath's Sexual/Textual Lives." In *The Iconic Page in Manuscript, Print, and Digital Culture*, edited by George Bornstein and Theresa Tinkle, 55–88. Ann Arbor: University of Michigan Press, 1998.

The Tretise of Miraculis Pleyinge. Ed. Clifford Davidson. Kalamazoo, MI: Medieval Institute Publications, 1993.

Tubbs, J. W. *The Common Law Mind: Medieval and Early Modern Conceptions.* Baltimore: Johns Hopkins University Press, 2000.

Tyndale, William. *An Answere unto Sir Thomas Mores Dialoge.* STC 24437. Antwerp, 1531.

———. *The Obedience of a Christen Man.* STC 24446. Antwerp, 1528.

———. *Tyndale's New Testament.* Edited by David Daniell. New Haven: Yale University Press, 1989.

Tyndale, William, and John Frith. *The Works of the English Reformers.* Ed. Thomas Russell. 3 vols. London: Ebenezer Palmer, 1828–31.

Vanhoutte, Jacqueline A. "Engendering England: The Restructuring of Allegiance in the Writings of Richard Morison and John Bale." *Renaissance and Reformation* 21, no. 1 (1996): 50–77.

Vauchez, André. "St. Birgitta's Revelations in France at the End of the Middle Ages." In *Santa Brigida Profeta Dei Tempi Nuove / Saint Bridget Prophetess of New Ages: Proceedings of the International Study Meeting Rome, October 3–7, 1991,* 176–87. Rome: Casa Generalizia Suore Santa Brigida, 1991.

Vergil, Polydore. *Anglica Historia.* London: Nichols, 1846.

Wakelin, Daniel. *Humanism, Reading, and English Literature, 1430–1530.* Oxford and New York: Oxford University Press, 2007.

Walker, Greg. *Plays of Persuasion: Drama and Politics at the Court of Henry VIII.* Cambridge: Cambridge University Press, 1991.

Wall, Sarah Elizabeth. "Racking the Body, Shaping the Text: The Account of Anne Askew in Foxe's 'Book of Martyrs.'" *Renaissance Quarterly* 54 (2001): 1165–96.

Wallace, David. *Cambridge History of Medieval English Literature.* Cambridge: Cambridge University Press, 1999.

———. "'Whan She Translated Was': A Chaucerian Critique of the Petrarchan Academy." In *Literary Practice and Social Change in Britain, 1380–1530,* edited by Lee Patterson, 156–215. Berkeley: University of California Press, 1990.

Walsham, Alexandra. "Inventing the Lollard Past: The Afterlife of a Medieval Sermon in Early Modern England." *Journal of Ecclesiastical History* 58 (2007): 628–55.

Walsingham, Thomas. *Historia Anglicana.* Edited by H. T. Riley. 2 vols. London: Rolls Series, 1863–64.

Warren, Nancy Bradley. *Spiritual Economies: Female Monasticism in Later Medieval England.* Philadelphia: University of Pennsylvania Press, 2001.

———. *Women of God and Arms: Female Spirituality and Political Conflict, 1380–1620.* Philadelphia: University of Pennsylvania Press, 2005.

Wawn, Andrew. "Chaucer, *The Plowman's Tale* and Reformation Propaganda: The Testimonies of Thomas Godfray and *I Playne Piers.*" *Bulletin of the John Rylands University Library of Manchester* 56 (1973): 174–92.

Wells, Stanley, and Gary Taylor. *William Shakespeare: A Textual Companion.* Oxford: Clarendon Press, 1987.

White, Hayden. *Metahistory: The Historical Imagination in Nineteenth-Century Europe.* Baltimore: Johns Hopkins University Press, 1973.

White, Helen. *Social Criticism in Popular Religious Literature of the Sixteenth Century.* New York: Macmillian, 1944.

White, Paul Whitfield. *Theatre and Reformation.* Cambridge: Cambridge University Press, 1993.

Williams, C. H., ed. *English Historical Documents, 1485–1558*. Vol. 5. London: Eyre and Spottiswoode, 1967.

Williams, Philip, Jr. "The 'Second Issue' of Shakespeare's *Troilus and Cressida*, 1609." *Studies in Bibliography* 2 (1949–50): 26–35.

Wilson, Richard. "'A Mingled Yarn': Shakespeare and the Cloth Workers." *Literature and History* 12 (1986): 164–80.

Wing, Donald. *Short-Title Catalogue of Books Printed in England, Scotland, Ireland, Wales, and British America, and of English Books Printed in Other Countries, 1641–1700*. Ann Arbor, MI: University Microfilms International, 1978. [Cited throughout as Wing.]

Womack, Peter. "Imagining Communities: Theatres and the English Nation in the Sixteenth Century." In *Culture and History, 1350–1600*, edited by David Aers, 91–145. New York: Harvester Wheatsheaf, 1992.

Wood, Andy. *Riot, Rebellion, and Popular Politics in Early Modern England*. Basingstoke, Hampshire: Palgrave, 2002.

Wood, Anthony á. *Athenae Oxonienses*. Edited by Philip Bliss. Vol. 1. London, 1813.

Woolf, Daniel. *The Social Circulation of the Past: English Historical Culture, 1500–1730*. Oxford: Oxford University Press, 2003.

Woolfson, Jonathan, ed. *Reassessing Tudor Humanism*. New York: Palgrave Macmillan, 2002.

———. "Burckhardt's Ambivalent Renaissance." In *Palgrave Advances in Renaissance Historiography*, edited by Jonathan Woolfson, 9–26. New York: Palgrave Macmillan, 2005.

Wormald, Patrick. *The Making of English Law: King Alfred to the Twelfth Century*. Oxford: Blackwell, 2001.

Wyrley, William. *The True Use of Armorie*. STC 26062. London, 1592.

Yates, Frances. *Astraea: The Imperial Theme in the Sixteenth Century*. London: Routledge, 1975.

Notes on Contributors

Rebecca Brackmann is Assistant Professor of English at Lincoln Memorial University. She is the author of *The Elizabethan Invention of Anglo-Saxon England*. She has also published articles on topics such as Old English law, Anglo-Saxon poetry, and J. R. R. Tolkien.

Kathy Cawsey is Associate Professor in the Department of English at Dalhousie University in Halifax, Nova Scotia. She is the author of *Twentieth-Century Chaucer Criticism: Reading Audiences*. She also has coedited (with Jason Harris) *Transmission and Transformation in the Middle Ages: Texts and Contexts*.

Dan Breen is Associate Professor of English at Ithaca College. He has written articles on Skelton, More, and early modern historiography. He is working on a book manuscript titled *Making the Past: History, Historians, and Literature in Tudor England*.

Sarah Kelen is Associate Professor of English and English Department Chair at Nebraska Wesleyan University. She is the author of *Langland's Early Modern Identities* as well as a number of articles on the early modern reception of Chaucer and Langland.

William Kuskin is Associate Professor of English and English Department Chair at the University of Colorado, Boulder. His most recent book is *Recursive Origins: Writing at the Transition to Modernity*. He has worked extensively on early English printing and is the author of a monograph, *Symbolic Caxton: Literary Culture and Print Capitalism*, and the editor of a collection of essays on Caxton, *Caxton's Trace: Studies in the History of English Printing*.

Jesse Lander is Associate Professor of English at the University of Notre Dame. He is the author of *Inventing Polemic: Religion, Print, and Literary Culture in Early Modern England*. He has also edited *Macbeth* for Barnes and Noble and *1 Henry IV* for *The Norton Shakespeare*.

Thomas Prendergast is Associate Professor of English and English Department Chair at the College of Wooster. He is the author of *Chaucer's Dead Body: From Corpse to Corpus* and has just completed a book entitled *Exhuming the Body Poetic: Public Culture and the Making of Poets' Corner 1066–2011*. He is also writing a book with Stephanie Trigg entitled *Medievalism and Its Discontents*.

Kellie Robertson is Associate Professor of English at the University of Maryland. She is the author of *The Laborer's Two Bodies: Literary and Legal Productions in Britain, 1350–1500*. She coedited (with Michael Uebel) *The Middle Ages at Work: Practicing Labor in Late Medieval England*.

Nancy Bradley Warren is Professor of English and English Department Head at Texas A&M University. She is the author, most recently, of *The Embodied Word: Female Spiritualities, Contested Orthodoxies, and English Religious Cultures, 1350–1700*. Her previous books are *Women of God and Arms: Female Spirituality and Conflict, 1380–1600* and *Spiritual Economies: Female Monasticism in Later Medieval England*.

Index

Abridgement of the Chronicles of England (Grafton), 178

accumulatio (heaping up of words): describing medieval conditions, 100–101; Foxe's use of, 94, 100–106, 107; Milton's use of, 93–94; monastic rules critiqued with, 107; periodization and, 94; use of in anti-Catholic polemic, 7, 94; visual equivalent of, 103; William Tyndale's use of, 101

Achilles (character in *Troilus and Cressida*), 157, 172n44; at Hector's tomb, 167–68; pride of, 154; representation and, 155

Achilles Shield (Chapman), 144, 168n6

Act in Restraint of Appeals (1533), 17

Acts and Monuments (*Book of Martyrs*) (Foxe), 7; *accumulatio* in, 94, 100–101, 102–5; ages of history in, 97–98; female saints in, 187–88; five-fold periodization in, 98–99, 103; iconography of, 103; medieval culture critiqued in, 99–100; polemical aspect of, 95; woodcuts in, 7, 103, 104 *fig.*, 105 *fig.*

Aers, David, 131

Agamemnon (character in Caxton's *Recuyell*), 153–54

ages of the church, 97–98

alliteration in *I Playne Piers*, 38–39, 40–41, 42–44, 45, 47

Alsop, Barnard, 159, 160, 169n8

alterations/rewriting: in medieval/Renaissance texts, 1–12; by printers, 84–85; of rhyme scheme in *I Playne Piers*, 43–44, 45, 48, 49–50

Amadis of Gaul (medieval romance), 189

The Anatomie of the English Nunnery in Portugal (Robinson), 7, 190–93

Anglo-Saxon law: common law's development from, 112–13; English identity and, 111–13; as foundation of courts, 115–17; Lambarde's knowledge of, 111; as living entity, 7; religion and, 10; restored by Magna Carta, 117

The Annales of England (Stowe): woodcuts in, 182, 183 *fig.*, 195n17

An Answere unto Sir Thomas More (Tyndale), 101

antecedent texts: Clerk's Tale and, 1–2; *I Playne Piers* and, 9; Knight's Tale as, 6; as living entities, 1–3, 12; Lydgate's *Fall of Princes* as, 3, 5

Antichrist, time of, 98

antiquarianism, 35n32, 85–86

antiquities, 76

antiquity: of common law, 7, 113–18; legitimacy as product of, 84; of *Piers Plowman*, 38; of Protestantism, 40

anxieties: about alteration of texts, 85; about dissolution of monasteries, 19; about female monarch, 179; about legitimacy, 174, 176, 177, 184, 190,

193; about loss of the past, 80; of Tudor writers, 11–12

anxiety of influence, 2, 6, 12

apocalyptic theologies of history, 95, 97

apparitions, Lydgate as, 3, 5, 13n8, 14n15

Archaionomia (Lambarde), 111, 112–13, 116, 119, 124

Archeion (Lambarde), 115–17, 120, 125n23, 125n24

Arthur, King, 115

artifice, 9, 143–44, 164, 166

Aston, Margaret, 108

authenticity: antiquity and, 84; of *Piers Plowman*, 82–83. *See also* legitimacy

Baldwin, William, 3, 5, 6

Bale, John, 10; antiquarian method and, 35n32; ascription of *Piers Plowman* and, 85; attitude of toward Henry VIII, 17; bibliography and, 35n43, 35n44; Brigham and, 9, 75, 89n23; censorship of, 71; as client of Cromwell, 33n8; dissolution of monasteries and, 19, 76; endings of plays by, 31, 36n57; English literary tradition and, 76, 159; Foxe influenced by, 97; on historical King John, 28, 30; historiography and, 6, 18; humanism and, 22, 34n28, 76, 89n34; on loss of manuscripts, 15n32; on need to revise chronicles, 35n35; "Newe Yeares Gyfte" and, 21–24, 34n22; notebook of, 72–75; reformed religion justified by, 83; as reforming historian, 35n45, 35n47; on Robert Langland, 70, 86; Robert Langland discovery and, 72–75, 77–78, 79–80, 89–90n39; Veritas as figure for, 36n57

Bale, John, works of: *Examinations of Anne Askew*, 85; *Illustrium Maioris Brytannie Scriptorum*, 81, 88n19, 144; *Image of Both Churches*, 97; *Index Britanniae Scriptorum*, 30, 35n33, 72, 73; *Laboryouse Journey and Serche of Johan Leyland*, 21–24, 34n22; *Scriptorium Illustrium Maioris Brittanie Catalogus*, 72, 73, 85. See also *Kynge Johan*

Barish, Jonas, 137

Bennett, Josephine Waters, 189, 196n32

Benoit de Sainte-Maure, 144, 167

Benson, Larry, 167

Bible, 26, 44, 48

bibliographies, Bales's, 23, 35n33

birds as symbols, 46

Birgitta, St., 186; linking of with Elizabeth I, 187–89; sexual corruption and, 192. *See also* Brigittine Order of nuns

Blanche of Lancaster, 180, 184

Blodgett, James, 77

Blundeville, Thomas, 3–4, 5

Boccaccio, Giovanni, 3, 5, 144, 167

bodies: body of the tale, 1, 3; books and, 8, 9, 12, 14n25; Catholicism and, 6–7, 102; female, 174, 190–91; gesture, 128, 130–31, 133–35, 137; hermeneutics of, 139n28; nation as (body politic), 118, 120–23. *See also* corpses; posthumous kiss; tombs

Bodleian Library MS Laud 581 (manuscript of *Piers Plowman*), 75, 77–78

Boethius, 164, 165

Bolingbroke, Henry (Henry IV), 132, 175, 179, 180, 184n1

Bonian, Richard, 146, 157

Book of Martyrs (Acts and Monuments) (Foxe). See *Acts and Monuments*

books: as bodies, 8, 9, 12, 14n25; durability of, 161; history of, 145; representation and, 161–64; transcending historical period, 141. *See also* texts

Bossy, John, 181

Bowers, John, 38–39, 81

Brackmann, Rebecca, 6, 7, 10, 13–14n14

Braham, Robert, 160

Brantley, Jessica, 145

Breen, Daniel, 4, 6, 89n34

Brigham, Nicholas: as Bale's source, 9, 89n23; books lent to Bale by, 75; cataloging/collecting impulses of, 80; Catholicism and, 9–10, 89n29; Chaucer's tomb and, 10, 75–76; conservatism of, 76; interest of in English literary history, 76; "De Venationibus Rerum Memoribilium," 75; manuscript lent to by Coppinger, 77–78; "Memoirs by Way of a Diary," 75; as source of information about Robert Langland, 74, 77–78

Bright, Allen, 78

Brigittine Order of nuns: female descent and, 186–87; Lancastrian support for, 10; licentiousness of, 7, 190–92, 196–97n42; Spanish match supported by, 189–90

British Library, MS Cotton Vitellius A.XVI (Vitellius manuscript), 129, 131, 138n5

Brown, Marshall, 94

Buckingham, 2nd Duke of (Henry Stafford), 175–76, 181

Burckhardt, Jacob, 95–96, 109n9, 109n10

Cade, Jack: accounts of, 8–9; demands of, 127; power assumed by, 134; Shakespeare's portrayal of, 127–28, 135–36; in Vitellius manuscript, 129

Cade's Rebellion (1450), 127, 128–29, 138n4

Calderni, Domizo, 84

Canterbury Tales (Chaucer): Clerk's Tale in, 1–2, 11, 14n26; narrative voice in, 13n3; Petrarch's name misspelled in, 14n26; Plowman's Tale in, 37, 51n3, 85; rewriting in, 1–2

cataloging, 23, 35n33, 80. See also *accumulatio* (heaping up of words)

Catholic church: common law's independence from, 115; criticized in *I Playne Piers*, 42; Foxe on decline of, 97–99, 103–5; textual dominion of, 26–27, 31; use of political authority by, 25–26; as whore of Rome, 190–91, 192

Catholicism: Brigham and, 89n29; Chaucer's tomb and, 76; corporeality and, 6–7, 102; devotional practices of, 7, 93–94, 100–103; Elizabeth I and, 179; Henry VIII and, 177, 179; Lancastrian line and, 186–87, 193; *Piers Plowman* and, 9–10; Spanish match and, 189–90. *See also* Catholic church; Protestantism

Cawsey, Kathleen, 6, 9

Caxton, William: ekphrasis of Hector's tomb translated by, 9, 143–44, 155, 166; literary history and, 145, 159–60; Lydgate and, 159–60, 164; "orgulous" used by, 152–53; typography used by,

143, 161. See also *Recuile of the Histories of Troie . . . Translated out of Frenche in to English by Wyllyam Caxton* (Copland); *Recuyell of the Histories of Troye* (Caxton)

Cecil, Robert, 115, 195n16

celibacy, clerical, 45

censors, 148–49

censorship, 71

centralization: political, 18, 19, 20, 34n15; of textual production/interpretation, 26

ceremonialism: critiques of using *accumulatio*, 7, 100–103; Milton's catalog of, 93–94; of monasticism, 106; reformers and, 109n18; as theatrical, 137

Chapman, George, 144, 168n6, 169n7

Charles I, 193

charters: granted by King John, 29–30, 35–36n49

Chaucer, Geoffrey: anxiety and, 6; *Canterbury Tales*, 1–2, 11, 13n3, 14n26, 37, 51n3, 85; Clerk's Tale, 1–3, 6, 11, 13n3, 14n26; Knight's Tale, 6; literary history and, 2, 161; Lydgate on, 167–68; Monk's Tale, 3, 164; narrative voice of, 13n3; Petrarch as distant from, 14n26; Plowman's Tale and, 85; Shakespeare and, 3, 6, 144, 156, 168n5; source texts of, 2; Thynne's editions of, 76–77; tomb of, 10, 75–76; on tragedy, 164–65; *Troilus and Criseyde*, 152, 161, 164, 167–68, 170n13

chiasmus, 100

children: Griselda's, 1–2; of nuns, 7, 191, 192, 196–97n42

chronicles: Bale on need to revise, 35n35; Cade's rebellion in, 128–31; Froissart's, 4; *Kynge Johan* and, 25, 26, 28–29, 32; *Piers Plowman* and, 10; value of for national tradition, 21–22. *See also* Holinshed, Raphael

Church of Rome. *See* Catholic church

Civil Order (character in *Kynge Johan*), 25

Clergy (character in *Kynge Johan*), 25, 26, 31

Clerk, the (character in Clerk's Tale): narrative voice and, 13n3; Petrarch's body and, 1–3, 11; references to Petrarch by, 14n26

Clerk's Tale (Chaucer), 1–3, 6, 11, 13n3,
14n26
Cohen, Esther, 134
Coke, Edward, 115, 124
Collectanea satis copiosa (manuscript
anthology), 17
comedy, 173n61, 173n62; Lydgate on,
164–65; *Troilus and Cressida* as, 146,
148, 149, 151
common law: Anglo-Saxon law and,
112–13; antiquity of, 7, 113–18; schools
of thought on, 113
The Complaynte of the Plowman. See *The
Plowman's Tale*
composite texts: *I Playne Piers* as, 9, 50–51
*A Conference About the Next Succession
to the Crowne of England* (Parsons),
179–81, 182, 186, 193, 194n10, 195n16,
195n23
congeries, 94, 101. See also *accumulatio*
(heaping up of words)
Consolation of Philosophy (Boethius), 164
Copland, William, 145, 151–52, 156,
160, 161, 162–63 *fig.*, 169n8, 171n21,
171n22
Coppinger, Ralph, knight of Davington
(Kent), 75, 77–78, 79, 80
corporeality. See bodies
corpses: Hector's, 143, 165, 166; King
John's, 6, 27–29, 31, 33; Polonius's,
14n25; preservation of, 35n45; punishment of, 133; reanimation of, 8. See also
posthumous kiss
Corpus Christi College MS 201, 78
Corpus Christi festival, 131, 139n11
Corthell, Ronald, 181
couplets in *I Playne Piers*, 38, 41, 43–44,
45–46, 48
courts, 115–17, 120
Coverdale, Miles, 39, 47, 59, 106
Creede, Thomas, 152, 157, 158 *fig.*, 159,
160, 169n8, 172n47
Cromwell, Thomas, 1st Earl of Essex, 21,
33n8, 34n20
Crowley, Robert: ascription of *Piers Plowman* and, 71; incipit to *Piers Plowman*
and, 74–75; John Bale and, 72–73;
medieval poetic form explained by,

38, 42; *Piers Plowman* authenticated
by, 82–83; *Piers Plowman* printed by,
39, 70; on Robert Langland, 70, 81;
treatment of historical evidence by, 79,
81–82; *Vision of Pierce Plowman*, 37
Crowmer, William (sheriff of Kent),
128–29
Curran, John, 115

Davies, Tony, 77
death: antecedent texts and, 6; Elizabeth I and, 181; Griselda's, 1–2; King
John's, 27; Leland's, 28; of partisans in
Cade's rebellion, 129; punishment after,
133–34. See also corpses; posthumous
kiss; tombs
De Casibus Illustrium Virorum (Boccaccio), 3
De institutione novitiorum (Hugh of St.
Victor), 133
depositions: of Charles I, 193; Elizabeth I
and, 181; Lancastrian heritage and, 175,
176; of Richard II, 5, 175, 179–80, 181,
182, 197n45; of Richard III, 175
Destruction of Troy (Whalley), 166
*Destruction of Troy . . . Translated out
of French into English, by W. Caxton*
(Creede and Simmes), 152, 157, 158
fig., 159
"De Venationibus Rerum Memoribilium"
(Brigham), 75
Devereux, Robert, 2nd Earl of Essex, 181;
rebellion of, 137–38, 169n7, 181
Diehl, Houston, 137
differentiation: Foxe's periodization as,
99–100
disease/sickness, 121–22, 155
Dissimulation (character in *Kynge Johan*),
26, 27
dissolution of monasteries, 8, 15n32,
19–20, 76; Foxe's justification of, 108;
as Lancastrian triumph, 193
Doleman, R. (Robert Parsons). See Parsons, Robert
doubt: in *Kynge Johan*, 25
Douglas, Gavin, 144, 168n6
dowry, 48
dramatic forms, 164–65. See also theater

dramatic representation: in *2 Henry VI*, 8–9
dramatic text: prose and, 157–59
dream visions: authorship of *Piers Plowman* and, 78–79
Dudley, Robert, 1st Earl of Leicester, 189
Duffy, Eamon, 100, 109n18
Duggan, Hoyt, 75

early modern studies: medieval studies and, 11
earnestness, 101
Edward III, 180, 182, 187–88, 194n4, 196n29
Edward IV, 175, 180, 187, 194n1
Edward VI: depicted in woodcut in *Annales of England*, 182; Grafton as king's printer to, 178; *Laboryouse Journey* dedicated to, 21, 22; *Piers Plowman* and, 71; reformism of, 103, 108; Yorkist lineage of, 180
Edwards, A. S. G., 39, 42
Eirenarcha (Lambarde), 113–14, 118–19, 124
ekphrasis: of dramatic performance, 164, 165; of Hector's tomb, 9, 143–44, 155, 165–66
Eld, George, 146, 147 *fig.*, 148, 157, 159, 170n17, 172n47
Elizabeth I: *Conference* and, 195n16; danger of antiquarianism and, 85–86; *Kynge Johan* and, 32; Lancastrian inheritance and, 177–82; ownership of history and, 174; as part of false Lancastrian line, 180–81; St. Birgitta linked with, 187–89; successors for, 184–86; in woodcut in *Annales*, 182
Elizabeth of York, 178, 180
emulation, 155
Eneados (Douglas), 144, 168n6
England (character in *Kynge Johan*), 25, 27, 28, 29
English Civil Wars, 193
English identity: Anglo-Saxon past and, 111–13; law and, 123
English literary tradition: Bale and, 76, 159; dissolution of monasteries and, 76; *Piers Plowman* and, 86–87; Simpson on, 159, 168n3

English subjects/citizens: law as determiner of, 118–19
epistle to reader in *Troilus and Cressida*, 146, 148–49, 151, 170n17
Erasmus of Rotterdam: Catholic superstition and, 101; on kissing, 132; on saints' lives, 82; scholarly community imagined by, 71, 72
Essex, 2nd Earl of (Robert Devereux), 181
Essex rebellion (1601): *Richard II* and, 137–38, 181; *Troilus and Cressida* and, 169n7
estates of council (in *Kynge Johan*), 6, 18, 25, 26–27, 30–32
The Examinations of Anne Askew (Bale), 85

Fall of Princes (Lydgate), 3, 5
female descent, 196n29; Brigittine spirituality and, 186–87; Lancastrian line and, 176–77, 184–85, 194n4, 196n24
Ferguson, Wallace K., 96–97, 109n13
feudalism: kissing and, 132–33, 134
Fiedler, Leslie A., 146
First Folio, 148, 160, 171n32; literary history and, 159; placement of *Troilus and Cressida* in, 149, 152; prologue to *Troilus and Cressida* in, 149–52, 154, 156–57
foreigners/resident aliens: Lambarde on, 118–19
foreign status: illegal behavior and, 119
formalism. *See* textual formalism
Foxe, John: apocalyptic interpretation of, 97; on binding of Satan, 97, 109n15; calculations of, 98–99; on ceremonialism, 100–101, 102–3; corporeality and, 6–7; on decline of church, 97–98, 103–5; on doctrine of good works, 102; on John Wyclif, 99–100; on monasticism, 105–8; on St. Birgitta, 187–88; use of *accumulatio* by, 94, 100–106, 107. *See also* *Acts and Monuments (Book of Martyrs)* (Foxe)
Fradenburg, L. O., 80
France: English claim to, 176, 177, 186, 196n26; foreign policy in, 127, 128; infanta Isabel's connection to, 184; vices attributed to, 119

Freud, Sigmund, 11, 14n24, 177
Froissart, Jean, 4

Galbert of Bruges, 133
The Game and Play of Chess (Caxton), 152–53
Gardiner, Stephen, 85
gates of Troy, 152
Genealogia deorum gentilium (Boccaccio), 144
genre: Achilles's mixing of, in *Troilus and Cressida*, 155; influencing reuse of medieval texts, 9; in prologue to First Folio version of *Troilus and Cressida*, 149, 151, 157; *Recuyell* and, 160; transformation of, 164–65; in *Troilus and Cressida* epistle, 148, 151
genres: comedy, 146, 148, 149, 151, 164–65, 173n61, 173n62; prophecy, 82; tragedy, 149, 151, 152, 157, 164–65, 173n61, 173n62
Gesetze (Liebermann), 111
gesture, 128, 130–31, 133, 134, 137
Gepyncþu (*Ranks*) (Saxon legal tract, in Liebermann's *Gesetze*), 111
God, 4, 41, 178–79
A godly dyalogue & dysputacyon betwene Pyers plowman, and a popysh preest (Tudor "plowman" text), 46
Gothicism, 113, 118
Gower, John, 151, 159
Grafton, Richard, 87n11, 178, 193
Greenwich, England, 189, 196n32
Grindal, Edmund (bishop of London, later archbishop of Canterbury), 86
Griselda (character in Clerk's Tale), 1–2, 14n26
Guido delle Colonne: Chaucer and, 161; *Historia destructionis troiae*, 144, 159, 161, 167; Lydgate and, 164, 165, 167; translated by Caxton, 143, 155, 159

Hadfield, Andrew, 17
hagiography, 27, 82
Hailey, R. Carter, 70, 87n8, 87n11
Hall, Edward, 4, 128, 136, 138n4, 139n6; *Union of the two noble and illustre famelies of Lancastre & Yorke*, 182

Hamlet, 11, 14n25
Hanna, Ralph, 75, 77
Harris, Jonathan Gil, 120
Harvey, John, 82
heaven, 41
Hector: double image of, 143; preservation of, 165–66. *See also* tombs, Hector's
Helgerson, Richard, 128
Henry II, 17, 117
Henry IV, 132, 175, 179, 180, 184n1
Henry V, 176–77, 186–87, 193
Henry VI, 128, 132, 175, 196n24
Henry VI, Part 2 (Shakespeare): antitheatricality in, 136–38; Jack Cade in, 127–28, 135–36; as metadramatic, 8–9; posthumous kiss in, 127, 135, 136–37
Henry VII, 175, 176, 177, 178, 179, 180, 194n4
Henry VIII: Catholic partisans and, 177; Catholicism and, 179; dissolution of monasteries by, 8, 76, 193; Elizabeth I as rightful heir of, 178, 182; historiography and, 16–17; Leland's historiography and, 20–21, 22, 34n21, 34n23, 34n24; political centralization and, 19, 20, 34n15; printers and, 47, 71; as problem point in Lancastrian history, 179–80; Reformation and, 16–17, 32, 33n9; reformers of, 197n42; Tudor rose tree and, 178, 182
Heraclitus, 112
Historia destructionis troiae (Guido delle Colonne), 144, 159, 161, 167
historians, 4–5, 19, 23–24, 115; of the book, 145; doing the work of kings, 16–17, 33n7. *See also* Bale, John; Holinshed, Raphael; Lambarde, William; Leland, John; Veritas (character in *Kynge Johan*)
historical narratives: Bale's focus on seeking out, 23; bias in (subjectivity of), 3–5; as literary fictions, 13–14n14; representation in, 8–9
Historie of Iason (Caxton), 152–53
historiography, 9; accessibility of, 30; challenging Catholic Church, 27; Elizabeth I and, 181; Foxe's, 6–7, 108; Holinshed's, 13n13; humanism and, 95;

memorialization and, 27–28, 29–30; morality and, 3–4; "Newe Yeares Gyfte" and, 20–21; as part of public domain, 18, 21–23, 24; periodization and, 93–94, 95, 96, 109n6; political agency and, 32–33; Protestant, 6–7, 96, 100; rebel kiss and, 8, 128, 131; reform of, 18, 27–29, 32; role of, 16–17; Royal Supremacy and, 19; as subject to correction, 10; Veritas and, 6

history: controlled by church, 26, 30; influence of on present, 30; instability and, 174–75; performance of, 136–38; political legitimacy and, 174; readers of, 22–23, 25, 32; reenactment of, 182. *See also* periodization

Holinshed, Raphael: Annabel Patterson on, 13n13, 135, 140n29, 195n20; on Cade's rebellion, 9, 128–29, 131, 135, 136, 138n4, 139n11; on gesture, 128, 130–31; on Richard II, 4–5

Holsinger, Bruce, 39, 143, 156

Howard, Henry, 82

How the Plowman lerned his pater noster (de Worde) (print), 37

Hudson, Anne, 39, 84, 91n68

Hugh of St. Victor, 133, 134

humanism: authorship of *Piers Plowman* and, 10, 71–72, 76, 80–83, 86; Bale and, 22, 34n28, 76, 89n34; enthusiasm for antiquities and, 76; at Henry VIII's court, 34n16; historiography and, 95–96; Leland's historiographic project and, 22; periodization and, 95–96; reformers and, 19

humors, the, 122

Hunne, Richard, 47

Huntington Library, MS Hm 128 (manuscript of *Piers Plowman*), 74–75, 77, 89n25, 89–90n39, 90n44

idolatry, 7, 8, 50, 100, 106, 137

Illustrium Maioris Brytannie Scriptorum (Bale), 81, 88n19, 144

Image of Both Churches (Bale), 97

immemorialism, 113

Imperial Majesty (character in *Kynge Johan*), 17, 18, 25, 31, 33n1, 35n40

Index Britanniae Scriptorum (Bale), 30, 35n33, 72–75

infantas, 184, 185–86, 189–90

Institvtiones ivris civilis (Justinian), 114

interpretive authority: in *Kynge Johan*, 22, 25–27, 30, 31, 32–33, 36n56

intertextuality. *See* antecedent texts

inventio (discovery of saints' lives), 82

invention of texts/authors, 82–84

inversion of convention: in *I Playne Piers*, 41–42

I Playne Piers (Protestant polemic), 37–69; alliteration in, 38–39, 40–41, 42–44, 45, 47; antiquity of Protestantism in, 40; church criticized in, 42, 45, 46–47; complexity of poetry in, 41; as composite text, 9, 50–51; couplets in, 38, 41, 43–44, 45–46, 48; dates of, 39–40; labor in, 41–42; medieval forms obscured in, 38–40, 43; origins of, 9; Plowman's Tale and, 38, 39, 48–50; printed in poetic layout, 39, 51n10, 52–69; printings of, 39–40; radicalism of, 50; theology in, 42. See also *Piers Plowman* (poem)

Isabel, Infanta of Portugal (Isabella Clara Eugenia of Spain), 184, 185–86

Itinerary (Leland), 28, 34n24

Jameson, Frederic, 93

John, King (character in *Kynge Johan*): corpse of, 6, 27–28, 31; death of, 27; estates and, 26–27, 30–31; London Bridge and, 29; memorialization of, 27–29; misperceptions of, 24–27; reforms of, 18, 24–26, 32; Veritas and, 16, 29–30, 35n46. *See also* John, King (historical figure)

John, King (historical figure): charters granted by, 29–30, 35–36n49; London Bridge and, 29

John of Gaunt, 180, 184, 194n4

John of Salisbury, 123

Johnson, Barbara, 38

Joye, George, 85

jury system, 114, 119–20

Justinian, 114

Kane, George, 72, 78–79, 79–80, 87n3, 88n16, 89n24, 90n44

Kastan, David Scott, 15, 35

Kelen, Sarah, 39, 83

King, John N., 81, 175

kissing: as public gesture, 132–33. *See also* posthumous kiss

Knight's Tale (Chaucer), 6

Koselleck, Reinhart, 94, 108n5

Kuskin, William, 6, 8–9

Kynge Johan (Bale), 6, 16–33; chronicles and, 6, 25, 26, 27, 28–29, 32; dates of, 33n3; interpretive authority in, 22, 25–27, 30, 31, 32–33, 36n56; memorialization in, 27–29; misperceptions in, 24–27; political centralization critiqued in, 18; reforms in, 18, 24–26, 32; revisions of, 32; uncertainty in, 35n39

labor: in *I Playne Piers*, 41–42

The Laboryouse Journey and Serche of Johan Leyland (Bale), 21–24, 34n22

Lagus, Conrad, 114

Lambarde, William, 111–24; *Archaionomia*, 111, 112–13, 116, 119, 124; *Archeion*, 115–17, 120, 125n23, 125n24; attitude toward Anglo-Saxon law, 111; charges to juries by, 114, 115, 117–18, 119–20, 121, 122; *Eirenarcha*, 113–14, 118–19, 124; Elizabeth I and, 181; on English legal history, 114–18; on foreigners, 118–19; ideology of, 10; influence of on later common lawyers, 124; on law as living entity, 7; on law as medicine, 120–23; on law as soul of nation, 123–24; literary elements used by, 13–14n14; on Magna Carta, 117; monastic sources and, 111; on Norman conquest, 115–17; *Perambulation of Kent*, 111; Roman law and, 114–15; on royal courts, 115–16

Lancaster, house of: house of York uniting with, 177–78, 180, 182

Lancastrian inheritance, 175–77; Elizabeth I and, 177–82; Iberian claim to, 184, 190

Lancastrian lineage, 174–93; Brigittine Order and, 186–87; Catholicism and,

10, 186–87, 193; false, 180–81; female descent and, 176–77, 184, 194n4, 196n24; Henry VIII as problem point in, 179–80; Protestantism and, 178–79, 187–89, 193; repression and, 11, 177; Tudor claim to, 175–80, 194n4; Yorkist claim to, 194n4

Lander, Jesse, 4, 7

Langland, Robert, 10, 70–87; authorship of *Piers Plowman* and, 77–78; Bale and, 70, 72–73, 86; Brigham and, 74, 77–78; controversy surrounding, 87n3; evoked in *I Playne Piers*, 43, 44; reformation and, 79–80, 86; sources of information about, 72–75, 77–78; Wyclif and, 70, 81, 86

Langland, William, 37, 77–80, 86

Langley, William, 70

Laste volume of the Chronicles (Holinshed), 4–5

Latin spoken by priests, 46–47, 50

Laud 581 (manuscript of *Piers Plowman*), 75, 77–78

law(s): common law, 112–18; English identity and, 123; as living entity, 7; as medicine, 120–23; Roman, 114–15; as soul of nation, 123–24; as walls, 112–13, 119–20. *See also* Anglo-Saxon law

lawbreakers: need to remove from national body, 122–23

Lefèvre, Raoul, 142 *fig.*, 144, 153, 158 *fig.*, 159, 162–63 *fig.*

legitimacy: as product of antiquity, 84; of Protestant cause, 83; of royal courts, 115–16; of texts, 82–84; of Tudor dynasty, 10, 174, 175–80; women and, 176, 184–86, 192–93

Leicester, 1st Earl of (Robert Dudley), 189

Leigh, Nicholas, lord of the manor of Addington (Surrey), 75

Leinbaugh, Theodore, 112

Leland, John: comprehensiveness of, 23; dissolution of monasteries and, 19–20, 76; English literary history and, 159; Henry VIII and, 20–21, 22, 34n21, 34n23, 34n24; historiography and,

18; humanism and, 22; *Itinerary*, 28, 34n24; in *Laboryouse Journey*, 24; letter to Cromwell by, 34n20; "Newe Yeares Gyfte," 8, 20–24, 28, 29, 34n21, 34n22; Plowman's Tale and, 85; power exercised by, 16; on preservation of texts, 8; Protestant nativism of, 34n16; Veritas and, 28–29

Lerer, Seth, 11

Levy, F. J., 115

Liebermann, Felix, 111

The Life and Death of Hector . . . Written by Iohn Lidgate monke of Berry (Purfoot), 160

light/darkness metaphor, 80, 99–100

literary history: Brigham's interest in, 76; Chaucer and, 2, 161; recursion and, 167; *Recuyell* and, 144, 157–61; reformation politics defining, 168n3; textual formalism and, 141, 145–46

Lollards: *Piers Plowman* and, 37, 38, 42, 47; on pilgrims' behavior, 133; as proto-Protestant, 115; writings of, 84, 91n68, 91n78, 137

London, England: kissing in, 132

London Bridge, 29

Lydgate, John: Caxton and, 159–60, 164; dramatic sensibility of, 164–65; editors of, 173n61; ekphrasis by, 164, 165–66; engagement with Chaucer, 167–68; *Fall of Princes*, 3, 5; *Recuyell* as prose alternative to, 144; as specter, 3, 5, 13n8, 14n15. See also *Troy Book* (Lydgate)

Magna Carta, 30, 117

Major, J. Russell, 132–33

Malcomson, Cristina, 190

Mallen, Eric, 155

Malvern, John, 70

Marcus, Leah, 145

Maria Anna, Infanta of Spain, 189–90

Marshe, Thomas, 145, 160, 164

martyrdom, 7, 27, 32

Mary I, 76, 89n29, 178, 179, 182

Massey, John, 47

Matthews, David, 6, 15n28, 15n31

Maude, Empress of England, 185

McKisack, May, 86

McMullan, Gordon, 6, 15n28, 15n31

medicine, 120–23

medieval poetic forms, 38, 42, 51. *See also* poetry

medieval studies: early modern studies and, 11

melancholia, 11

"Memoirs by Way of a Diary" (Brigham), 75

memorialization, 27–30

Methodica iuris vtriusque traditio (Lagus), 114

Milton, John, 93

mimesis, 144, 155, 161, 166, 167. *See also* representation

Mirror for Magistrates (Baldwin), 3, 5–6, 13n8

misperception: of *I Playne Piers*, 9; in *Kynge Johan*, 25, 26–27

monarchs: criticized in *I Playne Piers*, 45–46; as head of national body, 120–21; historians doing work of, 16–17, 33n7; importance of in reformation, 17–18; maintenance of common law as requirement of, 117; reading national history and, 24; right and duty of to provide justice, 115–16. *See also* specific monarchs

monasteries, dissolution of, 8, 15n32, 19–20, 76, 108, 193

monasticism: *accumulatio* representing, 94; Foxe on, 105–8. *See also* monasteries, dissolution of; Syon (exiled Brigittine monastic community)

Monk's Tale (Chaucer), 3, 164

monuments: to King John, 6, 28; texts as, 7–8, 9, 12; tombs as, 12

Moore, Samuel, 72, 74

morality: history as teacher of, 4

More, Thomas, 82

Le Morte Darthur (Malory), 153

MS 201 (Corpus Christi College, Oxford), 78

MS 687 (Society of Antiquaries, London), 78

MS Cotton Vitellius A.XVI (British Library, London), 129, 131, 138n5

MS Hm 128 (Huntington Library, San

Marino), 74–75, 77, 89n25, 89–90n39, 90n44
MS Laud 581 (Bodleian Library, London), 75, 77–78
Munday, Anthony, 137

Nashe, Thomas, 84
nationalism: *Piers Plowman* and, 37
"Newe Yeares Gyfte" (Leland): Henry VIII as patron of, 20; historiography and, 20–21; kingly virtue in, 29; in *Laboryouse Journey*, 21–24, 34n22; manuscript copy of, 34n21; on preservation of manuscripts, 8; unfinished work and, 28
nighttime, 41, 43
Nobility (character in *Kynge Johan*), 25, 26
Normans: Anglo-Saxon law and, 115–18
notebook, Bale's (*Index Britanniae Scriptorum*), 30, 35n33; information on Robert Langland in, 72–75
notoriously, 9
novelty, 83, 187
nuns. *See* Brigittine Order of nuns

objectivity, 94–95
OED (*Oxford English Dictionary*), 106, 153, 157
Olsen, Palle J., 98, 109n15
orgulty (orgulousness): of books, 161–64; in *Recuyell*, 153–54; in *Troilus and Cressida*, 154–55, 156, 157; usage of, 152–53, 171n28
Original & Sprynge of all Sectes, 106
Th' Overthrow of Stage-Playes (Rainolds), 137

Page, R. I., 112
The Painfull Aduentures of Pericles Prince of Tyre as it was lately presented by the worthy and ancient poet Iohn Gower (Wilkins), 157–59
Pandarus (character in *Troilus and Cressida*), 11, 149, 156
Parker, Matthew, 86, 112, 115, 116
Parsons, Robert (R. Doleman), 179–81, 182–87, 193, 194n10, 196n24; *A Conference About the Next Succession to the*

Crowne of England, 179–81, 182, 186, 193, 194n10, 195n16, 195n23; Lancastrians and, 10
Patterson, Annabel: reading of Cade by, 128; on reading of Holinshed, 13n13, 135, 140n29, 195n20
Patterson, Lee, 14n24, 94, 95, 108–9n6
Pearsall, Derek, 75–76
Perambulation of Kent (Lambarde), 111
Pericles (Shakespeare), 151, 157–59
periodization, 93–108; *accumulatio* and, 94; apocalyptic theologies and, 95, 97; fifteenth-century literature and, 141; five-fold scheme of, 98, 99, 103; humanism and, 95–96; as inconsistent/ unhelpful, 11; in literary histories, 168n2; in Milton, 93–94; nineteenth-century visions of, 108–9n6; as polemical, 94–95; as practical, 96–97; as project of differentiation, 99–100; Simpson on, 168n2
Petrarch, 1–2, 3, 11, 14n26
Philip II (king of Spain and Portugal), 184, 195n22
Philip III (king of Spain and Portugal), 189–90
Phiston, William, 152, 157, 159, 160, 169n8
Pierce the Ploughman's Crede, 37, 38
Piers Plowman (poem) (Langland): adaptability of, 37; antiquity of, 38; attributed to Robert Langland, 70, 77–78; attributed to William Langland, 77–79; attributed to Wyclif, 72, 75, 76, 88n19; authenticity of, 82–83; Catholicism and, 9–10; Crowley's edition of, 39, 70, 71; Crowley's preface to, 71, 73, 81–82; dating of, 83; incipit to, 73, 74–75; manuscripts of, 74–75, 77–79, 89–90n39, 89n25, 90n44; Plowman's Tale confused with, 85; poetic form of, 38, 42; reformism and, 37, 70, 71, 79–80, 86–87, 87n9. See also *I Playne Piers* (Protestant polemic)
plowman pamphlets, Protestant, 52n13
The Plowman's Tale: alterations to, 85; attributions to, 52n22, 52n23; bird symbology in, 46; introduced into

Canterbury Tales by William Thynne, 37; *I Playne Piers* and, 38, 39, 48–50; printings of, 51n3

PMLA, 145

Pocock, J. G. A., 112, 113

poetry: alliterative long lines, 38–39, 40–41, 42–44, 45, 47; complexity of in *I Playne Piers*, 41; couplets, 38, 41, 43–44, 45–46, 48; *I Playne Piers* printed as, 39, 51n10, 52–69; medieval forms of, 38, 42, 51; obscured in *I Playne Piers*, 38–40; prose intervening with in *I Playne Piers*, 38–39, 45, 47, 48; tail rhyme, 38, 43, 44–45, 46–47, 48, 51n10. See also *Piers Plowman*

polemic: *accumulatio* in, 7, 94; against monks, 106; periodization as, 94–95; of Reformation, 96; against theater, 136–37. See also *I Playne Piers* (Protestant polemic)

Policraticus (John of Salisbury), 123

political authority: exercised by historians, 33n7; in *Kynge Johan*, 25–26

political centralization: critique of in *Kynge Johan*, 18; Henry VIII and, 19, 20, 34n15

pope: Henry VIII challenging, 17; in *I Playne Piers*, 42, 46, 53, 56, 57, 60; in *Kynge Johan*, 26; St. Birgitta and, 188, 192

Portugal, 184

posthumous kiss, 127–38; in *2 Henry VI*, 127, 135, 136–37; in 1381 rebellion, 130–31, 133, 134, 138–39n6; antitheatrical polemic and, 136–37; audience's reaction to, 129–30; in Cade's rebellion, 128–30; Holinshed's account of, 129, 130; in medieval executions, 134; reanimation of bodies in, 8; in Vitellius manuscript, 129

poverty: in *I Playne Piers*, 42, 50

The praier and complaynte of the ploweman vnto Christe (early sixteenth-century text), 83–84

"Preface to the Reader from the Printer" (preface to *Piers Plowman*) (Crowley), 71, 73, 81–82

Prendergast, Thomas, 6, 9–10, 51n4

pride, 152, 153–54. See also orgulty (orgulousness)

priests: ceremonialism of, 137; corruption of nuns and, 192; criticized in *I Playne Piers*, 42, 45–46; Latin spoken by, 46–47, 50

printers: alteration of texts by, 84–85; Caxton as first in England, 144; imprisonment of, 47; of *Piers Plowman*, 37–38; of *Recuyell*, 169–70n8; Richard Grafton, 87n11, 178, 193; of Shakespeare's works, 172n47; Wynkyn de Worde, 37, 152. See also Caxton, William; Crowley, Robert; Eld, George

printing: Bale's call for, 23; of *I Playne Piers*, 9, 38–40, 42–43, 50–51, 51n10; of Plowman's Tale, 51n3; of *Recuyell*, 143–44, 152–53, 157–61, 169–70n8; royal proclamation about, 71; of *Troilus and Cressida*, 146, 148, 157–59, 170–71n17; variance in printed texts, 13n11; as vernacular, 145

prophecies, 81–82

prose: dramatic text and, 157–59; intervening with poetry in *I Playne Piers*, 38–39, 45, 47, 48; *I Playne Piers* printed as, 9, 38–39, 43; *Recuyell*'s third book as, 144

Protestantism: antiquity of, 40; attempt to give priority to, 83; authorship of *Piers Plowman* and, 79–80; Catholicism and, 10; English law as, 115; *I Playne Piers* and, 9, 42; Lancastrian line and, 178–79, 187–89, 193; law and, 112; novelty as threat to, 83, 187; Piers Plowman as symbol of, 37; Spanish match and, 189–90; textuality and, 7. See also Catholicism; Protestant Reformation

Protestant Reformation: Henry VIII and, 16–17, 32, 33n9; periodization and, 96, 98; polemic of, 96. See also Protestantism; reformation

Prynne, William, 192

Purfoot, Thomas, 159, 160

Puttenham, George, 101

Pyers Plowman's Exhortation, 37, 38

Pynson, Richard, 160

racial arguments for English purity, 118
Rainolds, John, 137
reading of history: in *Kynge Johan*, 25; nation building and, 22–23; as source of political unity, 32
rebellions: 1381 rebellion, 130–31, 133, 134, 138–39n6; Cade's Rebellion (1450), 127, 128–29, 138n4; Essex rebellion (1601), 137–38, 169n7, 181; tactics of, 139n12;
rebels: representation of, 127–28; use of theater by, 131, 137–38
reconciliation, kiss of, 132
Recuile of the Histories of Troie . . . Translated out of Frenche in to English by Wyllyam Caxton (Copland), 162–63 *fig.*; printing of, 152; as source for *Troilus and Cressida*, 156–57; temporality expressed in, 161; textual formalism and, 145; *Troilus and Cressida* prologue and, 151–52; *Troy Book* and, 160
Recuyell of the Histories of Troye (Caxton): Caxton's epilogue to book 2 of, 159–60; editions of, 152, 157–61, 169–70n8; ekphrasis of Hector's tomb in, 9, 142 *fig.*, 143–44; language used in, 156–57; literary history and, 144, 157–61, 160–61; orgulty in, 153–54; representation in, 143–44; as source for *Troilus and Cressida*, 144, 145, 156–57, 169n7; sources of, 144; *Troilus and Cressida* prologue and, 151–52; *Troy Book* and, 160
Recuyles or Gaderinge to Gyder of the Hystoryes of Troye (de Worde), 152, 169n8
Reform and Cultural Revolution (Simpson), 166, 168n6
reformation: as act of resurrection, 16–17; misperception and, 25; monarchs and, 17–18; *Piers Plowman* and, 37, 70, 71, 79–80, 86–87, 87n9; reading of scripture/history as mechanism for, 25–27, 30, 32. *See also* Protestant Reformation
reformers: Bale as, 35n45, 35n47; humanism and, 19
reforms: King John and, 18, 24–26, 31–32
relics: books as, 164; condemnation of, 79, 90n46, 93, 101; danger of, 137; kissing of, 133

religion: Henry V and, 176–77, 186–87; as soul of nation, 123. *See also* Catholicism; Protestantism; Reformation
Renaissance: Burckhardt's account of, 95–96
representation: in *2 Henry VI*, 8–9; books and, 161–64; in ekphrasis of Hector's tomb, 9, 143, 167–68; illusion of, 165; in *Recuyell*, 143–44; in *Troilus and Cressida*, 145, 155–56; in *Troilus and Criseyde*, 167–68
repression, 11, 177
reproduction, 144–45, 160–61, 166
rhyme scheme in *I Playne Piers*: alliterative long lines, 38–39, 40–41, 42–44, 45, 47; altered from original, 43–44, 45, 48, 49–50; complexity of, 41; couplets, 38, 41, 43–44, 45–46, 48; tail rhyme, 38, 43, 44–45, 46–47, 48, 51n10
Richard II: deposition of, 5, 175, 179–80, 181, 182, 197n45; Elizabeth I and, 181, 182; Holinshed on, 4–5; kiss of reconciliation and, 132
Richard II (Shakespeare), 137, 181
Richard III, 175–76, 179, 180, 181
Robertson, Kellie, 6, 8–9, 13n14
Robinson, Thomas, 7, 190–93, 196–97n42
Roman de Troie (Benoit de Sainte-Maure), 144, 167
Roman Invasions (Curran), 115
Roman law, 114–15
rose tree, Tudor, 177–78, 182
royal courts, 115–16, 117, 120
The royall passage of her Maiesty from the Tower of London, to her palace of Whitehall with all the speaches and deuices (anonymous account of Elizabeth I's coronation pageants), 177–78, 179, 194n6
Royal Supremacy: historiography and, 19

sainthood: in *I Playne Piers*, 42, 45. *See also* Birgitta, St.
saints, lives of, 82
Saye, James Lord (James Fiennes, 1st Baron Saye and Sele), 128–30
Scanlon, Larry, 70
Scase, Wendy, 38, 90n55

Schmitt, Jean-Claude, 134

Schoeck, R. J., 124

scholarship: community in, 10, 71, 72

Scoloker, Antony, 37

Scott, James, 131

Scriptorium Illustrium Maioris Brittanie Catalogus (Bale), 72, 73, 85

Seauen Bookes of Iliades (Chapman), 144, 168n6

A Second and Third Blast of Retreat from Plays and Theaters (Munday), 137

Sedition (character in *Kynge Johan*), 16, 25, 31

sexual corruption, 7, 190–91, 192

Shakespeare, William: Chaucer and, 3, 6, 144, 156, 168n5; Jack Cade portrayed by, 127–28, 135–36, 138; metadramatic elements and, 8–9; *Pericles*, 151, 157–59; prose texts matched with, 157–59; reading of *Recuyell* by, 161; reanimation of past by, 8–9, 11; rebel kiss portrayed by, 127–28; retrospection by, 144; *Richard II*, 137, 181; textual formalism and, 145; *The Two Noble Kinsmen*, 6, 15n31. See also *Henry VI, Part 2*; *Troilus and Cressida*

Sheaperdes Calendar (Spenser), 188–89

shepherds, 47–48

sickness/disease, 121–22, 155

Simmes, Valentine, 152, 157, 158 *fig.*, 159, 169n8, 172n47

Simpson, James: on English literary tradition, 159, 168n3; on idolatry accusation, 100; on *I Playne Piers*, 39; on light metaphor, 80; on periodization, 168n2; on political centralization, 19; reading of Hector's tomb by, 166; *Reform and Cultural Revolution*, 166, 168n6

Skeat, Walter, 72, 78, 87n3, 89n24

Society of Antiquaries, MS 687, 78

sonnet tradition, 3

Spain, 184, 186, 190

Spanish match, 189–90, 192–93

Sparks, William, 73, 75

specters, Lydgate as, 3, 5, 13n8, 14n15

Spenser, Edmund, 187, 188–89

Stafford, Henry, 2nd Duke of Buckingham, 175–76, 181

STC (*A Short-Title Catalogue of Books Printed in England, Scotland, and Ireland, and of English Books Printed Abroad, 1475–1640*) (Pollard and Redgrave), 39

Stow, John, 86, 182, 183 *fig.*, 195n17

Strohm, Paul: on definition of tragedy, 173n62; on Edward IV's return to England, 194n1; on exclusion of historical events, 182; on limitation/periodization, 168n2; on Lydgate as apparitional, 13n8, 14n15; on *Mirror*, 6; on rememorative reconstruction, 80

Stuart, Arabella, 185

subjectivity, 94–95

Syon (exiled Brigittine monastic community): Greenwich as former site of, 189; Henry V as founder of, 186–87, 193; lineage of nuns at, 191–92; sexual corruption of, 7, 190–91; support of Spanish match by, 189–90

tail rhyme in *I Playne Piers*, 38, 43, 44–45, 46–47, 48, 51n10

Tatlock, John, 160–61

A Testimonie of Antiquitie (Parker), 112

texts: alterations to, 84–85; circulation/use of, 8; collected by Leland, 20–21; genuineness of, 82–83; literary vs. nonliterary, 13–14n14; political control and, 25–26; possession of as dangerous, 85–86; preservation of as crucial for reformation, 18; stability of, 13n11; as tombs, 7, 12; truth of, 4. See also books

textual formalism: defined, 141; ekphrasis of Hector's tomb as, 143, 166–68; English formalism as, 145; persistence of, 160–61; *Troilus and Cressida* and, 145–46, 156

Textus Roffensis, 111

theater: history performed in, 135–38; as idolatrous, 8; polemic against, 136–37; rebellion as, 131. See also dramatic forms

theatricality: Cade's awareness of, 8–9

1381 rebels/uprising: *Piers Plowman* as representative figure of, 37, 42; posthumous kiss and, 130–31, 133, 134, 138–39n6

Thynne, John, 77
Thynne, William, 37, 76–77
tombs: Chaucer's, 6, 10, 75–76; King
    John's, 28; symbolic power of, 28; texts
    as, 7, 12. *See also* tombs, Hector's
tombs, Hector's: Achilles and, 167–68;
    Caxton's ekphrasis of, 143–44, 155; as
    metonym for art, 167; as metonym for
    literary formalism, 166; representation
    and, 9; Simpson's reading of, 166
topography, 18, 30, 32
tragedy, 173n61, 173n62; Lydgate on,
    164–65; *Troilus and Cressida* as, 149,
    151, 152, 157
transformation, 148–49, 151
trauma, 176, 177, 178, 179–80, 182
Troilus and Cressida (Shakespeare):
    epistle to reader in 1609 quarto of, 146,
    148–49, 151, 170n17; material form
    of, 146–48, 151; new title page to 1609
    quarto of, 146, 147 *fig.*, 148; orgulty in,
    154–56, 157; print history of, 157–59,
    170–71n17; prologue to in First Folio,
    149, 150 *fig.*, 151–52, 154, 156–57;
    Recuyell as source for, 144, 145, 156–57,
    169n7; representation in, 9, 145, 155;
    textual formalism and, 145–46, 156
Troilus and Criseyde (Chaucer), 152, 161,
    164, 167–68, 170n13
Troy Book (Lydgate): Achilles in, 167–68;
    dramatic genres in, 164–65, 173n61;
    editions of, 160–61; ekphrasis in,
    165–66; historical perspective of,
    173n64; literary history and, 156, 159,
    160–61, 167; orgulty not mentioned in,
    152; *Recuyell* as prose alternative to, 144
Troy Book (Richard Pynson's version of,
    1513), 160
Troy Book (Thomas Marshe's version of,
    1555), 145, 160, 164
*The true order and Methode of wryting and
    reading Hystories* (Blundeville), 3–4
Tudor, Henry (Henry VII), 175, 176, 177,
    178, 179, 180, 194n4
Tudor dynasty, legitimacy of: Catholi-
    cism and, 10; female bodies and, 174;
    Lancastrian descent and, 10, 175–80,
    194n4; medieval history and, 174

Tudor Historical Thought (Levy), 115
Tudor rose tree, 177–78, 182
Tuke, Brian, 77
The Two Noble Kinsmen (Shakespeare and
    Fletcher), 6, 15n31
Tyndale, William, 47, 59, 81, 84–85, 137;
    An Answere unto Sir Thomas More, 101
typography, 143, 145, 152, 155, 167,
    173n57

Ulysses (character in *Troilus and Cressida*),
    154–55, 156, 171n32
uncanny, the, 11
undead, 1, 10
*Union of the two noble and illustre famelies
    of Lancastre & Yorke* (Hall), 182
university culture, 76
usurpation. *See* depositions

Veldener, Johannes, 143
Vergil, Polydore, 175–76, 181
Veritas (character in *Kynge Johan*): as
    critique of political centralization,
    18; depiction of King John by, 29–30,
    35n46; on estates' treachery, 30–31; as
    figure for John Bale, 36n57; Leland
    and, 28–29; multiplicity of sources of
    authority and, 19; new historiographi-
    cal tradition and, 27–29, 32; power
    exercised by, 16; speaking on behalf of
    true history, 6
vernacular scriptures: in *I Playne Piers*,
    44, 48
vice figures in *Kynge Johan*, 25, 26–27, 31,
    35n42
The Vision of Pierce Plowman (printed by
    Crowley), 37. See also *Piers Plowman*
    (poem) (Langland)
visions: Bale's entries on, 74
Visio Petri Ploughman (Bale), 74, 78
Vitellius manuscript, 129, 131, 138n5

Walley, Henry, 146, 157
Walsham, Alexandra, 82, 91n68
Walsingham, Thomas, 130–31, 139n7
Warren, Nancy Bradley, 6, 7, 10, 11
Wawn, Andrew, 38, 39, 48, 52n23, 85
Weber, Max, 106

Whalley, John, 166
White, Hayden, 13n14
White, Helen, 39
White, William, 157–59
Wilkins, George, 157–59
Wilson, Richard, 128
Wisdom, John, 73
Wolfe, Reynald, 38
women: bodies of, 174, 190–91; descent
    through female line, 176–77, 184–85,
    186–87, 194n4, 196n24, 196n29; in line
    of succession, 176–77, 184–86; as sinful,
    190–91; Spanish match and, 190
Woolf, D. R., 93

Woolfson, Jonathan, 72
de Worde, Wynkyn, 37, 152
Wormald, Patrick, 111
Wrawe, John, 130–31, 139n11
Wyclif, John: censorship of, 71; Foxe on,
    99–100; *Piers Plowman* attributed to,
    72, 75, 76, 88n19; Robert Langland
    and, 70, 81, 86

York, house of: uniting with house of
    Lancaster, 177–78, 180, 182
Yorkists: female descent and, 185, 194n4,
    196n24, 196n29; Jack Cade as, 136;
    Syon and, 187

Typeset in 10/13 Adobe Caslon Pro
Composed by Tom Krol
Manufactured by Cushing-Malloy, Inc.

Medieval Institute Publications
College of Arts and Sciences
Western Michigan University
1903 W. Michigan Avenue
Kalamazoo, MI 49008-5432
http://www.wmich.edu/medieval/mip

 WESTERN MICHIGAN UNIVERSITY